# Radical Pacifism

Syracuse Studies on Peace and Conflict Resolution
Louis Kriesberg, *Series Editor*

1968 anti-Vietnam War demonstration. *Photograph courtesy of the WRL.*

# Radical Pacifism

The War Resisters League and Gandhian
Nonviolence in America, 1915–1963

## Scott H. Bennett

Syracuse University Press

First Edition 2003
03 04 05 06 07 08    6 5 4 3 2 1

The paper used in this publication meets the minimum requirements of
American National Standard for Information Sciences—Permanence of
Paper for Printed Library Materials, ANSI Z39.48–1984.∞™

**Library of Congress Cataloging-in-Publication Data**

Bennett, Scott H.
Radical pacifism : the War Resisters League and Gandhian nonviolence
in America, 1915–1963 / Scott H. Bennett.— 1st ed.
p. cm.—(Syracuse studies on peace and conflict resolution)
Includes bibliographical references and index.
ISBN 0–8156–3003–4 (hc)—ISBN 0–8156–3028–X (pbk.)
1. Nonviolence. 2. Nonviolence—United States—History.
3. Pacifism—United States—History. 4. War Resisters
League—History. I. Title. II. Series.
HM1281.B465 2003
303.6'1'0973—dc22                    2003018506

*Manufactured in the United States of America*

*For Cathy and Julia*

**Scott H. Bennett** is an assistant professor of history at Georgian Court College in Lakewood, N.J. He has published on radical pacifism, the peace movement, and World War II conscientious objectors. He spent ten years as an international educator in Denmark, Italy, and El Salvador.

# Contents

# Acknowledgments

WITH GREAT PLEASURE, I wish to thank those who have assisted me with this project. Many people read the manuscript and made valuable suggestions. At Rutgers University, New Brunswick, where I began this book as a history dissertation, Dee Garrison, John W. Chambers, David M. Oshinsky, Phyllis Mack, and Kathleen M. Brown all made thoughtful comments at various stages. Later, as I revised for publication, Charles Chatfield, John D'Emilio, and Lawrence S. Wittner (who served as the "outside" member of my dissertation committee) offered detailed critiques on the entire manuscript, while Wendy E. Chmielewski, Frances Early, David McFadden, Michael Foley, Larry Gara, Michael Pilz, Bob Flood, and Claribel Young commented on portions of it. Several WRL members, including Abraham Kaufman, Ida Kaufman, Albon Man, Ralph DiGia, and Vivien Roodenko Lang, also read it and offered suggestions.

Having conducted most of the research for this book at the Swarthmore College Peace Collection, I wish to thank its expert staff: Wendy E. Chmielewski (curator), Barbara Addison, Wilma Mosholder, and Anne Yoder. Besides processing an avalanche of green sheets, pink papers, and white slips, they steered me to unprocessed collections, recent acquisitions, and important documents.

The most rewarding aspect of this project was meeting the WRL members who "made" the history I am writing about. In taped interviews, informal conversations, and written communications, they provided important information, invaluable insights, and a window into the hidden world of American radical pacifism. Some of them permitted me to use their personal papers. I thank Charles Bloomstein, Ernest Bromley, Marion Bromley, Ralph DiGia, Seymour Eichel, Margaret Rockwell Finch, Roy Finch, Larry Gara, August Gold, Edward P. Gottlieb, Marion Gottlieb, George Houser, Philip Isely, Abraham Kaufman, Ida Kaufman, Vivien Roodenko Lang, Richard Lazarus, Brad Lyttle, David McReynolds, Albon Man, Jules Manson, Annabel Sidman, Craig Simpson, and Bill Sutherland. I am also grateful to non-WRL members Garry Davis, Carlos Cortez, and August Tyler.

Several people deserve special thanks. Dee Garrison supervised the dissertation, introduced me to the WRL, and encouraged me throughout the long process of research, writing, and revision. Larry Wittner, whose pioneering work on CO activism and resistance during World War II inspired me to write about radical pacifism instead of labor history, improved the manuscript and extended his friendship. Charles Chatfield took time from his own important work to help me halve the manuscript and sharpen its focus. Abe Kaufman's encyclopedic knowledge of the WRL before World War II was vital to my efforts to reconstruct the League's early history; he offered me his memories, papers, and friendship. Finally, during visits to New York City, Eddie and Marion Gottlieb opened their home to me.

I wish to thank Mary S. Evans, Brian McCord, and Therese Walsh, and the other dedicated artisans of Syracuse University Press who have made this book possible; my thanks also to Matthew Kudelka of Toronto University, who copyedited the manuscript.

I wish to thank my former and present colleagues at Rutgers-Camden, Chicago State University, and Georgian Court College for their encouragement. I particularly wish to thank Georgian Court College for providing the funding to index this book.

On the home front, I wish to thank Edward and Grace DeMarco, who provided extraordinary child care and, in the process, delighted—and spoiled— their granddaughter. Thanks also to Nancy and Bill DeLaura for saving the day—on many days. Above all, I wish to thank my wife, Cathy, who provided constant good cheer and read endless drafts, besides making my computer work—all while maintaining her own career. The birth of our daughter, Julia, has enriched my associations with this project and placed all else in perspective. It also makes the subject of war and peace, always compelling, more personal.

Parts of chapters 1 and 3 were first published in *Peace and Change,* and I am grateful to Blackwell Publishers for permission to reprint these materials.

# Introduction

War is a crime against humanity. I, therefore, am determined not to support any kind of war, international or civil, and to strive for the removal of all the causes of war.

> —WRL Declaration

Our object is to unite men and women who have determined to give no support to any war, irrespective of the reasons—political, religious or humanitarian—which have led them to take this stand.

> —WRL Objective

Those of us who founded the War Resisters' International insisted from the first that it must be anti-capitalist as well as pacifist. We repudiated "bourgeois" pacifism, wished to extend individual resistance to a general strike against war, and stood for "revolution by non-violence." The membership was both anarchist and socialist and, while assistance was given to religious objectors to war, the influence of the organisation was always exerted to emphasize the identity of the struggle against war and the struggle against the economic system which is its cause.

> —Fenner Brockway, WRI chair

IN ITS 1983 ANNUAL REPORT, the A. J. Muste Memorial Institute captioned a photograph of the New York City headquarters of the War Resisters League (WRL) "The Peace Pentagon."[1] Besides the WRL and the Muste Institute—itself a WRL offshoot named after America's leading pacifist, WRL leader A. J. Muste—the three-story, corner-lot NoHo building at 339 Lafayette Street housed Women's Pentagon Action, the Catholic Peace Fellowship, Episcopal Churchmen for South Africa, the New York Anti-Nuclear Group, the Infant Formula Action Coalition, Art for Social Change, Political Art Documentation/Distribution, and the Fund for Open Information and Accountability. As the center of a thriving peace culture, the Peace Pentagon offered "a nourishing atmosphere"—one that was "alive with the noises of people working for peace and social justice."[2]

The Peace Pentagon serves as a metaphor for the WRL's role in peace and social justice movements in the twentieth-century United States. As the organizational home for secular radical pacifists, the WRL has offered these dissidents fellowship and sanctuary from an often hostile American political culture; it has also nourished an alternative vision of radical pacifism and Gandhian nonviolence. In addition, to borrow sociologist Aldon Morris's term, the WRL has functioned as a "movement halfway house," assisting and shaping many better-known social reform groups and campaigns.[3] Most importantly, the WRL has contributed to the modern American peace movement, which emerged in response to the then-unprecedented horrors of World War I. Noting modern technological warfare's capacity to destroy humanity, historian Charles DeBenedetti has described this post-1914 peace movement as the "necessary" reform[4]—an assessment shared by the WRL.

The modern American peace movement dates from World War I. The prewar peace movement, led by male business and professional elites and supported by middle-class professionals, was practical, respectable, and prudently reformist. To resolve conflict and prevent war, the prewar peace movement promoted international law and justice, arbitration and conciliation, and multinational peacekeeping machinery. In contrast, the modern, post-1914 peace movement—characterized by citizen peace activists, women's peace organizations,[5] and a progressive reformist impulse—was a more militant grassroots movement that sought both peace and social justice.

Between the world wars, two branches of the peace movement emerged: antiwar peace advocates and radical pacifists. Both were opposed to war and militarism; however, antiwar peace advocates (among them liberal internationalists, liberal pacifists, and the Socialist Party of America [SP]) supported defensive wars and sometimes also "good" wars and armed social revolutions. They held that some wars and revolutions were necessary to defend the nation, preserve the peace, and promote social justice. Unlike antiwar but nonpacifist peace advocates, *absolute* pacifists—sometimes called war resisters or radical pacifists—repudiated *all* organized violence, war, and armed class revolution.[6]

This study highlights the role of the WRL. It is important, however, to emphasize that the WRL functioned as part of a larger peace coalition and movement. The WRL participated in coalitions with liberal and absolute pacifist groups, including the Women's International League for Peace and Freedom (WILPF), the Women's Peace Union (WPU), the Women's Peace Society

(WPS), the Catholic Workers, the Peacemakers, the Committee for Nonviolent Revolution, the National Committee for a Sane Nuclear Policy, the Committee for Nonviolent Action, and, most often, the Fellowship of Reconciliation (FOR). Working alongside the religious pacifist FOR and other groups, the WRL helped transform pacifism: by the time they were done, pacifism meant more than simply repudiating war; it was a nonviolent social movement that resisted war and promoted social reform.

Since its founding in 1923 by socialist pacifist Jessie Wallace Hughan, the WRL has been the most important secular, mixed-gender, radical pacifist organization in the United States. I use the term *radical pacifism* to mean opposition to all wars or armed social revolution, support for both peace and social justice, and—when applied to the WRL—support for nonviolent social and democratic "socialist" revolution. Though often termed Gandhian, the WRL had socialist and pacifist origins, though it later fused these traditions.

Aiming to unite all absolute pacifists "irrespective of the reasons—political, religious, or humanitarian—which led them to take this stand,"[7] the WRL enrolled socialists, anarchists, radicals, and even capitalists. Mindful of the sectarianism that plagued earlier radical groups and seeking to avoid political factionalism among its diverse membership, the WRL never established an explicitly socialist platform; until World War II it was a single-issue organization that seldom adopted official positions on issues other than war resistance. Notwithstanding its apolitical pluralism and diverse membership, most of its leaders and activists were "socialists," and most voted for the SP, at least through 1948. After World War II many younger WRL leaders championed nonviolent direct action. Although opposed to capitalism, these COs placed less credence in electoral strategies and institutional socialism than did the League's founding generation.

In addition, the WRL represents what John W. Chambers and Charles C. Moskos have termed the "secularization of conscience" and "new conscientious objection."[8] Although it welcomes both religious and nonreligious pacifists, the WRL remains a distinctly secular organization. It advances secular arguments to support its positions, and it advocates the right of individuals to base their conscientious objection on secular considerations. Thus, where religious pacifists usually reject collective violence on moral and theological grounds, the WRL emphasizes the futility of modern war and armed revolution. In the WRL's view, the mass strike or general strike—along with other forms of organized nonviolent noncooperation—is a more effective strategy for resisting invasion and pursuing social revolution.

Significantly, the WRL has been the keystone of the secular, radical pacifist, twentieth-century, democratic American Left. Moreover, it has constituted the left wing of the modern American peace movement. Since its inception, the WRL has promoted a radical pacifist alternative to the Left (of which it forms a part) *and* to the mainstream consensus advocating nation-state sovereignty, national self-interest, power politics, and the use of armed force in international relations. No surprise, then, that pacifists and peace advocates have often been perceived as subversive. As radicals whose pacifist convictions and activism prompted harassment and sometimes persecution, the WRL and its members have championed freedom of dissent and strengthened civil liberties in America.

The WRL was founded decades ago, yet it is also one of the "new" post–World War II social movements. Barbara Epstein notes (as do others) that the new social movements emphasize culture and community and favor anarchist, nonviolent direct action and civil disobedience outside the sphere of electoral politics. Following Antonio Gramsci, she rejects—along with other advocates of the new social movements—the traditional Marxist preoccupation with political economy. Furthermore, in yet another challenge to Marxism, the new social movements reject the working class as the historical agent for radical social change, affirming the "revolutionary" potential of other social classes and of such social movements as the peace, civil rights, civil liberties, environmental, and feminist movements.[9]

In his study of American peace activists, Charles DeBenedetti used John F. Kennedy's *Profiles in Courage* (1955) to make an important point. DeBenedetti compared Kennedy's political heroes, whose brave "moral heroism" served the "national interest," with courageous and principled twentieth-century "peace heroes."[10] To honor their convictions and promote global peace, DeBenedetti's peace heroes endured vilification, isolation, and disappointment. Affirming the importance of citizen peace leaders to peace reform, he asserted that the post-1914 "American peace movement has gained and maintained its existence through a shifting combination of individuals and groups committed to the notion that war is an intolerable but resolvable problem that governing authorities have refused to challenge."[11] Likewise, Charles Chatfield has argued that peace advocates have been "prophetic" and contended that "the importance of individual leaders and activists cannot be overemphasized."[12] Although primarily a social history of the WRL and secular radical pacifism in America, this study also relates the story of the WRL activists who nourished, legitimized, and popularized an alternative vision of radical pacifism and Gandhian nonviolence.

The WRL rejects quietistic passivism and advocates an active, radical pacifism that challenges military aggression, political tyranny, and social injustice through nonviolent means. Political scientist Gene Sharp has detailed nearly two hundred techniques of nonviolent action that have been used to advance social change and deter or defend against external aggression and internal rebellion. These techniques include demonstrations, strikes, boycotts, noncooperation, and civil disobedience. Sharp extends the classic pacifist literature written between the world wars and shows how nonviolent protest and resistance have been used to achieve social justice and political reforms, prevent internal coups, defeat invasions, expel foreign empires, and overthrow domestic dictatorships. In the last three decades, nonviolent "people power" has either toppled or contributed to the overthrow of repressive regimes or government policies in Iran, Poland, the Philippines, South Africa, the Baltic states, the Soviet Union, Yugoslavia, and Indonesia.[13]

Historians recognize the WRL's significant role in modern American nonviolent and post-1945 social reform movements; however, this is the first published history of the League. In this study I make four main arguments. First, the WRL, which represents the most important vehicle of secular, radical pacifism in the United States, has articulated an alternative vision of American society, international relations, and social revolution. The ends and means of this radical pacifist vision have challenged both the mainstream political consensus and the Left. Second, the WRL has evolved from a single-issue pacifist registry, educational forum, and political pressure group devoted exclusively to war resistance into an organization advocating nonviolent direct action and civil disobedience in promoting a multi-issue agenda for advancing peace and social justice. Third, the WRL has helped popularize the philosophy and techniques of nonviolent protest and resistance. Through its own program and by supporting other groups, the WRL has popularized, legitimized, and Americanized the Gandhian nonviolent direct action that has infused post-World War II peace and justice movements. Fourth, radical pacifism and organized nonviolence are a realistic and effective means of protest, resistance, and social revolution.

Finally, a brief statement regarding my position toward the WRL and pacifism: I am neither a League member nor a radical pacifist, and I began this project sharing the common view that, though morally admirable, pacifism remained irrelevant to the existing power relationships among nation-states (and social classes). As I researched the subject, however, my position changed. While I make no explicit argument here about the relative merits of radical pacifism, liberal internationalism, and "realism" in world affairs, I now contend that radical pacifism deserves serious consideration, offering one realistic strategy for defeating invasion, deterring aggression, resisting tyranny, and challenging social injustice. What changed my mind? First, like most observers, I had confused pacifism wth quietistic passivism and nonviolence with nonresistance. Second, I came to this project as a labor historian familiar with the collective power of the working class. Soon, I discovered that virtually all my preconceptions about radical pacifism were false; on one level, the WRL and radical pacifism offered much the same logic embraced by advocates of labor activism, who insist that such tactics as mass, disciplined, nonviolent shop-floor action, boycotts, demonstrations, and general strikes can effectively counter the power of capital, and even, at times, that of governments. My examination of the WRL and radical pacifism, together with the example of many other successful nonviolent social movements, revealed the power and efficacy of nonviolent protest and resistance. Thus the original title of this manuscript: "Pacifism Not Passivism."

# Abbreviations

| | |
|---|---|
| ACLU | American Civil Liberties Union |
| AEC | Atomic Energy Commission |
| AEL | Anti-Enlistment League |
| AFL | American Federation of Labor |
| AFSC | American Friends Service Committee |
| ATWA | Amalgamated Textile Workers of America |
| BLA | Bureau of Legal Advice |
| CCCO | Central Committee for Conscientious Objectors |
| CDPC | Civil Defense Protest Committee |
| CFA | Committee for Amnesty |
| CIO | Congress of Industrial Organizations |
| CLB | Civil Liberties Bureau |
| *CO* | *Conscientious Objector* |
| COPC | CO Problems Committee |
| CORE | Congress of Racial Equality |
| CNVA | Committee for Nonviolent Action |
| CNVR | Committee for Nonviolent Revolution |
| CNVR-NY | CNVR New York Local |
| CPLA | Conference for Progressive Labor Action |
| CPS | Civilian Public Service |
| DACANW | Direct Action Committee Against Nuclear War |
| FCDA | Federal Civil Defense Administration |
| FOR | Fellowship of Reconciliation |
| FOR-NY | FOR New York Local |
| GCD | Ghana Council for Nuclear Disarmament |
| ICBM | Intercontinental Ballistic Missile |
| IWW | Industrial Workers of the World |
| MCBO | Metropolitan Board for Conscientious Objectors |
| MIA | Montgomery Improvement Association |

| | |
|---|---|
| MOBE | National Mobilization Committee to End the War in Vietnam |
| MOWM | March on Washington Movement |
| NCF | No-Conscription Fellowship |
| NMWM | No More War Movement |
| NSBRO | National Service Board for Religious Objectors |
| NVAANW | Nonviolent Action Against Nuclear Weapons |
| NVDAC | Nonviolent Direct Action Committee |
| *NYT* | *New York Times* |
| PDC | Provisional Defense Committee |
| PNM | Peace Now Movement |
| PTL | Pacifist Teachers League |
| RCC | Resist Conscription Committee |
| SANE | National Committee for a Sane Nuclear Policy |
| SCLC | Southern Christian Leadership Conference |
| SCPC | Swarthmore College Peace Collection |
| SI | Socialist International |
| SNCC | Student Nonviolent Coordinating Committee |
| SP | Socialist Party of America |
| UWF | United World Federalists |
| WILPF | Women's International League for Peace and Freedom |
| WMWFG | World Movement for World Federal Government |
| WPP | Woman's Peace Party |
| WPS | Women's Peace Society |
| WPU | Women's Peace Union |
| WRI | War Resisters' International |
| WRL | War Resisters League |
| WRL-EC | WRL Executive Committee |
| WRL-IAC | WRL Interim Administrative Committee |
| WRL-NY | WRL New York Local |
| YMCA | Young Men's Christian Association |
| YPSL | Young People's Socialist League |
| YPSL-NY | YPSL Greater New York Federation |

# Radical Pacifism

# 1

# Jessie Wallace Hughan and the WRL

The Origins, Founding, and Philosophy of the WRL
and Radical Secular Pacifism in America from
World War I to 1925

DR. JESSIE WALLACE HUGHAN (1876–1955) distinguished herself as an
American educator, author, socialist, and pacifist who championed peace, radical pacifism, and war resistance. Throughout a half-century of global war, armed
revolution, and militaristic Cold War, she advocated nonviolent conflict resolution and nonviolent social revolution.[1] In the late 1930s one admirer called her
"the soul of the War Resisters' Movement in this country."[2]

A "pioneer"[3] in the modern American peace movement, Hughan challenged
the dominant ideology—professed by both the political mainstream and the
Left (of which she was a part)—that sanctioned war and revolutionary violence
to achieve peace and justice. She formulated a strategy of war resistance based on
the premise that a pacifist minority, pledged in advance to withhold support for
war, could mobilize public opinion and stop governments from declaring war
by persuading them that sufficient support to wage war did not exist. Hughan
also advocated nonviolent social (and socialist) revolution. She founded the War
Resisters League (WRL), a secular, mixed-gender, socialist-oriented radical pacifist organization that spearheaded nonviolent resistance and social reform in
America.

Hughan's personal story is compelling. She possessed a superior intellect and
superb leadership skills. She was highly cultured. She delighted in friendships,
conversation, books, poetry, music, opera, theater, movies, overseas travel, and
hiking and swimming during summers in Maine. She never married. She earned
an M.A. in economics (1899) and a Ph.D. in political economy (1910), but she
was prevented by political and gender discrimination from becoming a college
professor of economics. When she was even prevented from teaching economics

1

in New York City's public school system, she embarked in 1900 on a career teaching high school English. A gifted organizer, she founded many groups, including the Alpha Omicron Pi (female) fraternity (1894), the Anti-Enlistment League (1915), the WRL (1923), and the Pacifist Teachers League (1940).[4] Significantly, the gendered spheres of war and peace have rendered Hughan "invisible" to history.

### Origins of Jessie Wallace Hughan's Pacifism

When World War I began, Hughan was a pacifist; by the time it ended she had formulated a mature strategy of war resistance. The influences of family, Christianity, socialism, and feminism led her to embrace pacifism in 1914 at the age of thirty-seven. She wrote her first "mildly pacifist" poem in 1909;[5] however, she did not consider herself an "active pacifist" until April 1914, after American armed forces occupied the Mexican port of Vera Cruz.[6] In her diaries, which until then had been filled mainly with socialist matters, she began recording her pacifist activities.[7]

### Family

Hughan was raised in a stimulating family environment in which independent thought was valued. Both her parents were radicals, and this encouraged her interest in pacifism, politics, economics, and feminism. Jessie and her sisters Marjorie and Evelyn all became pacifists. Evelyn also became an active suffragist and had a successful career as head of the Foreign Department of Ginn and Company, a major textbook publisher.

Hughan's father, Samuel Hughan, emigrated to the United States from England in 1866 and two years later married Margaret Balieff West. Samuel, who held progressive views on gender, converted Margaret to the suffragist position and "encouraged her artistic side to develop."[8] Samuel was a Swedenborgian (a pacifist sect), a single-taxer, a suffragist, and a vegetarian. He was also a freelance journalist who wrote a study of the British land question that paralleled Henry George's analysis in *Progress and Poverty*. In 1886 he managed that reformer's New York City mayoralty campaign.

Margaret too was a Henry George devotee. She was also president of the Women's Single Tax Club of Brooklyn. With her husband's support she participated in a literary club, wrote literary pieces, and composed music. Margaret abhorred physical violence and corporal punishment and attended closely to her three daughters' "spiritual welfare."[9] Physically fearless, she was known to break up street fights between drunks. On at least one occasion she stopped a peddler from beating his cart horse.

Her parents' progressive ideas, cultural nourishment, and spirit of intellectual inquiry equipped Jessie Wallace Hughan to challenge prevailing truths and to embrace feminism, socialism, and pacifism. Like her parents she became a feminist and suffragist. In November 1917, Hughan, although not herself permitted to vote, received more than one thousand ballots as the Socialist Party candidate for the New York Assembly in an election that also granted women in the state the right to vote. She never became an active suffragist like her sister Evelyn; she did, however, play an active role during World War I in the emergent women's peace movement, which articulated the connections among feminism, suffrage, and peace.

Hughan was influenced by her parents' radicalism. For example, their involvement in the single-tax movement was directly reflected in Hughan's Columbia University M.A. thesis, "The Place of Henry George in Economics" (1899). Similarly, her Barnard College senior thesis, "Recent Theories of Profits" (1898), her Columbia Ph.D. dissertation, "The Present Status of Socialism in the United States" (1910), and her speeches and publications on socialism, pacifism, and international affairs reflected the political and intellectual influence of her parents. It is likely that her father's experiences in England and South America sparked her lifelong interest in international relations and global travel. Her parents' progressive attitude toward gender roles instilled in her the confidence to pursue public goals in a "man's world." Especially relevant to her peace activism, her mother taught her to hate violence.[10] This, Hughan later reflected, was "perhaps the strongest pacifist influence in my childhood."[11]

## Christianity

Hughan's pacifism was also shaped by Christianity. In the mid-1890s, at Evelyn's prompting, she joined the Unitarian Church. In response to the bloody Philippine insurrection and American conquest (1899–1902), Dr. Chadwick, minister of Brooklyn's Second Unitarian Church, influenced Jessie and Evelyn toward pacifism. In 1915, Hughan became a charter member of the Fellowship of Reconciliation (FOR), at the time a decidedly Christian pacifist group.[12] By World War I the religious dimension of her pacifism was obvious.

In a postwar review of a pacifist play written by her close friend and fellow pacifist Tracy D. Mygatt, Hughan welcomed the "revival of Christian martyrdom" that was one result of the war. The heroes of Mygatt's play were religious

conscientious objectors (COs), who won martyrdom not through death in battle but by choosing "manacles and solitary confinement" and refusing to compromise their Christian ideals by serving in the military. "Jesus has been here
with us in Leavenworth," Hughan mused, referring to the federal prison where
many COs were incarcerated and mistreated.[13]

Hughan portrayed her Christian pacifism as revolutionary and nonviolent.
Her Jesus was a "Jewish workingman who in the age of imperialist aggression
taught and practiced nonviolence."[14] During the revolutionary days of 1919 she
cautioned that Christians "committed to the principle of love cannot join our
'red' comrades in their project to take . . . the kingdom of Heaven by violence."[15]

However, her radical pacifism also differed from Christian nonresistance,
which renounced all force and coercion, even of the nonviolent kind. She repudiated war ("the organized killing of one group by another"),[16] yet she did not reject all force ("the exertion of power") to resist evil and advance social reform.[17]
Nor did she preclude legitimate police powers, shooting violent criminals in self-
defense, or even the idea of assassinating of Adolf Hitler.[18] In sum, she did not
disavow all force—only "that form of force known as war."[19]

## Socialism

Besides family and religion, socialism was a critical element in molding Hughan's
pacifism. Despite her parents' radicalism, she saw herself as a political conservative
when she started her doctoral program at Columbia University in 1905. Two years
later she became a socialist while researching her dissertation on American socialism. Consistent with her intention to write a thesis that would "smash socialism,"[20] she spent a year preparing "The Case Against Socialism" for a competition
sponsored by the Hart-Schaffner-Marx department store. Part of her research involved attending socialist meetings. Believing that socialists were wild radicals
who "threw bombs,"[21] she found the initial encounters "terrifying."[22] Within the
year, however, she had discarded her fears and embraced socialism. Her academic
adviser, the economist Edwin R. A. Seligman, a prominent supporter of capitalism, refused to endorse Hughan for a faculty post. Indeed, during her dissertation
defense, Hughan answered "the questions twice—first, as I believe you [Selig-
man] would desire them to be answered; then, what I really think."[23] After her dissertation was published as *American Socialism in the Present Day* (1911), the SP
appointed Hughan—now a respected socialist intellectual—to party positions.
One of these was a seat on the executive committee of the Intercollegiate Socialist
Society, on which she served with Jack London and Upton Sinclair. In addition,
the SP several times nominated or endorsed her for public office.[24]

Marxian analysis and organized socialism's response to World War I shaped Hughan's strategy of war resistance as well as her interpretation of international relations. Reflecting socialist principles, her analysis of the war emphasized economic factors and the causative links among capitalism, colonialism, and war. Imperialism, she held, resulted from capitalism's need for raw materials, markets, and cheap labor. Faced with a crisis of overproduction, European nations erected protective tariff barriers against one another. Unable as a consequence to sell their surplus production in Europe, they established (and later defended) new economic empires of colonies, protectorates, and spheres of influence. In this way, she argued, economic imperialism led to political imperialism and colonialism.[25]

Hughan saw economics as the main cause of the war. However, she rejected economic determinism, pointing out that there were also noneconomic causes of war, such as nationalism, racism, fear, secret diplomacy, and the armaments race. Furthermore, she repudiated the following socialist syllogism: Capitalism causes war; socialism will eventually abolish capitalism; so peace must await the socialist victory over capitalism.[26]

In assessing socialism's failure to prevent World War I, Hughan contended that the critical mistake of the Socialist International (SI) was that it failed to devise a concrete plan to avert war. The socialist parties of the various nations were equally to blame in this regard. While large and spirited at first, the antiwar demonstrations of July 1914 had proved pitifully inadequate as a means of preventing armed conflict. After hostilities broke out, the absence of a clear plan for uniting and directing a war resistance movement left individual resisters on their own.[27]

Hughan observed that despite their general opposition to war and preference for the arbitration of international disputes, as of 1914 European socialists had neither formulated a concrete plan for common action nor adopted an antienlistment pledge. Moreover, they retained the distinction between offensive and defensive war. But Hughan did praise one socialist proposal—the general strike against war.[28] Significantly, Hughan's endorsement of the general strike and her reading of the SI's debate on the issue situates her war resistance within the international socialist mainstream on war and peace.

Between 1891 and 1914 the SI debated the general strike against war. At meetings in Stuttgart (1907) and Copenhagen (1910), British Independent Labour Party leader Keir Hardie and French socialist Edouard Vaillant championed the measure. At the Copenhagen Congress they proposed the following resolution: "Among the means to be used in order to prevent and hinder war the congress considers as particularly efficacious a general strike, especially in the industries that supply war with its implements (arms, munitions, transport, etc.), as well as agitation and popular action in their most active forms."[29] After a spirited debate the Copenhagen Congress tabled the Hardie-Vaillant proposal and referred it to the International Socialist Bureau for further study in preparation for renewed consideration at the 1914 Vienna Congress.

In mid-July 1914, shortly before the scheduled Vienna meeting, the French Socialist Party, led by Jean Jaures, reiterated its support for the general strike to avert war and compel international arbitration. In response to the impending European crisis, the Socialist International moved the Congress from Vienna to Paris and brought the date forward to 9 August. But before European socialists could meet to formulate collective antiwar action, Jaures was assassinated, German Social Democrats voted for war credits, the European working class succumbed to nationalism, and general war erupted.[30] Although European socialists disregarded their antiwar and internationalist principles and voted for the war credits to finance the juggernaut of death, Hughan maintained that the socialist parties—including the American SP—were the closest the world had to a peace party.[31] Socialism remained "the one international political language," she asserted.[32]

Like their European comrades, American socialists were faced with the task of transforming general antiwar principles into a concrete strategy. Hughan urged the SP to adopt a specific plan of action that endorsed the general strike against war, and to include in its membership statement a declaration repudiating both offensive and defensive war. At its April 1917 St. Louis Convention, called to determine its position toward American participation in the conflict, the SP condemned the war, opposed American intervention, and vowed to support "all mass movements" against conscription.[33] Although recognizing that the American Federation of Labor's accommodationist policies precluded a general strike and mass action against the war, Hughan contended that the St. Louis Resolution provided comfort for secular COs, who predicated their war resistance on political, economic, and humanitarian rather than religious grounds.[34]

The historian George Haupt has detailed the SI's failure to transform general principles into concrete, collective antiwar action. He provides evidence that supports Hughan's strategy of war resistance: "Obviously one of the factors that any government must bear in mind before accepting the risk of a war is public opinion in general, and in particular that of the sectors that have for years displayed militant pacifism. As a key-point, social democracy and the workers' movement had great weight in the governments' decisions."[35]

Confident that the Austrian-Serbian crisis would remain a local conflict, the International Socialist Bureau opted for caution. At its meeting on 29 and 30 July its members decided not to mobilize workers for an organized antiwar campaign or a general strike against war. Instead they chose to defer decisions on these matters to the upcoming Socialist International Congress. That meeting never convened; it was preempted by the outbreak of World War I. According to Haupt, European governments noticed the socialists' hesitation and realized that the SI would not be able quickly to overcome its indecision, counter a patriotic groundswell, and mount an effective antiwar campaign.[36]

Haupt's interpretation of prewar events supports the contention of Hardie, Vaillant, and Jaures (and Hughan) that the public threat of a coordinated general strike would have comprised a powerful deterrent and might have compelled European governments to reevaluate their decision to declare war. Moreover, it validates Hughan's emphasis on public opinion and her premise that an uncompromising radical pacifist minority, publicly pledged in advance to refuse to support war, could deter governments from waging war.[37]

## Women's Movements and Peace Movements

The women's and peace movements did not shape Hughan's core pacifist beliefs; they did, however, provide a rich heritage of female and antiwar activism that nourished her post-1914 pacifist leadership. Historians have found a direct link between the suffragist movement and the feminist pacifism of the World War I and postwar eras. They have also detailed the suffragist movement's influence on the prewar socialist movement, the wartime women's peace movement, and postwar female activism. The suffragist movement provided the education, skills, confidence, and political experience that empowered women to exercise leadership in the public sphere of war and peace—a role previously reserved for men. More broadly, the suffragist movement and feminist activism helped to shape the new peace movement spawned by World War I and to create a network of sisterhood that sustained women's postwar reform activism.[38]

Historians have also demonstrated the links among the nineteenth-century antebellum peace, abolitionist, and women's movements, especially among the Garrisonians. Harriet Alonso has established a continuous historical line connecting the abolitionists, Seneca Falls, the suffragist-infused Woman's Peace Party (WPP), and the contemporary feminist movement. Similarly, Margaret Hope Bacon has linked female abolitionism to the women's rights movement and emphasized the importance to both of nonviolence. Bacon contends that from the Civil War to the Nineteenth Amendment (1920), the women's rights movement relied on nonviolent methods—picketing, marches, hunger strikes, civil disobedience, and tax resistance—to promote gender equality. Fanny Garrison Villard, the daughter of William Lloyd Garrison and the founder of the

Women's Peace Society (WPS), symbolizes the link between the abolitionist and women's rights movements and the nineteenth- and twentieth-century peace movements.[39]

Hughan illustrates this connection between suffrage and social radicalism. There are obvious links between the radicalism of the suffragist movement and her socialist and pacifist activism. Hughan suffered sex discrimination before she converted to socialism (1907) and pacifism (1914), and her commitment to socialism and suffrage preceded her pacifism. After earning her Ph.D. in political economy (1910), Hughan placed first on the high school certification exam to teach economics, but her gender and politics prevented an appointment.

Hughan was active in the prewar suffragist and socialist movements, and both informed her pacifism. With other suffragists and feminists she formed an important element of the wartime pacifist movement. She enlisted in and sometimes helped lead groups comprised of or shaped by activist women, including the American Union Against Militarism, the Emergency Peace Federation, the People's Council, and the WPP. Moreover, the political ties and personal friendships she formed in the wartime feminist-suffragist movement and in the mixed-gender peace and justice movements sustained and strengthened her peace activism over the next four decades.[40]

### World War I and Radical Pacifism

World War I baptized Hughan's nascent pacifism and transformed it into a specific strategy of war resistance. With its demand for total war, the conflict deepened and shaped her pacifism in important ways. After August 1914, Hughan participated in the American antipreparedness and nonintervention movement. In addition to her involvement in the SP, between 1914 and 1918 Hughan helped establish or participated in the FOR, the Emergency Peace Federation, the American Union Against Militarism, the WPP, and the Anti-Enlistment League (AEL).

#### Women's Peace Movement

During World War I, Hughan was the secretary and a board member of the feminist pacifist Woman's Peace Party-New York Branch. Formed in January 1915, the WPP was a key link between the peace and suffrage movements. Its Preamble proclaimed that women, as the "mother half of humanity," had a special role to play in the struggle for peace and justice.[41] Jane Addams, the president of the organization, asserted that "sensitiveness for human life is stronger in women than in men." Moreover, she claimed that women had developed special skills in the "treasuring," "protection," "nurture," "fulfillment," and "conservation" of human life.[42] The group's platform urged the enfranchisement of women to secure their political equality and permit them to influence political decisions on war and peace. Hughan wrote for and helped edit *Four Lights,* the radical newsletter of the New York branch of the WPP.[43] Likewise, in the immediate postwar period she worked with female activists to promote feminism and radical pacifism. When absolute pacifists split from the Women's International League for Peace and Freedom to form the Women's Peace Society (1919) and the Women's Peace Union (WPU) (1921), Hughan joined both groups and served as vice chair of the WPS.[44]

Hughan was not herself a nonresistant. However, the Women's Peace Society letterhead carried a William L. Garrison quotation that expressed the militant nature of the radical pacifism she admired and championed:

> Non-resistance is not a state of passivity. On the contrary, it is a state of activity, ever fighting the good fight or faith, ever foremost to assail unjust power, ever struggling for liberty, equality, fraternity, in no national sense, but in a worldwide spirit. It is passivity only in this sense—that it will not return evil for evil, nor give blow for blow, nor resort to murderous weapons for protection or defense.[45]

In a 1920 article published in the socialist press, Hughan articulated the socialist feminist element of her pacifism:

> It is the work of us women, moreover, to inspire this attack [on capitalism and war]. We have learned pretty thoroughly that the chief interest of men, even radical men, does not lie in human life as such . . . .
>
> We know, as Socialists, that the economic is the foundation—but we know, as women, that the foundation is not all.
>
> For us socialist women the fight for the sacredness of life is the greatest issue in the world and more than a by-product of the economic struggle.[46]

Hughan served as a link among the pacifist, feminist, and socialist movements. For instance, in 1921 the WPU had difficulty persuading socialist and radical women to march in a peace parade since, they contended, disarmament was "futile" until "after the revolution."[47] The WPU asked Hughan to urge radical women to march in the disarmament parade.[48] She was an ideal choice: not only had she pioneered the argument that peace need not await revolution, but she was respected by her socialist, feminist, and pacifist sisters and comrades.

Hughan spoke and wrote against the preparedness movement that sought to take the United States into World War I. Maintaining that war was rooted mainly in economics, nationalism, and militarism, she argued that reform, not military preparedness, was the best guarantee of national security. And to address the primary economic causes of war, she advocated a democratic socialist alternative to the capitalist status quo.[49]

### The No-Conscription Fellowship

British war opposition, manifested in the antiwar Independent Labour Party (ILP) and the absolute pacifist No-Conscription Fellowship (NCF), shaped the direction of Hughan's war resistance. Although the ILP renounced the war, many younger party members such as Fenner Brockway pursued a more radical war resistance.[50] In November 1914, Brockway established the socialist pacifist No-Conscription Fellowship, a mixed-gender, absolute pacifist organization that embraced war resisters of diverse political, economic, and religious persuasions. The NCF gained distinction as the first British group to collect pledges to resist conscription and for related war work. Socialists comprised 75 to 80 percent of its fifty thousand members, including most of the six thousand British COs who were imprisoned.

Although British conscription law allowed conscientious objection and civilian service, the absolutist NCF repudiated all cooperation with the war system and resisted the draft. When the government cracked down, its members endured persecution, jail, and the threat of execution. Brockway and Clifford Allen served prison terms, while Bertrand Russell lost his Cambridge lectureship and was denied permission to leave Britain to accept a post at Harvard. Suffragette Catherine E. Marshall assumed a leadership role in the No-Conscription Fellowship, which benefited from the experience, skills, and political knowledge she had acquired in the women's movement. To resist the war system and win release, imprisoned COs often used the suffragist technique of hunger strikes.[51]

In 1921, two years after the NCF disbanded, veterans of the organization founded as its direct descendant the socialist pacifist No More War Movement (NMWM). Affiliated with the War Resisters' International (WRI), the NMWM required members to sign a pledge declaring their intention never to participate in war.[52]

## The Anti-Enlistment League

Meanwhile, in May 1915, influenced by the NCF, Hughan founded the Anti-Enlistment League (AEL), the forerunner of the WRL. Headquartered in her Brooklyn home, the AEL was the first American organization devoted to collecting individual pledges of war resistance. As Hughan remembered it:

> During that winter [1914–15], I visited the heads of the various peace societies in New York trying to find out some aggressive peace action on the part of some existing group. Meeting with discouragement from all, I decided to do what I could myself and planned an *Anti-Enlistment League,* which should line up all men and women who should promise never to enlist voluntarily or to give approval to such enlistment on the part of others.[53]

Frances M. Witherspoon, a lifelong friend of Hughan and a socialist pacifist collaborator, recounted the origins of the AEL: "I was among those who heard Jessie Hughan on a June night in 1915 tell a group of tense listeners in New York's old 14th Street Labor Temple that there was but one way to stop war—categorical, individual refusal to participate. From that unforgettable night sprang the Anti-Enlistment League."[54]

Hughan quickly gained the support of Unitarian minister John Haynes Holmes and Tracy D. Mygatt. Frances Witherspoon and Evelyn Hughan then became the first to sign the AEL pledge: "I, being over 18 years of age, hereby pledge myself against enlistment as a volunteer for any military or naval service in international war, offensive or defensive, and against giving my approval to such enlistment on the part of others."[55] The AEL collected pledges and enlisted members without regard to their gender or their religious or political affiliation. Hughan distributed most of the group's literature and pledges at socialist meetings.

The AEL gained national attention in 1916 after an exchange between Hughan and Theodore Roosevelt, the jingoistic former president. Denouncing "pacifists and poltroons," Roosevelt declared that "any man who signs a pledge . . . should be promptly disenfranchised and then sent to the front to dig kitchen sinks, bury dead horses and do other jobs which would relieve brave men of the unpleasant but necessary hard work of a campaign." Writing in the New York newspapers, Hughan replied: "You may think it odd, Mr. Roosevelt, but there are a few of us who have so far outgrown the soldierly ambitions of our childhood as really to find more agreeable the task of burying a dead horse than of bayonetting a live man."[56]

Before disbanding in April 1917, the Anti-Enlistment League collected 3,500 pledges. This sparked opposition out of proportion to its small membership. Having been established to thwart voluntary enlistment, the league disbanded when the United States entered the war and introduced conscription. Government persecution, exemplified by the Justice Department's seizure of its files, contributed to the league's decision to disband. So did disagreement among pacifists over the limits of resistance to conscription. After the United States entered the war, Hughan hoped to transform the AEL into a militant no-conscription group similar to the No-Conscription Fellowship in Britain. But pacifist leaders led by John Haynes Holmes, Norman Thomas, and Roger Baldwin rejected her proposal, opting instead to help COs secure exemptions under the conscription law.[57]

## Wartime and Postwar Red Scares

Hughan's wartime commitment to pacifism and socialism developed in the context of the virulent Americanism, patriotism, nationalism, and general antiradicalism that accompanied World War I and fostered political conformity as well as loyalty to the war effort. During the Red Scare that accompanied the war, governments, private agencies, and "patriots" conducted repressive campaigns against radicals, pacifists, and liberals who challenged the war and the basic structures of American society. The repression was particularly severe in New York City, where local authorities, fearing the large immigrant and radical communities, enacted coercive municipal measures. The Industrial Workers of the World (IWW, whose members were known as Wobblies), the SP, the American Union Against Militarism, the People's Councils, the Anti-Conscription League, and other opponents of war were battered by legal and extralegal measures. When the United States entered the war in April 1917, the public equated pacifism with treason, and efforts to impose political conformity intensified.

Federal legislation such as the Espionage and Sedition Acts restricted dissent and bred conformity, besides making it easier to prosecute radicals. Pacifists were kept under surveillance. The postmaster general suppressed many radical publications, including two issues of *Four Lights,* the newsletter of the WPP–New York Branch, which Hughan wrote for and edited.[58]

Hughan was criticized by prowar socialists as well as by nationalists. "You may imagine my shame and humiliation as a Unitarian," a coreligionist wrote, "to discover that two of the promoters of the scheme to prostitute American loyalty and manhood were identified with the church."[59] Another critic, in a vitriolic note to Hughan, displayed the passion that pacifists provoked and expressed the common assumption that women personified weakness and subversion: "You are a *Traitor* to your country[,] a Contemptible Woman & a Cowardly Pacifist. You disgust all true Americans & it is to be hoped that the Board of Education drives you out of the School, such Miserable Female Characters as you are, should be driven out of the country." [60]

Hughan often observed that pacifists required courage. Responding to those who poured scorn on " 'rabbit' pacifists," she noted that most pacifists were exempt from conscription because of age or gender, yet "face ridicule and risk imprisonment in order to prevent other people from being sent to the trenches." [61] True courage, she contended, was "the willingness to suffer and die, rather than the willingness to inflict suffering and death on others." [62] COs and nonviolent ("passive") resistance campaigns exemplified this courage. Hughan noted that nearly six thousand COs had been court-martialed in Britain. Thirty of them had been sentenced to death, which prompted them to "declare their readiness to be shot rather than shoot other men." [63] Similarly, but on a collective scale, nonviolent labor strikes, German opposition to French occupation of the Ruhr (1923), and Gandhi's *satyagraha* movement in India combined "physical courage and the refusal of combat." [64]

In New York, where the wartime antiradical crusade focused special attention on education, Hughan suffered harassment and persecution as a result of her pacifism, socialism, and union activities. The New York Education Act of 1917 authorized officials to fire public teachers for "treasonable or seditious statements." [65] New York City required teachers to sign loyalty oaths, although eighty-seven teachers refused to do so. School officials used harassment, dismissal, and the denial of teaching licenses to enforce decrees forbidding teachers from criticizing the war or supporting socialism and communism. Several pacifist teachers and professors were fired, including future WRL members Mary S. McDowell and Scott Nearing. [66]

As a socialist, a pacifist, and an advocate for the teachers union, Hughan was an obvious target for persecution. The New York City school superintendent repeatedly warned her that she might be terminated for her pacifist opinions and activism. Although other teachers were leading class debates on preparedness, in 1916 Hughan's principal directed her not to discuss with her students "any subject connected with war and peace or radical controversy." [67] In July 1918, when she affirmed her war resistance in a newspaper interview on the occasion of her nomination by the SP for the post of New York secretary of state, the associate superintendent requested a meeting to discuss her political views. [68]

The postwar Red Scare, which extended the wartime persecution of pacifists and radicals, targeted Hughan. In January 1919 the Senate Judiciary Committee, chaired by Lee Overman, included Hughan on a list of sixty-two radicals who refused to support the war. Archibald Stevenson, an investigator for the Military Intelligence Division and the Lusk Committee, which had furnished the names, portrayed the list as a "Who's Who in Pacifism and Radicalism."[69] When asked about her inclusion on this list, Hughan replied, "I am glad to appear on any list that begins with Jane Addams' name."[70]

On the recommendation of the Lusk Committee (1919–21), New York passed the Lusk Law to remove radicals from classrooms. The law required teachers to sign a loyalty oath and established a committee to examine the loyalty of teachers. In 1922, after she qualified her loyalty on a questionnaire, the committee summoned Hughan. "I am a loyal American," she testified, "but my loyalty is subject to the dictates of my conscience." She refused to sign the loyalty oath unconditionally; however, the Lusk Law was repealed in 1923 and she was able to keep her job.[71] In a witty poem, "The Bolsheviks'll Git You," Hughan parodied Archie Stevenson:

> Little Archie Stevenson has come here to stay,
> To sweep the agitators out and keep the Reds away,
> To shoo-oo the revolutions off and put the folks to sleep,
> And chase the I.W.W. and earn his board and keep.
> But when we hear the soap-box a-shrieking in the dusk,
> And the bombs begin to rattle in the brain of Papa Lusk,
> And the headlines flare and flicker and we dream about the Hun,—
> We huddle in committees and have the mostest fun,
> A'listenin' to the witch-tales that Archie tells about—
> For the Bolsheviks 'll get you ef you don't—watch—out!
>
> Once there was a working-class that wouldn't say its prayers;
> It mocked at all its masters and it shocked its millionaires,
> But when it waved the red flag and the neighbors ran to hide,
> There was two-big-black-things a-standing by its side;
> The one it was a Trotzky and the other a Lenine,—
> And when the neighbors peeped again, no master could be seen,
> And you couldn't find a millionaire in all that land about,—
> For the Bolsheviks'll git you ef you don't—watch—out!
>
> So you'd better mind your manners and your masters kind and true,
> And vote for all the millionaires who make the jobs for you;
> And don't you wear a red tie, and don't you go on strike,

And don't you join a union that the old man doesn't like,—
But when the boss comes riding by, throw up your hats and shout,—
Or the Bolsheviks'll git YOU, TOO, ef you DON'T—WATCH—OUT![72]

Hughan endured harassment throughout her life. In her hysterical 1934 compilation of American "Reds," Elizabeth Dilling smeared Hughan and the WRL as communist allies.[73] Despite outstanding scores on the requisite examinations, Hughan never received the promotion to department head she sought. "I was denied the appointment to which I was entitled by my first examination," she explained in the 1930s, "solely because of my religious and political opinions regarding war and peace."[74]

## Jessie Wallace Hughan's Strategy of War Resistance

Influenced by World War I, Hughan formulated a strategy of war resistance that posited the power of citizens—led by a radical pacifist minority—to prevent war. Marked by total warfare and mass mobilization, the war profoundly shaped her thinking. With its unprecedented reliance on propaganda campaigns, modern total warfare required the mass mobilization of public opinion and near 100 percent support. Hughan contended that a "revolutionary" (or "irreconcilable") pacifist minority,[75] by galvanizing the peace movement and public opinion, could withhold the popular support that governments required in order to wage war.[76]

Her strategy emphasized the importance of a public, written declaration proclaiming one's intention to oppose war. But if it was going to succeed in pressuring the government to reject war, the declaration—and the enrollment of war resisters who signed the pledge—had to be publicized during peacetime. World War I had demonstrated that once hostilities threatened, nationalism, patriotism, racism, propaganda, repression, and "popular frenzy"[77] made reasoned judgment and antiwar dissent difficult. Declarations were the most direct method of making each pacifist voice count; they also underscored the responsibility of individuals for war and peace. Since those who signed declarations risked persecution, their action showed a psychological commitment to pacifism. Thus Hughan viewed these declarations as an "acid test,"[78] holding that those who pledged resistance would likely honor their intention in the event of war. Also, by establishing a principled opposition to *all* war, declarations offered enrollees some protection against charges of antipatriotism in the event of hostilities.[79]

Paradoxically, Hughan's antiwar strategy, though it was based on the socialist "general strike against war," challenged orthodox socialism. She emphasized the need for concrete action and repudiated the socialist axiom that peace must follow socialism. Citing the abolition of dueling, cannibalism, slavery, and child sacrifice, she contended that peace also could *precede* socialism. "Wars will cease when men refuse to fight—and women refuse to approve," [80] she later observed. War could not be ended by international agreements such as those that had been made—and broken—before both world wars.[81]

Important socialist, anarchist, and pacifist leaders rejected Hughan's strategy of war resistance, especially her emphasis on written declarations and her conviction that peace could precede socialism. "I do not believe in the social efficacy of pledges, and cannot support the proposed pledge gathering campaign," declared New York SP leader Morris Hillquit. "Not by individual promises and pledges but by collective enlightenment and above all by political and economic power will we minimize the danger of war." [82] Norman Thomas, the future SP leader and at the time a pacifist minister, argued that the "preparation of such a list" of pacifists pledged to resist war would be ineffective.[83] He urged Hughan to concentrate her efforts on international war and to ignore social revolution—which she termed "civil war" in her antiwar declaration.[84] Thomas affirmed his pacifism but also confessed: "I feel myself in some ways to be more sympathetic with the revolutionaries who say frankly that under certain conditions that they would support organized violence." [85] Roger Baldwin, a philosophical anarchist and World War I CO who defended other COs before heading the American Civil Liberties Union (ACLU), summarized the classic position of the secular radical Left: "Surely if the causes of war lie in the present economic system, then only the abolition of that system will abolish war." [86] Hughan, who remained active in the pacifist and socialist movements, was by now devoting her life to challenging this axiom.

### The Founding and Ideology of the War Resisters League

After World War I, Hughan spearheaded efforts to establish a radical pacifist organization that would unite men and women of diverse political and religious convictions who repudiated all war. Consistent with her radical pacifist position, she rejected postwar liberal peace activism, communist antimilitarism, and the new League of Nations, which sanctioned armed force to maintain peace. Hughan recounted:

> There existed after the Armistice, however, no organization comparable to the war-time No-Conscription Fellowship in Great Britain, which should enroll

men and women of differing political and religious beliefs under the refusal to give support to war. Peace advocates of the liberal type were inclined to place their hopes in the League of Nations, those on the radical wing in the Soviet Republic. . . . With only a few did the growing reliance of the Soviets upon violence and of the League upon the militarist powers, strengthen the conviction that the war regime would not end until substantial numbers in each nation should make clear in advance their unconditional refusal to engage in the next suicidal folly at government bidding.[87]

The WRL had organizational roots in the Fellowship of Reconciliation and the female peace societies. Most accounts contend that the WRL emerged from an FOR committee. Although this is true, it ignores the important role the women's peace movement played in the birth of the WRL. In the years immediately following World War I, the Women's Peace Society and the Women's Peace Union constituted the most radical elements of the pacifist movement. Hughan, one of the leaders of this absolute pacifist current, drew on a wartime and postwar network of radical pacifists to found the WRL, which welcomed those war resisters excluded from the FOR and the female peace societies.

Hughan led the postwar movement to establish a radical pacifist federation that would appeal to a wider constituency than the FOR and women's peace societies. The WRL emerged in part from this attempt to gather absolute pacifist groups into a federation. "There are indications of a strong desire among nonresistants to resume the agitation and organization which were checked in 1917," Hughan observed in 1921.[88] She was a leader in the WPS and the WPU, yet she also realized that the female membership and "feminist basis"[89] of these two groups restricted their appeal. To organize pacifist men she recommended the formation of either a companion male society to the WPS or, even better, a new, mixed-gender pacifist organization. She also understood that the FOR's influence was limited by its Christianity and that its multi-issue reform agenda diluted its focus on pacifism.[90] Besides this, some wartime pacifists and COs had injected a militant impulse into the postwar pacifist movement; they were uncomfortable in a Christian-based organization and receptive to a secular alternative.[91] Having been victimized herself by the wartime and postwar Red Scares, Hughan wanted to provide pacifists with an institutional sanctuary from hostility, isolation, and persecution.[92] So she formed the WRL, an organization committed to unifying all radical pacifists, whatever their sex, religion, or politics. It would be an American affiliate of the War Resisters' International.[93]

Beginning in 1920, Hughan proposed that the FOR sponsor a pacifist organization that would be open to members without regard to religion, gender, or politics. At the FOR's 1920 conference she promoted her strategy of war resistance, based on the conviction that a well-organized, absolute pacifist minority could marshal public opinion to pressure the government not to wage war. In accord with this vision, she proposed the creation of a new, inclusive, radical pacifist enrollment agency.[94]

At its 1921 conference the FOR authorized Hughan to establish a Committee for Enrollment Against War. Between January and April 1922 that committee collected one hundred antiwar pledges. Later that year it listed the benefits of a federation of war resisters. Federation would conserve scarce resources by providing a clearinghouse for pacifist ideas, activities, and literature. Also, by uniting absolute pacifists, a federation would foster "courage," "strength," "dignity," and a "sense of solidarity."[95] Finally, in the event of war a federation would help war resisters gain recognition that their opposition rested on principle rather than expedience.[96]

Around the same time, similar socialist pacifist developments were taking place on the other side of the Atlantic. In 1921 a European pacifist federation was formed, uniting the British No More War Movement with several smaller pacifist groups on the continent. This federation took the name "Paco"—Esperanto for peace. Soon after, the group transferred Paco's headquarters to England, elected H. Runham Brown honorary secretary, and renamed itself the War Resisters' International. Fenner Brockway, chair of the WRI, later explained the organization's radical nature:

> Those of us who founded the War Resisters' International insisted from the first that it must be anti-capitalist as well as pacifist. We repudiated "bourgeois" pacifism, wished to extend individual resistance to a general strike against war, and stood for "revolution by non-violence." The membership was both anarchist and socialist and, while assistance was given to religious objectors to war, the influence of the organisation was always exerted to emphasize the identity of the struggle against war and the struggle against the economic system which is its cause.[97]

This European socialist pacifist vision motivated Hughan and would characterize the WRL, whose members were also members of the WRI. It also distinguished the WRL from conservative prewar peace groups and reformist but less radical postwar peace organizations.[98]

From 1921 to 1924 the NMWM, which had promoted the general strike against war, organized worldwide No More War demonstrations on the anniversary of the outbreak of World War I. In New York City the WPS, the WPU, and the FOR—acting together through a federation committee of absolute pacifist groups—organized annual demonstrations marking the same event. Female peace activists, including Hughan, provided the primary leadership for the No More War parades. The women of the WPS and the WPU who organized the No More War demonstrations sustained Hughan and supported the creation of the WRL. Elinor Byrns and Olivia Torrence joined Hughan on the first WRL executive committee, as did two male No More War activists. In summary, female peace activism was an important source of Hughan's war resistance.[99]

Meanwhile, in February 1923, the FOR again endorsed Hughan's proposal for a new, inclusive organization and appointed a committee to establish a pacifist federation. On 15 March 1923 this committee met in Hughan's Manhattan apartment and formed the War Resisters League (though this name was not yet used consistently). The members adopted the declaration of the No More War Movement, the British section of the WRI: "I declare it to be my intention never to take part in war, offensive or defensive, international or civil, whether by bearing arms, making or handling munitions, voluntarily subscribing to war loans, or using my labor for the purpose of setting others free for war service."[100] Significantly, the declaration also pledged "to strive for the removal of all the causes of war, and to work for the establishment of a new social order based on co-operation for the common good."[101]

Calling itself the War Resisters Committee, the group extended to the WPS and the WPU a proposal for federation. Both accepted. With the FOR, the enlarged federation reorganized itself as the American Section of the War Resisters' International. As secretary, Hughan maintained contact with the WRI and other war resistance groups. In a letter to Runham Brown several months after the formative March meeting she reported: "We have at last succeeded in forming the *War Resisters' League,* which we request you consider as the American section of the War Resisters' International."[102] She explained that the newly constituted WRL had granted membership to members of the FOR, the WPS, and the WPU and was seeking to enroll individuals not connected with these pacifist groups.[103] The relationship between the *separate* WRL and the federation committee (under various names) would sometimes remain confused and blurred over the next two years; even so, the 15 March 1923 meeting marks the birth of the WRL as the oldest secular, mixed-gender, radical pacifist organization in the United States.[104]

Several weeks after this pivotal March meeting, the federation committee, representing the FOR, the WPS, and the WPU but for some reason not yet the WRL, took action on several matters. To emphasize its commitment to assertive pacifism the committee substituted "non-violent resistance" for "passive resistance."[105] It also voted to affiliate with the WRI. On 4 May 1923 the committee recommended to its constituent organizations that they join the WRI.[106]

Meeting on 11 February 1924, with only three members in attendance, the federation committee (renamed the War Resisters Committee) voted to discontinue regular meetings and to empower Hughan to conduct its business. Before adjourning, the committee observed: "The purpose for which the Committee was appointed has been accomplished,—namely the establishment of an American Section of the War Resisters' International, including the F.O.R., the W.P.S., and the W.P.U., and the putting into circulation of anti-war declarations to be signed by any person regardless of sex or religion." [107]

Within a year Hughan and other war resisters, spurred by Runham Brown and the No More War Movement, were leading the effort to resurrect and revitalize the absolute pacifist coalition. In response to Brown's "thrilling" manifesto of early 1925, urging pacifists to pressure their governments to endorse unilateral disarmament,[108] the WPU organized the first conference of all American absolute pacifist groups affiliated with the WRI. This meeting was held in the New York City home of FOR leaders Kathleen and John Sayre on 5 March 1925.[109] Participants discussed creating a loose federation of absolute pacifist organizations, elected delegates to the spring WRI London conference, drafted recommendations on strategies to abolish war to present at the London meeting, and planned an April "no more war" rally. Hughan observed that a similar committee, independent of the WRI, had been formed two years earlier but had lapsed. It is unclear whether she was referring to the WRL; however, she declared that this new federation represented a "revival" of the previous effort.[110]

On 13 March 1925 the representatives reconvened and established a permanent joint committee, temporarily named the War Resisters' International-United States Section. This group would represent absolute pacifist groups (the WRL, FOR, WPS, and WPU); provide a clearinghouse for information and communications both within the United States and in Europe; and promote collective peace action. In response to a motion by Hughan, the committee also decided to require an antiwar pledge for membership. By the end of April the group had renamed itself the War Resisters International-United States Committee and made Hughan its secretary. Yet the members of this committee remained preoccupied with their own separate organizations, and as a result the group fell into dormancy within two years. Even so, within the pacifist community, the reemergence of a federation committed to radical pacifism and to a declaration of war resistance amounted to an endorsement of Hughan's strategy of war resistance.[111]

Radical pacifists in America and England discussed the issue of gender and expressed support for Hughan's call for a mixed-gender organization of war resisters. Male and female pacifists alike saw that in the United States women were the most militant pacifists and dominated the emergent war resisters' movement. Radical pacifist leaders, including Hughan, valued the role of women but lamented that men and World War I COs were largely absent from the war resisters' movement in the United States. From London, Brown wrote: "I agree with Miss Hughan that it would be of very great value to get more men into the American groups." [112]

Indeed, gender informed Hughan's war resistance in significant ways. She retained membership in the Woman's Peace Party, the Women's International League for Peace and Freedom, the Women's Peace Society, and the Women's Peace Union. Her strategy of war resistance (which she did not expressly state until the late 1930s), based on collective individual refusal and mass nonviolent resistance, empowered women to participate in the historically male-dominated sphere of war and peace. Despite her feminism and her leadership in gender-exclusive women's peace groups, however, she championed mixed-gender organizations to promote pacifism, most notably the AEL and the WRL. In the context of a separate-spheres society, she argued that a male-led pacifist movement would prove more politically effective than a female-dominated movement. For this reason, although she led the WRL until World War II, she selected a man to hold the positions of chairman and (usually) vice chairman, retaining the title of secretary for herself. By remaining in the background, she hoped to protect the WRL from being "smeared as a woman-run organization." [113] In this way, patriarchy shaped her organizational strategy and rendered Hughan "invisible" to history. [114]

In the fall of 1925, Hughan informed WRI secretary Runham Brown that, with "exactly one dollar" in its bank account, the "small and struggling" WRL, [115] "which until this year has been only a committee with a few hundred scattered names enrolled by them, has now gotten fairly started as a real society for aggressive work." [116] With its radical pacifism, antiwar declaration, and acceptance of both men and women as members, the WRL embodied Hughan's vision of a pacifism both radical and practical and constituted a key part of the postwar pacifist movement.

In the late 1920s the League modified the declaration it had adopted at its historic March 1923 meeting. With minor changes, this revised declaration remains in effect today: "War is a crime against humanity. I, therefore, am determined not to support any kind of war, international or civil, and to strive for the removal of all the causes of war." [117] The WRL Declaration mirrored the No More War Movement pledge but differed from the declaration of the Anti-

Enlistment League. The AEL pledged to refuse support for international wars; in contrast, the WRL Declaration affirmed the intention of League members to oppose both international and civil war. According to Abraham Kaufman, the WRL's longtime executive secretary, the texts diverged in this way for two reasons. First, the declaration of the AEL had been written during the preparedness campaign, so it focused on World War I—an international war—with the goal of preventing American involvement in that conflict. Second, the pledges were circulated at socialist meetings and would have garnered less support if they had renounced civil war—a term encompassing class war.

Written after the 1917 Bolshevik Revolution, the WRL/WRI declaration condemned the violent class war of the Bolsheviks and others. While socialists had initially welcomed the Russian Revolution, by the early 1920s the Bolsheviks had resorted to repression and the socialists and communists were engaged in bitter political and ideological struggles. By condemning all wars, international and civil, the WRL Declaration had the unintended consequence of bolstering socialists and excluding communists, who supported both class war to advance socialism and defensive war to defend the Soviet Union.

The WRL Declaration retained the NMWM pledge "to strive for the removal of all the causes of war,"[118] which to the League meant capitalism, imperialism, militarism, nationalism, racism, and other social and economic causes of war and violence. Since 1923, as part of an international pacifist movement (WRI), the WRL has offered a radical pacifist critique of the existing order. Moreover, it has articulated an alternative to an international system based on national armed power; and to a capitalist system that, it argues, fosters rivalry and conflict, produces poverty and inequality, and represents class rather than democratic rule. In summary, the WRL has been the primary expression in America of the secular, radical pacifist Left—one with a pronounced democratic socialist orientation.[119]

# 2

# Consolidation and Growth

The WRL Between the World Wars, 1923–1941

FROM ITS BEGINNINGS as little more than "one corner of Jessie's bedroom,"[1] by the mid-1930s the War Resisters League had consolidated its operations, achieved organizational status, and expanded its peace activism. It had rented an office, hired a full-time executive secretary, recruited an impressive executive committee, published literature, sponsored pacifist projects, and participated in the powerful interwar peace movement. Between the world wars the WRL registered significant growth, began advancing the ideas of radical pacifism and Gandhian nonviolence, and consolidated its leadership of the secular pacifist Left.

World War I had spawned both liberal and radical pacifist groups, but the WRL would be the only secular, mixed-gender, absolute pacifist organization to survive the interwar years and World War II. Before World War I, the American peace movement had been dominated by conservative organizations controlled by male elites; in contrast, the post-1914 peace movement consisted of progressive social reformers, social-gospel clergy, feminists, and socialists committed to both peace and social justice.[2] Having established itself as the left wing of this postwar citizens' peace movement, the WRL espoused a secular, socialist-orientated, absolute pacifism. The League's secular radical pacifism differed from religious pacifism, Christian nonresistance, liberal pacifism, and communist peace advocacy, as well as from the antiwar but nonpacifist platforms of organizations such as the Socialist Party. This chapter examines the ideology and activism of the WRL and representative League leaders.

## WRL Peace Leaders: Experiences, Ideas, and Activism

Despite its modest size and resources, the WRL attracted talented men and women to its banner during the interwar years. In accord with its inclusive phi-

23

losophy, the WRL enrolled radicals, socialists, anarchists, liberals, and even conservatives—whoever repudiated all war and armed revolution. "Our goal," the WRL declared, "is to unite men and women who have determined to give no support to any war, irrespective of the reasons—political, religious, or humanitarian—which have led them to take this stand."[3] Because it welcomed all absolute pacifists, the League had a diverse membership that held various views on pacifism and politics. The WRL was a democratic, libertarian, and nonhierarchical organization. It emphasized consensus, rejected a party line, and allowed internal dissent.

For the sake of targeting its limited resources and preserving its unity, before World War II the WRL remained a single-issue group, that issue being war resistance, and did not take official stands on general social, economic, and political issues. Hughan believed that such issues should be addressed by the Socialist Party and in other multi-issue venues and that the WRL should avoid general issues of social justice that would divide its membership and interfere with its primary mission. Accordingly, the WRL seldom issued official statements on specific world events or foreign policy matters. Notwithstanding its diverse membership and organizational policies, the impulse behind the WRL's radical pacifism was secular and socialist-oriented.[4]

To assess the League's significance, historians must examine the experiences, perspectives, and contributions of its individual members. There are several reasons why. First, although it restricted itself to peace activism in order to concentrate its scarce resources and avoid factionalism over the most effective means to eradicate "the causes of war,"[5] the League helped construct a vibrant peace culture—which nourished both peace and justice. WRL activists shared a radical, mainly socialist vision, worked for both peace and social justice, and were involved in various liberal reform and socialist projects outside the League. Second, through the League's broad social justice activism, its members advocated radical pacifism and Gandhian nonviolence within the American reform movement. Third, the experiences, ideas, and activism of key WRL members illustrate the different strands of pacifism within the League, the main constituencies within the League or related to it, and the contributions of its members to the peace, civil liberties, labor, and socialist movements.

Even a brief examination indicates that most members of the WRL were middle-class professionals[6] and that the WRL was a secular organization with progressive roots that strove to popularize radical pacifism and Gandhian nonviolence through its literature and its activism. It exerted influence beyond the pacifist movement. Moreover, despite its official stance of apolitical pluralism, the WRL leaned strongly toward socialism. When its members worked to eradicate social injustice, they were honoring the League's pledge "to strive for the removal of all the causes of war."[7] To most League members, this meant abolishing capitalism.

### Abraham Kaufman and Secular Jewish Socialist Pacifism

For nearly two decades, Abraham Kaufman (1908– ) was the WRL's executive secretary and administrative backbone. Besides being Hughan's surrogate son, he and Hughan were close friends and political partners for thirty years. In the mid-1970s, Kaufman summarized his role: "[I] have not been one of the prophetic voices of pacifism as have Jessie Hughan or Evan T[homas] or Isidor Hoffman or J[ohn] H[aynes] Holmes. I have been the administrative, working executive in the WRL who tried to make best use of the excellent people who really ran the League."[8]

Kaufman was exposed to socialism from childhood. Like many Jews, his father had fled Russian oppression in 1905 or 1906. In the Jewish immigrant community of the South Bronx, Kaufman grew up listening to socialist debates in his father's dry goods store. By the time he was ten or twelve he was attending socialist street-corner meetings and open-air debates between the SP and the Socialist Labor Party (SLP). In 1924 he joined the Young People's Socialist League (YPSL), whose members were known as Yipsels. Two years later, through his involvement with the Yipsels, he met Ida Yavner, who became his wife and his comrade in both the SP and the WRL.

Spiritually, Kaufman considered himself an atheist and a humanist. In 1926 he joined the Unitarian Bronx Free Fellowship, a group cofounded by Hughan and led by the Rev. Leon Rosser Land, a future member of the WRL executive committee. In the 1930s Kaufman also joined the Brooklyn Ethical Culture Society. He viewed rabbis as a reactionary force in the Jewish community—at least he did until the 1930s, when he met progressive rabbis in the WRL such as Isidor Hoffman, Sidney Goldstein, and Abraham Cronbach. Though he remained a secular Jew, after World War II he began to appreciate the relevance of the Jewish prophets to his socialism and pacifism.

Kaufman met Hughan in 1922, when he attended her tenth-grade English class at Textile High School. Besides teaching, Hughan served as the school disciplinarian, acting English Department chair, and textbook custodian. Once, when Kaufman was sent to Hughan for talking in chemistry lab, she had him serve the standard five days' after-school detention by helping her in the bookroom. In 1924 he noticed that she was wearing a campaign button promoting Robert LaFollette, the Progressive Party candidate for president, whom he and the SP supported. When he asked her about the button, she told him she was a socialist. This led to a political discussion, which led to a thirty-year friendship.

Kaufman and Hughan formed a "Veritas Club" at the school. Even after he graduated he attended the club meetings at Hughan's apartment; the discussions there led him to embrace pacifism. "From her I learned about Gandhi's use of truth as a weapon and I became a pacifist as well as socialist," he later recalled.[9] On his eighteenth birthday, 5 December 1926, he signed the WRL Declaration and joined the League.

After graduating from Textile, Kaufman worked his way through the City University of New York. In October 1928, Jessie and her sister Evelyn, contributing $5 a week each, hired Kaufman as Jessie's assistant. That made him the WRL's first paid employee. Until then, he recalls, Jessie had expedited League work "from her bedroom typewriter with the advice of an advisory committee which she had gotten together and which met occasionally—I would guess 3 or 4 times a year."[10] At the time, the League possessed only two pieces of literature—a *Life* magazine antiwar cartoon and a WRL membership card with its declaration. With Kaufman's administrative assistance, Hughan wrote the first four-page League folders: "What is the WRL?" and "What Is War Resistance?" Although Kaufman had earned Jessie's respect, both she and Evelyn told him that he had been hired, in part, because he was a man.[11]

During the late 1920s and 1930s, Kaufman participated in United Front organizations. This bitter experience shaped his staunch anticommunism as well as his strong distrust of the Communist Party. In 1928 he served as treasurer of the United States Committee of Youth Against War and Fascism, a United Front group that dissolved when it failed to take over the SP and YPSL. He chaired a YPSL investigation into the disruptive role of communists in two New York Yipsel circles. In 1933 he represented the WRL in meetings with Earl Browder, SP representatives, pacifists, and other radicals; these led to the founding of the Congress Against War and Fascism, another United Front organization and precursor to the American League Against War and Fascism. The WRL never joined the American League Against War and Fascism, which championed (armed) collective security; however, the League did cooperate with it on specific projects. Like most WRL members who debated affiliation versus cooperation with the American League Against War and Fascism, Kaufman urged organizational separation from the group. Having been "burned" by sectarian communist politics,[12] he retained an intense distrust of the Communist Party and communists.[13]

During the 1930s and 1940s, Kaufman assumed several administrative positions in the peace movement. He was secretary of the United Pacifist Committee and the Joint Peace Board (later renamed the Peace Strategy Board). Formed in

1938, the United Pacifist Committee promoted cooperation among absolute pacifist individuals and organizations in the New York area. In 1942, the WRL initiated the formation of the Joint Peace Board to provide a venue for peace groups to exchange information on specific projects. In addition, in response to the 1940 draft, Kaufman cofounded the Metropolitan Board for Conscientious Objectors, which provided free, nonsectarian counseling and sometimes legal aid to COs in the New York region.[14]

### John Haynes Holmes: Religious Pacifism and Gandhian Nonviolence

The Reverend John Haynes Holmes (1879–1964), cofounder of the Anti-Enlistment League (1915) and the WRL's chair or honorary chair from 1929 to 1943, was one of America's most prominent religious pacifists and Christian nonresistants during the interwar decades.[15] From his powerful pulpit at the Unitarian Church of the Messiah (reconstituted in 1919 as the nondenominational Community Church of New York), Holmes trumpeted pacifism and condemned both world wars. Besides being a peace activist, Holmes was an influential socialist, social gospel reformer, author, and editor. Most significantly, he was the earliest champion of Mohandas Gandhi in the United States.

Holmes participated in many reform movements. He cofounded and remained a leader in the FOR, the National Association for the Advancement of Colored People (NAACP), and the American Civil Liberties Union. He championed free speech and birth control; he worked to free Sacco and Vanzetti and Tom Mooney; and he helped expose political corruption in New York City. Portraying socialism as "political Christianity,"[16] he was a member of the SP. In 1935 he broke with the Soviet regime over the purge trials and became a vocal critic of the Bolsheviks and pro-Soviet liberals: "I am unwilling to condemn ghastly horrors in Nazi Germany, and denounce dreadful crimes in my own country, and then remain silent when I see these horrors and crimes, or even worse, being perpetrated in Russia."[17]

In response to World War I, Holmes turned to the teachings of Jesus, the Quakers, Romain Rolland, and Leo Tolstoy. The experience made him a pacifist. He cofounded the Anti-Enlistment League with Hughan, joined the American Union Against Militarism, and opposed the preparedness campaign. He crystallized his pacifist views in *New Wars For Old* (1916). Writing to rehabilitate nonresistance and to preserve American neutrality, he argued that nonresistance offered a "reasonably efficacious substitute for the more or less futile method of force."[18] Force and violence, he asserted, generated counterforce and counterviolence and inevitably led to new conflict. Even when the side of good won, war perpetuated war and was for that reason incapable of fostering lasting peace and security. Challenging the popular view that equated nonresistance with cowardly, passive acquiescence, he contended that nonresistance demanded positive nonviolent resistance to injustice and aggression, including love, reason, and "passive" resistance.[19]

In a powerful sermon on 1 April 1917—the day before President Wilson was to deliver his war message to Congress—in front of an anxious overflow crowd, Holmes declared himself a war resister. He condemned the nation's impending entry into the conflict, declared his opposition to war, and detailed an alternative pacifist program for fostering international brotherhood and preserving American democratic ideals and liberties: "When hostilities begin, it is universally assumed that there is but one service which a loyal citizen can render to the state—that of bearing arms and killing the enemy. . . . This I cannot and will not do."[20]

Holmes was the first leader to popularize Gandhi in the United States. By the winter of 1918, more than two years before Gandhi and his noncooperation campaign captured the attention of the American press, Holmes had become the Indian's preeminent American disciple. Over the next three decades he eloquently popularized Gandhi's significance and relevance through sermons, articles, and books and through his personal involvement in the WRL and other nonviolent reform organizations and projects.[21] In 1926 *Unity* magazine, which Holmes edited, serialized Gandhi's autobiography, making it available in English for the first time. In sum, Holmes pioneered the Americanization of Gandhi.

"Who is the Greatest Man in the World?" Holmes asked in an April 1921 Community Church sermon. Then, honoring a man unknown to most of his audience, he preached about Gandhi. Holmes proclaimed the little-known Indian as "unquestionably the greatest man living in the world today, and one of the greatest men who has ever lived."[22] He described Gandhi's earlier, two-decade-long passive resistance campaign to win social and political rights for the South African Indian community and his current struggle to secure Indian independence from British rule. He stressed that nonresistance was not passive acquiescence but "a positive and aggressive policy"[23] and that its techniques, which included noncooperation and boycotts, were both moral and realistic. He quoted Gandhi on the link between courage and pacifism: "I believe in the doctrine of non-violence as a weapon not of the weak but of the strong."[24] Significantly, in view of its key role in the WRL's ideology, Holmes portrayed Gandhian nonresistance as a strike.[25]

A year later, Holmes preached on the "World Significance of Mahatma

Gandhi." The previous year, most members of the Community Church had never heard of "the greatest man in the world";[26] by 1922, as Holmes noted, the press was featuring Gandhi on its front pages as the leader of the growing movement for Indian independence. Holmes endorsed Gandhi's anti-imperialist message but added that his true significance was in his spiritual leadership, his doctrine of nonresistance, and his challenge to Western capitalist materialism.

Most importantly, Holmes emphasized the social relevance of Gandhian passive resistance to the American pacifist movement. Nonresistance by then had a long tradition, but Gandhi was the first leader to adopt it as a method for promoting social change and solving social problems on a vast scale. Holmes declared that those traditional nonresistants who "solved the problems of life by running away from them"[27] were irrelevant to efforts to end modern industrial conflict and international war. Gandhi, however, was a new type of nonresistant who "demonstrated the feasibility of non-resistance as a method of political and economic reform, and . . . [like] Newton or Darwin, opened up a new era in human history." "If Gandhi succeeds [in obtaining Indian independence]," Holmes continued, "we shall see that non-resistance is a sound method of social action, [and that] resort to violence for any cause is no longer necessary."[28]

Besides shaping the enduring image of Gandhi as a nonviolent nationalist, around 1919 Holmes began portraying him in a manner consistent with his own Christian nonresistance. In doing so he created a lasting interpretive symbol of Gandhi in America. "But when I think of Gandhi," Holmes professed in 1921, "I think of Jesus Christ."[29] Like a modern Plutarch, he popularized the parallel lives of Gandhi and Christ. Both men exemplified nonresistance, love for mankind (including one's enemies), personal sacrifice and suffering, and spiritual leadership, and both identified with the masses. In 1922, Holmes dubbed Gandhi the "Christ of our age."[30]

Holmes popularized radical pacifism and Gandhian nonviolence in a Broadway production. On his way home from London in 1931 after his first meeting with Gandhi, Holmes outlined *If This Be Treason*, a pacifist play that anticipated Pearl Harbor. It was presented on Broadway during the 1935–36 season. The play featured a newly elected pacifist American president confronting a Japanese attack on the U.S. fleet in Manila harbor. Learning that his predecessor had provoked the attack by issuing an ultimatum to the emperor and by dispatching the fleet in accordance with a secret preparedness plan, the new president defied prowar sentiment and ordered that the fleet be withdrawn and that mobilization be canceled. Furthermore, he proclaimed the Kellogg-Briand Pact (outlawing aggressive war) to be as "sacred"[31] as the Constitution and vowed "to make peace, instead of war."[32] Like Gandhi in London, the pacifist president traveled to Japan; there, in meetings with the recalcitrant premier and his militarist advisers, he declared his refusal to make war and desire to seek peace. For a season at least, the audience at the Music Box Theatre (which the WRL leafleted) witnessed the triumph of pacifism over war—a stark contrast to the U.S. response to the events at Pearl Harbor six years later.[33]

In early 1938, ill health forced Holmes to resign from the chairmanship of the WRL, and the League offered him the post of "honorary chairman." Holmes accepted, and continued to lend the WRL his great prestige.[34]

## Devere Allen and Political Pacifism

Devere Allen (1891–1955), a leader in the pacifist and socialist movements, provided a vital bridge between the SP and both the WRL and the broader pacifist community.[35] From his initial religious impulse and Quaker roots, he became one of the most prominent political pacifists of the interwar period. As a student at Oberlin College, Allen opposed American entry in World War I, joined the Intercollegiate Socialist Society, supported suffragists, edited antiwar publications, and participated in campus peace and justice movements. Between 1928 and 1940 he served on the WRL's executive committee, usually as vice chair; he also served a term on the WRI world council. Allen was also an influential editor, journalist, lecturer, author, and peace historian. More than any member of the WRL, he publicized the complex and challenging issues that the Spanish Civil War raised for war resisters.

Allen played a leading role in interwar peace and justice movements. Besides working with the WRL, he served on the FOR's executive committee and international council, the Pacifist Action Committee, and the Emergency Peace Campaign. He also cofounded the League for Independent Political Action and the American League for India's Freedom. He held important positions in the SP: he sat on its national executive committee, attended the Labor and Socialist International as an SP delegate, and was a member of the boards of both the League for Industrial Democracy and the *American Socialist Quarterly*. The SP nominated or endorsed Allen as a Connecticut candidate for senator (1932 and 1934) and governor (1938). Finally, Allen wrote the controversial "Declaration of Principles" (1934), which sparked fierce debate over the meaning of war resistance and the role of violence in the class struggle and which did much to generate the factionalism that shattered the SP between 1934 and 1940.

During the interwar period, Allen became a well-known and influential journalist and editor. Between 1921 and 1933 he edited the FOR's magazine, the *World Tomorrow*, which advocated pacifism and a radical, multi-issue agenda for social reform. Impatient with the "christocentric"[36] orientation of the *World Tomorrow* and of staff members Kirby Page and Reinhold Niebuhr, he moved over to the *Nation* in 1931 before returning to the *World Tomorrow* the following year.

During a working trip to Europe in 1930–31, Allen investigated current developments, wrote articles for the *Nation* and other American journals, and cultivated contacts with assorted radicals, socialists, and members of the WRI and International FOR. Notably, he interviewed Gandhi, then attending the London Round Table Conference.

In Europe, Allen experienced firsthand the 1931 Spanish Revolution. Invoking John Reed and the Bolshevik Revolution, he dubbed his sojourn in revolutionary Spain the "Ten Days That Shook DA."[37] But what most struck him about the Spanish Revolution was its relative lack of violence. In a dispatch published in the *World Tomorrow*, he emphasized the role of nonviolence—a strategy that received little support five years later during the Spanish Civil War. "A nonpacifist people," he observed in 1931, "led by men who have hardly given a thought to pacifism . . . conducted one of the greatest overturns of history with almost perfect self-control, with marvelous solidarity, with passion entirely devoid of violence."[38] For Allen, pacifism could not accomplish enough as long as it limited itself to religious ethics and personal witness. Spain gave him an opportunity to develop his views on the task ahead for political pacifists. "The pacifist . . . must ally himself . . . with the great world movement for economic change, seeking frankly to bend it away from the violent views . . . but aiding in the building up everywhere of disciplined working-class bodies for the overthrow of privilege," Allen argued. "For in the combination of non-violent principle with revolutionary aims is a power that can shake thrones and systems, and equally hold men's minds to the creation of new worlds."[39]

In 1933, Allen launched the No-Frontier News Service, an international news agency that would provide independent alternative news, especially about world events and the peace movement. Initially he envisaged the project as a global peace news service, "construing peace news to include economic relations, of course, as well as all the other factors involved in war."[40] Believing that economic justice was the bedrock for peace, he hoped the service would promote peace and social justice. Broader than a pacifist press agency, the venture (which would later be renamed Worldover Press) was sympathetic to the peace movement. Perhaps one-third of its reporters worldwide were pacifists. Eventually nearly seven hundred newspapers from sixty-two countries subscribed to the service, which often provided more insightful news and analysis than the mainstream press. As historian Charles Chatfield has concluded, Allen provided a respectable source of transnational news to promote international understanding, and thereby served both the peace movement and the general public.

Besides all of the above, Allen was a pioneer peace historian. In 1930 he published *The Fight for Peace,* a classic analysis of the American peace movement and alternative peace strategies. Written from the perspective of a secular socialist pacifist, his study combined historical scholarship, contemporary analysis, and spirited polemic. Several themes dominated his account: the primacy of economics in determining war and peace, support for the radical wing of the peace movement, and the imperative to oppose *all* war. In addition, Allen marshaled arguments in support of pacifism and war resistance. Indeed, *The Fight for Peace* offers an eloquent statement of the secular, radical pacifist assumptions, philosophy, and techniques of the WRL.

Allen championed the radical wing of the historical peace movement. He approved its repudiation of *all* war—international, offensive, defensive, and internal, as well as those conflicts fought for "noble" ends.[41] For instance, he praised William Lloyd Garrison's antebellum New England Non-Resistance Society, a radical rival to the American Peace Society: "At last, there was a peace organization that was almost super-pacifist, you might say and without any bars of sex or color." [42] But he reserved his highest praise for Elihu Burritt, founder of the League of Universal Brotherhood (1846) and one of the few pacifists who opposed the Civil War. Like the WRL, Burritt endorsed political action (which Garrison rejected), supported the labor movement and a general strike against war, welcomed women, and required members to pledge in writing not to enlist in the military and not to support the preparation or prosecution of any war.

Allen criticized the middle-class peace movement for failing to forge close ties with the labor movement and for failing to emphasize sufficiently the importance of economic justice to world peace. He asserted that workers had the most to gain from peace and could form the "raw materials" [43] for a "strike" against war. He called for a peace-labor alliance, arguing that peace did not have to await socialism. Wars would cease only when citizens refused to fight for their nation. Not surprisingly, he praised Burritt's written peace pledge, a tactic that became central to the strategy of war resistance adopted by Hughan and the WRL some seventy-five years later.

In *The Fight for Peace,* Allen did more than write a history of the American peace movement. The concluding chapters championed war resistance and nonviolent resistance as the most *effective* strategies for attaining peace and justice. He cited many examples of nonviolent resistance, endorsed the "general strike for peace," [44] and emphasized that passive resistance—despite the term's unfortunate and erroneous connotation—actually constituted active nonviolent resistance. In a powerful polemical chapter that spoke to current conditions, he rebutted the common objections to war resistance and marshaled the contributions that pacifism had made in the fight for peace.

Allen observed that World War I spawned a new type of nonreligious political pacifist, or war resister. These pacifists founded the transnational WRI to resist war *and* address the social conditions that caused conflict. Allen now wanted to transcend conscientious objection and build a secular, nonviolent social movement that could abolish war and promote justice by transforming existing social and economic conditions. He insisted that such a social movement would require middle-class radical pacifists to embrace the working class, "who bear the brunt of war and settle its bills." [45]

In August 1940, Allen resigned as WRL vice chairman to serve the peace movement through the No-Frontier News Service.[46]

## Frances Witherspoon, Tracy D. Mygatt, and the Women's Peace Movement

Frances Witherspoon (1887–1973) and Tracy D. Mygatt (1885–1973) illustrate the WRL's links to the women's peace movement and the civil liberties movement. Sharing a lifelong "Boston marriage" partnership, Witherspoon and Mygatt were active pacifists, socialists, suffragists, social reformers, and writers. Friends of Jessie Wallace Hughan, they were charter members of the Anti-Enlistment League (1915) and the WRL (1923), serving on League's executive committee in 1930 and during and after World War II. Both women came from upper-middle-class families. Witherspoon's father, who represented Mississippi in Congress (1913–15), shaped her pacifist views. He opposed military spending, the Spanish-American War, Theodore Roosevelt's jingoistic foreign policy, and Woodrow Wilson's 1914 seizure of Veracruz, Mexico, which led to bloodshed and near war. Mygatt's ancestors had come to America in the 1630s.

After graduating from Bryn Mawr College in 1909, Witherspoon and Mygatt moved to New York City and plunged into social activism. In 1910, Mygatt established the Chelsea Day Nursery for working mothers and their children. On the eve of World War I they became Christian socialists, joined the SP, and participated in the 1913 "Church Raids," which sought to persuade churches to provide food and shelter to unemployed men. In 1915 they joined the SP's Socialist Suffrage Committee and organized the Socialist Suffrage Brigade to mobilize support for a New York referendum on women's suffrage, which failed to pass.

During World War I, Witherspoon and Mygatt helped lead the antiwar movement, the women's peace movement, and the civil liberties movement. Both of them joined the Anti-Enlistment League, the Emergency Peace Federation, the SP, the American Union Against Militarism, the People's Council, the FOR, and the Woman's Peace Party (WPP); they also coedited *Four Lights,* the publication of the WPP-New York Branch. Like Hughan, they demonstrate the link between prewar suffragist activism and the wartime and postwar women's peace movement. After the war, as well as their work for the WRL and FOR, they enlisted in the Women's International League for Peace and Freedom and the Women's Peace Union. Expert writers, they also publicized pacifism through books, plays, and articles.[47]

In addition to all this, Witherspoon made an important contribution to the First World War civil liberties movement through the New York Bureau of Legal Advice. Formed in May 1917 by feminist pacifists and supported by the SP, labor radicals, and radical pacifists, this organization has often been confused with or overshadowed by the American Union Against Militarism's Civil Liberties Bureau (later the independent National Civil Liberties Bureau led by Roger Baldwin). After it was reorganized on a broader basis in July, the Bureau of Legal Advice took responsibility for all civil liberties cases in the New York City area. Witherspoon served as the group's executive secretary, while Mygatt performed volunteer work.

The Bureau of Legal Advice provided free counseling and legal assistance to thousands of conscientious objectors and their families as well as to people who found themselves being persecuted for expressing unpopular opinions. It also functioned as a legal clearinghouse and counsel for pacifist organizations and publicized legal and legislative developments involving civil liberties. The bureau maintained contact with COs after they had been assigned to military camps and thus was able to wage a successful campaign to abolish army brutality. (In one incident, some uncooperative COs were punished by being manacled and hung by their wrists from prison bars for nine hours a day.) After the war, Witherspoon and the bureau participated in a campaign to extend amnesty to the three hundred COs and 1,500 political prisoners still incarcerated. Finally, the bureau provided legal services for legal aliens (often Wobblies) victimized by the postwar Red Scare and awaiting deportation. In 1920, however, the Bureau of Legal Advice folded its tent. In this same period, the National Civil Liberties Bureau reorganized as the American Civil Liberties Union. Still headed by Roger Baldwin, the ACLU absorbed some of the Bureau of Legal Adivce's work.

According to historian Frances Early, during World War I, Witherspoon, Mygatt, and the Bureau of Legal Advice helped build a democratic "peace culture,"[48] a culture that would benefit the WRL and the peace movement in the interwar period. The counseling and legal aid that the bureau provided COs closely resembled the activities the WRL would perform during World War II. The WRL thus continued the peace and civil liberties legacies of Witherspoon, Mygatt, and the Bureau of Legal Advice.[49]

### A. J. Muste and Nonviolent Labor Radicalism

Netherlands-born A. J. Muste (1885–1967) became one of America's most important activists for the Left, labor, and pacifism. He served on the WRL's executive committee from 1937 to 1953 and was quite influential in the League, but he was more closely identified with the FOR, which he joined during World War I, later serving as its national chair (1926–29) and executive secretary (1940–53). Ordained into the Dutch Reformed Church in 1909, he became a Quaker in 1918.

In 1919, Muste headed the strike committee that led the Lawrence textile strike on behalf of thirty thousand workers. During the four bloody months of conflict that followed, the police clubbed strikers (including Muste) and positioned machine guns along major thoroughfares to intimidate and provoke the strikers. Aware that worker violence would discredit the strike and prompt overwhelming state violence, Muste urged—and the strike committee adopted—a nonviolent strategy. The strike ended in a victory for labor. Roger Baldwin, a World War I CO and longtime leader of the ACLU, observed: "That Lawrence strike was especially significant because it was one of the first examples of collective, pacifist pro-labor activity led by ministers."[50]

The Lawrence workers rejected the United Textile Workers (an AFL union) and in 1919 helped organize the rival Amalgamated Textile Workers of America (ATWA), a more militant and radical union. Between 1919 and 1921, Muste served as general secretary of the ATWA and edited its journal, *New Textile Worker*. Over the next two years he organized many strikes before resigning to head the Brookwood Labor College in Katonah, New York.

Between 1921 and 1933, Muste directed Brookwood, the nation's first residential school for workers. Brookwood offered adult education to labor leaders and advocated industrial unionism. Brookwood's socialist-oriented instructors trained their students in the skills and techniques they would require to mobilize workers, organize strikes, and administer unions. During his time at Brookwood, Muste moved farther and farther left, becoming increasingly involved in revolutionary labor activities. By the late 1920s he had abandoned the FOR, Christianity, and pacifism.

In 1929, Muste cofounded the Conference for Progressive Labor Action (CPLA) to challenge and reform the AFL. Its platform endorsed industrial unionism, an end to discrimination within unions, unemployment benefits and social insurance, a five-day week, recognition of the Soviet Union, formation of a labor party, and opposition to imperialism and militarism. The CPLA led and supported strikes in textiles, steel, and coal. Because of these activities, it found itself confronting John L. Lewis, who at that time was defending craft unions. Communist Party leader William Z. Foster felt threatened by the independent Left position of the CPLA (often referred to as the Musteites), and dubbed its members "little brothers of the big labor fakirs."[51] Muste resigned from Brookwood in 1933 after his efforts to align the college with the CPLA inspired a faculty revolt.

In 1933, Muste and the CPLA established the American Workers Party, a democratic, independent, revolutionary party that sought a "third way" between socialism and communism.[52] The American Workers Party supported the Scottsboro boys and led the 1934 Toledo Auto-Lite strike, a militant labor campaign that prompted the Communist League of America (Trotskyists) to propose a merger. In December 1934 the two united to form the new Workers Party, U.S.A., led by Muste. In 1936 the party participated in the Akron Goodyear Rubber strike, the first CIO strike to resort to sit-down tactics. At that time, Muste appeared to have broken with pacifism; the Workers Party constitution asserted that "the policy of folded arms, passive resistance, 'conscientious objection' etc. is completely futile as a means of struggle against imperialist war, regardless of the sincerity and courage of those who resort to it."[53]

In August 1936, Muste took a European vacation, during which he visited Leon Trotsky in Norway and attended a Trotskyist meeting in Paris. He also visited Paris's Left Bank Church of St. Sulpice, where he had a mystical conversion. While remaining a socialist, he rejected Marxism-Leninism and returned to Christianity. Back in America he announced his break with Trotskyism and rejoined the FOR, which elected him to its national council and appointed him its industrial secretary, charged with applying nonviolent techniques to labor disputes. Muste served as the FOR's executive secretary from 1940 until he retired in 1953. Between 1937 and 1940 he also headed the Presbyterian Labor Temple in New York City. Located in a working-class slum, the temple sponsored public forums, classes, and speakers, besides providing a meeting place for unions.

By the beginning of World War II, Muste had undergone a dramatic odyssey from pacifism to Marxist-Leninism and back to pacifism. Perhaps more than any other WRL leader, he had participated in the labor movement at both the grassroots and leadership levels. Likewise, he had led several independent revolutionary socialist organizations. Allen had urged the peace movement to forge closer links with the labor movement, but it was Muste who actually led this effort. As a result of these experiences he developed superb organizing skills and excellent contacts in the labor movement, which he later tapped to obtain funding for pacifist projects. In mid-1939, *Time* magazine dubbed Muste "The Number One U.S. Pacifist."[54]

## Evan W. Thomas and Conscientious Objection

Evan Thomas (1890–1974) was a World War I conscientious objector who chaired the WRL during and after World War II. He was also a doctor with expertise in syphilis. Despite his individualistic bent and his aversion to organizations, Thomas joined the WRL and FOR in the late 1930s and remained a WRL leader until 1950.

Thomas enrolled in Union Theological Seminary on the eve of World War I. Embracing its social gospel doctrines, he acted on these principles through his work at the American Parish Among Immigrants in New York City's East Harlem. He worked with his brother Norman, who was the FOR's secretary at the time and a member of the National Civil Liberties Bureau. In order to witness the Great War from a closer vantage point, Thomas decided to continue his theological studies in Edinburgh, Scotland.

In 1915 and 1916, while a student in Britain, Thomas became a pacifist; he also grew more and more ambivalent toward organized Christianity. Influenced by the New Testament, Jesus, Leo Tolstoy, and social gospel thought, he adopted an opposition to war based on religious nonresistance. By talking with soldiers and by reading letters that classmates received from brothers at the front, he learned how the barracks and the battlefields crushed individualism and conscience—a realization that was central to his rejection of war and militarism. He found the COs' refusal to kill appealing; significantly, he observed that most COs operated outside the church. In May 1916 he wrote his mother: "It is the 'conscientious objector' in the countries now at war that opens up the only way to permanent peace."[55] Criticizing the churches for "their intolerance, their emphasis on externals rather than the spirit, their smug self-satisfaction and self-righteousness," he suggested that Christian work and ethics be secularized, applied to social issues, and advanced outside the organized church.[56]

Between November 1916 and September 1917, under the auspices of the Young Men's Christian Association (YMCA), Thomas carried out volunteer work in German prisoner-of-war camps in England. To provide Christian service and to meet the requirements of the Hague Conventions, the YMCA had established social centers and service programs in the camps to meet the POWs' religious, educational, and recreational needs. Thomas visited these camps and spoke with the prisoners, noting that the camps' thriving social life (schools, theater, choirs, and gymnastics) was organized mainly from within by the POWs themselves. The prisoners' efforts empowered them and provided Thomas with examples of community organization that he later promoted in American CO camps during both world wars.

Thomas and several American YMCA secretaries administering the POW programs became increasingly disillusioned with the war and began meeting for monthly discussions. These secretaries provided Thomas with a pacifist network; all but one of them would be imprisoned as COs in American military jails and camps.[57] Thomas returned to the United States in September 1917 in a mood of disenchantment, aware that he was facing conscription.

In Britain, Thomas continued to sharpen his thinking on his own role in advancing pacifist, humanitarian, social, and ethical ideals. He accepted the need for governments and organizations, yet he also realized that he was a radical individualist unwilling to compromise his principles. This led him to reject a career in the church and to turn away from institutions generally. According to Charles Chatfield, Thomas's YMCA experience "solidified" his pacifist ideas [58] and provided "a bridge to active war resistance."[59] Thomas soon had the opportunity to transform his ideals into action.

On being inducted in April 1918, Thomas took an absolutist CO position, refusing to cooperate in any way with the military authorities administering the CO camps. He was one of the 3,989 American COs drafted during the war and one the 450 COs court-martialed and imprisoned for their absolutist refusal to cooperate with the system. Thomas, who was strikingly tall at six feet seven inches and had a keen sense of humor, became a CO leader. In a letter to his brother from Fort Leavenworth, Kansas, Thomas explained his position. "I am a C.O. because of freedom, first, last, and all the time," he wrote Norman. "I think disarmament and leagues of nations . . . futile. . . . War will end when the people refuse to be conscripted."[60] This last phrase anticipated the WRL's motto.[61]

In 1918, Thomas participated in two hunger strikes to protest the militarization and denial of individual liberty that conscription and the army-administered CO camps entailed. The first lasted three days. On 19 August 1918, at the Fort Riley CO tent colony five hours from Fort Leavenworth, Thomas and more than twenty other absolutists (including Howard Moore, Harold Gray, and Erling Lund) began a second hunger strike to obtain prepared food instead of raw food rations, which required processing and cooking. The next day, Moore broadened the strike into an anticonscription protest, vowing not to eat until he was released. Thomas, Gray, and Lund joined him in this. In a letter to the secretary of war, Newton D. Baker, the four men explained: "We are unalterably opposed to the principle of conscription and believe it to be un-American as well as the very backbone of militarism and war, hereafter [we intend] to resist any restrictions on our liberty under the Selective Service Act." [62] In a letter to his brother the same day, Thomas exclaimed: " 'Give me liberty or death.' " [63] Six days into the strike, Thomas was hospitalized and force-fed through a tube inserted down his throat. Opposed to suicide and realizing that the strike would not achieve its goal, Thomas quit his fast after fourteen days.

Thomas and his cohorts soon announced that they would begin yet another hunger strike on 16 September if the camp's food policies did not change. When they didn't appear for roll call on that day, Thomas and Moore were arrested, imprisoned, and placed in the "hole" (solitary confinement), where they were fed bread and water. A month later, Thomas's court-martial convened. The court ignored the prosecutor's request for the death penalty and sentenced Thomas to life imprisonment; this was later reduced to twenty-five years hard labor in the Ft. Leavenworth Disciplinary Barracks. At Leavenworth, as prisoner #14822, Thomas experienced his most difficult wartime years.

On entering Leavenworth, Thomas considered himself a political prisoner and agreed to work. However, on 6 November 1918, after working for two weeks, Thomas started a work strike to protest the treatment of the Molokan COs. The Molokans were a Christian sect from Russia whose religion forbade them to obey military orders. When they refused a work order, they were court-martialed and locked in solitary confinement.

Thomas suffered the same fate. He was confined to the "hole"—a windowless, five-by-nine-foot cell—for two weeks with only several thin blankets infested with bedbugs and a sleeping board eighteen inches wide. The floor was cold, damp concrete; the diet was bread and water. Like the other prisoners in the hole, he was handcuffed to the crossbars of his cell door in a standing position for nine hours each day, his hands locked either over his head or at waist height. Following intervention by the Bureau of Legal Advice and the National Civil Liberties Bureau, President Wilson abolished manacling on 6 December. Thomas was removed from solitary during Christmas week, and released from Leavenworth on 14 January 1919.

After his discharge, Thomas campaigned for amnesty for still-imprisoned COs, worked in the labor movement, and drifted around the country. On Thanksgiving Day 1920 the last thirty-three COs in American prisons were pardoned and released.

For several months Thomas served as secretary of the militant Amalgamated

Textile Workers of America local in Paterson, New Jersey, where silk workers were engaged in a strike action. However, Thomas was uncomfortable with organizations generally and with the hard-nosed organizing techniques used to build a labor movement. He also found himself able to understand the perspectives of both workers and decent bosses and frustrated by disruptive communist elements. So he resigned his position.

In the year that followed he crossed the Atlantic from Liverpool to New Orleans as a merchant seaman, rode the rails and befriended hoboes, and worked in warehouses, lumber camps, and wheat fields. In late 1922 he returned to New York, where he became a lab technician and attended medical school, from which he graduated in the late 1920s. As a doctor he pioneered the use of penicillin to treat venereal diseases. Eventually he would head the penicillin program at New York's Bellevue Hospital and advise the U.S. government and the World Health Organization on the treatment of syphilis.[64]

WRL activists of the interwar period came from various backgrounds and had different perspectives, yet they shared many convictions, positions, and experiences, a commonality that would foster an alternative radical pacifist vision and community. The WRL, FOR, WPU, and WPS were all absolute pacifist groups, and all were affiliated with the WRI. Their often overlapping memberships constituted a New York-centered pacifist subculture. This pacifist community became deeply involved in the broader movement for social reform in America, which in turn allowed the League to reach a larger, more diverse audience with its radical pacifist message. During the 1920s and 1930s the WRL formulated a radical critique of the existing social system and its impact on war and peace, articulated a pacifist alternative to war and violence, and developed arguments to illustrate the efficacy of nonviolent resistance.

### The Peace Activism of the WRL

The WRL distributed literature and sponsored a program of peace action to promote radical pacifism and to attract new members pledged to resist war. It advocated nonviolent methods, some of which had already been developed by the peace, labor, and suffragette movements. Between 1923 and 1940 the League expanded from several hundred members to nine hundred active, dues-paying members and nineteen thousand enrolled members (who had signed the WRL Declaration). The WRI congratulated the League for growing more quickly than any other section in the world.[65] In 1930 the League began holding annual conferences on radical pacifism in New Jersey's Watchung Hills. Soon after that it began hosting annual dinners as educational and fundraising events. On a project-by-project basis, it also began participating in coalitions with other peace and justice reform movements, both pacifist and nonpacifist.

The WRL organized parades, peace walks, peace teams, street corner meetings, radio talks, affidavits for European refugees, and dozens of protests and political actions condemning militarism and war.[66] William Floyd, a WRL member, wrote *War Resistance* (1931), a pamphlet summarizing the League's position.[67] He also conducted poster walks with his "antiwar" dog.[68] Hughan published *The Challenge of Mars* (1932), a volume of peace poems dedicated to the WRL, and invented two pacifist games. Advertisements touted one of these, "Guns or Disarmament," as "a lively card game that will go far to break down the war psychology"[69]—"Just the thing for [a] YPSL or SP branch social!"[70] Edward P. Gottlieb, who changed his middle name to "Pacifist," established an active WRL-New York local.[71]

Albert Einstein lent his prestige to the WRL. In late 1930 he expressed his views at New York's Ritz-Carlton Hotel: "True pacifists must publicly declare in time of peace that they will not take up arms under any circumstances. . . . Even if only two per cent of those assigned to perform military service should announce their refusal to fight, governments would be powerless, they would not dare send such a large number of people to jail."[72]

Einstein's speech was acclaimed by pacifists all over the world. "Thrilled" by his "magnificent statement on War Resistance,"[73] the WRL distributed a flyer entitled "Einstein on War Resistance," along with "2%" buttons to promote war resistance and radical pacifism. Unfortunately, the public confused the buttons with a campaign to repeal the Volstead Act so as to permit beer with a 2 percent alcohol level, so League members had to stop wearing them. In late 1932 the League invited Einstein to become an honorary chairman. But after the Nazis were elected in Germany the following year, he abandoned pacifism and resigned from the WRI.[74]

Besides its 2 percent campaign and standard enrollment form pledging signatories to resist war, the WRL promoted similar declarations through the American Peace Letter and the Oxford Pledge. These initiatives reflected the League's conviction that public opinion could influence government policies and prevent war. Hughan wrote the American Peace Letter, basing it on a 1927 letter that Sir Arthur Ponsonby had posted to the British prime minister over the names of 130,000 peace lovers who pledged to resist war. The WRL circulated the American Peace Letter, and each year shortly before Armistice Day forwarded to the president the names of those who had pledged to resist war.[75]

The WRL also endorsed the Oxford Pledge. In 1933, Oxford (University)

Union undergraduates voted that "this House will not fight for King and country in any war." In the United States the Oxford Pledge provided the impetus for mass student strikes for peace. In April 1934, 25,000 students, mainly in New York City, walked out of their classes to attend rallies where they repeated an adapted version of the Oxford Pledge. The following year, 175,000 students participated in similar actions nationwide. In 1936 the Emergency Peace Campaign opened with a student strike against war. In late 1937 the WRL's Student Enrollment Committee, along with other pacifist youth groups, endorsed a statement that reaffirmed support for the Oxford Pledge. The Student Enrollment Committee cofounded the Youth Committee for the Oxford Pledge to collect signatures. Like the WRL, the statement asserted that collective security—which relied on armed force—provided "the slogan that is being used for the mental mobilization of the people behind the imperialist aims and war plans of their government."[76] According to two prominent student peace leaders, the Oxford Pledge, like the WRL Declaration, sought "to restrain American warmakers by convincing them that there is a likelihood of non-support at home."[77]

The League took creative action to protest militarism and promote peace and disarmament. During its poster walks, from two dozen to several hundred activists marched single file on the sidewalks, with posters aloft. In 1937 the WRL cosponsored a New York City demonstration and parade to show "HOW PACIFISM WORKS—120 YEARS OF UNARMED BORDER BETWEEN UNITED STATES AND CANADA."[78]

In May 1931, in response to a military air show over New York City, the WRL helped organize a peace parade. For the airshow, an armada of 672 airplanes left its Chicago base and overflew various cities before arriving at Washington, D.C., for Memorial Day. In New York City, millions either watched the planes perform acrobatics and mock duels over the Hudson River or saw the armada during its 160-mile sweep over the metropolitan area. In response, the WRL sponsored a large demonstration at Cooper Union Square and a protest march to Madison Square led by John Haynes Holmes. A. J. Muste ridiculed attempts to justify the exhibition on the grounds of national security, charging that the display glorified war and distracted the unemployed from their economic plight.[79]

Several times during the 1930s, the WRL organized elaborately scripted Armistice Eve ceremonies at the Eternal Light in Madison Square. Tracy Mygatt and Frances Witherspoon scripted these pageants. The ceremonies honored World War I veterans, both the soldiers who were killed and the heroic COs, the "other soldiers in the Liberation-war of humanity."[80] Four young torchbearers, representing nations from each compass point, converged at the center of the forum and raised their torches as the audience reaffirmed their pledge to re-nounce war. The script praised the Kellogg-Briand Pact (which prohibited ag-gressive war) and the Frazier Amendment (which called on the United States to outlaw all war and abolish the armed services). Before the closing prayer, the of-ficiating minister proclaimed the WRL slogan: "Wars Will End When Men Refuse to Fight!" The League's leaders understood that both emotions and logic governed human behavior. So the pageant sought to harness the thrills, the ritu-als, and the drama associated with militarism to the more challenging war against war.[81]

Working with other peace advocates, the WRL reached millions through projects such as No More War parades and the Emergency Peace Campaign. In the early and mid-1930s the WRL, alongside other peace and progressive groups, organized four No More War parades in New York City. Three hundred people marched in the first parade; fifteen thousand participated in the final pa-rade and rally. Watching a film of the May 1934 parade, which boasted ten thou-sand marchers, Hughan commented: "It seemed as never before that we were really in a small way making history."[82]

Elaborate preparations, colorful posters and banners, and participation by four dozen groups made the 1934 and 1935 No More War parades spectacular successes. Peace and socialist groups were especially prominent. The WRL donated Kaufman's services for six weeks to help plan the 1935 parade. Decora-tions transformed cars into peace floats dramatizing wars' causes and conse-quences. Approved antiwar slogans included: "End War Through War Resistance," "War Is Idiotic Mass Murder," "Mothers Pay the Heaviest War Tax," "Abolish the CMTC and the ROTC," and "Wars Will Cease When Men Refuse To Fight."[83] Organizers filmed the parade for propaganda work; Hughan's response to the film illustrates the parades' publicity value.

At a mass meeting in Union Square following the 1935 parade, which re-ceived plenty of media attention, WRL chair John Haynes Holmes declared that if "compelled to choose between the uniform of a soldier and that of a convict he would take the convict's."[84] He then led a litany, which the large crowd shouted back line by line: "If war comes, I will not fight. If war comes, I will not enlist. If war comes, I will not be conscripted. If war comes, I will do nothing to support it. If war comes, I will do everything to oppose it. So help me God!"[85] Later, the socialist-dominated crowd sang the "International." To foster community and promote the WRL's message, Hughan and Frank Olmstead wrote pacifist songs for the occasion, including one that echoed the socialist pacifist perspective of most League members by vowing not to fight for the profits of munitions corpo-rations: "By and by we will smash their profits," one Hughan poem vowed. "We won't fight for the Slovak Skoda . . . Krupp von Bohlen . . . Bethlehem Steel . . . Dupont Powder . . . [or] Colts-revolvers." [86]

Olmstead, a member of the WRL's executive committee from 1931 to 1947, was also an FOR leader and YMCA official. Between 1927 and 1941 he was the YMCA's intercollegiate secretary in New York. During World War I he witnessed the Russian Revolution and heard Lenin and Trotsky outline the Bolsheviks' goals. He served as YMCA secretary to the army of Alexander Kerensky, leader of the provincial government (which was overthrown by the Bolsheviks), and later to the U.S. Army in Russia. For months he carried $40,000 in emergency funds. Many times the Bolsheviks discovered the cash at checkpoints, but he never lost a dime. He later explained: "I found that a sense of good will and a recognition of brotherhood was far more protection than though I had carried a revolver." [87]

The No More War Parades involved a coalition of peace, liberal, radical, labor, and religious groups; they pointedly excluded communists from participation. (In 1934 the WRL decided not to affiliate with the communist-controlled American League Against War and Fascism, though it would cooperate with it on specific projects). In 1935 the parade organizers denied credentials to both the American League Against War and Fascism and the Young Communist League. A year earlier the same organizers had prohibited slogans "expressing approval of any type of armed conflict";[88] this effectively excluded communist slogans advocating "good" wars or violent class warfare. Consistent with its radical pacifist ideology and anticommunist democratic socialist orientation, the WRL generally chose not to cooperate with communists until the Vietnam War.[89]

The WRL also participated in the 1936–37 Emergency Peace Campaign, a broad, pacifist-led coalition that brought together the antiwar (and internationalist) and the pacifist wings of the peace movement. Five members of the WRL's executive committee served on the campaign's national council; they were also members of other pacifist groups. To further the coalition's projects, the League again donated Kaufman's services.

The Emergency Peace Campaign sought to keep the United States out of war, build a strong antiwar movement, and promote the political and economic reforms that a peaceful and stable international order would require. In a major political-educational effort, the Emergency Peace Campaign formed local peace committees in twelve hundred cities, sent letters and telegrams to influential political leaders, lobbied Congress, and promoted its agenda through press releases and Devere Allen's No-Frontier News Service. The Emergency Peace Campaign did much to ensure the passage of the 1937 Neutrality Act. It also championed the Oxford Pledge-inspired student strike for peace and collected twenty-three thousand pledges to renounce war. Significantly, the campaign's emphasis on antiwar pledges to influence public opinion did much to validate Hughan's and the WRL's strategy for preventing war. Differences between pacifists (who advocated neutrality) and antiwar internationalists (who supported collective security) led to tensions within the coalition that brought about its demise. Charles Chatfield has argued that despite these differences and its brief existence, the Emergency Peace Campaign was "the greatest united effort made by peace advocates until at least the Vietnamese war." [90]

## The Challenge of Fascism and Militarism

During the 1930s, armed aggression threatened the international order. Militarist Japan occupied Manchuria (1931 and 1937); fascist Italy invaded Ethiopia (1935); and Nazi Germany defied the Versailles settlements with its program of rearmament and remilitarization and its demands for territorial concessions in Europe. Between 1936 and 1939, in a prelude to World War II, Spain became an international battleground, with Germany and Italy provisioning General Franco's reactionary rebellion and the Soviets supporting the elected Republican government through material aid and the International Brigades. In the United States, this armed aggression sparked fierce debates over collective security and neutrality legislation and whether the United States should involve itself in the war.

The WRL repudiated the League of Nations, collective security, and the shipment of munitions to belligerents. However, it found itself divided over whether to endorse boycotts and sanctions. Although it opposed armed collective security—in part because of fears that it would precipitate war—the League failed to reach a consensus on the use of economic sanctions to punish aggression in China, Ethiopia, and Spain.

Rabbi Sidney E. Goldstein, chair of the WRL's executive committee, pressed the League to endorse the boycott movement. He served at New York's Free Synagogue as the assistant rabbi to Rabbi Stephen Wise, another boycott champion and WRL member. Arguing that the WRL must substitute nonviolent alternatives for war lest it become politically irrelevant, Goldstein advocated economic and diplomatic sanctions and the prosecution of aggressor nations in the World Court.

Other members of the League disagreed with Goldstein. Led by Frank Olmstead, they asserted that boycotts would harm the innocent along with the guilty, provoke militarism and revenge inside sanctioned countries, and fail to prevent or reverse determined aggression; they could even spark a world war. Moreover, they argued, the Spanish and Chinese governments had also killed civilians; this blurred the moral distinction between themselves and the aggressors and further weakened the case for boycotts.

When the boycott debate threatened to split the League, Hughan reminded the members of the WRL's primary function: it was meant to be a single-issue educational and enrollment organization dedicated to war resistance. The WRL, she emphasized, united war resisters who had chosen for religious, humanitarian, or political reasons to repudiate war. This consensus, however, was never meant to extend to other political issues. Hughan was keenly aware that the League's members had divergent political views, and she warned that the WRL must avoid taking positions on political issues (such as boycotts) that would threaten its unity. Two WRL questionaires revealed the League's divisions over boycotts and economic sanctions to thwart Japanese aggression. In October 1937 the League drafted and debated a statement on boycotts. Unable to reach consensus, it tabled the statement.[91]

Were nonviolent responses to armed aggression realistic? The rise of fascism and militarism forced both pacifists and nonpacifists to consider this question. Most observers, including theologian Reinhold Niebuhr, dismissed pacifism as a utopian and irrelevant response to the organized and aggressive tyranny represented by Japan, Italy, and Germany. On the eve of World War II, Niebuhr— himself a socialist and former pacifist—emerged as perhaps the most respected American critic of pacifism. In *Moral Man and Immoral Society* (1932), he distinguished between individual and social ethics: individuals could advocate absolute pacifism, but society must give priority to justice and power. Stated differently, pacifism was a personal philosophy of nonviolence, not a prescription for public policy. In 1934, Niebuhr resigned from the FOR's executive committee and endorsed violence in certain situations to improve social conditions. After the 1938 Munich Conference he broke entirely with pacifism, advocating "realism" in foreign policy and supporting armed force and war to thwart aggression. For him, Munich demonstrated pacifism's failure and irrelevance: only military force (war), not morality (pacifism), could stop Hitler.[92]

In the interwar decades the WRL and radical pacifists developed a literature that presented nonviolence as a realistic alternative to war and violence. Jessie Wallace Hughan, John Haynes Holmes, Devere Allen, and William Floyd all made important contributions to this classic literature on war resistance. So did WRL member Richard B. Gregg and other radical pacifists such as Bart de Ligt, a Dutch anarchist, and Krishnalal Shridharani, an Indian disciple of Gandhi.

In *The Power of Non-Violence* (1935), Gregg explained Gandhian *satyagraha* in terms of Western social science, arguing that nonviolent resistance ("moral jiujitsu")[93] transformed a conflict and kept opponents off balance and contending that it could prevail against superior armed force. In 1934, de Ligt, a member of the WRI International Council, presented detailed plans for a war resistance campaign to the triennial WRI conference. In *The Conquest of Violence* (1938), he argued that nonviolent direct action, as expressed by the workers' soviets in Russia (1905 and 1917) and the factory occupations in Italy (1919–20), was an effective method for achieving social revolution and defending the nation. Observing that governments and elites typically commanded greater armed force than their opponents and that violence often guaranteed defeat, he warned: "[T]he more of violence, the less of revolution."[94] In *War Without Violence* (1938), Shridharani rejected traditional pacifism and acknowledged that force was necessary to preserve national sovereignty and abolish social injustice, but he also championed nonviolent direct action as an effective substitute for war and violence.[95] Finally, in a cogent essay, Hughan illustrated the WRL's interwar shift from individual war resistance toward collective nonviolent resistance.[96]

### From War Resistance Toward Nonviolent Resistance

Six months before the Nazis invaded Poland in September 1939—which marked the beginning of World War II—Hughan elaborated her strategy of war resistance in *If We Should Be Invaded: Facing a Fantastic Hypothesis*. Emphasizing the realism of radical pacifism, this pamphlet resembled previous proposals for nonviolent resistance developed by Western war resisters such as de Ligt and Gregg. But Hughan went beyond the WRL's standard opposition to war and armed revolution and formulated a comprehensive strategy of Gandhian nonviolence and noncooperation as a response to a hypothetical invasion of the United States. Her plan shifted responsibility for national defense from the military to the civilian sphere and from male soldiers to the entire civil population—men, women, and children. In the past, Hughan had promoted mixed-gender organizing for peace. Now she explicitly championed a strategy that would grant women a role equal to that of men in defending the republic.

A pacifist foreign policy, Hughan emphasized, would seek to prevent war through a program that removed "incentives to invasion" and addressed the root causes of modern war: fear and economics. She endorsed gradual "complete disarmament," the open inspection of former military bases, the Kellogg-Briand Pact, the Frazier Amendment, and the settlement of disputes through arbitration, conciliation, and the World Court. To eliminate the economic sources of aggression, she called for the removal of all restrictions on American trade and raw materials and for the granting of independence to American colonial possessions. Finally, she argued that a pacifist nation would use education to "prepare" a nonviolent defense. Pacifist reforms to the curriculum would define courage, heroism, and patriotism in nonviolent rather than military terms. Pacifist education would also seek to make "anti-militarism" a "sacred national ideal" with the power to stir "patriots" to "sacrifice personal interest and if necessary life itself."

In the event of invasion, Hughan counseled "resistance to the bitter end." But instead of armed defense, she advocated mass nonviolent resistance staged by a united citizenry, men and women alike. Citizens would treat invaders with respect, but civil leaders would not surrender and neither would they obey enemy commands. Public officials and workers would carry out their duties as long as orders came from elected authorities. If invaders removed the legitimate civil leaders and issued dictates, public workers would ignore orders, cease work, and destroy documents. A nonviolent response such as this would paralyze vital public services including police, fire, public utilities, telephone and telegraph systems, airports, and railroads. In the same vein, citizens would offer "passive" resistance—a "general strike raised to the nth power"—and refuse all cooperation with the enemy. A conquering general had the power "to torture striking workers, execute disobedient citizens and deliberately starve the resisting community," yet brute force could not provide the foodstuffs, supplies, and services an occupation army required. Forced to choose between "terrorism or compromise," the invader would discover that self-interest dictated moderation. Hughan understood the political nature of warfare: "All victory consists in breaking down the will of the enemy people. Military defense tries to do this through fear, which frequently produces the opposite effect. Non-violent defense works through self-interest, slower to arouse but more reliable in the long run." [97]

Hughan acknowledged that no pacifist strategy could ensure victory or prevent casualties, but neither could a military strategy. Ruthless aggressors might use bombs, explosives, and poison gas to break the will of civilian populations. Unlike nonviolent resistance, however, armed resistance would entail enormous military and civilian casualties. *"Under military defense,"* Hughan warned—invoking the examples of Spain and China, where "civilians were slaughtered as part of war routine"—*"such bombardment would not be a mere possibility, but a certainty."* [98] She agreed that armed aggression must be defeated, but she also maintained that nonviolent measures offered a humane, effective, and realistic alternative to military defense, which produced certain carnage and uncertain results.

Although their beliefs were rooted in moral and ethical principles, between the world wars radical pacifists invoked realism and historical experience to advance nonviolent alternatives to war and violence. They argued that organized, disciplined, mass-based, nonviolent direct action had successfully resisted foreign aggression and promoted social reform under both liberal and authoritarian conditions. Citing case studies, they pointed out that nonviolent tactics had prevented war, frustrated internal revolt, resisted foreign occupation, and advanced radical social change. They noted that mass strikes, demonstrations, boycotts, noncooperation, civil disobedience, worker soviets, and factory occupations had helped prevent war between Korea and Japan (1904), Norway and Sweden (1905), and England and Bolshevik Russia (1919–20). The same tactics had empowered workers in Russia (1905 and 1917) and in Italy (1919–20), defeated the Kapp Putsch in Germany (1920), shortened the French occupation of the Ruhr (1923), and shaped Gandhi's many campaigns for Indian independence and social justice.

While condemning violence and war as futile, the WRL also repudiated passive acquiescence and championed active resistance to defeat aggression and bring about social reforms. Unlike militarists—whether capitalist, socialist, or communist—the League advocated resistance without violence and believed that nonviolent techniques could triumph. To the WRL, radical pacifism was pragmatic. Thus, when it advocated pacifist defense and nonviolent revolution in the Spanish Civil War, its vision and program were based on historical precedent and "realism"—not moral utopianism.[99]

# 3

# Socialist Pacifism and Nonviolent Social Revolution

The WRL and the Spanish Civil War, 1936–1939

FOR THE LEFT the Spanish Civil War was a conflict between democracy and fascism, revolution and reaction, darkness and light, good and evil.[1] "Spain," the *Socialist Call* editorialized in July 1936, "is now the battle-ground between savagery and civilization."[2] Most historians concur, depicting the emotional drama as "the wound in the heart" and a "crusade of the left."[3] Although she shared this view, Jessie Wallace Hughan also posed the central question confronting those socialist pacifists who supported the Spanish Loyalists and revolution in Spain: "What about Spain? Opposing war is a comparatively simple matter as long as war means capitalism, aggressive imperialism, exploitation of workers. Socialism stood for this long before war resistance appeared on the horizon. But what about war carried on by the workers against counter-revolution and in defense of legitimate government?"[4]

Thus Hughan raised the question of revolutionary *means*. How should the Left advance and defend social justice and revolution—through armed struggle or nonviolent measures?

Almost alone among the secular Left in America, the WRL repudiated the use of armed violence to promote social revolution and defeat fascism in Spain. The League viewed international wars as the product of capitalist rivalries and power politics; in contrast, it saw the Spanish conflict as a class war and a social revolution and in that light championed a Republican victory. The Old Left—centered in the Communist and Socialist parties—endorsed armed force and recruited volunteers to fight in Spain; the WRL repudiated armed intervention and violence in the Spanish Civil War and formulated a pacifist critique of the SP and of those radicals who embraced war as a means to advance the class struggle and bring about social revolution.

50

The Spanish Civil War seriously strained the relationship between the WRL and the SP. The radical pacifist strategy of the League brought it—along with its socialist members—into sharp conflict with the SP, which supported armed struggle in Spain to defend and advance a workers' regime and revolution. Most accounts of the SP in the 1930s acknowledge a pacifist current that contributed to the debate over the Spanish Civil War and to the relationship among pacifism, Spain, and the bitter factionalism dividing the party during that decade. Previous studies have ignored the role of the WRL in those debates, underestimated the influence of war resisters within the SP, treated radical pacifism and socialist pacifists in a cursory manner, and confused radical pacifism with isolationism; furthermore, they have often collapsed the critical distinctions among various types of pacifism. Existing accounts also fail to explain the principles and techniques of war resistance and reinforce the view that radical pacifism, while moral and even admirable, offered neither a serious nor a realistic strategy for defeating fascism and advancing social revolution in Spain.[5] This chapter seeks to redress past scholarly neglect and to demonstrate that socialist pacifist war resisters within the SP played a prominent role in the party's internal debates over the Spanish Civil War. Though largely unknown, this socialist pacifist current amounts to an important alternative vision in the American socialist and radical tradition.

## Before Spain: The WRL and Class Violence

The debate over the use of armed force in the Spanish Civil War took place in a context of crisis and urgency, of previous debate over violence to promote social justice, and of the development of a coherent pacifist literature and program based on realism rather than morality. For much of the 1930s—a decade marked by economic depression and competing fascist and communist challenges—pacifist and radical groups such as the WRL, the SP, and the FOR considered, debated, and often experienced internal divisions on the issue of violence in the class struggle. The FOR and the SP—whose multi-issue agendas fomented conflict between the competing demands of peace and justice—split over the use of violence to promote social justice and revolution.[6]

Confronted with the plight of its embattled Republican "comrades" and their request for arms, the WRL did not escape this dilemma.[7] Fenner Brockway, the chairman and cofounder of the WRI, resigned to support the Loyalists and armed class war.[8] Abraham Kaufman recalls that the Spanish Civil War, with its promise of social revolution, tested the resolve of the WRL's leaders and other radical pacifists more than either world war.[9] Unlike the SP and the FOR, however, the League never wavered from its rejection of violence in the class struggle, allowing it to avoid serious discord over the issue. Even Devere Allen, who advocated armed "police power" in Spain,[10] avowed his pacifism in a late 1936 letter to Hughan: "Am I not right in thinking that we have to draw the line at participation in armed violence, even in a more or less 'holy cause?' "[11] The WRL's single-issue agenda and Hughan's leadership and emphasis on unity helped the League to hold firm to its pacifist principles.

Even before the Spanish Civil War, the WRL unequivocally repudiated violence to advance social revolution. The delarations of the WRI and WRL expressly rejected class warfare.[12] Hughan stated the WRL's position in a flyer and two pamphlets: "How About Civil War?", *Revolution and Realism,* and *War Resistance in the Class Struggle.*[13] Hughan argued that violent social revolutions had failed to secure permanent reforms and had often provoked counter-revolutions that actually retarded social progress. Also, although violence often accompanied revolution, British history and the French and Russian revolutions demonstrated that it was not essential to the actual transfer of power from one class to another. In Britain, for instance, the liberation of the serfs, the transfer of power from the aristocracy to the bourgeoisie, the emancipation of slaves, and the political enfranchisement of workers and women had all been achieved through gradual, nonviolent revolution. Even in Russia, the actual March and October revolutions that deposed the czar and brought the Bolsheviks to power were quite bloodless events. Although guerrilla warfare might win isolated victories, Hughan argued, permanent social revolution on a mass scale was usually futile in the twentieth century and could not prevail against modern technological armies. As for the United States, Hughan regarded an armed uprising there as "the extreme of Utopianism."[14] She advised supporters of social revolution to be realistic: "Let us choose the weapons where numbers count, where we have the advantage,—the strike, the ballot, the organization of non-violent resistance."[15] For Hughan and the WRL it was the political and economic organization of the masses, not the violent and romantic "propaganda of the deed,"[16] that would make social revolution.

The FOR and the SP also confronted the dilemma of class violence, though with more calamitous results. For nearly a year in 1933 and 1934, the FOR debated the issue of violence to promote social justice. Its two executive secretaries, Joseph B. Matthews and John Nevin Sayre, took opposing positions on this question. Matthews, whose commitment to nonviolence was tactical, was a political pacifist who had spent time in the Socialist and Communist parties. Convinced that violence was necessary in order to overthrow capitalism, he resigned from the FOR in March 1933. Sayre, a principled religious pacifist who opposed violence to advance social justice, also resigned to allow the FOR to resolve its stand on class violence. After a referendum in which 90 percent of its membership endorsed "non-violence in the class war as well as in international war," [17] the FOR accepted Matthew's resignation while rejecting Sayre's. While Matthew's camp was defeated, by mid-1934 at least one-third of the FOR's National Council and more than fifty members had resigned in apparent protest. Hughan and Kaufman were among the WRL members active in the FOR who opposed Matthews and his turn toward class violence. [18]

The SP suffered from bitter factionalism between 1934 and 1940, prompted in part by debates over the role of violence and the meaning of war resistance in the class struggle. At the party's 1934 National Convention, the Declaration of Principles composed by Devere Allen precipitated factional warfare. The declaration was adopted by the convention and later ratified in a membership referendum; even so, the sharp debate it triggered shattered the party.

The debate over the declaration centered on the SP's response to international conflict and class war. At issue was the socialist view of democracy. Affirming the St. Louis Proclamation (1917), the antiwar plank repudiated militarism, imperialism, and international war; pledged to support socialists who refused "to perform war service"; [19] and advocated "massed war resistance, organized so far as practicable in a general strike of labor unions and professional groups in a united effort to make the waging of war a practical impossibility and to convert the capitalist war crisis into a victory for Socialism." [20] Turning from international war to class struggle, the declaration committed the SP to organize a disciplined labor movement and general strike to fight fascism. "Capitalism is doomed," it proclaimed. "If the capitalist system should collapse in a general chaos and confusion . . . the Socialist Party . . . will not shrink from the responsibility of organizing and maintaining a government under the rule of the producing masses." [21]

Radicals denounced the declaration as too cautious, while the conservative old guard declared that the document was endorsing violent communist revolution. Actually, the declaration neither departed from the SP's historical position on international war nor advocated violence in the class struggle. Defending his draft, Allen argued that in calling for "massed war resistance" the declaration was not advocating armed force;[22] rather, it was reaffirming the SP's traditional efforts to mobilize workers in opposition to war. Mass war resistance and general strikes, he observed, were nonviolent alternatives to armed violence.

Neither Allen's explanation nor the declaration's ratification put an end to the factionalism. Indeed, it intensified. In 1936 the old guard seceded from the party to form the rival Social Democratic Federation. Meanwhile, Trotskyites were admitted into the SP, only to be expelled the next spring. After 1936 the Trotskyites and other "revolutionary" factions, which were particularly strong in New York, provoked new factional battles, championed violence in the class war, and displayed sharp intolerance toward war resisters in the SP.[23]

### The Eugene V. Debs Column: Solidarity or Folly?

Reluctantly, the SP endorsed armed force as a means to defeat the fascists in Spain. This presented a challenge for the Roosevelt administration, which had adopted a policy of nonintervention out of concern that the Spanish conflict might spark a general European war. [24] The SP continued its long-held opposition to international and capitalist wars and its support for neutrality in such wars; but now it also argued that civil wars should be subject to different criteria, insisting that Spain's legal, elected Republican government had the right to purchase arms to defeat an internal rebellion. Confronted with the Spanish Civil War and expansive fascism, SP leader Norman Thomas abandoned his liberal pacifism and endorsed armed force in Spain.[25] More eventful, the SP organized the Eugene V. Debs Column to fight fascism in Spain.

On 12 December 1936, Jack Altman, executive secretary of the SP's New York local, announced plans to raise a five-hundred-member legion to fight in Spain with the International Brigades. Named the Eugene V. Debs Column, this battalion would include technical experts, engineers, aviators, and fighters.[26] Altman and the New York local had taken this remarkable action without consulting the national party. However, several days later the SP's National Action Committee approved his decision. In order to comply with U.S. neutrality laws, which the project violated at least in intent, the SP claimed that it was not recruiting volunteers but only helping those who wished to enlist. In January 1937 the SP created the Friends of the Debs Column to raise $50,000 to transport the volunteers to Spain. Although legally independent, the Friends of the Debs Column remained under SP control while recruiting volunteers to fight in Spain. The Friends had also been established (on Thomas's advice) as a means of easing the strain on socialist pacifists in the party who opposed the Debs Column. "Among them are valuable Party members," Thomas observed, "and we cannot afford to take a position that here in America one cannot be a pacifist and a loyal, hardworking Socialist." [27]

WRL members of the SP responded to all this with a blistering attack on the Debs Column. In letters to the *Socialist Call* and the *New Leader,* socialists in the League condemned the plan and advocated nonviolent alternatives to defeat fascism and bring about social revolution. Edward P. Gottlieb, a New York City teacher and member of both the SP and the WRL, invoked Spain and the 1934 Austrian civil war to question whether armed force could achieve the transfer of class power. He endorsed the nascent American sit-down labor strikes as "more revolutionary avenues of non-violent struggle" than violent rebellions that "went out of date with the Paris Commune."[28] Caroline F. Urie, a Quaker and a member of the SP, the WRL, and the FOR, pointed out that means and ends were related and warned that even a Republican armed victory would militarize society and repress civil rights and liberties. Likewise, Elisabeth Gilman, who headed the SP in Baltimore, expressed her disenchantment with the Debs Column.[29] In a colorful letter to the *Socialist Call,* Joseph M. Coldwell, a member of the WRL and the SP who had shared an Atlanta prison cell with Eugene V. Debs during World War I, repudiated the Debs Column: "If I thought I could hasten the coming of the social revolution by shooting some one there are several in the U.S. whom I would like to practice on. But I do not believe that the social revolution will be ushered in by a lot of nit-wits, who if given guns will shoot as crooked as they have been voting, and probably kill themselves and their comrades."[30]

In an open letter to Thomas published in the *New Leader,* WRL chairman John Haynes Holmes expressed "amazement," "outrage," and "shock" over the project.[31] His dramatic letter, which is cited by most biographers of Norman Thomas (although without mentioning the WRL), remains an eloquent statement of pacifist sentiments:

> When did Socialism thus become identical with militarism? . . . Let us send food, clothing, medical supplies in abundance, but not a gun, not a bomb, not an airplane, to prolong the war and extend the area of devastation and death.
>
> You and I, Norman, have been through this business before. We stood fast when Belgians lifted cries as pitiful as those lifted by Spaniards today, and when Paris was beset no less terribly than Madrid. We refused to listen to the specious pleas of 1917 that the world should be made safe for democracy, civilization saved, and war forever ended by use of arms for the killing of men in battle. . . . I appeal to you as the successor of Gene Debs, and as yourself an uncompromising pacifist of consistent and heroic record, to save the Party and the nation from this madness before it is too late.[32]

In the *Socialist Call,* Hughan, Winston Dancis, and A. J. Muste continued the WRL's critique. They argued that the Debs Column was poor tactics and alleged that several hundred men would provide only marginal military value, but might open a breach through which reactionaries could pour money, arms, and recruits to the fascists. Furthermore, the project increased the likelihood that the

United States would be drawn into the conflict, compromised efforts for stringent neutrality legislation (which the WRL endorsed), and positioned the SP as supporting the achievment of socialism through "bloody warfare." All of this would strengthen the "increasingly prevalent psychology that war in the modern world is inevitable and the only means of solving social conflicts." Finally, they contended that if socialists did not teach workers to refuse to participate in war, for "whatever honorable motives, [and] are tricked into transforming the struggle AGAINST war and Fascism into a struggle FOR war against Fascist countries, Fascism wins,—Socialism and humanity lose." [33]

Although it generated a great deal of publicity for the SP, the Eugene V. Debs Column proved a failure and made no meaningful contribution to defeating the fascist rebellion in Spain. Evidence suggests that about two dozen volunteers reached Spain, where they joined the Communist-led International Brigades. In April 1937, Ed Melnicoff, a member of the Debs Column who claimed that only twenty SP recruits had reached Spain, observed that "the Debs Column has been a horrible flop and should be liquidated at once." Similarly, former SP national secretary Harry Fleischman later declared the Debs Column "weak and ineffective"; historian Frank Warren termed the enterprise a "flop"; and Norman Thomas biographer Bernard Johnpoll concluded: "The Debs Column was hardly worth the effort; it was, in fact, never organized." [34]

### WRL Voices on Spain

In accord with its single-issue agenda and its reluctance to adopt positions on political issues that might divide its membership, the WRL did not issue an official statement on the Spanish Civil War. It did circulate four pamphlets on the Spanish conflict to publicize different pacifist perspectives, but those pamphlets represented the opinions of the authors rather than official League policy. [35] In addition, Devere Allen spoke and published widely on the Spanish fratricide for pacifist, socialist, and liberal audiences. Despite the absence of an official WRL pronouncement on the Spanish Civil War, and notwithstanding disagreements over the question of "police action" and over how much support and of what type to extend to the Loyalists, a consensus about Spain did exist within the WRL. Devere Allen, John Haynes Holmes, and Jessie Wallace Hughan all expressed this consensus, even while airing the differences in position on Spain within the League.

The WRL consensus had four elements. First and most important, the WRL argued that war and armed revolution were futile in the twentieth century. World War I and modern, mechanized warfare in general had made international war suicidal and inefficient and the defense of civilians nearly impossible. Indeed, in a direct rebuttal to the stirring Republican battle cry "No Pasaran!" Hughan contended that soldiers could no longer defend "home and country" by declaring, "They shall not pass."[36] The League insisted that armed revolution could no longer prevail against organized governments, which could always marshal more power, more guns, more force, and more violence than rebels or guerrillas—though Spain was unique in that the Army was leading the revolt. Allen concurred with this. To socialists who insisted that the class struggle permitted the sole choice of "spineless defeatism or the upbuilding of revolutionary armies," Allen replied, "The tragic thing about this fallacious alternative is primarily its guarantee that, under most crises likely to arise in modern industrial nations, the working-class is doomed to defeat and that Fascism is destined to triumph."[37] Rejecting "the counterfeit philosophy of military romanticism"[38] and leaving aside moral considerations, Allen explained that the pacifist case against "armed social revolution"[39]

> is based . . . upon the transformation . . . in the ratio of power between organized governments and revolutionary movements. The mechanization of armament, the declining chances of a successful *coup d'etat,* and the lessening numbers of military strategists required to crush a rebellion must profoundly change our estimates of revolutionary tactics. The occasional exceptions, particularly in countries still primarily agrarian, do not affect the general trend. To most of the world at the present time, the ratio of Authority-power to Revolutionary-power has shifted so that Authority-power is developing by geometric progression while Revolutionary-power is progressing at an arithmetical pace.[40]

Though viewing organized killing as unethical, the central WRL argument against war was that in the twentieth century it remained futile, ineffective, and suicidal.[41]

Second, Spain confirmed the importance of pacifist education. "Our ideal," Allen stated, "would be a Spanish working class, trained in non-military resistance, disciplined in pacifist courage (which must be of a tougher steel than military courage) acting in solidarity for non-cooperation with the foe."[42] The Loyalists had embraced military measures, yet it was wrong to condemn them for this, because they lacked exposure to pacifist experience and ideas. To be effective, nonviolent resistance required prior training in pacifist principles and tactics; it could not suddenly be adopted or imposed during a crisis. The Spanish comrades had succumbed to violence; American workers and socialists, through pacifist education, might yet develop nonviolent strategies to build disciplined solidarity among the working class. Accordingly, the WRL urged the SP to initiate a pacifist study program.

During the 1938 Sudetenland crisis, Allen bluntly told Norman Thomas that both passivity and armed defense guaranteed doom for the Czechs. Lamenting that the party had done nothing to develop nonviolent alternatives that might prove more effective than armed defense, he encouraged the SP to examine nonviolent strategies and experiences. "Instead, all we do, convention after convention," he complained, "is to mouth the conventional phrases that may have had some relevance during the days of the Paris Commune, but which are scarcely at all related to our present-day world."[43]

Third, the WRL asserted that massive armed violence would militarize Spanish society and increase the likelihood of another world war. Hughan warned that even if the Republicans won, the pervasive "civil execution" and "military slaughter" would deepen the bloody political fissures within the Loyalist movement, perpetuate violence for generations, and make a tolerant, democratic, and socialist "workers' commonwealth" unlikely. At best, she predicted, a Republican military victory would result in a "regime of rigid suppression punctuated with 'Moscow trials.' " Most important, she asserted that the Spanish Civil War and the alignment of nations into "two rival dictatorships"—fascist and communist—was making another world war more feasible.[44] Even if armed force succeeded in establishing a Spanish "millennium," its achievement would amount to nothing next to the "catastrophe" that would result from a single year of a second world war.[45] Holmes concurred, portraying Spain as Armageddon.[46]

Fourth and finally, the League advocated a nonviolent strategy in Spain to advance social revolution and defeat internal rebellion. The WRL counseled disciplined nonviolent resistance, mass noncooperation, political and economic "agitation, education, organization,"[47] and especially the mass or general strike. Pointing to recent sit-down strikes by American workers, the League argued that mass strikes tapped the power of the working class and in Spain would provide the most effective alternative to violence, which was outmoded. In an effort to convince skeptical socialists, Allen linked the Indian *hartal*—which he credited with "revolutionary implications"—to American sit-down strikes and European labor disputes: "It is highly instructive to note how appreciative of the sit-down strike and its implications are many of those who have been loud in their jeers at the Gandhi-Nehru methodology, in view of the positive historical development of the sit-down strike from its practice on a substantial scale by the non-violent strugglers of India."[48] In the same vein, he argued that the 1935 strike in Mâçon, France, where several dozen men and women sat on railroad tracks to block the movement of materials and scabs, demonstrated the success of Gandhian techniques in labor disputes and the class struggle.[49]

In response to socialists who insisted that class struggle required violence, Allen noted that Marx and Engels themselves had deemphasized the role of violence after they witnessed the defeat of violent revolutionary movements. He also rebuked socialists for romanticizing violence and for their intolerance of pacifist comrades. Regarding the Left's response to Spain, he lamented:

> I am tempted to say "allegedly" thoughtful persons—have been staging a precise imitation of the wartime reactionaries of 1917. Not only are we witnessing the circulation of stale phrases as if they were newly minted; not only do we see the counterfeit philosophy of military romanticism; but we are experiencing the same stupid and uncomprehending attacks on pacifism, this time from the left, that we went through during the World War. . . . This proves how scandalously our American radicals are imbued with the capitalist philosophy they have absorbed at the knee of bourgeois education.[50]

Finally, Hughan suggested that the "workers' republic" might have ensured its survival if it had "sued" for peace with Franco before war devastated the nation and "internal dissensions set the People's Front groups to imprisoning and executing one another."[51] Holmes agreed, commenting that though the fascists might take power, the Left, through mass nonviolent resistance and noncooperation, could prevent the rebels from governing and remaining in power.[52]

Within this broad consensus, the League maintained three broad positions regarding the proper pacifist response to the Spanish conflict: armed police power, neutral nonresistance, and nonviolent partisan support for the Republicans. Allen defended the right of the legitimate Republican government to use armed police power to protect itself against violent rebellion. However, he distinguished between legitimate armed police action exercised by the elected Spanish government, and violent civil or class war, which he rejected. He linked police power to a second source of tension that was emerging within the League and the pacifist movement—the one between political pacifism and religious nonresistance. He contrasted his own political pacifism, which he considered realistic, with traditional religious pacifism and nonresistance, which in his view had been made obsolete by modern, depersonalized warfare. "I have never been a Tolstoyan pacifist," he declared, "though of course I can highly respect this point of view. I am a political pacifist . . . who believes in government and, if necessary, the use of armed power to exercise the chief responsibility of government—the protection of its citizens and their human rights."[53]

This doctrine of police power raised troubling questions for the WRL. How were political pacifists to determine the boundary between police action and civil or class war? Here, both Allen and Hughan quoted H. Runham Brown, the British anarchist and WRI honorary secretary. Brown supported limited police power and physical force but drew the line at "armed mass murder," contending that police power is exceeded when the government finds it necessary to "destroy" those whom it sought to "restrain." [54]

Within the WRL, Holmes represented a minority position of religious non-resistance. He repudiated all armed force and urged pacifists to withhold economic and military assistance from both sides. He noted the escalation from money and supplies to munitions and planes to the volunteer international battalions that fought, bled, and died in each camp. He lamented what he viewed as either compromises or desertions within the pacifist movement. In this he must have been thinking of Allen, Brown, Thomas, and other comrades who had endorsed armed police action. "Even the pacifists," he bemoaned, "long since solemnly pledged to the war against war, are one by one caving in before the Spanish crisis, and confessing that perhaps once more, just once more, we must kill for our ideals." [55]

Hughan rejected nonresistance, adopting instead a middle position on police action between that of Holmes and that of Allen and Brown. She accepted police action in theory, but she also challenged Brown's compromise over armed force and sought to express "the point of view of the war resister who is also a social radical." [56] Although she championed the Loyalists, she rebuffed pleas for armed intervention on behalf of "our struggling comrades in Spain" [57] and refused to sanction war either to support a "workers' revolution" or to arm legitimate "resistance to counter-revolution." [58] She contended that a democratic, socialist revolution could not be imposed by war; it required the "transfer of power from one social class to another" [59] and would be achieved through economic forces rather than by armed might. According to Hughan, fascism was a mass movement, not a "military coup." [60] The Franco-led counterrevolution demonstrated that "inadequate popular support" existed for the revolution in Spain.[61] Although never wavering in her belief that modern war was both unethical and futile, she acknowledged that "if war is ever ethically justifiable, this one is justifiable." [62]

## The WRL and the SP

During the Spanish Civil War the SP was suspicious of and often hostile toward both the WRL and its own pacifist minority. The debate between socialist war resisters and advocates of armed support for the Loyalists created deep political divisions within the SP and its youth organization, the Young People's Socialist League, whose members were known as Yipsels. Despite sharp criticism from elements of the party and attempts by Yipsels to expel pacifists, socialist war resisters resolutely defended their right to advocate nonviolence within the SP. In the socialist press and in various socialist forums, the WRL debated its SP and Yipsel opponents regarding the Debs Column, the possibility of nonviolent resistance and revolution in Spain, and the role of pacifists in the party.

The Trotskyite-influenced YPSL-Greater New York Federation (YPSL-NY) adopted an especially intolerant and aggressive stance toward the WRL and socialist pacifists. In July 1936, YPSL-NY empowered a subcommittee to consider this question: "Is membership in the War Resisters League by Party members incompatible with the decisions and resolutions of the Party?"[63] Allen, the most influential WRL member in the SP at the national level, and Winston Dancis, a former YPSL national secretary who championed the League's position within YPSL-NY, led the counterattack. YPSL-NY rejected the Dancis-authored minority report, which upheld the WRL's view. Instead it adopted the majority report, which declared that official party resolutions were binding on all members and must be obeyed. This included resolutions endorsing armed force in support of colonial wars and in situations (such as Spain and the 1934 Austrian socialist revolt) where workers were battling reactionaries to win political power and to defend democracy and socialism. Individual pacifists were welcome in the party, the report concluded, but members could not belong to both the SP and the WRL, which as an organization opposed pertinent SP resolutions and all war.[64] Although they were not punished, Kaufman, Dancis, Gottlieb, and Hughan were charged with violating party discipline and threatened with censure or expulsion.[65]

Irving Barshop, the executive secretary of YPSL-NY, was especially zealous in his insistence that WRL members of the SP must accept party discipline and submit to the SP's position on armed resistance and war. He warned that both the SP and YPSL must avoid the "swamp of absolute pacifism . . . and clean our own house."[66]

Replying to Barshop, Allen denied that existing SP policy precluded pacifist war resistance; he also defended the position of socialist pacifists in the party. He acknowledged that modern struggles involved "marginal and even central unplanned violence," but he also argued that the SP should allow pacifists to resist fascism in (often dangerous) noncombatant positions and through nonviolent means as an alternative to participating in "planned violence." Indeed, Allen added, nonviolent general strikes might promote "aggressive class struggle" more effectively than "the traditional resort to the barricades." He repudiated "civil war" and "armed insurrection," but he also defended legitimate police power and asserted that the WRL's pledge did not preclude "the use of armed governmental force against counter revolution, for the preservation of the Socialist state." Finally, in a postscript, he listed the names of nearly four dozen WRL and/or FOR members of the SP and asked whether the party could afford to lose them through resignations. Although not comprehensive, this roster highlights the important role that socialist pacifists played in the SP.[67] None of this persuaded Barshop, who insisted that "under certain circumstances absolute pacifism becomes reactionary in content and action."[68]

The debate over Spain also received prominent attention in the *American Socialist Monthly,* an SP journal that published exchanges between WRL socialist pacifists and advocates of the Debs Column and armed class struggle. One such exchange, between WRL and SP member Caroline F. Urie and SP firebrand James Burnham—a Trotskyite intellectual who brought charges against Gottlieb—raised an important Marxist criticism of pacifism. Burnham leveled a stinging attack against pacifism, which he declared was highly influential in the SP. Invoking historical materialism, he argued that pacifism was a " 'fight for peace' independent of the class struggle for workers' power. Pacifism . . . lifts war out of its concrete historical context, views it as a thing apart from the relations of cause and effect, and thus looks on the struggle against war as supra-class and supra-historical."[69] He reiterated the orthodox socialist axiom that the WRL rejected: capitalism caused war and socialism alone could abolish the causes of war and institute peace. Although he admired many individual pacifists, he condemned pacifism as a dangerous diversion from the class struggle and proclaimed it "the duty of socialists to attack pacifism sharply and uncompromisingly."[70]

In rebuttal, Urie admonished Burnham for failing to distinguish between bourgeois pacifism and WRI-type socialist pacifism. She declared that WRI war resisters repudiated liberal and bourgeois pacifism, emphasized the social and economic roots of war, and sought a socialist society. The real difference between Burnham and socialist war resisters, she contended, was over means not aims. Like other League members, she repudiated violence on the dual grounds that it hindered socialism and *"that it is ineffective—*that it does not permanently settle any conflict but leads only to further violence,—that victories won by violence require force and violence to maintain them, and that in such an atmosphere of restraint the spirit of Socialism and its ideas cannot survive."[71] She charged that "sniping with chance weapons from behind barricades—is futile and childish in this day of highly disciplined and specialized technical warfare, aerial attacks, armored tanks, etc."[72] Both peace and justice, she maintained, would come

through collective nonviolent action such as strikes, boycotts, and noncooperation. Thus, Burnham and Urie shared an economic and class analysis of the
Spanish conflict but disagreed on the most effective means of resistance.[73]

Shortly after the Spanish Civil War erupted, Dancis and Kaufman organized
the New York Socialist War Resisters Group. Their action was prompted by
events in Spain, by the YPSL-NY declaration that WRL membership was incompatible with membership in the SP/YPSL, and by the need to counter mis-
information about and opposition to pacifism within the SP. Reiterating the
WRL's consensus on Spain, this new group set out to stimulate discussion on
pacifism, explain pacifism to socialists, promote pacifist tactics during strikes,
and support both pacifist positions within the SP/YPSL and socialist positions
within the peace movement. Most important, it led opposition to the Debs Column within the SP.[74]

On the last day of 1936, this group convened a special meeting in Hughan's
home to consider whether pacifists should resign from the SP over the Debs Column and the persecution of pacifists within the party. To prevent a split, Thomas
and Allen submitted statements. Although no longer a pacifist, Thomas was still
personally and politically close to Hughan and Allen. He respected war resisters
and wanted to keep them in the SP. Contending that pacifism was built upon religious or philosophical foundations that most socialists did not share, he asserted that a contradiction existed between pacifism and effective political
leadership—a distinction that was especially relevant in Spain. "There is no
background in Spain," he declared, "which makes possible a Gandhi-like resistance to fascism."[75] He assured his audience that he would protect the right of
war resisters to express their position, but he also maintained that pacifists did
not have the right to denounce the SP in the capitalist press. The New York Socialist War Resisters decided unanimously to remain in the SP so long as free expression of pacifism was permitted, "since even with its faults and inadequacies,
the Party is the best available political instrument for anti-war action and independent working class action to establish a Socialist commonwealth."[76] The
WRL and the New York Socialist War Resisters succeeded in triggering discussion on nonviolent alternatives in Spain. Even so, pacifism remained a minority
position within the national SP and its New York local.

### Devere Allen: Bridge or Compromise?

Devere Allen illustrates the keen dilemma of the socialist pacifist struggling to
resolve conflicting loyalties to the WRL and the SP, to nonviolent means and socialist ends, to peace and justice. He held executive positions in both the WRL

and the SP; thus, he had to find ways to balance the contending responsibilities these leadership roles entailed. He served as a vital bridge between the WRL and the SP, yet at times he found himself at odds with elements of both. At the national level, he was the most influential of the WRL members in the SP. From inside the party he fought for freedom of expression for pacifists, promoted nonviolent alternatives to violence both in Spain and in the class struggle generally, and persuaded Norman Thomas to resign as leader of the SP if the party decided to expel the pacifists. He asserted that "nothing could be more harmful than the severance of relations, or even of sympathetic understanding, between Socialists and the peace organizations with realistic programs."[77] For Allen, the WRL, with its radical pacifist analysis and prescriptions, was the most realistic of all these peace groups.

When talking to war resisters, Allen espoused a similar message of tolerance and unity. Late in 1936, before a combined WRL-FOR audience, he quoted Gandhi in advocating tolerance toward nonpacifists. (In the same way, when talking to socialists, he invoked Marx and labor strikes to establish common ground with socialists in order to promote peaceful coexistence with pacifists within the SP.) In this speech he declared his fervent support for the Republican forces, his commitment to nonviolence, and his tolerance for socialist comrades in America and Spain who chose a different course from his own:

> Six years ago I heard Gandhi . . . describe his position as an advocate of nonviolence, and especially his relations with those who shared his aims of freedom and self-development for India but who did not share his faith in non-military means to a common end. "I wish to express," he said, "my solidarity with them."
>
> I think this is what most war resisters feel about the Spanish workers and peasants, who are locked in a grim struggle with fascist reaction—a fascism peculiarly ruthless, peculiarly medieval, peculiarly irresponsible toward those decencies of life without which a peaceable world is only a fantastic illusion. We want, in Spain, the triumph of the Loyalist cause . . . Our solidarity must be unquestioned, our support not capable of being challenged.[78]

Despite these sentiments, Allen denied that "an iron duty" bound pacifists to endorse the Republican military strategy in Spain. Indeed, he contended that "blind surrender" to conventional armed resistance would constitute the "greatest disservice" to the noble Spanish cause.[79]

Besides opposing the Debs Column (which the party allowed to languish), Allen shaped the SP's Spanish policy in other ways. He campaigned successfully against the slogan "Arms for Spain," suggesting that "Help Spain" represented a wiser policy, especially with the general public and the nonsocialist groups the SP was counting on to finance its Spanish relief program. He and Thomas called for the formation of a new group, the Friends of the Debs Column, to administer the volunteers. Although Allen refused to serve on this "independent" committee, he endorsed fundraising for Spain, citing media reports that the Republicans needed food and medical supplies more than munitions. He frankly acknowledged that any supplies and money donated would make it easier for the Republicans to purchase arms; but he also pointed out that their military actions represented legitimate police power.[80]

So Allen supported the SP campaign to provide money and supplies to the Republican government, knowing these donations would be used for war purposes. Furthermore, he drew a distinction between police action and armed war/revolution. Both these stances generated tensions between political pacifists and religious nonresistants within the WRL, tensions that in 1937 prompted him to submit his resignation as the WRL's vice chairman. All of this illustrates the different strands of pacifism that existed within the League, as well as the role of radical pacifist WRL members in the antiwar but nonpacifist SP.

It was Kaufman who precipitated the rift between Allen and the WRL. In a 1937 letter to Runham Brown forwarding American nominations for the WRI international council, he implied that several members of the WRL's executive committee who opposed Allen's support for SP policies had lost confidence in his commitment to war resistance. Kaufman was a supporter of Allen and was not trying to sink his nomination; he was merely reporting that differences of opinion over Spain had arisen within the WRL's executive committee. The clash really started when three of the twenty-four members of the WRL's executive committee, including Holmes and Rabbi Sidney Goldstein, questioned Allen's "logic" in endorsing armed police action and raising cash for Spain, cash that was helping the Republicans buy arms.[81] Because of their doubts about him, these three abstained from voting when it came time to support Allen's nomination to the WRI international council.

In spirited letters to Kaufman and Brown, Allen reiterated his commitment to war resistance, defended his SP positions, and argued that he had advanced pacifist interests within the party. He assured Brown that despite his "difficult situation"—one caused by his sitting on both the SP national executive committee and the Labor and Socialist International executive board—his "fundamental convictions" were intact.[82] Within the SP's national executive committee, Allen reported, he had articulated the radical pacifist perspective, promoted freedom of expression for pacifists, and persuaded Thomas to resign should "the small minority who are hell-bent on attacking war resisters and pacifists, get to the point where they choke off freedom of action for war resisters in the S.P." [83]

Allen's rebuttal to Kaufman was rather more polemical. He detailed his SP record and disputed Kaufman's own portrayal of it. He also pointed out how difficult it was for socialist pacifists in the WRL and SP to reconcile the competing claims of peace and justice at a time when their Republican comrades were dying in Spain:

> *Never* have I . . . given my support to work for Spain which included armament. That is to say, never my personal support. I am a member of the Socialist Party, a majority of whose members have decided upon a policy in favor of contributing not only for humanitarian relief, but for arms; though, thanks to the pressure employed by some of us, added to the sad experience with the so-called Debs Column, the Party is now, on my motion in [the] National Executive Committee, carrying on all its work for Spain through the North American Committee for Spanish Democracy, whose relief activities are entirely humanitarian. Every other member of the Socialist Party, including yourself and Dr. Hughan, is in precisely the same category as I am. I have never formulated an appeal, a statement on Spain, a Party resolution, nor a policy in the National Executive Committee, without expressly making my own personal abstention from the use of arms perfectly clear. At the same time, I have not wished to resign my membership from the Party just because I am in the minority, any more than you and Dr. Hughan have felt like doing so.
>
> It is true that I have never been an absolutist in the sense of taking the Tolstoyan position of abstaining from all use of physical force in every circumstance; but I have never changed my position on war, international or civil, nor with regard to the employment of arms in either type of conflict. I do not, however, feel that I can properly refrain from assisting the government of Spain, which most accurately represents, I am convinced, the people's will, merely because the majority of Spaniards have never been exposed to ideals of war resistance and can hardly be expected to embrace these principles in the mass. . . . If anything, I am more convinced today of the folly of armed violence than ever before.[84]

Further communication clarified views and repaired the damage. Both Kaufman and Hughan told Allen they had total confidence in him. They emphasized that Holmes and Goldstein, although challenging his logic, had never doubted his sincerity as a war resister and that they had withheld their votes only to register their disagreement with his stance. Kaufman pointed out that Allen himself had questioned the logic of Holmes and the Trotskyites in the SP, without confusing intellectual differences with a lack of sincerity. Kaufman also acknowledged that, according to the absolute nonresistance standard, he and Hughan were as illogical as Allen; for instance, although both had refused to support the SP campaign to muster funds for Spain, they had raised money that enabled the WRI to provide humanitarian relief for Spanish noncombatants, which in turn allowed the Republican government to divert scarce resources and labor to the war. "As long as the Socialist Party does not expel you and Abe and myself as pacifists," Hughan wrote Allen, "I am anxious for us all to remain active both in the S.P. and the W.R.I. You as a member of the Socialist N.E.C. are, I believe, particularly valuable in the W.R.I."[85] Satisfied that any differences were only ideological and that his loyalty was not in question, Allen withdrew his resignation. Soon after, he was elected to the WRI international council.[86]

There was more to the American response to the Spanish Civil War than war resistance and armed international brigades. While the WRL was advocating nonviolent social revolution to defend the Republican regime, radical pacifist comrades in Spain were honoring their nonviolent principles by carrying out relief work. The WRI-affiliated and pro-Loyalist Spanish League of War Resisters, founded by Professor Jose Brocca, provided humanitarian assistance to dispossessed victims of the civil war. The WRL supported Brocca through the WRI-established Spanish Relief Fund.

With the WRI's support, the Spanish League of War Resisters helped refugees. The WRI established two foreign bank accounts that enabled Brocca to purchase milk and food, which were unavailable in Spain. The WRI also distributed food, clothing, and supplies through its own dock in Valencia and through local committees organized by the Spanish League of War Resisters. In Madrid, Brocca organized a women's committee to distribute food and to collect information on people who were not able to reach relief centers. He also established refugee centers to help those who had been driven from their homes by bombs and bullets. He disliked traditional orphanages, which to him resembled prisons, so he established "homes" that sheltered up to twenty-five children in the care of a surrogate mother and father. He also founded several children's colonies in southern France, and with WRI support settled five hundred children in Mexico. The WRL provided only modest financial assistance to the Spanish Relief Fund; even so, its contributions saved lives, reduced suffering, and nurtured solidarity within the international war resisters' movement.

Brocca and his family made great sacrifices to honor their pacifist convictions. Brocca quit his university post in Madrid to apply pacifist principles in the midst of the slaughter. His teenage son helped him with his relief work and died from tuberculosis induced by strain and malnourishment. After the war the rebels interned Brocca in a concentration camp in southern France. In 1942 the

WRI arranged for his passage to Mexico, though he had to leave his family behind. Five years later the WRI helped pay the passage for Brocca's wife to join him there. Brocca's story demonstrates that pacifist courage is no less heroic than the military kind.[87]

## Beyond the Gun and Umbrella

The story of the WRL and the Spanish Civil War is important for several reasons. First, it illustrates that during the 1930s the SP contained an influential bloc of socialist pacifists who rejected armed class warfare and military defense while articulating an alternative vision of nonviolent social revolution. Recovery of this forgotten socialist pacifist tradition enriches our understanding of the SP and radicalism in the 1930s. It also challenges the view that radical pacifism was an irrelevant moral critique; in fact, it was an ideology and social movement that rejected violence on ethical *and* pragmatic grounds while offering a serious though embryonic alternative program of nonviolent resistance. Second, the WRL's critique of the Spanish Civil War offers a challenge to the "realist" school that advances the idea that military force is the only way to defend national interests. The League failed to persuade the SP and American radicals—and the Spanish themselves—to defend the Republic and pursue social revolution through nonviolent means. That being said, the defeat of the Spanish Republic neither invalidates pacifism nor proves that military measures are more realistic. After all, the Loyalists never tried a pacifist strategy. Moreover, armed warfare by pro-Loyalist Spaniards and foreign volunteers also failed to defeat the fascist rebellion and preserve the Republic.

During the 1930s the WRL was too small to seriously challenge the dominant view (which the SP shared) that military power was the most realistic means for ensuring national defense and advancing social revolution. The League did, however, succeed in voicing an alternative nonviolent strategy that fused socialist and Gandhian methods. As the debate over Spain illustrates, the WRL contributed a vital socialist pacifist current to the SP. This challenges the notion that Left radicals must embrace violent revolution. During and since the Spanish Civil War, the League pioneered and promoted a middle way between the umbrella and the gun—between appeasement and war—one of radical "pacifism" rather than quietistic "passivism."

# 4

# Dissent from the "Good War"

The WRL and World War II, 1939–1945

AFTER THE JAPANESE ATTACK on Pearl Harbor, most Americans embraced the "Good War." The Japanese attack, the fascist threat, and the evil specter of Hitler seemed to offer no alternative. The WRL, however, remained steadfast in its absolute pacifism. Representing the secular *and* left wings of the pacifist movement, the League during the war worked hard to encourage a negotiated peace, to provide fellowship for pacifists, to help conscientious objectors, to protest the shortcomings of Civilian Public Service (CPS), and to oppose conscription. League members also edited the left-wing, social actionist, pacifist press and spearheaded nonviolent direct action techniques to champion civil rights. The League had always admired Gandhi and promoted his ideas; now, during World War II, the Indian was even more of an inspiration, especially to the younger COs within the WRL and the radical pacifist movement.

World War II was a watershed for the WRL.[1] Various events in those years radicalized the League. It began to broaden its focus from a single issue to many issues of social justice and to shift its tactics from political and educational protest to nonviolent direct action. COs provided the major impetus for these changes; their social activism and strikes in CPS camps and prison, combined with pacifist-led, nonviolent direct action projects in the outside world, contributed to and also illustrated those shifts. All of this would have a powerful impact on postwar peace and justice movements, especially the civil rights movement. The League had always opposed racism, but it took little action until the war started, when its CO members found themselves in racially segregated jails and CPS camps and began leading strikes against Jim Crow. The COs' revolt radicalized the League. It represented a rebellion not only against the state, which controlled Selective Service, CPS, and the prisons, but also against the pacifist movement, which until then had been largely traditional, religion-

69

based—and cautious. The COs' revolt, led by members of the WRL and the FOR, marked the birth of a more activist radical pacifism, one that embraced direct action.[2]

In addition, CPS camps and prisons served as laboratories for developing, testing, and refining techniques of nonviolent direct action. Through their common experience, COs forged a permanent pacifist network that transformed the postwar WRL and shaped postwar pacifist—and nonpacifist—social reform and radicalism. The COs' wartime revolt provided a critical link between the WRL's prewar theory and its postwar action.[3]

### Before Pearl Harbor

Even before Pearl Harbor the WRL had formulated a response to World War II. In 1939, in *If We Should Be Invaded,* Hughan offered a strategy for nonviolent defense and resistance. In September 1939, after the Germans invaded Poland and World War II began, she pointed out critical issues that the League would have to confront if the United States entered the war. Mindful that the U.S. government had repressed dissent during World War I, she anticipated similar efforts against the WRL once war broke out. Under such circumstances, Hughan asked, should the WRL disband? conduct public meetings? go underground? recruit new members? advocate war resistance? circulate antiwar literature? relinquish its membership lists?[4]

A May 1941 WRL questionnaire revealed a consensus on these important questions. If either the government or events forced the League to disband, it should not go underground, for that would violate its principles. Rather, members should continue to communicate with pacifists in America and abroad, provide assistance to pacifists and COs in need, and promote an equitable peace. Anticipating that the government might seize its records, the WRL copied its membership list on onion paper and distributed duplicates to several members for safekeeping. In an interview, Kaufman confided that he expected to be arrested within a year.[5]

The WRL's radical pacifist ideology shaped its explanation of and response to World War II. Emphasizing economic causes of war while recognizing other contributing causes, the WRL did not view Nazi Germany, fascist Italy, or Japan, even after Pearl Harbor, as the sole culprits. The League charged the United States, the Allies, and the capitalist system with partial responsibility for the onset of the war. It argued that World War I and the Versailles Treaty had led to the rise of Hitler, the collapse of the interwar international system, and the new war. Furthermore, this new war would only sow the seeds of future armed conflict.

The WRL also argued that the Allies were fighting to defend colonial empires (with their markets and raw materials) from Axis imperial ambitions. During much of the 1930s, the WRL contended, the U.S. government and American corporations had supported Nazi Germany as a bulwark against communism. According to the League, opponents within Germany would eventually overthrow the despotic Nazi dictatorship. In summary, the WRL did not view World War II as a Manichaean struggle that compelled its support. Rather, the League's role was to abolish war's root causes by promoting a just peace and radical reform of the political, social, and economic conditions that were responsible for war and violence.[6]

In 1940, in a special congressional election in New York City, Hughan stood for office on an antiwar platform. A. J. Muste chaired her write-in campaign, which garnered support from pacifists and socialists, including WRL members and Norman Thomas. Hughan, who entered the race two weeks before the February election, was trying to publicize the peace movement and mobilize antiwar sentiment for the November general election. She endorsed an immediate armistice, a negotiated peace, American neutrality, armament reduction, and a provision to make American entry into the war contingent on a referendum. "Keep America out of War,"[7] Hughan urged voters. The campaign lambasted Earl Browder, the Communist Party candidate, as a communist "fuehrer"[8] who had supported collective security until Stalin and Hitler signed a nonaggression pact in August 1939 and who had defended the Soviet invasion of Finland in the winter of 1939–40. Although Hughan declared that her campaign achieved its goals, the *New York Times* ignored her in its election-day coverage.[9]

Also in 1940, Hughan initiated the Pacifist Teachers League (PTL) as an informal caucus within the New York Teachers Guild. The PTL claimed between 100 and 150 members. During World War I, pacifist teachers—including Hughan—had been harassed, penalized, and fired. The PTL sought to protect teachers who might be persecuted for opposing the war or for refusing to participate in draft registration, war bond campaigns, aluminum collections, air raid drills, civil defense rehearsals, and other war work. It also provided fellowship for pacifist teachers, disseminated pacifist ideals, and (looking forward to the postwar era) promoted "the spirit of international conciliation."[10]

Led by Hughan and Edward P. Gottlieb, the PTL fought for the reinstatement of pacifist teachers who had been fired by the Board of Education, as well as for the admittance of teachers who had been denied licenses because of their pacifist views. When the board decided to close schools and require teachers to register draft-eligible males, some pacifist teachers objected or refused. After written appeals and a meeting with the superintendent, pacifist teachers were excused from war-related work. Hughan's principal honored her pacifism and had told her earlier that instead of draft registration she could perform other tasks. Nonetheless, Hughan did not report to school on draft registration day (16 October 1940), since she believed that she should forfeit her daily pay of $13 to assume some sacrifice.[11]

The WRL also mobilized to block—or at minimum influence—the first peacetime draft in American history. On 16 September 1940, President Roosevelt signed into law the Selective Training and Service Act of 1940. After pacifist lobbying, Congress amended the original Burke-Wadsworth bill to include more liberal provisions for COs. Pacifists won two major concessions. The law granted CO status to any "person who by reason of religious training and belief, is conscientiously opposed to participation in war in any form." This language broadened the Selective Service Act of 1917, which had effectively restricted CO status to members of the historic peace churches (Quakers, Mennonites, and Brethren).

In addition, the 1940 law permitted COs to choose either "non-combatant service" under military control or "work of national importance under civilian direction." But the law did not grant conscientious objector status to absolutists or secular objectors. Furthermore, the 1940 act authorized the Selective Service System to administer the conscription program.[12]

The WRL denounced the Burke-Wadsworth bill and the Selective Service Act. With other peace and civil liberties organizations, it sent a delegation to Washington to lobby Congress. Kaufman, a member of the delegation, testified against the Burke-Wadsworth bill and declared the League's opposition to all military conscription. In more practical terms, the League sought revisions that would bring the legislation closer to the more liberal British Conscription Act of 1939. In particular, the League wanted the American law to grant CO status to nonreligious objectors who resisted war on "humanitarian, intellectual, or moral" grounds.[13] It also requested complete exemption for absolutists—that is, for those who refused all cooperation with conscription, including alternative civilian service.[14]

The Selective Service System, in concert with the historic peace churches, created Civilian Public Service to provide alternative service under civilian control for COs who rejected noncombatant military service. In October 1940 the peace churches established the National Service Board for Religious Objectors (NSBRO) to coordinate the administration of CPS camps. NSBRO appointed

Paul Comley French, a Quaker, as its executive secretary and began talks with Selective Service to settle the details of alternative service.

The 1940 law authorized alternative civilian service but left the conditions of that service for the president to determine. NSBRO submitted a proposal for civilian service to Selective Service that called for both government and private religious camps. Clarence Dykstra, the first director of Selective Service, and Colonel (later General) Lewis B. Hershey, its future leader and then a top official in the agency, endorsed the NSBRO plan. In November 1940, Dykstra discussed the proposal with Roosevelt, who opposed the plan on the grounds that it treated COs too leniently. He suggested that the army run the camps. Dykstra, alarmed at the president's reaction, returned to NSBRO and urged the peace churches to drop the idea of a dual system of government and private camps. He advised the churches to administer and finance the entire civilian service program. In Dykstra's view this would avoid congressional appropriation hearings and the government control that would accompany government-funded camps. In addition, he calculated that the "voluntary assumption" of financial and administrative responsibility for civilian service by the peace churches would neutralize public opposition to the plan and win Roosevelt's approval.[15]

Confronted with the choice between government *or* private religious camps, the peace churches, the FOR, and other religious groups accepted Dykstra's proposal on a six-month trial basis (later renewed for the duration). The government would contribute equipment and camps; church groups would care for the COs and maintain the camps. Roosevelt approved the agreement in mid-December, and the plan was formalized in February 1941 by Executive Order 8675. The first CPS camp, at Patapsco, Maryland, opened on 15 May 1941. Over the next six years nearly twelve thousand men would serve in 151 camps nationwide. The last CO was discharged on 31 March 1947.[16]

The pact between the government and the peace churches combined political pragmatism with recognition of the right of conscientious objection. Government decisions on alternative service were influenced by public opinion, which was hostile to lenient treatment for COs. At the same time, the government had learned from the experience of World War I. It extended more liberal treatment to COs not only because it was right to do so, but also to avoid the administrative burden of handling principled and often difficult COs. In December 1940 the peace churches viewed the CPS agreement as the best deal available and a vast improvement over the policy that had been in place during World War I. Later, as problems with CPS emerged, the WRL and other critics charged that the churches had conceded too much to the government.

The WRL refused to join NSBRO but did participate on its consultative council. The peace churches assumed financial and administrative responsibility for CPS; however, Selective Service officials in each camp retained policy control. Along with other complaints, the issue of military control, symbolized by the appointment of General Hershey to head Selective Service in July 1941, sparked a momentous debate between the pacifist movement's "service" (religious) and "resistance" (political) wings.[17]

## Pearl Harbor and the "Good War"

"Do not let Japan lead us into disastrous war," Jessie Wallace Hughan telegraphed President Roosevelt immediately after the 7 December 1941 Japanese attack on Hawaii. "We urge peace in spite of the Pearl Harbor events."[18] Meeting two days after Pearl Harbor, the WRL executive committee reaffirmed its antiwar stand. Hughan later characterized this as the League's "most important decision" to date.[19]

Less than two weeks after Pearl Harbor, the WRL issued a statement on World War II that reaffirmed its commitment to pacifism. The League condemned fascism and Japan's "murderous" attack, but it also argued that "all nations must share responsibility for the causes leading up to the struggle." Furthermore, the United States had contributed to the outbreak of hostilities by supporting the Versailles Treaty, by enacting anti-Asian measures such as the Chinese Exclusion Act and the segregation of Japanese and other Asians in San Francisco's schools, and by failing to honor its own neutrality laws. Finally, consistent with its democratic principles and respect for those who saw war as a "patriot duty," the WRL announced that it would not obstruct the war effort.[20]

The WRL's decision not to resist the war effort reflected several concerns. The League recognized that pacifists stood no realistic chance of preventing war. "We are such a small group," Evan Thomas confessed, "that we would kid ourselves if we think we are of any social importance."[21] Ideologically, most WRL leaders were socialists committed to majoritarian political rule. Moreover, some League members opposed coercion, including direct action by a pacifist minority to block the majority will. On a more personal level, John Haynes Holmes declared that he had neither a "martyr complex" nor "the slightest desire to go to prison."[22] Legal factors also contributed to the League's caution. After the United States declared war, the WRL adjusted its literature and activities to comply with the Espionage Act. It also decided to cease public demonstrations and to stop soliciting enrollments, although in 1943 it reversed this decision. Aware that they were a small minority, WRL members never considered resisting or obstructing the war effort.[23]

During World War II the League's membership and budget increased. It enlisted new members, including COs, at a modest rate: 1,436 in 1940; 696 in 1941; 692 in 1942; 443 in 1943. Extant WRL membership totals show wartime increases in both active membership (those who paid dues and had signed the WRL Declaration) and enrolled membership (those who had only signed the declaration). Active members are listed first: 1940 (896/18,850); 1941 (1,343/19,402); 1942 (1,606/11,369); 1943 (217 new active members, 190 new CPS CO members, 28 new enrolled members); and 1944 (nearly 2,500 active members). During the war the League's budget also increased, from $4,500 in 1939 to $21,000 in 1943.[24]

The relationship between the WRL and the FBI illustrates the League's desire to remain legal as well as its reluctance to hamper the war effort. Between 1939 and 1945 the FBI monitored, investigated, and advocated prosecution of the League. One historian has concluded that the FBI considered the WRL a national security threat because of its pacifist convictions, political ideas, and opposition to war and conscription. Although the Justice and State Departments absolved the League of all charges, the FBI investigated the WRL on eight separate occasions for allegedly violating the 1938 Foreign Agents Registration Act, interfering with the 1940 Selective Service law, threatening internal security, practicing sedition, and serving as a communist and fascist front.

Initially, the FBI was interested in the WRL-WRI relationship and the League's technical violation of the Foreign Agents Registration Act (by its nonregistration). The WRL cooperated with the FBI, opened its files, explained its history and philosophy, and provided information on its members and other COs. Subsequently, the FBI visited League offices on at least 166 occasions during the war to obtain information on CO claimants appealing decisions of their local draft boards and to verify their membership in the WRL. Unlike World War I, however, the federal government did not persecute pacifists. "Frankly," Hughan confided in mid-1942, "pacifism in the United States is unhindered so far, chiefly because it has not yet proved dangerous to the war regime."[25]

The League organized peace teams and local chapters to encourage peace action and education as well as fellowship among pacifists. In weekly or bimonthly meetings, peace teams discussed pacifist texts, current affairs, and the use of nonviolent techniques to advance global justice. These teams sang peace and labor songs, wrote to congressmen, and planned peace projects. They sponsored public meetings, organized study groups, circulated petitions, provided financial support to COs, staged simulated draft board tribunals so that COs could rehearse their responses, participated in WRL, WRI, and FOR fundraisers, and distributed pacifist literature, newspapers, and periodicals. In general, these teams fostered an autonomous pacifist culture and community.[26]

WRL locals, which served the same purpose as peace teams, extended the League's presence. When the war began, the WRL announced plans to establish locals in thirty-one cities and sixteen states. The joint WRL-FOR local in Washington, D.C., the largest chapter outside New York, claimed four hundred members and pursued an active peace and justice program.[27] Besides all this, the WRL joined coalitions with pacifist and antiwar groups to assist COs, to encourage a prompt, just, and lasting negotiated peace, and to challenge proposals for postwar conscription.[28]

WRL members were an important component of the wartime pacifist press, through which the League disseminated its own views and influenced the broader pacifist community. Besides providing organizational support, League members edited, wrote for, and managed the major national left-wing pacifist publications.[29]

The *Conscientious Objector* (1939–46), which covered national and international pacifist developments, was the most important voice for COs. Although independent, the paper reflected the WRL's views and those of its militant CO members in CPS and prison. In October 1939, under the auspices of the United Pacifist Committee, the WRL helped launch and finance the paper. The paper was sponsored during its first two years by the New York sections of the WRL, the FOR, and the Friends, and later by the national WRL. By March 1942, differences between the League and the FOR had developed over CPS and other issues; also, the sponsoring groups wished to avoid legal responsibility for the publication's hard-hitting articles. At that point the *Conscientious Objector*, which by then had a circulation of thirty-two hundred, was made an independent entity with its own board.

The WRL and its members made important contributions to the *Conscientious Objector*. The WRL provided money and subsidized office space and loaned the paper Abraham Kaufman as a part-time adviser. Newspaperman Jay Nelson Tuck of the *New York World Telegram* edited the paper until 1945, when he was drafted and entered CPS. Roy Finch of the *New York Herald Tribune,* a CPS conscientious objector, wrote articles and served as assistant editor. James Peck, a prison CO, contributed a labor column, and CPSer Max Kampelman commented on general affairs. The paper covered COs' disillusionment and radicalization over CPS, and their activism in CPS and prison. In June 1946, the paper discontinued publication and transferred its assets to the League.[30]

WRL members were the leading force in *Pacifica Views* (1943–47), a four-page weekly published by COs at the Glendora, California, CPS camp. The founding editor of this paper was Henry V. Geiger. Controversial, erudite, and iconoclastic, *Pacifica Views* was the "gadfly of C.P.S."[31] "PV" raised social and philosophical questions and provided pacifists (especially secular CPSers) with a forum for discussing pacifist ideas and methods of applying nonviolent action to social reform.[32]

A. J. Muste, the FOR executive secretary and a member of the WRL executive committee, edited *Fellowship,* the well-established FOR journal. In sum, League members played a prominent role in the social action, radical pacifist press, and this gave the WRL influence within the pacifist community out of proportion to its size.

### Peace Now: The WRL Appeal for a Negotiated Peace

Throughout World War II the WRL opposed the Allies' policy of unconditional surrender and advocated a just, immediate, and negotiated peace. Pointing out the disastrous consequences of the Versailles Treaty—a document of vengeance that had been imposed on the defeated Germans after World War I—the League asserted that only a negotiated peace could stop the present mass slaughter and avoid or abolish the conditions likely to cause future wars. Similarly, the WRL's Peace Aims Committee called on the American and British governments to "Win-the-Peace-by-Waging-Peace-Now."[33] WRL literature warned that unconditional surrender would prolong the killing and perpetuate the causes of war. In independent venues, individual WRL members also advocated a negotiated peace.[34]

In April 1942 the WRL published a pamphlet calling for an immediate negotiated peace. The author was the League's vice chairman, George W. Hartmann, a prominent SP member and professor of educational psychology at Columbia University. Hartmann, who was more concerned with the consequences than the causes of World War II, proposed a world charter to guarantee the entire global population "Peace, Plenty, and Freedom."[35] The Peace Now Movement (PNM), which Hartmann formed in July 1943, advocated a similar program.

The WRL's relationship with the PNM illustrates the League's commitment to a negotiated peace as well as the divisions within the pacifist movement over coalitions with nonpacifist groups. The PNM sought to unite pacifists and nonpacifists for the purpose of promoting a negotiated end to the war in order to save lives and create a peaceful and more equitable world order. Hartmann, the PNM chairman, along with John Collett, Bessie Simon, and Dorothy Hutchinson, were the principal founders of the PNM. WRL members Hughan and

Theodore Walser attended the PNM's charter meeting and at first supported the group.[36] The PNM sought pacifist and socialist support; however, the WRL, the SP, and most pacifist organizations had doubts about certain individuals and elements within the PNM, so they kept their distance. The League never joined the PNM; however, it shared its views on the origins of World War II as well as its commitment to a negotiated peace. So it supported its aims and distributed its literature.

The League rejected formal association with the PNM (and with the America First Committee and the Communist Party) both from principle and for pragmatic reasons. The WRL expressed concern over the backgrounds of key PNM leaders, some of whom were tainted by their involvement in the America First Committee and its right-wing, anti-Semitic, and isolationist sentiments. The WRL abhorred such groups and views and feared that by aligning itself with them through the PNM it would be compromising the pacifist movement and exposing itself to political attacks. Earlier, in mid-1941, the League had adopted a resolution repudiating the America First Committee's "nationalist and isolationist" position.[37] The League also charged the PNM with duplicating its own efforts and with taking inadequate political precautions, thereby threatening the League's reputation. For reasons like these, Hughan resigned from the PNM within two months.[38]

In Newark, New Jersey, several months before the PNM was founded, David Dellinger initiated the more radical Peoples Peace Now Campaign. On 6 April 1943, the anniversary of America's entry into World War I, the group staged a small demonstration at the Capitol in Washington. In its leaflets it rejected unconditional surrender, arguing the Allies should support the German people, who wanted peace and would overthrow Hitler. The same leaflets called for the democratic social ownership of the means of production, the distribution of wealth according to need, and an end to colonial exploitation, anti-Semitism, and Jim Crow racism. The police seized the leaflets and picket signs but made no arrests. During a follow-up action in Newark, the police confiscated the group's materials. When Dellinger refused to report for an army physical, federal authorities—no doubt unhappy with his protests—arrested him. He was sentenced to two years in Lewisburg Penitentiary.[39]

The WRL sought a negotiated peace partly in order to save European Jews from certain death. Earlier than most, the WRL was warning Americans about the Nazis' "extermination" campaign in progress against European Jews. It insisted that only a "speedy, negotiated peace" could save them from further destruction.[40]

Confronted with the systematic Nazi annihilation of the Jews, Hughan warned that "neither vengeance nor victory can save them."[41] An Allied military victory and demands for an unconditional surrender would prolong the war and prove a "Jewish death warrant." [42] Furthermore, a German defeat might provoke a "pathological" response and prompt the Nazis to "exterminate all Jews." [43] Writing to the *New York Times* in February 1943, she observed that one-third of Europe's six million Jews had already perished and that another two million were likely to die before the war ended. She urged the United States to offer the Nazis an immediate armistice, subject to the safe transfer of Jews to an Allied guardianship. "We *must act now*," she warned "*for dead men cannot be liberated.*" [44]

In April 1945 the WRL took action to promote a negotiated peace with Japan. The following month it adopted a statement on peace terms with Japan and a just postwar settlement in Asia. It also decided to cooperate with the FOR in a petition drive urging American-Japanese peace and to consider other political and educational activities for mobilizing public opinion for a negotiated peace.

The WRL statement on Japan was written by Theodore D. Walser, a member of the League's executive committee. It proposed the following: a peace based on the liberation of Asia from Japanese imperialism and Western colonialism; revocation of the Chinese Exclusion Act and other laws based on racial discrimination; U.S. support for economic reconstruction in Japan and Asia; and the inclusion of Japan and Asia in a world federation. Walser was an expert on Japan, having spent twenty-six years there as a missionary before the Japanese interned him after Pearl Harbor. In mid-1942 the Japanese evacuated him and more than 430 enemy aliens by ship. [45]

In the spring and summer of 1945 several WRL members and CPS veterans, led by Lew Hill, discussed a dramatic "Japanese Project." They considered sailing a boat to Japan to demonstrate the "moral principle of brotherhood" and to encourage a negotiated end to the Pacific war. The dropping of atomic bombs on Hiroshima and Nagasaki rendered this quixotic plan moot. One participant later declared: "There are times when only acts, however revolutionary and even adventuresome they may seem, can give reality to ideas and win support for principles." [46] His explanation amounted to a preview of postwar pacifist activism, which would emphasize that the personal was political and that individual, subjective protest had the potential to transform political realities.

### Odyssey of Disillusionment: The WRL and Civilian Public Service

Most WRL leaders took a caustic view of CPS, the program of civilian service created by the peace churches and Selective Service in 1940. The League refused to help administer conscription and opposed the lack of choice for COs between government and church camps. It also refused to join NSBRO, the agency created by the peace churches to run the camps. But in order to retain a voice on CO matters, the WRL served on NSBRO's consultative council.

## CPS Origins and Shattered Promises

Key WRL leaders noted that both NSBRO and Selective Service originally endorsed paid work and maintenance for COs, though individuals could still decline government support in accordance with "the second mile" principle,[47] which taught Christians to assume sacrifice during times of national crisis. The agreement also required the peace churches to support all COs who could not pay their own maintenance costs; and it called for parallel government and church camps. However, the peace churches soft-pedaled government camps once they realized they had underestimated the number of secular objectors.

The WRL was almost the only pacifist organization to oppose the agreement between the peace churches and Selective Service. In February 1941 the League conducted an influential referendum among its draft-age members to determine which type of camp they preferred. The referendum offered three forms of alternative civilian service, which were based on the Selective Service's own categories: government camps that paid men for their work; NSBRO-operated but government-funded camps that paid no wages; and a CPS system of church operated and financed camps that paid no wages and required COs (or churches and pacifist organizations) to pay a $35 monthly maintenance charge. The referendum demonstrated the League's support for government operated and/or financed rather than church camps and for a choice between government and religious camps. The referendum results seemed to undermine support for the agreement between the peace churches and the Selective Service, which was scheduled to expire in six months. This raised fears within the religious pacifist community.[48]

During a visit to discuss the referendum, Paul French "begged"[49] the WRL to drop its demands for government camps until after private church camps were established. Once church camps were operating, French promised, the peace churches would work to obtain government camps for COs who wanted them. Meanwhile, the understanding between the peace churches and the Selective Service on civilian service collapsed after it became obvious that the resources to provide government pay and maintenance were not available. NSBRO was worried that Congress, if asked to fund the agreement, might reopen the entire issue and scrap religious camps. In response to requests by the peace churches, the League agreed to suspend its opposition to CPS and to wait for government camps—a development expected to take several months. However, the first government camp was not established until 1943, and then without pay. The WRL blamed NSBRO and Selective Service for the lengthy delay and for failing to implement the provisions of the original agreement and understanding on CPS.

The WRL's hostility toward NSBRO and Selective Service intensified between 1940 and 1943 for several reasons. First, the promises of wages, maintenance, and "meaningful work of national importance" were never kept. The WRL demanded that military and CPS conscripts be compensated equally, and it condemned Selective Service for refusing to pay for CPS work or to make allotments for CO dependants. Furthermore, the League advocated a more robust program of "detached service" that would allow COs to perform the "work of national importance" promised by the Selective Training and Service Act of 1940 outside camps—in hospitals, public health research projects, fire-fighting brigades, and the like. It endorsed Britain's civilian service program, and it criticized NSBRO for not championing an American version of that plan. The British model required no government funding; British COs lived at home, worked in approved jobs, kept their wages, and supported dependants themselves.

Second, it became obvious that camp policy was being made by Selective Service officials operating under military control, not by the church-appointed civilian camp directors, who were pacifists or sympathetic to pacifists. Third, after trying hard to persuade French and NSBRO to honor the original WRL–peace church understanding that promised parallel government camps with paid work and maintenance, the WRL concluded that NSBRO had failed to address its concerns with sufficient vigor. Similarly, the League criticized Hershey's decision to administer civilian service through either the government or private religious agencies, but not both. It argued that COs of different religious and political persuasions should be able to choose between religious and government camps. Finally, by 1943, as more COs rejected CPS and opted for prison rather than camps, the League's hostility toward NSBRO, CPS, and Selective Service heightened.[50]

Within the WRL, COs took three distinct positions toward CPS: service, resistance, and absolutist. Those who took the service position accepted alternative service as a good-faith attempt by the government to honor individual conscience. These men welcomed the opportunity to apply religious principles and serve humanity through hospital work, participation in medical experiments, conservation projects, relief activities, and other meaningful service. Those who chose resistance—mainly radical political and religious COs—emphasized liberty, civil rights, and social reform in CPS, in prison, and in the broader society. These COs also tended to spurn the service wing, which they viewed as a complicit tool of the war-making state. Finally, a small number of absolutists, who repudiated any compromise with conscription or the war effort, accepted prison. Absolutists refused to register for the draft, submit to a military physical examination, or report to CPS. Some COs initially chose CPS before the experience of camp life led them to embrace absolutism and wage hunger strikes and walkouts to express opposition to a "slave system" that supported the mass murder of war.[51]

### Evan Thomas and CPS: The Radicalization of an Absolutist

Evan Thomas and Frank Olmstead, the WRL's wartime chairmen, illustrate the initial divisions over CPS within the League and how CPS radicalized the WRL and prompted it to break formal ties with NSBRO. (In January 1941, Thomas became chairman when Olmstead stepped down to become the WRL field work director.) Thomas had consistently rejected giving the peace churches a monopoly over CPS camps; in contrast, Olmstead at first supported the peace church-run religious camps. The CPS experience radicalized both men, however, and led them to modify their positions and to issue searing indictments of CPS.

In an example of rank-and-file pressure, militant and discontented COs provided the main impetus for Thomas's and Olmstead's radicalization. Conversely, A. J. Muste, the FOR's executive secretary and a member of the WRL executive committee, defended CPS throughout the war. Muste feared that "compulsory government-managed service is in the present historic context a fascist one." He asserted that CPS offered "an important opportunity for pacifist service, witness against war and conscription, growth in the pacifist way of life, and preparation for future volunteer services including nonviolent direct action to achieve basic social change."[52] His (and the FOR's) defense of CPS prompted many pacifists to resign from the FOR, including WRL/FOR members David Dellinger, Paton Price, and Evan Thomas.[53]

Thomas had been an absolutist prison CO during World War I. From the beginning he was a strong and influential opponent of CPS. In a 1940 letter to Muste he expressed the militant resistance spirit that came to infuse and radicalize the wartime League: "There are worse places than jail under the circumstances."[54] At one point he stopped criticizing CPS in public in order to avoid jeopardizing approval of the religious camps, which most pacifists favored. Then, in late 1941, he started up again, condemning the agreement between the peace churches and Selective Service and calling CPS a system of "totalitarian" "slave labor" camps.[55] In a November 1941 memo to NSBRO and CPS camp directors that prompted a spirited response from religious pacifists, Thomas bluntly attacked NSBRO and CPS. He acknowledged that religious camps "perform[ed] a very useful and desirable function *unless they are the only forms of alternative service available,*" but at the same time he denounced NSBRO for imposing a religious monopoly on CPS and for denying COs a choice between government and religious camps.[56]

Thomas also condemned coercive CPS "government labor camps" that failed to offer meaningful work of national importance.[57] According to the 1940 Selective Service Act, conscription operated under military control and COs were required to perform alternative service under penalty of jail; from this, Thomas concluded that CPS was a coercive rather than a voluntary system. And since the peace churches had negotiated the CPS agreement and were administering the camps, he charged them and NSBRO with helping the government enforce the draft: "In other words, are pacifists going to aid the government to put other pacifists in jail?"[58] Answering his own question, he replied that "pacifists have no business . . . trying to run conscription for the government," adding, "Coercion, bureaucracy and authoritarianism do not become good when accepted by pacifists."[59] Like Muste, he recognized the dangers posed by collectivism and government control. Even so, he favored government camps, arguing that should the government restrict liberties, "the C.O.s can always practice what so many of us talk about—nonviolent resistance." In September 1944, disillusioned by four years of dealing with CPS, Thomas resigned from the FOR over its membership in NSBRO.[60]

## Frank Olmstead and CPS: A Barometer of Radicalization

CPS also radicalized Olmstead, who moved from support to sharp criticism of CPS. Like many religious pacifists, he welcomed CPS as a positive attempt by the government to honor conscience. CPS permitted COs to do meaningful work under pacifist direction; it also offered them the opportunity to transform ideals into action and construct humane, democratic, self-governing pacifist communities based on pacifist values and relationships. But for Olmstead, the reality of CPS would fall far short of its promise.

In November 1942, Olmstead wrote an influential report on a tour he made of CPS camps. This report marked a key transition in his thinking on CPS and tells us much about the WRL perspective on CPS. According to Olmstead, one-third of COs voiced "considerable dissatisfaction" with the camps; the other two-thirds sympathized with the minority and themselves welcomed "more significant work." Unhappy COs lambasted the trivial work assignments, the lack of compensation and maintenance, and the churches' administration of the camps. Most CPS work did not use the COs' "trained minds and established skills"; nor did it match in importance the firefighting work performed by COs in several camps. Olmstead estimated that "70% of the projects could be done by able-bodied morons." At the same time, he reported that COs would accept routine manual work, "if every shovelful of dirt were doing something for the refugees of Europe."[61]

Olmstead blamed NSBRO for the COs' disillusionment and for the conflict within CPS. Congress had authorized compensation for CPS work, yet after the peace churches recommended that COs work without pay in church-financed camps, the government decided not to fund CPS camps. The lack of compensation and maintenance created hardships, and some COs walked out of the camps in protest. Many COs blamed the peace churches for their bleak living standards: clothing and shoes often were inadequate, dental problems were left untreated, and no provision had been made for dependants. Criticizing the influence of religion in CPS, rebellious COs also claimed that requiring men to work under church direction violated the separation of church and state.

Olmstead reported that despite these problems, some camps were offering excellent educational opportunities and were serving as laboratories of democracy and social cooperation. In one camp, COs who planned to participate in reconstruction programs in Europe after the war were developing the skills they would require to dissolve social barriers and help mutually antagonistic groups. But in Olmstead's view, CPS's most valuable educational benefit was the democratic, experiential, and participatory process of helping operate the camps.

Olmstead's report contained internal contradictions. Indeed, there was an odd dissonance between his damning evidence and his positive conclusions. He detailed the serious problems in CPS, yet he also declared that "despite all the imperfections, morale in the camps is at a high level." His double perspective did not last long, however. Six months later he concluded: "NSBRO has become intolerable for many."[62] What accounts for his transformation?

Toward the end of the war, Olmstead wrote several biting assessments of CPS and discussed the evolution of his own thinking on the subject. He explained that as the League's director of field work he had visited eighty-five camps. Meeting COs, sharing their work and quarters, and listening to their complaints and shattered dreams transformed his perspective and led him to repudiate CPS. He catalogued the poor camp conditions, compared CPS to slavery, and declared CPS "a story of idealism and tragic blunder."[63] Echoing Thomas, he charged the Quakers (and by implication the other peace churches) with becoming "a cog in the conscription machine . . . and serving the institution of the church rather than putting above all other considerations concern for the individual pacifist."[64] In summary, Olmstead, Thomas, and the WRL itself were radicalized by the discontent with CPS among the League's secular, radical, and activist members and by their grassroots revolt within the camps.

### Mental Hospital Orderlies and Human Guinea Pigs

Disappointment with typical CPS assignments, the desire to perform "work of national importance," and the urge to demonstrate their willingness to assume dangerous risks and sacrifices, led more than three thousand COs to volunteer for work in mental hospitals and five hundred more to serve as human guinea pigs in medical experiments.

Perhaps the COs' greatest contribution to the national welfare was their work in public mental hospitals and in state training schools for the retarded. More than three thousand COs served in forty-one mental hospitals in twenty states, and in seventeen schools for the mentally deficient in twelve states. COs, and in some cases their wives and girlfriends, ameliorated the acute wartime labor shortages that led to understaffing and worsening conditions for the nearly six hundred thousand people confined in these institutions.

After visiting several mental hospitals, Olmstead published an account of one. Left alone in the building where incontinent patients were housed, he was surrounded by three hundred inmates. Half were naked, most had huge sores but no shoes, others had swollen feet from urine poisoning, and some acted out perversions. A nauseating odor cloaked the room. "I have been in storms at sea, in train wrecks, and in Moscow during the Bolshevik revolution," Olmstead confessed, "but I have never had quite the feeling that I had when I turned from that locked door to face three hundred insane incontinents."[65] Similarly, Roy Finch, a CO who worked at Eastern State Hospital in Williamsburg, Virginia, recalls that mental hospitals were "unbelievable hell holes" where horrid conditions and abuse were common.[66]

COs humanized mental hospitals by applying nonviolent principles and treating inmates with respect. Following the arrival of CO attendants, hospitals reported a decline in inmate "accidents." Olmstead urged the government to accommodate COs who instead of wasting their talents on trivial tasks, "want to put their faith to work at a point of real need and welcome the disagreeable and often dangerous work of the mental institutions."[67]

Alex Sareyan worked at Connecticut State Hospital as a CO and became a mental health professional after the war. He contends that COs led a "revolution in mental health care" during and after the war. In 1950, for instance, COs helped found the National Association for Mental Heath, which improved the training of mental health care professionals and the standards of care for the mentally ill. The association also sponsored many programs to promote awareness of mental illness and effective treatments for it. COs also led dozens of other postwar initiatives to improve mental health care. "The important consideration," Sareyan concludes, "is that small bands of dedicated individuals can initiate and facilitate social change on a grand scale."[68]

Five hundred COs volunteered to serve as human guinea pigs for medical and scientific experiments. Using COs as live subjects, scientists conducted uncomfortable and often dangerous experiments relating to the cure, control, or treatment of malaria, typhus, pneumonia, and jaundice (infectious hepatitis). Other experiments tested the effects of extreme heat, cold, and altitude, as well as malnutrition and starvation.

By 1943 at least two dozen WRL members in CPS and prison had participated in these experiments. Charles Bloomstein took part in a malaria experiment at Massachusetts General Hospital. Max Kampelman enlisted in a starvation and rehabilitation experiment at the University of Minnesota. Nathaniel Hoffman joined an experiment designed to address malnutrition in postwar Europe. Bent Andresen took part in an experiment on the relationship between a high-protein diet and extreme cold. Jim Peck participated in a yellow jaundice experiment that permanently damaged his liver. Peck later explained: "I viewed it as an opportunity to do a small part in helping to discover a cure [for an illness] which . . . plagued people in many parts of the world, particularly in the east."[69] By volunteering as human guinea pigs, COs demonstrated that pacifists no less than GIs risked their lives to advance ideals and serve humankind.[70]

## The WRL and CO Issues

Within the WRL, differences existed between the service and resistance currents and among resistant COs themselves. These differences came to a head over the League's policy toward NSBRO and CPS, as well as over the protest strikes that CO radicals were waging in CPS and prison. As government control became obvious and heavy-handed, CO radicals spearheaded "direct action" work and hunger strikes to challenge the racism, censorship, state control, and trivial rules they were encountering in CPS and prison. Wartime developments also fueled the COs' revolt. By 1943 the shock of Pearl Harbor had faded and American victory seemed likely. At the same time, the Allies' obliteration bombing of European cities and demands for unconditional surrender were mobilizing pacifists to protest the mass slaughter and to save the postwar peace.[71] Departing from the League's traditional function as a single-issue enrollment, educational, and fellowship organization, the resistant current embraced direct action to advance a multi-issue agenda of both peace and justice.

The WRL maintained a close relationship with COs and championed their cause; it was keenly aware of the growing unrest and disillusionment in the CPS and prison systems. The League spent much of its time aiding COs, both secular and religious, League and non-League members alike.[72] Limited resources permitting, it helped COs appeal draft board decisions and win probation and parole from the Justice Department. It also developed a network of correspondents within CPS and the prisons to publicize COs' living conditions and protests, collected books for CPSers and encouraged them to join the League, and dispatched WRL representatives to visit the camps and prisons.[73]

Initially the WRL called for the creation of independent agencies to provide counseling and legal aid to COs. In this vein the League helped establish the Metropolitan Board for Conscientious Objectors, which advised COs in the New York City area; the National Council for Conscientious Objection; and the Legal Service for Conscientious Objectors, later absorbed by the ACLU. When these and other bodies proved insufficient, the League formed its own CO Problems Committee (COPC) to assist COs. To provide draft-eligible men with information and counseling, the League published a series of ten leaflets on conscription, conscientious objection, Selective Service forms, draft boards, and the appeal process. It also administered a valuable clipping project on COs, draft objectors, and draft resisters for the United Pacifist Committee. Through its work for COs the League gained influence out of proportion to its numbers.[74]

In late 1943 the WRL polled representative members in the camps to gauge the "status of morale" in CPS. Based on responses submitted by ten COs, the League concluded that morale in CPS was still a "serious" problem and that camp conditions paradoxically fostered both resistance and resignation.[75] Several examples illustrate the discontent with CPS among League members. Rex Corfman confessed "that there is considerable deception and sabotage such as reading on project time and not putting in a full day's work." Max Kampelman attributed work slowdowns to the widespread belief that the camps were not trying to match COs' skills to meaningful jobs; rather, "the camps are created to keep them occupied and under surveyance while they are 'mildly incarcerated.'" The report described one CPSer with a Ph.D. who, when ordered to sort nails, responded with a slowdown. Roy Finch expressed what militant COs perceived as the essentially authoritarian nature of CPS: "The camp is rather like a mule—beaten all day and if beaten enough will take one more step but absolutely no more than necessary."[76]

The report supported the WRL's contention that CPSers, when treated with respect and given important tasks, were productive workers. Charles Bloomstein recognized that COs were inner-directed men motivated by conscience and principle rather than material incentives or coercion: "Most of the men, like myself, do what *we* consider to be a worthwhile day's work, for personal reasons of self-respect and pride, and not because of any compulsion."[77] In particular, COs assigned to detached service units exhibited good morale and a sense of purpose. "There is very little discontent in this camp," stated one WRL member assigned to a Weather Bureau project, "because we all came here by our own choice, and find it a big improvement over the camps where we had been."[78] Much discord had resulted from conscription, yet the report contended that changes within the CPS system could foster a more positive atmosphere. But these changes were not forthcoming. As a result, more and more COs were disobeying rules, refusing to work, walking out of CPS, and opting for jail over CPS. One particular case focused the attention of pacifists on COs in CPS and prison, and led to momentous decisions within the League. Significantly, the radicalization of COs would radicalize the League.

### Reversing the "Great Mistake": The WRL and the Murphy-Taylor Hunger Strike

On 12 February 1943, CPS walkouts, imprisoned absolutists, and WRL members Stanley Murphy and Louis Taylor staged an eighty-two-day "liberty or death" fast[79] at Danbury Federal Correctional Institution to protest conscription and the treatment accorded COs. Their dramatic hunger strike became an "absolutist cause celebre."[80] The Murphy-Taylor strike prompted the League to sever its relationship with NSBRO. It also mobilized elements within the League who supported direct action over more traditional protest measures. In these ways it marked an important watershed for the League.

On 16 October 1942 (the second anniversary of registration under the 1940 conscription act), after sixteen months at Big Flats, a New York CPS camp, Murphy and Taylor walked out to protest their trivial work assignments. Taylor was a Henry George devotee; Murphy was the camp personnel man and former labor organizer, actor, and poet. Both were popular among other COs. On 12 February 1943, the same day they started serving their two-and-a-half-year sentences at Danbury, they adopted a policy of noncooperation with prison authorities and began a "fast unto death" against the conscription system.[81] After seventeen days they were force-fed with tubes and wrapped in sheets to prevent them from deliberately vomiting. They continued their fast for eighty-two days until 5 May, when Selective Service agreed to provide significant work and liberalize CO paroles.

Within the WRL, Evan Thomas and David Dellinger led the absolutists' response to the strike. Julius Eichel also championed an absolutist position. Eichel was a past member of the League who had resigned over its refusal to adopt an absolutist stance toward the 1940 Selective Service law; he was also the leader of the Absolutist War Objectors Association and one of only two COs who had been imprisoned during both world wars. With his wife Esther, another absolutist, he published the two leading wartime absolutist publications, the *Weekly Prison News Letter* (1943) and its successor, the *Absolutist* (1943–47). Both of these publications lionized the strikers.[82]

On 10 March nearly three hundred members of New York WRL and FOR chapters met at the Labor Temple in Greenwich Village to discuss the Murphy-Taylor hunger strike. After long discussion, plans for further action were entrusted to a committee dominated by League members. This committee recommended that pacifists launch a letter-writing campaign and dispatch a delegation to Washington to pressure the administration to release Murphy and Taylor and permit them (and all COs) to perform work of national importance consistent with their training and choice. More significantly, it recommended that the WRL and FOR "immediately withdraw from NSBRO."[83]

Three committee (and League) members—Dellinger, Philip Isely, and Charlotte Bentley—also advocated more radical direct action. They argued that Murphy and Taylor "have gone beyond the traditional methods of resolutions, speeches and letter-writing." Their actions have infused "a new vigor in the pacifist forces" and "we make a great mistake if we limit our support of them to the traditional methods which they have already surpassed."[84] In a separate statement, Dellinger and six other COs and pacifists emphasized peace and justice and called on the League, the FOR, and others to support Taylor and Murphy, who were "offering their lives . . . to dramatize their unsurrendering opposition to war and conscription . . . and . . . to stir the pacifist movement out of its present complacency."[85]

The same statement chided pacifists who "ourselves have been sitting in bourgeois parlors and wooded hills quibbling over how far our own compromise can go—whether to buy war bonds, conduct medical experiments for the military, or support the USO. . . . We are learning that pacifism implies not alternative service or noncooperation, but a vigorous, unsparing attack on evil." The authors called on pacifists to converge on Washington between 4 and 6 April to lobby government officials. In a controversial direct action protest, they would also picket the Senate to stop the war, to adopt "a constructive program of Food, Freedom and Justice everywhere," and to end "appeasement to [imperialist] Fascism" in India and North Africa. The statement also denounced the absence of democracy in the Soviet Union, India, and Jim Crow America. Acting through an April Six Action Committee, CO radicals, emulating Gandhi, planned "meetings of preparation and dedication" [86] and urged nationwide direct action in CPS camps and jails to support the Washington protest. [87]

The Murphy-Taylor strike inspired other WRL members and pacifists. COs attending the Chicago Conference on Social Action expressed their "solidarity" with Murphy and Taylor and recommended specific action, including a collective CPS and prison CO work strike. [88] Five days later, from a CPS camp at Powellsville, Maryland, Igal Roodenko announced that he would commence a work strike on 3 May unless the Danbury men had ended their fast. He had contemplated such a protest and fasted intermittently for six weeks. "With no further action on my part," he declared, "should Murphy and Taylor die, their blood would be on my hands." [89]

Opponents of withdrawal argued that the WRL could more effectively promote its demand for government camps with compensation and more detached service through continued participation in NSBRO. But the Murphy-Taylor strike did not enjoy unanimous support within the WRL. Although Hughan applauded the strikers' "high integrity and spirit of sacrifice," [90] she objected to their fast on moral and practical grounds. Writing from Florida, she explained her opposition toward both the strike and the absolutists response to it:

> I believe the hunger strike to be contrary to the pacifist system of non-violence. It is a form of suicide, quieter but not less suicide than a pistol shot. . . . I believe that the hunger strike is of no value to our Cause. . . . They are risking death to *stop the war.* I consider this wholly impracticable, *because,* such a strike may be effectual in startling the public to action *if* a large majority are in general sympathy but merely inactive or unaware of the facts. This is true of Gandhi and was true more or less in the suffragette agitation in Britain and the Irish Revolution. Our case, however, is the exact opposite. The general public, even in peacetime, was not sympathetic with us extremists, and now because of war propaganda they are thoroughly opposed. [91]

The contrast between Hughan's disapproval of the Murphy-Taylor protest and her praise for Gandhi's contemporaneous hunger strike is interesting. "What a wonderful thing that Gandhi held out!" she wrote to Abraham Kaufman in March 1943, the same month she repudiated the Murphy-Taylor strike. She acknowledged that Gandhi "did accomplish drawing the world's attention" to the Indian independence movement; however, she expressed less enthusiasm toward "other hunger strikes" that might end in failure or death. [92] Unlike

Hughan, the absolutists asserted that readiness to risk death to protest conscription and war represented a logical—even heroic—example of pacifist commitment. Indeed, hunger strikes seemed consistent with the radical pacifist ideal—articulated by Hughan herself four years earlier in *If We Should Be Invaded*—of enduring nonviolent "hardship and death" in social struggles.[93]

On 17 March the WRL executive committee discussed reports produced by the Labor Temple committee and the COPC. In particular, it considered whether the League should withdraw from NSBRO's consultative council and endorse the Labor Temple committee proposals that sought support for "action well beyond our resolve not to obstruct or interfere with the war effort."[94] Unable to reach a decision, the executive committee scheduled another meeting for 22 March to resolve the issues. According to Kaufman, this would be the "most important" meeting since Pearl Harbor.[95]

Opponents of withdrawal argued that NSBRO was the most effective vehicle available to the League in its campaign for government camps with compensation and more detached service. They noted that despite the League's preference for government camps, most COs preferred the existing religious camps. They emphasized how important it was for pacifists to cooperate and saw NSBRO, for all its imperfections, as a means to unite most pacifists, both religious and secular.[96]

Those who favored withdrawal from NSBRO argued that the League must repudiate the "Great Mistake"—the original pacifist agreement to take all COs into church-operated camps without compensation or government support. Despite its good intentions, CPS was denying COs the right to choose between religious and government camps and between paid and unpaid work. Though it had never joined NSBRO, the League did serve on its consultative council. Furthermore, its name appeared on NSBRO letterhead and it made a small ($15) monthly contribution. Impatience with conditions in CPS and the prisons had been building, and the Murphy-Taylor strike made even this limited relationship unpalatable to many League members. "Can we be related," the COPC asked, "to an arrangement which is primarily responsible for three of the conditions which drove these men to prison and a hunger strike ["work under the Church, work with no government support, and work without pay"]?" The COPC recommended that the League withdraw from NSBRO's consultative council: "The War Resisters League has from the start refused to approve the initial mistake. The League was the only pacifist organ to take that stand, possibly because it was most free from obligation to a broader religious institution. Now Murphy and Taylor force us to question the continuation of our limited cooperation."[97]

At its 22 March meeting the WRL executive committee voted overwhelmingly to resign from NSBRO. It also endorsed the Labor Temple committee recommendations; however, it refused to allow the April Six Action Committee—the group organizing the direct action picketing in Washington—to use the League's mailing list.[98]

In response to the WRL's decision to withdraw from NSBRO's consultative council, three leaders who had championed the service orientation within the League resigned: John H. Holmes, Sidney E. Goldstein, and Isidor B. Hoffman. In his letter of resignation, Holmes called NSBRO's policies "wholly wise and good." He regretted that the League had injected "division and dissension into the pacifist movement at the very time when united action is most needed." Finally, he complained that the decision signaled a preoccupation with the "conscription question" and the abandonment of the League's traditional focus on the causes and cures of war.[99]

Evan Thomas and Hughan appealed to Holmes, Goldstein, and Hoffman to reconsider their resignations. Replying to Holmes, Thomas observed that despite his own opposition to the accord between the peace churches and Selective Service, he was not going to resign or attempt to impose his views on the League. In a letter to Hoffman, Hughan blamed the League's decision on the "younger and hot-headed members . . . the 'New Blood' "; she also denied that these people represented the "mature sense" of the executive committee, many of whose members had been absent from the meeting of 22 March.[100] Furthermore, she wrote Holmes, the resignations would deprive the League of the experienced counsel it needed to "balance" the "inexperienced members" who had voted to sever ties with NSBRO.[101] Holmes, Goldstein, and Hoffman refused to reverse their decision.[102]

The withdrawal from NSBRO and subsequent resignations did not end the League's involvement in the Murphy-Taylor case. In May 1943, Murphy and Taylor ended their eighty-two-day hunger strike, agreeing to accept parole to a public service institution in return for maintenance and a stipend of $2 per month. When this agreement collapsed, they were transferred to the Prison Medical Center in Springfield, Missouri, where inmates with mental problems were housed. The abuses they encountered there led them to challenge the prison authorities, and a second stage of their saga began. The WRL defended the two men, publicized their mistreatment, raised money for Elizabeth Murphy to visit Springfield, and successfully pressured officials to launch two investigations into conditions at Springfield.

After visiting her son twice in Springfield, Elizabeth Murphy informed Thomas in early August that both men were being kept in strip cells and sometimes beaten. In response to agitation by the WRL, the pacifist movement, and civil libertarians, the Bureau of Prisons director, James V. Bennett, reversed his previous denials and admitted that Murphy and Taylor had been confined to solitary, padded strip cells. Continued pressure forced Bennett to launch an investigation, which criticized their confinement in strip cells but reached no conclusion as to whether the two men had been beaten.

In September 1943, Murphy smuggled out a letter to his mother claiming that both he and Taylor had been badly beaten. In the year that followed, explosive articles in the *New York World-Telegram* and *St. Louis Post-Dispatch,* and a pacifist campaign led by Evan Thomas publicized the wrongful use of force at Springfield. The WRL denounced the Bureau of Prisons report as a whitewash. In March 1944, Thomas wrote a blistering letter to each member of Congress detailing the abuses—which included at least one inmate death—that prisoners suffered at Springfield. In October 1944, Murphy sued Bennett and the former warden on charges that he had been beaten, choked, kicked, dragged, held down while guards jumped on his stomach ("stomping"), confined naked to a strip cell, fed a punishment diet (of oatmeal, bread, and water), and threatened with a declaration of insanity. In early August 1945 the two men completed their sentences and were released. On 7 August the Families and Friends of Imprisoned COs, a group led by Julius and Esther Eichel, organized a party at the Labor Temple for the now-famous COs.[103]

The Murphy-Taylor case illustrates the WRL's concern about COs, prison conditions, and conscription. Furthermore, it represented a tentative but discernable broadening of the League's agenda beyond peace action and war resistance. The hunger strike radicalized the League by mobilizing its absolutist and resistant elements, who spurred it to resign from NSBRO's consultative council.

The same strike highlighted divisions within the WRL among its service, resistant, and absolutist factions. Disagreements existed over whether to work through NSBRO and whether the League should limit its activities to legal action. Resistant members themselves were split over whether to support the absolutist position, especially when doing so entailed civil disobedience. Both the service current and the more cautious of the resistant members lost on the issue of NSBRO. The debate over tactics between those favoring direct action and those supporting political-educational means of protest and resistance had not yet been resolved.[104]

Although it continued to reject civil disobedience, the WRL had been radicalized by the strike. In September 1943 the League relaxed the restrictive recruitment and enlistment policies it had adopted immediately after Pearl Harbor. It now mailed unsolicited literature and membership forms to civilians, as well as to noncombatants stationed at army camps who requested such materials.[105] More significantly, the League now showed greater tolerance for nonviolent direct action, and had broadened its single-issue agenda to address conscription, Indian independence, and African American civil rights.

### From Single-Issue War Resistance Toward a Multi-Issue Agenda and Nonviolent Direct Action

The WRL's wartime campaign against conscription, criticized by some members as peripheral to its focus on war resistance, represented a subtle broadening of its agenda. John Haynes Holmes expressed this position in his March 1943 letter of resignation: "The League seems to have forgotten that its prime business is with war, its cause and cure. . . . From all this the League has more and more turned away, and become absorbed in the conscription question, which is not properly our concern at all, or at least only in a subsidiary and relatively unimportant way." [106]

During 1944 and 1945 the WRL continued to campaign against postwar conscription. Disillusioned and radicalized by CPS, it also decided in the future to seek complete exemption for COs and not to request alternative service. In June 1945, Edward Richards and Evan Thomas repudiated peacetime conscription before a congressional committee. [107]

The WRL's wartime radicalization and broadened agenda is best illustrated by its support for African American civil rights. Gandhian nonviolent direct action has been central to the modern civil rights movement, which was invigorated during World War II. [108] Members of the League either led or contributed to the March on Washington Movement (MOWM) and the Congress of Racial Equality (CORE). In addition, COs who were members of the WRL led strikes against Jim Crow policies in prisons and protested racial discrimination in CPS (see chapter 5). Much of the emphasis on Gandhian nonviolent direct action to advance racial equality came from COs; however, female pacifists and older male pacifists who were exempt from the draft also experimented with direct action to promote civil rights. This link between the League, Gandhian nonviolent direct action, and the civil rights movement was exemplified by Jay Holmes Smith and the role that League members played in the MOWM and CORE.

Jay Holmes Smith, a prominent advocate of nonviolent direct action to achieve social justice, was a former missionary expelled from India because of his association with Gandhi and the Indian independence movement. He was elected to the WRL executive committee in 1942. He founded the Harlem Ashram (1940–47), a cooperative pacifist community that became a center of New York City's nonviolent direct action movement. Under the FOR's auspices, he also established the Nonviolent Direct Action Committee (NDAC) and the

Free India Committee to explore the application of Gandhian principles and techniques to American social conditions.

Based at the Harlem Ashram, NDAC members studied Krishnalal Shridharani's texts and experimented with Gandhian techniques to promote direct action, Indian independence, and civil rights. Smith and NDAC members picketed the British embassy (and then fasted once arrested) to support Indian independence and to protest Gandhi's imprisonment. Smith led a 170-mile pilgrimage from Pennsylvania to New York City to publicize the plight of near-starving European civilians, a 160-mile trek from New Jersey to Washington for the same purpose, and a 240-mile interracial walk from New York City to the Lincoln Monument to promote racial equality. The Harlem Ashram offered courses on nonviolent direct action (which combined classroom discussions with direct action projects) to attack racial discrimination.

The WRL endorsed Smith's commitment to nonviolent direct action. "Jay Smith made us feel that we have done much less than we might in our opposition to war," a 1943 WRL report observed. "Non-violent direct action offers a method whose effectiveness has been demonstrated and which can be adapted to the American scene." Influenced by Smith, the League appointed a committee to oppose conscription by direct action. Despite its support for direct action, however, the League continued to shun civil disobedience.[109]

WRL members (operating through the FOR) worked with A. Philip Randolph, president of the Brotherhood of Sleeping Car Porters—the nation's most important black union—and influenced the emergent nonviolent strategy of his March on Washington Movement. In the spring of 1941, Randolph announced plans to lead a mass black march on Washington, D.C., to force an end to racial discrimination in defense employment. In June 1941, in response to this specter, President Roosevelt issued Executive Order 8802, which created the Committee on Fair Employment Practices. Randolph canceled the march but founded the MOWM to maintain the threat of a mass black march to pressure federal officials to advance civil rights. Answering critics who charged him with bluffing, Randolph announced that in July 1943, at MOWM's maiden national convention, he and the MOWM would launch a national civil disobedience campaign to secure black civil rights. To support Randolph and nonviolent social reform, A. J. Muste and the FOR assigned Bayard Rustin and James Farmer to help the MOWM organize its watershed convention. Muste, Rustin, and Smith—the outside pacifists who did the most to shape the MOWM's Gandhian strategy— were WRL and FOR members.

The black community divided over the wisdom and efficacy of militant nonviolent tactics. In response to the MOWM's proposed civil disobedience campaign, the *People's Voice,* a prominent black newspaper, raised the issue of Gandhian nonviolence in its weekly debate forum: "Does a non-violent, civil disobedience campaign similar to that of Mohandas Gandhi in India offer the Negro in the U.S. an effective method of protest?"[110] Writing for the affirmative, Smith asserted: "Old methods have about petered out. Words alone are too weak. Violent revolt would be suicidal . . . The Gandhi method appeals to the best in the opponent, and wins over public sentiment."[111] At the convention, Rustin delivered a major speech on the power of nonviolent direct action. In the end, two thousand MOWM delegates voted to adopt Gandhian direct action to abolish racial discrimination in public accommodations. The MOWM never realized its potential as a mass movement, however. Militant black social protest, represented by the MOWM and the 1943 race riots in Detroit and Harlem, spawned a conservative backlash. Combined with wartime political pressures, this conservative counter-movement contained and defused the militant black protest of Randolph and the MOWM.[112] Radical pacifists also founded CORE, which had a more lasting influence than the MOWM.

Under the FOR's sponsorship, radical pacifists established CORE in 1942. CORE emerged from an interracial FOR discussion group on race relations at the University of Chicago. All six founders were FOR members. Four of them—George Houser, James Robinson, Joe Guinn, and Homer Jack—were WRL members; the other two, James Farmer and Bernice Fisher, were close to the League. All six were pacifists; four were white and two black; three were former or future COs. Bayard Rustin, destined to play prominent roles in both the WRL and the FOR, was CORE's first field organizer.[113]

Houser provided the most important link between the WRL and CORE. One of eight Union Theological Seminary students sentenced to jail for refusing to register for the 1940 draft, Houser left prison in 1941 and went to Chicago to complete his studies. A member of the postwar WRL executive committee, Houser was one of the COs who helped move the League toward a more radical, direct action, multi-issue orientation. Though he served as a top FOR staffer, Houser was less interested in particular organizations than in building an effective nonviolent *movement* to advance both peace and justice.

Writing to Muste from Danbury prison, Houser explained his social actionist pacifist philosophy:

> It seems to me that the time has definitely arrived for those of us who are opposed to war, and who favor the creation of a society with greater justice for all to create a movement which can take us in that direction. . . . This means that we

must raise up a movement based on non-violence as a method, with the immediate aim of opposing the war, of promising as much democracy as possible here at home, and of working ultimately for a more socialist society.[114]

Shortly after CORE was founded, Houser argued that the WRL should change its name to reflect a broader concern consistent with "a non-violent approach to all [social] problems."[115] In his view, civil rights offered the best opportunity for nonviolent techniques and pacifist-nonpacifist cooperation. In late 1943 he observed that "CORE is the most fruitful organization for pacifists to work through . . . as far as social movements are concerned. CORE can have real power, but it will remain non-violent only to the extent that pacifists are within it."[116] From World War II to the mid-1960s, nonviolent tactics marked the civil rights movement. WRL members made important contributions to CORE, the civil rights revolution, and the use of nonviolence to promote social justice (see chapter 8).

During World War II the WRL underwent a subtle but significant transformation on several levels. First, the WRL and radical pacifists started to shift from political-educational to direct action techniques of agitation and protest. This represented a move away from prewar radical pacifist theory toward wartime action. Second, while the touchstone of the League's founding generation remained socialism and the socialist general strike against war, the new generation of COs who joined the League shortly before or during the war was inspired by Gandhi and adopted him as their model. The wartime pacifist press lionized Gandhi, the Indian independence movement, and the relevance of both to America and the world. Third, the WRL's increased involvement in the anticonscription and civil rights movements amounted to a broadening of its traditional program, which was the single issue of war resistance, to embrace a multi-issue agenda of social justice.[117]

# 5

# Toward Direct Action

The WRL and the CO Revolts
in CPS and Prison,
1940–1945

DURING WORLD WAR II, 12,000 conscientious objectors served in Civilian Public Service and 6,000 others went to prison. At least 550 WRL members worked in CPS, while another 100 spent time in jail.[1] More significantly, the League and its "articulate and energetic" members had a disproportionate influence among COs in CPS and prison.[2] Some prison COs had refused to register for the draft. Others had been denied conscientious objector status by draft boards, often because they opposed war on political, philosophical, or humanitarian rather than religious grounds. Still others enlisted in CPS, became disillusioned and radicalized by their experiences in the camps, and began walking out and refusing to cooperate with CPS officials and regulations. They were jailed as a result.

The CO community was diverse. The vast majority were religious COs, who represented over one hundred denominations. Many belonged to the historic peace churches—the Quakers, the Mennonites, and the Brethren. Some belonged to various other Protestant sects and were motivated by social gospel theology. There were also Catholics, Jews, Black Muslims, Hopi Indians, and Jehovah's Witnesses. More than 60 percent of all COs were Jehovah's Witnesses, who were willing to battle for the Lord at Armageddon and were not absolute pacifists. There also were a handful of political, philosophical, and humanitarian COs, both pacifist and nonpacifist, who did not meet the religious test established by the Selective Training and Service Act of 1940. The WRL was the major champion of these secular COs, who totaled less than 6 percent of all objectors. Nonpacifist political objectors included assorted socialists who opposed the war on Marxist grounds but did not repudiate all war. The nonpacifist Socialist Party (SP) did contain a pacifist current, which included WRL members, who organized several SP locals within CPS.[3]

Among both political and religious COs there were several fundamental impulses. These included the service, the resistant, the social actions, and the absolutist positions. Except for those religious objectors committed to a narrow service orientation, most of these resistant, social action, and absolutist COs were influenced by Gandhi and advocated active nonviolent resistance and social struggle. Resistant COs spearheaded protests for reform in CPS and prison; they also championed individual liberty, civil rights, and fundamental social reform. Social action COs—an articulate and impassioned subset of resistance impulse—maintained that pacifists should promote social justice and transform society along general socialist lines. Finally, the absolutist COs—the most uncompromising pacifists—refused all cooperation with Selective Service.

The WRL represented the left wing of the pacifist movement and encouraged CO revolt in CPS camps and prisons. Evan Thomas expressed this support in letters he wrote in April 1943 to League members in CPS camps: "Surely the time has come for the men in the camps to take action aggressively and in accordance with principle. . . . C.O[.]'s will come alive and understand the meaning of freedom only when they lose this timidity and are willing to risk even prison and death for the principles which we all cherish." In another letter he wrote: "I am convinced that if all the men in the CPS camps who have expressed dissatisfaction with the present set-up were to act by refusing to cooperate with the present totalitarian administration of the Selective Service Act, some sort of constructive action might be taken by the government."[4]

Resistants, absolutists, and social action COs typically were WRL members or were associated with the League or the FOR. The League, which embraced a radical pacifist ideology and supported nonviolent Gandhian resistance, provided a congenial home for radical, activist COs. League members within CPS and prison were more than ready to engage in nonviolent resistance and social activism, and this brought them into conflict with the Selective Service, the Bureau of Prisons, and most religious pacifists, the great majority of whom accepted wartime civilian service and rejected resistance and social transformation.[5]

The cohort of radical pacifist World War II COs would have a powerful impact on the WRL. During the war, resistant, social action, and absolutist COs staged nonviolent direct action protests—which included sabotage and work and hunger strikes—to protest Jim Crow racism, censorship, conscription, and the array of policies that dehumanized prison and gutted the original vision of CPS. In the postwar decades these radicalized COs would provide the WRL with much of its leadership, applying the techniques of Gandhian nonviolent di-

rect action that they had honed in prison and CPS to advance both peace and social justice.

This chapter focuses on COs who radicalized the WRL by participating in
the wartime revolt in CPS and prison and who helped lead the League after the
war. Their experiences—and their protests in CPS and prison—illustrate the
idealism, disillusionment, radicalization, and activism of many social action, resistant, and absolutist COs. Igal Roodenko, James Peck, Bayard Rustin, David
Dellinger, and Ralph DiGia, and others who participated in this grassroots,
rank-and-file CO revolt radicalized the wartime WRL and led its postwar peace
and justice activism. (Unless otherwise noted, all COs discussed in this chapter
were WRL members.)

## CO Protests by WRL Members in Civilian Public Service

Although most COs supported and cooperated with CPS, a minority of resistant COs denounced and challenged it. Resistant COs—most of them political
objectors, religious pacifists outside the peace churches, or atheists—were often
members of or close to the WRL. Many resistant COs registered for the draft, received conscientious objector status, and entered CPS, only to find themselves
disillusioned and radicalized by the experience. Historians have catalogued CO
complaints: the absence of paid work, support for dependants, medical insurance, and workmen's compensation; the lack of meaningful work of national importance; the military control and regulation of CPS camps, and the militaristic
outlook of the army officers who supervised the program; the often inefficient
and arbitrary camp management; the denial of freedom that conscription entailed; and the role of the peace churches and religious pacifists in administering
the camps against the will of secular and nonsectarian COs.[6]

To protest the failings of CPS, resistant COs resorted to work strikes, work
slowdowns, hunger strikes, "sabotage," walkouts, individual appeals, and mass
petitions. They also sent a barrage of critical letters to NSBRO, Selective Service,
the WRL, and the FOR. COs who were WRL members led this revolt against
CPS, with the League's support.[7] One League member, a nineteen-month veteran of CPS who refused to accept a transfer to another camp, declared: "I entered camp with a burning desire to make CPS a vital positive and creative
alternative to the way of blood-shed [sic] and distruction [sic]." Donald Rockwell, the nephew of Jessie Wallace Hughan, confessed: "I can conceive of a type
of benevolent, democratic, peace-time conscription, so beneficial to man, to society, to the world, that I might submit to it, but that is very far from anything to
which I have been subjected up until now." In late 1942, "after months of work-

ing on a glorified leaf-raking project," Wallace Hamilton proclaimed: "The CPS system reeks with decayed vision."[8]

In mid-1943 another League member, an eight-month veteran of CPS, made this complaint: "Speaking from experience I found the CPS system in practice characterized by threats, coercion, force and threats of force, lies, deceit, treachery, stool pigeon tactics, spying, misrepresentation, intimidation and a whole book of nonpacifist techniques." With less vitriol, Roy Finch observed in April 1943 that "CPS appears to be simply one prolonged crisis." Paton Price noted that a fissure had developed between radical COs and the established peace leaders who administered CPS. In late 1942 he offered a prediction that proved to be prophetic: "It may very well be that CPS will stand in pacifist history as a monument to the disintegration of one generation of pacifists during World War II."[9]

In 1942, COs began to walk out of camps and refuse transfers to other camps. In numerous statements they expressed their disillusionment with CPS, detailed their grievances, and declared that they would no longer compromise with CPS, conscription, NSBRO, Selective Service, and the wartime government. In their walkout statements they emphasized the importance of acting on their ideals and refusing to support—even implicitly—the war machine, totalitarianism, and slave labor. Philip Isely remarked: "By remaining in CPS, I not only acquiesce (and thereby give tacit support) to conscription and continued war, but I also fail to make the positive choice of devoting my full-time efforts towards ending the war and building a peaceful and cooperative society." Paton Price was determined to end all cooperation with CPS and conscription: "I have assumed the role of civil disobedience. . . . To withdraw, to be silent, to acquiesce to the military machine is not only to approve it, but actually to sponsor it." Like many COs, Julian Jaynes anticipated the moral imperative behind the Nuremberg principle: "In so far as I accept public decisions, I am responsible for them unless I remove my guilt by opposition. . . . [and by] civil disobedience against all war enactments." John H. Abbot denounced the insignificant leaf raking, the "involuntary servitude," and the "unhealthy state-church-individual relationship" that marked CPS: "I ask for the freedom which our men are fighting for on many shores, not to sit idle for the duration, as I would be in jail, but [to] serve fellowmen [sic] to the limit of my ability. I can not do that while confined in C.P.S." Hughan, whose nephew walked out of CPS and served a one-year prison sentence, later saluted COs who walked out: "Those boys . . . are the shock troops of war resistance."[10]

At the camp in Big Flats, New York, in October 1942, a dozen men—most of them WRL members—initiated a work strike. The dispute started over the lack of car insurance for COs who drove government trucks during work assignments. Without insurance, the men would be personally liable if someone were injured in an accident. COs driving government vehicles submitted a letter to the project manager explaining their position and turned in their driver's licenses. The situation deteriorated the following morning when the project manager arrived and found the work crew still in camp because Louis Taylor, their driver and labor representative, had relinquished his license. The manager bellowed, "So you're refusing to work?" Taylor quietly replied, "I'm not refusing to work . . . but I am unable to drive since I do not have a license." Enraged, the manager threatened, "Well, if you want to get tough, I can be the same way." The conflict escalated. The manager tried to dismiss Stanley Murphy, the camp personnel man. Then, when another crew reported to pull weeds, their project manager disciplined two men for insufficient work and ignored the labor representative's attempt to resolve the dispute. This provoked the work strike.[11] Two of the COs, WRL members Taylor and Murphy, later escalated their protest against CPS with their celebrated hunger strike (see chapter 4).

Walkouts and refusals to work openly defied the authorities. Some COs took a different tack, waging work slowdowns to resist CPS while avoiding prison. John Lewis circulated a mimeographed study of the work slowdown at the Lapine, Oregon, government CPS camp. He viewed the slowdown—the "stepbrother" of the general strike—as an effective nonviolent technique for thwarting the conscription system, promoting social justice, and resisting impending American fascism. Like most radical pacifists, he embraced the nonviolent slowdown tactics that the Wobblies and French syndicalists termed sabotage. The "imaginative use of passive resistance," he declared, could make forced labor "the world's most inefficient way of getting work done." He advised COs to reduce the work tempo by requesting detailed instructions before starting assigned tasks. He cited "one man [who] hacked at a 3-inch log all morning with a foreman standing over him constantly." Addressing fellow COs on the pacifist Left, he argued that "it is absolutely essential that we achieve a reputation as effective fighters for social justice with nonviolent methods. This is necessary if we ever hope to provide an effective answer to the charge of 'passivism.' "[12]

Roy Kepler recounted a similar situation at the Germfask, Michigan, CPS camp operated by the government:

> At Germfask we were organizing a work slow-down. We got to be experts at not working. This was one of the radicalizing experiences. . . .
> The effort was made to show that slave labor was not an efficient way to get

things done. We had the responsibility to develop alternatives to it, rather than to go an [sic] acquiescing in the slavery. We became experts at digging a hole that never got dug, or a trench. I remember one day we were sitting in the barracks looking out the window and one of our number was in effect being punished for something he had done. The camp foreman ordered him to dig a ditch from one building to another for the camp plumbing. This guy—Hugh Hammond—was a big pleasant guy, with a smile on his face; he never said anything about being a resister. But somebody noticed that Hugh was out digging where he had started digging, and an hour later he was still in the same spot. We started watching him as he went through the motions. To all appearances he was digging, nobody seemed to notice. Nothing ever happened! Finally the foreman heard of this and came rushing down. Hugh was just as mild as he could be. He said, "Well I've been digging here all afternoon." The foreman said, "You haven't gotten anything done!" Hugh bantered with him about it. He said, "Well you know I'm not a very good digger, I can't use the shovel very well, nobody has shown me how to use it." And pretty soon here was the foreman showing him how to use it.[13]

Indirect refusals to work were yet another form of sabotage and resistance. COs could thus protest without major risk of imprisonment. Martin Ponch, a CPS CO, related the following situation:

> For a while there I would report to work, because there were technicalities, you know, if you didn't report to work you obviously were refusing to work. But I didn't want to refuse, because you get several years in jail just for refusing to work. I didn't want to go to jail. So I would come out in the morning with my dungarees and whatever you needed to get out in the woods, and I'd say to the Forest Service man, "Mr. McCloskey, you have any work of national importance today?" And he'd say, "Same as we had yesterday." And I'd say, "Sorry, that is not work of national importance according to my books, so I'll go back to my editing." It was funny, because I did this a number of days in a row, and finally when he saw me coming out of the corner of his eye, he'd just find something to interest him off somewhere else, he didn't want to talk to me.[14]

Henry Dyer related the experience of a group at Camp Lagro, Indiana, that sang labor and antiwar songs en route to work. The men formed an unchartered union—the "Post Hole Diggers and Dirt Stompers Union, Local 6, United Conscientious Objectors of America." When supervisors prohibited them from removing their shirts in hot weather, they responded with a creative protest. "Bit by bit the workers tore off pieces of their shirts," Dyer reported. "The offending garments stayed on but grew smaller and smaller until at last they consisted of somewhat unevenly fringed, but nonetheless dainty, brassieres. And when the situation had grown thoroughly ridiculous, the shirts came off." [15]

During the war, nonviolent tactics like these remained in the experimental stage. In a statement on the Germfask and Lapine slowdowns, Frank Olmstead observed that Germfask "brought to a head a new technique of opposing conscription which might be called nonviolent nonproduction." The idea, he explained, was "conceived" at Mancos and "nursed along" at Lapine, and spread to Germfask, where most of the COs were transferees from Mancos and Lapine. Significantly, Mancos, Lapine, Germfask, and (later) Minersville, California, were government camps, which attracted the most radical CPS COs. Olmstead, who reported that work productivity had been cut by two-thirds, considered the slowdown a successful method for reforming CPS. Even more important, he demonstrated how a CO network linked COs in different camps, facilitating the spread of the ideas and techniques of nonviolent direct action and resistance. [16]

Rebellious COs also resorted to mass petitions to press their demands. WRL members helped lead several mass petition campaigns. In October 1941, WRL and other COs at the San Dimas, California, camp sent a petition to all CPS camps urging NSBRO and Selective Service to reform CPS and to provide COs with maintenance provisions, compensation equal to that of GIs, and a choice between religious and government camps. Another petition requested remuneration and work of national importance; it circulated through the camps and secured more than nine hundred signatures by February 1943. In 1943, Henry Dyer circulated a mass petition asking the president to "appoint a civilian board to place each man in suitable and useful work in the public welfare at regular wages." [17] Eighteen hundred COs (about 20 percent of CPS's population) signed the petition, which represented the largest CPS action. The White House rejected the petition. [18]

In November 1942, R. Boland Brooks and George B. Reeves resigned from NSBRO. This underscores the disenchantment with CPS and NSBRO. Both were important NSBRO officials as well as members of the WRL executive committee. Brooks, a successful New York lawyer, headed the NSBRO's appeals section and handled CO appeals pro bono; Reeves led the detached service section. Both resigned over NSBRO's failure to respond adequately to COs' pressing concerns and their conviction that CPS was ignoring the rights of secular pacifists. After leaving NSBRO, they headed the Legal Service for Conscientious Objectors, which provided free legal assistance to COs involved in disputes or appeals over paroles, draft classification, prison conditions, special projects for CO parolees, bail, or a draft board's refusal to grant CO status. The

WRL supported the Legal Service for Conscientious Objectors, and League members sat on its board. In January 1943, when the National Committee on Conscientious Objectors of the American Civil Liberties Union absorbed Legal Service for Conscientious Objectors, Brooks and Reeves took jobs in its Washington office.[19]

Drafted in 1944 and ordered to report to CPS, Brooks and Reeves continued their protests. In May 1944, Brooks refused to report to CPS and received a three-year jail sentence. In a statement to the court—which hours later he repeated before the WRL executive committee—Brooks distinguished between his commitment to uphold the law and Constitution and his disobedience of the Selective Service Act. The 1940 conscription law, he charged, violated the First, Fifth, and Thirteenth Amendments and constituted an "integral part of war."[20]

Similarly, on 15 May 1944, Reeves staged a symbolic one-day fast at the Lapine camp to "expiate" the guilt he felt over his role in establishing the "crime" of CPS. "Three years ago today the first Civilian Public Service camp opened in Maryland," he stated. "It is a day to be remembered with weeping and gnashing of teeth, a black day in the history of American freedom. For three years this illegal, unconstitutional system of punitive servitude has continued, and pacifists by and large have been silent," Reeves declared. "Because I had a part in the beginnings of CPS—as an executive of NSBRO—I feel guilty of a crime against the American public. Today I shall fast at noon and keep silence during the noon hour."[21]

Philip Isely, a member of both the WRL and the SP and a social action CO at Cascade Locks, Oregon, organized an SP local in camp that promoted intercamp social action. In August 1942 he circulated a statement throughout the camps titled "Towards Greater Opportunity in C.P.S." Criticizing the unsatisfactory CPS work projects, he proposed a program of expanded CPS work and educational opportunities that would emphasize social reconstruction and the building of a "peaceful and cooperative society."[22] He called for increased detached service to promote cooperatives, community service, housing projects, and wartime relief; looking beyond the war, he also urged postwar peace, reconstruction, and full employment. Besides requesting significant work, he outlined an educational program for CPS camps involving seminars, lectures, traveling faculty, and courses on subjects such as postwar reconstruction, cooperatives, and "pacifist techniques for obtaining social changes."[23] He also suggested that COs organize an intercamp conference to discuss CPS issues. Finally, he invited other camps to submit responses to the Cascade Locks proposals, circulate their own statements, and communicate their positions to NSBRO. The Cascade Locks SP local dropped its sponsorship of the campaign, and subsequent action was taken in the name of social action CPS COs, many of whom were WRL members.[24]

The Cascade Locks statement sparked a lively intercamp discussion. After an outpouring of letters, communications, and statements from COs in three dozen camps, and from other pacifists, the initial proposals were refined. This revised statement in turn led to the Chicago Conference on Social Action (April 1943), which was organized despite General Hershey's prohibition. Here, CPS COs and other pacifists met to discuss the problems within CPS. From New York, Evan Thomas wrote: "I am especially delighted that you men in the C.P.S. camps are beginning to act for yourselves. Frankly, it has disturbed me greatly in the past that the CPS campers seemed to be content to let others solve their problems for them. Up to the present, the campers have won little or nothing for themselves." The Cascade Locks initiative demonstrated a number of things: that the COs were becoming more and more dissatisfied and militant; that they were beginning to resort to collective action to address individual concerns and social reform; and that WRL members were playing a prominent role in the social action movement.[25]

William G. Webb, a Cascade Locks CO, illustrates how pacifist principles, camp democracy, and the CO rebellion were all linked. In a February 1943 letter to the camp director, he announced his refusal to continue unpaid work or to accept "slave status."[26] In part, he attributed the conditions that led to his refusal to the lack of democratic decision making in CPS. COs could discuss issues, but it was Selective Service that held the power and made the decisions. Addressing a camp meeting the following month, Webb emphasized the importance of "local self-government that embodied all of our principles of freedom, justice, and democracy" to "show the world" that men could govern themselves and resolve problems without "war, violence, coercion, or force." Comparing Selective Service with Hitler, he asked: "How can we deplore fascism in Germany and yet condone it here, in this very camp?"[27]

WRL members fought racial discrimination in some camps, including Powellsville (formerly Patapsco) and Cheltenham, both in Maryland. At Patapsco State Park, where Powellsville was located, African Americans were forbidden to use the picnic areas; COs protested this segregation in meetings with and letters to state officials. Some COs responded with work strikes. In another incident, when local residents opposed the transfer of two black COs to Powellsville, COs urged the American Friends Service Committee, which administered the camp, to ignore the racist complaints. Compromising, the Friends allowed one black CO to remain at Powellsville and transferred the second to another camp.[28]

The Cheltenham School for Delinquent Boys, a reform school for three hundred black adolescents in six cottages on twelve hundred acres of farmland, provided the venue for another CO protest, this one against segregated dining and living facilities. In October 1942, an interracial CO unit arrived to serve as cottage masters, psychologists, social workers, and night watchmen. Charles Butcher was dismissed for objecting to the brutal conditions at the school, which disciplined the boys by whippings and other coercive measures. The COs also challenged the school's Jim Crow eating and living arrangements. Forced to eat in the kitchen, Wally Nelson, a black CO, transferred back to his previous camp to protest the segregation. The protest spread, with both COs and non-CO staffers defying the Jim Crow arrangements. From a camp in Coleville, California, nearly fifty COs wrote the AFSC to denounce racial segregation at Cheltenham. Protest had failed to reverse Jim Crow at Powellsville; however, after two years of protest by COs and others at Cheltenham, a new superintendent ended racial segregation there.[29]

The WRL also supported the formation of the CPS Union. Max Kampelman and several other League members led this effort. In June 1944, delegates from some twenty CPS units met at New York City's Labor Temple to organize the CPS Union to attain recognition and collective bargaining rights, abolish CPS "waste and injustice," and win satisfactory wages and benefits. In particular, the union targeted Selective Service Directive 16, which required CPS men to work on private farms without pay and farmers to forward their wages directly to the U.S. Treasury. Although it enlisted five hundred members and organized twenty-five locals, Selective Service never recognized the union. Within the labor movement, however, the CPS Union did raise some awareness that unpaid CPS conscription was violating civil liberties and undermining the standards of a free labor movement.[30]

Even some camp directors and authorities became disillusioned with CPS. Paul G. Voelker resigned to protest scurrilous charges about Germfask COs in a *Time* magazine article. He was the fourth Germfask camp director to quit. "I have found the Selective Service treatment of men in this CPS camp to be the re-establishment of slavery in our nation and the punishment of men whose conscience does not permit their participation in war," he explained. "As a liberty-loving American citizen and ex-serviceman, I cannot take part in the administering of a system of unpaid, forced labor." Similarly, the superintendent of another facility told a WRL member jailed after walking out of CPS: "You COs may be glad when [the] war's over, but not half so much as I who yearn for [the] good old days of simple murderers and bankrobbers for prisoners."[31]

## Igal Roodenko: From CPS to Prison

Igal Roodenko (1917–91), a WRL member for fifty years, typifies the radical, social actionist, resistant CO who fought to promote individual freedom and social reform in CPS. Born and reared in New York City, the son of Jewish Ukrainian immigrants, Roodenko credited his parents with shaping his pacifism, socialism, Zionism, and agnosticism. His father immigrated to Palestine but left when the Ottoman Turks tried to draft him during World War I. The socialist-Zionist movement and Yiddish folk schools reinforced Roodenko's belief in democratic socialism. He joined the Young Poale Zion Alliance in 1930, and he supported the SP beginning in 1932, though he did not join the party until 1942. Planning to settle in Palestine, he studied horticulture at Cornell University (1934–38) to acquire the skills to develop the Jewish homeland.

Horrified at the sight of slaughtered animals hanging in butcher shop windows near his boyhood home, Roodenko became a lifelong vegetarian at the age of eight. In later years he would quote George Bernard Shaw to illustrate that his vegetarianism, pacifism, and nonviolent attitude toward life were all linked: "I am opposed to slaughter whether on the battlefield, the butcher's yard, or the sports arena."[32]

During the 1930s, Roodenko was active in student, peace, socialist, Jewish, and Zionist organizations. As secretary of the Cornell chapter of the American Student Union and as a member of the Cornell Peace Council, he helped organize annual student strikes against war. In 1935 he signed the Oxford Pledge. Working that summer as a camp counselor, he administered the pledge to three hundred children during a peace ceremony. Between 1940 and 1943 he worked in Georgia for the U.S. Agriculture Department and in Washington, D.C., for the Census Bureau and the CIO War Relief Committee. In Washington he attended regular meetings of the local WRL chapter, which embodied his socialist pacifist principles. In a 1941 statement to his draft board he quoted a League pamphlet that blamed modern wars on capitalism and the drive for markets and profits.[33]

Already a radical at the start of World War II, Roodenko became further radicalized through his wartime experiences and association with other COs. A resistant and social action CO leader, he exemplifies the nonviolent activism that the radical CO movement staged in CPS and in prisons. Moreover, his experience is representative of those COs who initially chose CPS but later rejected it for prison. During World War II he served in CPS camps at Powellsville, Maryland, and Mancos, Colorado. As a result of his protests in CPS, he also served time in the federal penitentiary at Sandstone, Minnesota.

At Powellsville (February to June 1943), Roodenko emerged as a leader of the radical social action wing of the CO movement. Critical of and impatient with CPS, he played a leading role in the Taylor-Murphy hunger strike and the Chicago Conference on Social Action. To support Murphy and Taylor's hunger strike he staged two fasts—a three-day sympathy fast (with fourteen other camp COs) in March and another hunger strike in April. At Powellsville the men elected him to represent them at the Chicago conference. Although Hershey prohibited COs from participating, Roodenko risked imprisonment and attended anyway. On his return he was penalized by the loss of furlough credits. In a letter to Evan Thomas after the Chicago conference, which he penned while on a work strike, he wrote: "My RTW [refusal to work] has started at a very opportune moment: there is an enormous amount of work to be done in mimeographing and distributing the results of the Conference."[34]

Disillusioned at Powellsville, Roodenko requested a transfer to an AFSC overseas relief and rehabilitation unit or to Mancos, the first government camp, which was scheduled to open in July 1943. Although he harbored feelings of "strong personal responsibility to eastern European Jewry," he thought the founding cohort of Mancos COs could shape conditions in the government camp and perhaps influence the direction of CPS. After the AFSC rejected him on the grounds that he was "too much of the protestor and not enough the negotiator to be able to fit nicely into their program," Roodenko chose Mancos. Though he had requested a transfer, he considered government camps inadequate and anticipated "a few months of vain storming against the iron walls of conscription" at Mancos.[35] Although Mancos was an insufficient solution to the demands raised by radical COs, Roodenko declared that the new camp "would leave us free to act directly with the government instead of thru a bunch of religious shock absorbers."[36]

Continuing his nonviolent activism at Mancos (July to November 1943), Roodenko waged various protests during his first two months. In response to a foreman who called a CO "yellow" and then knocked a prohibited cigarette from his hand, Roodenko and four other men quit work.[37] On another occasion, a CO (and WRL member) was arrested for refusing to work without pay, and Roodenko joined a collective one-day work and hunger strike to protest "forced labor without compensation."[38] Similarly, Roodenko and more than one hundred COs submitted a petition to Hershey urging the Selective Service, at minimum, to pay COs the $50 permitted by law. "To exact labor without compensation is the equivalent of slavery," they asserted.[39] The petition protested the allowance differentials at Mancos (which ranged from $3 to $7.50 per month), arguing that the "ridiculously inadequate" allowances should be equalized or that higher stipends should be paid to men with dependants.[40]

During September and October 1943, Roodenko grew more and more impatient and disillusioned with CPS. In letters to his sister Vivien, he spoke of his frustration and confided that he was seriously considering walking out, even though that meant prison. "CPS is so wrong that no matter how well minor problems are adjusted, the thing is wrong basically," he wrote in early September. "A man is a slave if he is forced to work at a job and in a place against his will . . . sooner or later, I will have to make a definite choice." [41] Two weeks later he wrote that "it is merely a matter of time before I go along with the rest." [42] In mid-October, fed up with and weary of the "petty irritations," [43] he considered transferring to an AFSC camp, though he recognized that such a decision entailed "just that which I condemn in the Friends' attitude: a tendency to forget the basic problem of conscription and war and trying to get as much out of the program in a personal way as possible." [44] He was faced with having to choose between the "opportunism" [45] of a more comfortable AFSC camp, Mancos's benevolent dictatorship, and his strong impulse to walk out. In the end, he remained committed to principle and radical action over personal advancement: "I will find it quite difficult to face myself for the rest of my life if the end of the war finds me still in CPS." [46]

Vivien Roodenko provided both a sounding board and emotional and intellectual support for her older brother. These things became even more important to him in 1945, when he went to prison. In 1943 she corresponded with him, and explained to their parents his willingness to court jail. She also did volunteer work for the WRL and the pacifist, socialist, and civil liberties movements. In September 1943, in response to his stated wish to take a more radical course of action and walk out of camp, Vivien wrote to him to express her sisterly and political support for whatever action he took, though she shared his preference for radical social action and rejection of CPS. "It is also extremely difficult for me to just glibly send you on to the clink," Vivien confided. "Yet I cannot refrain from viewing the entire situation in a broader sense than the narrow personal one. The pacifist movement is weak enough," she observed, "& with the percentage of social action people practically infintesimal [sic] it is all the more necessary for each one to go the limit that his conscience dictates." "Darling Igal," she concluded, "tho I hate like hell to say this—I must support your proposal to walk out of Mancos—but remember if you don't—my support of you will not diminish or retract one iota." [47]

Responding two weeks later, Roodenko paid tribute to his sister: "Your letter was so perfect a reply . . . and different from those others have received from their families, that one of the boys made a number of copies of it and several of them sent these home." In contrast to her support, he continued, "everywhere the answer is the same: you have suffered enough here in CPS; why should you assume even a greater burden?"[48] Vivien illustrates the gendered role of wartime pacifism and the gendered lens of historians writing about this period. During World War II the pacifist movement lionized male COs and their heroic sacrifice and resistance in CPS and prison. The contribution of draft-exempt male and female pacifist activists, who were also conscientious objectors, often lost its luster next to foxhole COs. To historians writing about COs and wartime pacifism, the role of women who supported sons, husbands, lovers, and brothers has remained either invisible or neglected.[49]

Fellow COs nurtured Roodenko's radicalization. Lively intercamp and CPS/prison exchanges were conducted through letters, pacifist newspapers, and CPS camp publications such as *Action,* the official organ of the Social Action Committee, which Roodenko coedited. All of these promoted COs' resistance and buttressed Roodenko's willingness to break with CPS and accept prison. For example, Paton Price, who had walked out of camp and into a jail sentence, depicted prison as preferable to CPS. In a July 1943 letter to Roodenko, Price confided that "the farther [sic] away I get from CPS the more appalled I am at what has happened and the more convinced I am that the Friends have performed an irremediable and catastrophic service to pacifism." "Pacifism's Paul 'Pierre Laval' French," Price predicted, "will not get far with his double-header appeasement program."[50]

On 29 October 1943, in his last CPS protest, Roodenko started a work and hunger strike to support six Lewisburg COs who were conducting a fast against prison censorship.[51] In letters to President Roosevelt and to Selective Service, CPS, and penal officials he explained that due to "the gravity of the moment—the lives that are endangered—I have no moral alternative but to express my concern as forcefully as possible."[52] On 6 November, to mark the birthday of Eugene Debs, he visited the dining room to quote the socialist leader: "While there is a lower class, I am in it; while there is a criminal element, I am of it; while there is a soul in prison, I am not free."[53] That Roodenko had a sense of humor and a flair for drama is clear from one account he gave of his Mancos work and hunger strike:

> After a week or so one of them [a Mancos official] said, "How're you doing, Roodenko?" And I said, "Well, I'm getting kind of weak. Oh, incidentally I think you ought to requisition a coffin from Selective Service. You know the red tape they have. And if you wait until I die, by the time you get it you will have a stinking corpse on your hands." The guy's face just blanched. On the 11th [sic; 13th] day I was arrested and taken to Denver and processed and released on bail.[54]

On 9 November 1943, the thirteenth day of his protest action, Roodenko was arrested for refusing to work and detained in the Denver County Jail.

Roodenko's arrest prompted a lengthy legal battle. Carle Whitehead, an attorney and leading Colorado socialist, represented Roodenko as well as three other COs who were challenging their arrests (for refusing to return to CPS from furlough). Roodenko argued that the Selective Service Act of 1940 imposed "involuntary servitude," restricted the "free exercise of religion," and placed the camps under military rather than civilian control, which exceeded congressional authority and violated the Constitution.[55] Following their convictions in March 1944, the defendants unsuccessfully appealed. Roodenko and his codefendants were sentenced in June 1944 to three years imprisonment. They then appealed to the U.S. Supreme Court.[56]

While his case was being appealed, Roodenko worked at the WRL's New York headquarters on prison CO issues and wrote a "News from the Prisons" column for the *Conscientious Objector*.[57] In April 1945 the Supreme Court declined to hear his case, and Roodenko entered Sandstone Federal Penitentiary, where he remained until his release in January 1947.

At Sandstone (1945–47), Roodenko continued the nonviolent protests that marked his CPS experience. Most notably, he made efforts to end Jim Crow at Sandstone and to obtain amnesty for imprisoned COs. In August 1945 he and his CO dorm mates integrated their Jim Crow dormitory and dining tables. Forty-two COs, including Roodenko and other WRL members, circulated a petition asking prison officials to assign Paul Gamble, a black CO, to their dormitory and dining tables. When all the COs in Roodenko's dormitory had signed the petition, the officials acquiesced. Since dorm residents ate together, Roodenko's dining table was also integrated. Significantly, Roodenko was aware of COs' past protests against Jim Crow at Sandstone and other prisons—most notably Danbury, where a work strike by COs resulted in an end to racial segregation in the dining room.[58]

The CO revolt, though it grew stronger as the war continued, was never strong enough to compel Selective Service and NSBRO to reform CPS. The COs did bring about some changes; by war's end, four government CPS camps had been established and detached service was available more often. But the rebellion did not succeed in obtaining higher compensation, more meaningful work, or greater liberty. NSBRO turned out to be too weak and hesitant, and Selective Service, which did have the power to reform CPS, viewed the CO revolt as a challenge to its authority. On the other hand, CPS provided a forum where resistant COs could develop personal relationships, mold pacifist networks, and experiment with methods of nonviolent direct action—methods that would infuse postwar radical pacifism. Roy Kepler captured the idealism that many COs harbored on entering CPS in his description of the radical community they forged from their shared experience and collective struggle in the camps. Writing later, Kepler emphasized the importance of meeting "all these interesting, congenial people. . . . The biggest single mistake the government made was introducing us to each other. We're still in touch! They helped build the pacifist network indeed!"[59]

## CO Protests by WRL Members in Prison

Like COs in CPS, prison COs waged dramatic nonviolent direct action protests to honor their convictions and advance social justice. Consistent with its official position of supporting all COs in whatever action they chose, the WRL defended and publicized these prison revolts; dispatched its representatives to prisons; intervened with the Justice Department and the Bureau of Prisons to obtain pardons, paroles, and better prison conditions; established a network of CO prison correspondents; mailed Christmas cards to prison and CPS COs; comforted families and provided a forum for COs' wives to meet in fellowship; and led a postwar campaign to win amnesty for COs convicted for their refusal to submit to conscription.[60]

Imprisoned COs were more difficult to help than those in CPS. Because prison correspondence was restricted to designated persons, the League was unable to initiate contact. Furthermore, the Bureau of Prisons refused to provide the names and addresses of a CO's relatives unless the inmate specifically requested it. In 1943 the League started a "WRL Fighting Fund" for prison COs, soliciting contributions under the slogan: "While One CO Remains in Prison *You Are Not Free.*"[61] As it turned out, League members' prison revolts were more significant than the WRL's level of financial support.

### James Peck and the Danbury Work Strike Against Jim Crow

Consistent with the prevailing "separate but equal" doctrine, the Bureau of Prisons maintained racial segregation in most of its housing and dining facilities. Thus, radical pacifist COs found themselves interned in segregated jails. On being confronted with racism, often for the first time, COs—WRL members among them—led a nonviolent wartime civil rights movement. The most significant prison rebellions against Jim Crow were organized by COs at the Danbury Correctional Institution in Connecticut, the Lewisburg Federal Penitentiary in Pennsylvania, and the Ashland Correctional Institution in Kentucky.[62]

On 11 August 1943, eighteen Danbury COs began a 135-day work strike to end Jim Crow in the prison dining room.[63] Five other COs soon joined them. The prison authorities placed the striking COs in administrative segregation. While they were being escorted by guards to the isolated punishment cells, the COs informed other prisoners of their strike by singing the chorus of the labor movement's best-known song: "So-li-dar-I-ty For-ever, So-li-dar-I-ty For-ever, The Union Makes Us Strong."[64] Jim Peck, Albon Man, and Ralph DiGia were among the WRL members who participated in the Danbury Jim Crow strike.[65] Man later identified Peck as the strike's "prime instigator" and "strongest personality."[66]

One of America's most colorful radicals, Jim Peck (1914–93) was a rank-and-file unionist, civil rights activist, and radical pacifist. In a Dickensian phrase that provided the title of his autobiography, Peck proclaimed that "the struggle for more social justice has been—and from the evidence of history always will be—one of underdogs versus upperdogs."[67] Born an upperdog, Peck devoted his life to championing the underdogs.

Peck was born into a wealthy New York City family and baptized in the prestigious Little Church Around the Corner (Episcopalian). When he was eleven his father died and his relationship with his mother turned poisonous. It would stay that way. Peck's mother was an ambitious social climber who married for money. She was also a racist and classist who snubbed Jews, blacks, and the working class. As a teenager, Peck lived with her and three servants in a seven-room apartment off Park Avenue. He vacationed with her on the French Riviera. He was educated for two years at a Swiss boarding school and later at an elite prep school in Lawrenceville, New Jersey, before entering Harvard.

During the 1930s, Peck embraced militant unionism, democratic socialism, and radical pacifism. His radicalization was kindled by a Lawrenceville friendship, reading, his experiences as a seaman, and his loathing for his mother and her "repulsive" social views. He was also influenced by Erich Maria Remarque's *All Quiet on the Western Front,* Helmuth Englebrecht and Frank Hanighen's *Merchants of Death: A Study of the International Armament Industry,* and George Seldes's *Iron, Blood, and Profits: An Expose of the World-Wide Munitions Racket.* At Lawrenceville, Peck pledged that in the event of war he would become a CO. In 1932, soon after he graduated, he coauthored, published, and distributed an antiwar leaflet. During his one year at Harvard he thumbed tradition and took a black prostitute to the freshman prom (having met her at Bottom Dollar George's whorehouse). "This would be my chance to act—not just talk—against racial discrimination," he explained. Unhappy with university education, Peck quit Harvard, dissociated himself from his mother and the luxurious upperdog life, and "cast my lot with the underdogs."[68]

After working for a year as a messenger and shipping clerk, Peck became a seaman. On his maiden voyage to Australia he gained exposure to labor's perspective and participated in a brief sit-down strike. He joined the International Seamen's Union, which was a conservative union, but became active in its Rank-and-File group, a militant faction that sought to replace bureaucratic leadership with grassroots union democracy. He also worked on the faction's publication, *Rank-and-File.* While walking a picket line in 1936, Peck helped establish the National Maritime Union (CIO). In the mid-1930s he was arrested twice for his labor activism before taking a nonpaying job with the Federated Press, a news syndicate serving union weeklies. There he learned to write human interest news stories—a skill he put to good use later on, while writing a labor column for the *Conscientious Objector,* editing WRL and CORE publications, and doing publicity work for various postwar peace and justice campaigns.

In 1940, Peck attended a meeting of the WRL-organized Upper West Side Peace Team and immediately joined the League. On draft registration day, Peck, who had arranged for the press to witness his defiance, declared his refusal to join the army. He then scribbled "conscientious objector" on his draft card and issued a statement that, with his photo, made the newspapers. He was convicted for refusing induction and in November 1942 began serving a three-year sentence at Danbury.[69] There, he repeatedly challenged the prison authorities. Drawing on his labor background, he waged many protests against war, Jim Crow, parole procedures, and prison conditions.

Peck received the first of many stints in solitary when he struck over an increased work week. He participated in food boycotts to protest foul food, which was removed from the menu. During the Murphy-Taylor hunger strike he organized several other food boycotts—one of which involved nearly all six hundred inmates—to demonstrate solidarity and protest their mistreatment at Springfield. On another occasion he refused to paint red, white, and blue signs for the prison victory garden. For this, officials sentenced him to ten days in isolation; furthermore, he would have to serve the remainder of his twenty-one months in administrative segregation. In 1944, Peck and other COs unscrewed the metal window screens overlooking the prison courtyard and hung a banner proclaiming "May Day 1944." During the hour it took guards to fetch a ladder and cut down the banner, inmates cheered and sang "Solidarity [Forever]."[70]

The Danbury work strike against Jim Crow was one of the most successful wartime applications of nonviolent direct action. Even before resolving to challenge Jim Crow, the COs had elected a committee to represent their concerns in meetings with Danbury's warden, Myrl E. Alexander. This committee called a strike to integrate the mess hall. The men elected Albon Man—"the professor-like Socialist"—permanent chairman of the strike committee.[71] The twenty-three strikers included socialists, anarchists, independent radicals, and rank-and-file unionists.

To isolate them from other inmates, officials confined the strikers to the entire second floor of "Upper Hartford." They were assigned individual five-by-eight cells, which lined both sides of the hallway. Daily yard time was permitted in good weather. Mail was delivered daily except Sundays. The strikers were authorized to read books from the prison library and to receive newspaper and magazine subscriptions. Supervised visits and correspondence were permitted.

Throughout their prolonged isolation the strikers refused to compromise and demonstrated an impressive tenacity and creative resistance. Confined to their own cells, they developed study groups, leisure activities, and a covert communication system. In the evenings they engaged in spirited debates, which often focused on religion and the labor movement. Peck, an atheist, often baited John Mecartney, a religious objector. Lowell Naeve, an anarchist CO, related one typical exchange that started with Peck shouting: " 'Hey Mecartney!' We all knew what was to follow. 'How are ya doin'? Readin' the book?' (the bible). . . . The beard-anti-beard argument would begin. God had been labeled by atheist Peck 'the man with the beard.' Mcecartney would try and hang a beard on atheist Peck, Peck would try to 'shave' Mecartney."[72]

These bull sessions, with their running arguments and good-natured kidding, dissolved frustrations, relieved the monotony, and made the time pass more quickly. The striking COs occupied themselves with various other activities. Naeve started a handmade newspaper, which Peck named the *Clink*. The men quickly learned that the pages of *Life* magazine, once hand-washed, yielded enough ink to print their own paper's cartoons, poetry, drawings, and articles.

To buttress morale and solidarity, Peck composed a protest poem for one of the prison shows. Entitled "Jimcrow Must Go," Peck's lyrics compared German Nazism to American Jim Crow:

> When in a correctional clink
> They teach you that colored guys stink
> We say that this sham
> Must take it on the lam—
> Jimcrow must scram.
>
> Whenever you go to eat grub
> The Negroes you have got to snub

In teaching to hate
They rehabilitate—
Jimcrow must gate.

They say that Hitler is wicked
To persecute race in his way
But when it's done in the U.S.
It's quite perfectly OK.

The blacks are as good as the whites
Why shouldn't they have equal rights
The warden says no
But we tell him it's so—
Jimcrow must go.[73]

In the evenings, COs also sang the poem, accompanied by a guitar. Naeve spent eighteen months crafting the guitar from a mixture of oatmeal and ground newspaper cooked on a radiator, and guards allowed him to purchase strings from the outside.

During their four-and-a-half-month work strike to abolish Jim Crow, the COs mounted parallel strikes. Through hunger strikes they obtained newspapers, magazines, books, longer yard periods, open cell doors, and hot food. They also waged a successful strike against the segregated prison barbershop, whose white and black barbers limited their endeavors to the heads of their own race. Even scissors were segregated. The strikers refused Jim Crow haircuts. Peck noted that after seven weeks "our hair had outgrown the patience of the prison officials."[74]

The COs also challenged the guards. Albon Man recalls the COs taunting a mustached Jewish guard. Pointing to Nazi persecution of the Jews, they would demand, "How can a Jewish guard help perpetuate racism in prison?" Peck dubbed the guard's moustache "the brush," and to aggravate him they would do things to "crush the brush"—for example, confront him with the contradiction that a Jew was enforcing racism. More generally, to protest a guard's objectionable actions, COs would greet his appearance by simultaneously flushing their toilets to create a deafening, Niagara Falls-like roar.[75]

After six weeks, the Danbury COs were discouraged by the lack of publicity for the strike. Peck would later praise Evan Thomas and Julius Eichel for their unqualified individual support, but he also wrote: "We were also disgusted by the failure of the pacifist organizations to support us. They were leery of a prison strike." In view of its support for CO prison activism, it is unclear whether Peck's charge included the WRL. Indeed, during the strike, the WRL's CO Problems Committee (COPC) supported the campaign to persuade the Bureau of Prisons to change its racial policies.[76]

To gain publicity, the COs named as their press agent League member and former staffer Ruth MacAdam, the fiancé of Ernest Smith, one of the Danbury COs on strike. MacAdam persuaded Adam Clayton Powell, the black congressman from Harlem, to organize a special committee to support the strike. She also helped convince the liberal and black press to publicize the story. Both the American Civil Liberties Union and the Workers Defense Fund belatedly supported the strike.[77]

Three months into the strike the warden accepted the mediation offer of Edward and Agnes Wieck, Illinois labor activists and the parents of Dave Wieck, one of the COs on strike. Their efforts prompted improved conditions. In a poststrike editorial, the *Conscientious Objector,* while praising the WRL's "Fighting Fund" for supporting prison CO protest, complained that the Danbury and Lewisburg strikes showed "that the great body of pacifists outside prison are not doing all they could do to support the men inside."[78]

On 22 December the warden unexpectedly summoned the COs and agreed to integrate the prison dining room if they ended their strike before Christmas. Starting on 1 February 1944, he promised, inmates would be free to sit wherever they liked. Elated, the COs terminated their strike. "It's over, it's over," Peck exclaimed, "we've smashed 'em." Although a few whites, a black Jamaican fascist, and several Black Muslims greeted the new policy with hostility, within days "mixed tables" were taken for granted. Peck later reflected: "It seems to me that the campaign against racial discrimination may be counted as one of the most important accomplishments of COs in World War 2."[79]

The 1943 Danbury strike against Jim Crow showed the potential of nonviolent protest, even under the authoritarian conditions of a "closed" prison system. Like the March on Washington Movement and the Congress of Racial Equality, the Danbury strike represented a limited but significant victory in the wartime civil rights movement—a full decade before the more celebrated, post-1954 movement for desegregation and legal equality, to which Peck and the WRL also contributed. The Jim Crow strike was also a harbinger of the social activism and direct action tactics that radical pacifists and the WRL would embrace after the war.

Peck was released from prison on April Fools Day, 1945. The next morning he went to the WRL office to mimeograph an exposé he had written on the privileged treatment that upperdog "bigshots" were receiving at Danbury. The wartime prison protests and his experience in the 1930s labor movement had shown Peck the methods and power of nonviolent social protest, which would guide his actions for the next three decades in the peace, civil rights, and labor movements. Throughout that time, the WRL would be his organizational base.[80]

### William Sutherland and the Lewisburg Protest Against Jim Crow

On 31 May 1943, eight COs at the Lewisburg maximum security prison refused to eat in the Jim Crow dining room to protest racial segregation. The protest began when a black CO in the prison's farm section was forced to eat alone in the kitchen when the table reserved for blacks was filled. Other COs joined the protest, including Bill Sutherland.[81]

Sutherland was reared in a middle-class New Jersey home. He became a pacifist in high school. While in high school, he became involved with the NAACP and youth groups interested in international relations and socialism. At Bates College, in Maine, he considered himself a Christian pacifist; he had heard of the FOR but not the WRL. After college he completed a brief stint with the AFSC before moving to New York and becoming involved in the WRL. At about the same time—the fall of 1940—he joined the Newark Ashram, a Christian pacifist group organized by David Dellinger. There he remained until July 1942, when he was convicted of violating the draft. During his stay at the ashram he deepened his pacifism by reading Gandhi and Krishnalal Shridharani and through conversations with members of the Newark and Harlem ashrams.

Sutherland registered for the draft and completed the physical exam and questionnaire, but he refused to report to CPS when called. At his July 1942 trial, the visiting (and presiding) judge from Tallahassee asked him in a southern drawl: "Young man. What is more important than fighting for your country?" Then he looked at a list of Sutherland's civil rights activities and, without waiting for a reply, pronounced: "Young man. Your education has been your undoing. Four years." According to Sutherland, this was the first time a World War II CO had received a jail sentence over two years. He realized then that black COs would receive harsher penalties than white COs.[82]

Sutherland spent one-third of his prison tenure on work or hunger strike, often protesting Jim Crow. Although he had expected racism in the South, the racial segregation at Lewisburg shocked him, and he joined other COs in protest actions. Elaborating on his CO stance, he later declared: "If I believe[d] in the use of violence to bring about democracy, I would never have to start in Germany. I would go to Alabama and Mississippi. . . . I didn't need to go overseas as far as fighting what I considered to be fascism." [83]

Meanwhile, at Lewisburg, to protest the black CO's Jim Crow banishment to the kitchen, eight COs in the prison's farm section refused to eat in the white dining room and attempted to subsist on food purchased in the prison commissary. After several days, the COs, weakened from the poor commissary food, informed officials that they were unable to work. The authorities transferred the strikers to the hole, where they resumed eating regular prison fare. Later, they were housed together in administrative segregation. Sutherland and four other COs from the main prison announced a solidarity hunger strike and also were sent to the hole; later they were placed in administrative segregation with the original eight.

On one occasion the COs were removed from isolation for a haircut. While waiting their turn they noticed that Sutherland had been taken to a different part of the room, where a black barber was cutting his hair. Confronted with Jim Crow haircuts, the men went limp, which created problems for the barbers and guards, who struggled—while laughing—to cut their hair.[84] The strikers also wrote to James V. Bennett, the Bureau of Prisons director, protesting the Jim Crow dining policy and conducted a brief hunger strike over the issue.

During a visit to Lewisburg the mothers of two striking COs met with Warden Hiatt, who permitted their sons to join the meeting. When the two men refused to end their strike, Hiatt became belligerent. He charged them with "stirring up race feelings where there had been none" and called one of them a "big mouthed trouble maker." "You aren't telling me how to run my business!" Hiatt thundered. "When you came inside those gates, you left *all your rights* behind, . . . I have absolute authority over everything but your thots [thoughts]." [85]

By mid-August the original Jim Crow protest had been transformed into a broader strike against general prison conditions, especially censorship and reliance on the hole. This broader strike, which involved several WRL members, is discussed below. In a letter to the mother of one of the strikers, Evan Thomas explained the significance and novelty of the emergent turn toward direct action: "Apparently the men who have gone on strike as a protest against racial discrimination are using a form of nonviolent direct action in order to correct this. I am sure that many pacifists do not understand such action as yet, but how are we ever going to get them to understand unless we inform them of the action and make them think about it?" [86]

Bayard Rustin and the Ashland Hunger Strike Against Jim Crow

In June 1945, in the first major action against Jim Crow in a Southern prison, fourteen men—twelve of whom were COs—at the Ashland Federal Correctional Institute in Kentucky refused to eat in the segregated mess hall. The strikers included three blacks and a Japanese American. Bayard Rustin (1912–1987), a black CO and the most prominent of the protesters, was a WRL member and the FOR's national race secretary. This was not the first CO protest in Ashland. In 1944, several COs, including WRL members Rustin and Larry Gara, had defied racism at the prison.[87]

First elected to the WRL's executive committee in 1943, Rustin was a Quaker, a pacifist, a socialist, and a civil rights leader. He held top positions in the WRL, the FOR, the March On Washington Movement, and CORE. He was also a gifted coalition builder and would be a prominent leader in the peace and civil rights movements for nearly five decades. Rustin was gay. He had striking good looks, enormous charm, and an exuberant love of life. He was a skilled musician who played the guitar, piano, and harpsichord; he also possessed a wonderful voice and sang Negro spirituals, Elizabethan songs, blues, and opera with equal polish and dramatic effect. Later, in the peace and justice movements, he often used his voice and debating skills to make his points and bring people together. All of these qualities made him a beloved and influential WRL leader.

Rustin was born out of wedlock in West Chester, Pennsylvania, and raised by his maternal grandparents, Janifer and Julia Rustin. Julia, a NAACP charter member and one of the few black Quakers in eastern Pennsylvania, was the biggest moral and religious influence on Bayard. When he and some school friends teased a Chinese laundry owner, Julia made Bayard work after school in the laundry for two weeks. At West Chester High School, where he was one of the few black students, he was an outstanding athlete and class valedictorian (1932). Later he attended several colleges, including the City University of New York, but he never graduated.

While still in high school, Rustin led several nonviolent protests against segregation. He was arrested for the first time when he refused to sit in the "Nigger Heaven" balcony at the local movie theater and took a seat in the white section instead.[88] Another time, the evening before a high school football game, he persuaded his black teammates not to play unless they were moved from their Jim Crow accommodations and united with their white teammates, which they were. Led by Rustin, some black classmates began entering white restaurants, soda fountains, department stores, and movie theaters, as well as the YMCA.

They were always ejected; even so, Rustin's leadership potential and social activism were by now apparent.

In the late 1930s, Rustin maintained his commitment to peace and justice activism. In 1937 he worked in the Emergency Peace Campaign. In debates with peace workers supporting armed defense of the Republic in the Spanish Civil War, he advocated nonviolence. Impressed by militant communists' support for the Scottsboro boys and for black civil rights in general, he moved that winter to New York, enrolled at the City College of New York, and joined the Young Communist League. More interested in politics than academics at City College, Rustin did organizing for the Young Communist League, joined rallies supporting the Scottsboro boys, and directed the Young Communist League's 1941 campaign to abolish segregation in the military. He frequented interracial Greenwich Village political cafés that attracted communists and left-wing intellectuals. In June 1941, the Nazis invaded the Soviet Union, and the Young Communist League ordered Rustin to cease the campaigning against Jim Crow in the armed services. Disillusioned, he realized that the communists were placing Soviet interests before those of blacks. He resigned from the Young Communist League, broke with the communist movement, and became a democratic socialist and critic of communism.

Rustin joined A. Philip Randolph's campaign to integrate munitions factories through a mass black protest march on Washington. When Roosevelt issued Executive Order 8802 banning the exclusion of black workers from armament plants, Randolph canceled the march. This angered his young organizers, who like Rustin argued that the executive order should have also integrated the armed services. In mid-1941, Rustin broke with Randolph, but two years later he again joined Randolph and his March on Washington Movement.

In September 1941, A. J. Muste named Rustin and two other gifted young pacifists to the FOR's staff: Rustin as student and general affairs secretary, George Houser (also a WRL member) as youth secretary, and James Farmer as race relations secretary. Rustin was a favorite of Muste and a rising star. Dubbed by their coworkers "Muste-Rusty," [89] the two shared a common political perspective and developed a father-son relationship. During his first year with the FOR, Rustin traveled extensively, addressing groups, conducting workshops on nonviolence, visiting CPS camps, and assisting interned Japanese Americans. During this time he gained a reputation as a militant on civil rights, which led the FBI to investigate him. By all accounts he was a talented, dynamic representative for the pacifist movement. Between 1941 and 1944 he was also working with the March on Washington Movement and CORE to advance civil rights.

In 1940, Rustin registered for and won classification as a conscientious objector; however, subsequent events radicalized him. In 1943 he refused a directive from his draft board to report for a physical exam. Influenced by Evan Thomas and John Haynes Holmes, he believed that religious and secular COs should be treated equally and that both should receive conscientious objector status. He also adopted a more radical attitude toward Selective Service and CPS. At the June 1942 WRL conference, during a panel discussion on CPS, Rustin—who visited CPS camps as an FOR staffer—argued that COs should adopt civil disobedience measures to develop alternatives to war.[90] He also discussed "the relative *strategic* merits of prison vs. CPS" within the League and supported the 6 April 1943 direct action picketing in Washington, D.C.[91]

Rustin opted for jail over CPS. In February 1944 he was arrested, convicted, and sentenced to three years in prison. During the two weeks he spent at the Federal Detention Center in Manhattan en route to the prison at Ashland, he applied nonviolent direct action to challenge racial discrimination. He was placed in solitary for protesting the Jim Crow dining room. At this, the prison choir—which Rustin organized and directed—refused to sing in the weekly religious services unless he was released to lead them. The warden complied.[92] Rustin entered Ashland in March 1944 and promptly joined the COs' struggle for racial equality.

Looking back on his prison experience, Rustin remembered the COs' optimism and sense of purpose, which transformed imprisonment into a liberating struggle for justice:

> We used to say that the difference between us and other prisoners was the difference between fasting and starving. *We* were there by virtue of a commitment we had made to a moral position; and that gave us a psychological attitude the average prisoner did not have. He felt either that he had done something wrong, and that he should be punished for it, or that he had done nothing wrong, and society was brutalizing him. We had neither the guilt nor the feeling of being brutalized. We had the feeling of being morally important; and that made us respond to prison conditions without fear, with considerable sensitivity to human rights. We thought we were making a contribution to society, in the same way that Gandhi, who was our hero, had said to a British judge: "It is your moral duty to put me in jail." That was our feeling. It was by going to jail that we called the people's attention to the horrors of war.[93]

This spirit of nonviolent moral warriorship infused the Ashland protests to abolish prison Jim Crow.

In June 1945, not long after several rebellious social action COs were transferred from Germfask CPS camp to Ashland, Rustin renewed his attack on Jim Crow by leading COs on a hunger strike. Unlike most in earlier Jim Crow strikes, the Ashland COs did not refuse to work. After two black nonpacifists on strike were transferred to other prisons, the remaining twelve COs were punished with administrative segregation. Linking their act to the earlier Danbury strike against prison racism, they sang "Jim Crow Must Go." Upon his arrival at Ashland in 1944, Rustin was placed in a segregated cell block, separated from the white COs on the floor above. Most (Southern) black inmates at Ashland abided racial segregation; Rustin and the northern COs objected to it. After many protests, Rustin was permitted to visit the white COs on the upper floor on Sunday afternoons. A white prisoner from Kentucky named Huddleston opposed racial mixing and warned Rustin not to return. The following week, Rustin appeared anyway. An inmate recorded a remarkable encounter:

> Huddleston went to the utility room and got a stick, the size . . . of a mop handle, and came back to hit Bayard over the head. . . . Huddleston hit Bayard with a mighty blow. . . . They [the COs] jumped and got between Huddleston and Bayard, and started taking the club from Huddleston. But Bayard asked them to stop, which they did. Huddleston continued to beat him with the club. . . . The club splintered and broke, but was still large enough to use, [when] Huddleston stopped. . . . Huddleston was completely defeated and unnerved by the display of nonviolence, and began shaking all over, and sat down.[94]

Although Rustin suffered a fractured wrist, Huddleston's violence against him actually advanced pacifism and integration. Reversing prison policy, the warden permitted interracial visits at any time. Rustin would later offer the incident as an example of effective nonviolent resistance.

In August 1945, after two months, prison authorities tried to break the strike by transferring four COs, including Rustin, who was sent to Lewisburg where he continued his "Ashland" hunger strike for several days. When officials placed him in administrative segregation with other striking COs, Rustin resumed eating. Paradoxically, when administrative segregation sealed off radical COs from the general prison population, it integrated their living and eating quarters. At Lewisberg, Rustin continued to wage hunger strikes and other protests against Jim Crow and other prison ills.

Rustin later recalled that prison officials seemed to surrender, at least tacitly, to the troublesome pacifist inmates: "They simply washed their hands of us. They said, 'Give them what they want. Keep them to themselves. We don't want them infecting others with their liberal ideas.' "[95] On his release in June 1946 after serving twenty-eight months of his three-year sentence, Rustin took up his new position as the FOR's race relations secretary (with George Houser).

The Ashland strike received outside support, and focused public attention on racial segregation in federal prisons. Black newspapers such as the *Amsterdam News, Pittsburgh Courier,* and *People's Voice* covered the Ashland saga. Rep. Adam Clayton Powell became involved. When the Bureau of Prisons' acting director justified Jim Crow and the treatment of the Ashland COs, Powell offered a detailed rebuttal.[96]

The WRL supported the Ashland strike. In a letter to the Fair Employment Practices Committee, it protested the "unfair racial policies" of the Bureau of Prisons.[97] At Ashland and elsewhere, the League complained, the bureau was maintaining Jim Crow dining facilities and assigning blacks to undesirable and lower-paying jobs. In November 1945, to protest racial segregation in prisons, the League joined ex-Danbury Jim Crow strikers and pacifist and civil rights groups in picketing a New York meeting of the American Prison Association. On the eve of the demonstration, NAACP leader Walter White wrote President Truman to protest the continued solitary confinement suffered by eight Ashland COs and to urge an immediate end to Jim Crow in federal prisons.[98]

Confronted with a nonviolent prison revolt against Jim Crow, which was led by COs, James Bennett—a moderate on race—asserted that black and white inmates were receiving equal treatment. He also defended limited racial segregation in prisons on pragmatic grounds. He insisted that racial segregation did not indicate racial discrimination, and he pointed out that although many prison activities were integrated, segregation in housing and dining facilities was still necessary in order to maintain order and prevent violence. Bennett invoked prominent sociologists—black *and* white—who argued that separation was the best means for promoting racial equality. He also attacked pacifist tactics. Writing to a participant in the Danbury Jim Crow strike, Bennett charged him with resorting to "undemocratic methods of coercion to force a change." "Strikes, boycotts, and civil disobedience," he argued, "certainly are not the democratic method of accomplishing the solution of racial problems. They merely engender discord and race riots."[99]

The WRL repudiated all racial discrimination and adopted wartime resolutions that endorsed human equality and condemned racism against blacks, Jews, and Japanese Americans. For instance, six months after Pearl Harbor the WRL denounced discrimination against blacks and Jews and urged the government to repeal the Chinese Exclusion Act and restore the civil rights and property of Japanese Americans. Three years later the League passed a resolution affirming the right of Japanese Americans freed from internment camps to reside anywhere in the country. In mid-1944 the League presented a resolution on racial equality to the Republican and Democratic conventions for possible inclusion in their platforms. It urged the repeal of all Jim Crow laws (including the poll tax), the strict enforcement of fair employment laws, and the extension of civil rights. And in its "Pacifist Plan of Action," which it issued the same month, the League pledged "to strive to end all exploitation and discrimination based on race color or religion." Surprisingly, however, the League did not pass resolutions specifically denouncing prison Jim Crow or expressing solidarity with COs—often WRL members—who challenged racism in the prisons.[100]

Though it did not pass specific resolutions, the WRL supported the striking COs and their efforts to abolish Jim Crow in prison dining facilities. It did this by publicizing the issue, by writing letters, and by meeting with prison authorities in Washington.[101] Individual League members spearheaded nonviolent direct action to promote civil rights, and the League as a whole sometimes extended direct support to prison COs who challenged Jim Crow. These things aside, the WRL continued to devote its limited resources to peace issues. However laudable anti-Jim Crow prison strikes might be, the League did not view endorsing them as one of its top priorities. Similarly, though it supported the Lewisburg COs' strike against prison censorship, the League did not adopt specific resolutions or earmark special funds to promote this protest action. Nevertheless, the COs' commitment and the League's attention to wartime civil rights presaged a broader agenda for the WRL after the war.

### David Dellinger and the Lewisburg Hunger Strike Against Censorship

At Lewisburg, six COs waged a sixty-five-day hunger strike against prison censorship. The protest originated in a May 1943 work strike to abolish racial segregation in the dining room. Five COs in the main prison went on a hunger strike to support eight COs from the prison farm who were on a work strike against Jim Crow. Those five were transferred to the hole. When they started eating again, they were moved to administrative segregation with the eight from the prison farm. By 11 August only seven of the original thirteen COs were still on strike, and that strike had broadened into a general protest against the prison system. On 28 September, five (later six) striking COs—David Dellinger, Paton Price, William Lovett, Thomas Woodman, William Kuenning, and Jack Dixon (the first three of whom were WRL members)—announced a hunger strike and narrowed the protest to an attack on prison censorship. Dave Dellinger (1915–), who played a leading role in the strike, was perhaps the most charismatic and influential leader of the militant COs who transformed the WRL during and after the war.

Dellinger was reared in a conservative, middle-class home in a Boston suburb, the son of an attorney. Both sides of his family had roots in prerevolutionary America. His mother filled her time with concerts, afternoon teas, and bridge and garden clubs. His father was a self-made man who disliked atheists, anarchists, and labor leaders. He was also chairman of the local Republicans. True to his conservative views, he helped defeat the 1919 Boston police strike and supported the execution of Sacco and Vanzetti. Yet he was also a compassionate man and a community leader who opposed prejudice. Dellinger loved him.

In the 1930s Dellinger attended Yale, where he captained the cross-country team, met radical Christians, and majored in economics. He discussed communism with classmate Walt W. Rostow, and though he gained some insights from Marxism, for him it lacked the spiritual dimension and nonviolent techniques of the sort offered by Richard Gregg and Gandhi. Unlike the communists, Dellinger did not believe that armed struggle, with its "bloodshed and hatred," [102] would advance social and human progress. He became involved with radical Christians in the University Christian Association, headquartered in Dwight Hall. After graduating in 1936, he spent a year in England at Oxford University on a graduate fellowship.

Back in the United States, Dellinger took a job at Dwight Hall from 1937 to 1939. During this time he worked with Yale students, union organizers, radicals, the poor and unemployed, and the Steel Workers Organizing Committee in a New Jersey company town. He joined the Socialist Party and became a leader in its adult and youth sections. After his stint at Dwight Hall, he enrolled in Union Theological Seminary in New York. Disregarding the seminary's threat of expulsion, he and several other students moved off campus and lived in Harlem. In the summer of 1940 he moved to Newark, New Jersey, where he organized a neighborhood activity program and served as minister for an inner-city church. With two Union roommates from Harlem and their female companions, he established the Newark Christian Colony, whose program reflected his interest in Christian communism and Gandhian ashrams. Better known as the Newark Ashram, it was home to eight to ten people who shared money, performed community work among the poor in the neighborhood, and—like the Catholic Workers—offered hospitality to all who knocked. The Selective Service Act of 1940 interrupted his Union studies and the Newark experiment. [103]

Eight seminarians at Union Theological Seminary, including Dellinger, George Houser, and other WRL members, denounced the draft, rejected ministerial exemptions as a "bribe," [104] and refused to register. The Union Eight linked conscription to totalitarianism and the "war system." They also repudiated CPS, which in their view was coopting dissent and preventing widespread opposition to the 1940 peacetime draft. "We do not expect to stem the war forces today;" they declared, "but we are helping to build the movement that will conquer in the future."[105] Dellinger was critical of A. J. Muste for his absence during the "decision-making crisis";[106] however, once the Union Eight confirmed their nonregistration, Muste and Evan Thomas issued a statement of support. The eight seminarians were convicted and sentenced to one year in Danbury prison. Speaking for the WRL, Frank Olmstead called them "the true heroes of this period."[107]

At Danbury, Dellinger challenged racism and the dehumanizing prison routine. Attending his first weekend movie, he deliberately sat in the black section and was punished with the hole. On other occasions, he received solitary for refusing to respond when summoned by his prison number and for not remaking his bed after a guard tore off the sheets and ordered him to make it as soldiers did. Dellinger and several COs, including star pitcher Don Benedict, a member of the Harlem Ashram and Union Eight, played on the prison softball team. Before the season's final game, which the warden badly wanted to win, Dellinger and other COs were confined to the hole for demanding a one-hour work break to demonstrate support for a nationwide student strike against conscription and military preparedness. Benedict refused to pitch unless the COs were removed from solitary, and the warden capitulated shortly before the game. Benedict threw a no-hitter, and they won.[108]

During the prolonged pregame strike, James Bennett, who considered Dellinger the COs' "ringleader," visited Danbury "to straighten [him] out." In response to Dellinger's complaints about prison fascism and racism, Bennett responded: "Dellinger, the American prison system is the most authoritarian institution in the world, and if you don't straighten up and obey every order that it gives you, no matter what it is, the full weight of that system will come down on you."[109] This incident confirmed Dellinger's belief in the justice of the COs' struggle against the "totalitarian" state.

Following his release from Danbury, Dellinger returned to the Newark Ashram, where he remained for the next year and a half, until his second arrest and jail term. Several months after his release from Danbury he married Elizabeth Peterson. With Don Benedict and Meredith Dallas, the Dellingers made the Newark Ashram a center of peace and justice activism in a neighborhood blighted by racial tensions and gang violence. The Newark Ashram attracted visitors interested in their communal, nonviolent "laboratory," as well as draft resisters seeking refuge.[110] Working at night in a bakery, Dellinger arranged to be paid off the books to avoid the 1943 war tax. He also initiated the Peoples Peace Now Campaign. After the 6 April 1943 Peoples Peace Now demonstration in

Washington and subsequent leafleting in Newark, federal authorities arrested Dellinger, who had refused to report for an army physical. He was sentenced to two years in Lewisburg Penitentiary. Benedict and Dallas also were arrested, and the Newark Ashram folded.

At Lewisburg, Dellinger and five other COs began a hunger strike against censorship. They demanded the right for all inmates—including those on punishment status—to receive uncensored reading and unfettered writing materials. They also demanded an end to censorship of incoming and outgoing mail. The COs took a reasonable position on censorship, one that the WRL publicized. While they accepted the right of officials to screen mail to detect escape plots, blackmail, drugs, and pornography, they objected to officials censoring either descriptions of prison conditions or inmates' political and religious opinions (through the exclusion of select books and magazines). In a letter to his family, Dellinger explained: "We are not eating because under the prison system it is the only method we have of calling for an end to [a] censorship" that perpetuated "prison abuses" and "a totalitarian [prison] system." [111]

In what seems to have been a concerted effort to publicize their case, Paton Price—an articulate CO leader and professional actor—repeated these charges verbatim in a letter to his family. In it he compared prison totalitarianism to Nazi fascism, and he invoked fidelity to one's convictions:

I feel compelled to fight such an evil with the most powerful weapon I have: my life. . . . If I were in Germany I would not submit to Fascism; nor am I able to do [so] in this community in which I am now living. Millions of men are valiantly giving their lives in the halocaust [sic] of war for what they believe is a fight for freedom. I believe differently. I believe that real freedom will come only when men refuse to submit to tyranny wherever they are & refuse to cooperate—non-violently, of course—with those who would enslave them. Believing so, should I be less willing to pay the same price for obtaining it that my military friends are paying—and vainly? . . . I realize that fighting an evil non-violently & taking suffering upon oneself rather than inflicting it upon others is a whole new area for you, but I sincerely hope that you will recognize its validity as contrasted to the bloody military way. Pacifism is not "a way out," it is another, a better way of fighting evil. [112]

Prison officials force-fed the COs during their hunger strike. Like many CO hunger strikers, Dellinger continued to resist symbolically, by refusing to open his mouth. The prison doctor responded by inserting a feeding tube into his nose. In an effort to persuade him to eat, prison authorities subjected Dellinger to a range of temptations and threats. He resisted "psychological warfare" and "bribes" and eventually received a conditional ("good time") release two months before his two-year sentence was up. At Ashland, eleven COs waged a one-week sympathy hunger strike.[113]

Thomas and Muste both sat on the WRL's executive committee, but they took different positions on the Lewisburg strike, which reflected differences between the WRL and the FOR. The League publicized the strike; moreover, as a mark of their trust in the WRL chairman and to honor his support for CO activism, the strikers named Thomas to represent them. As the FOR's executive secretary, Muste maintained close contact with the strikers. He advised them to end their fast, contending that prison censorship did not warrant a "fast unto death"—a tactic that should be reserved for urgent crises and even then only as a last resort.[114]

The sixty-four-day hunger strike ended in a compromise settlement on 1 December 1943. On 6 November, Bennett reversed his earlier refusal to negotiate while the strike continued. In a letter to the warden he suggested changes in the censorship rules. Following clarifications from Bennett, the strikers ended their protest. The Bureau of Prisons refused to guarantee correspondence and reading privileges to inmates in administrative segregation; however, wardens would decide each case individually, and inmates would usually be allowed these privileges. Furthermore, Bennett promised that "inspection" of personal mail and reading materials would not censor religious or political opinions.[115] The *Conscientious Objector* editorialized that on balance, the hunger strike had won "substantial gains.[116]

A report issued by Bennett during the strike made plain the narrow-mindedness of prison policy and acknowledged that COs and their nonviolent protests were a "perennial headache" for prison authorities. In it, Bennett labeled COs a discipline problem and declared that the "absolutists' " objection to war was "only a part of a program for changing the social, political, economic and cultural order of the world." Resorting to pop psychology, he contended that COs "are constitutional rather than conscientious objectors and are frequently motivated by an over-protective home or a mother fixation, or by revolt against authority as typified in the home and transferred to society at large. They are problem children, whether at home, at school, or in prison."[117] The motives Bennett ascribed to the COs were fatuous; even so, he had sufficient insight to understand that rebellious prison COs were seeking to challenge the war system and the status quo on every front. Radical pacifist COs were not "problem children"; in fact, they were the vanguard of a nonviolent social movement that was seeking peace, democracy, justice, and equality during the war and would continue to do so after it ended.


### Ralph DiGia and the Danbury and Lewisburg Parole Strikes

Ralph DiGia (1914–) was reared in a radical Italian American family in New York City. DiGia has alternatively defined the politics of his father—a friend of Carlos Tresca, the Italian American anarchist who was assassinated by fascists in 1943—as anarchist and socialist. The DiGias were part of the socialist-anarchist Italian American community that fostered a dissident political culture through political meetings and social activities. The DiGias protested Mussolini's rise, repudiated Italian fascism, and mourned Tresca's death. In 1927, DiGia accompanied his father to protest the execution of Sacco and Vanzetti on the day the two anarchists were electrocuted. Later, DiGia participated with other radicals in annual Columbus Day demonstrations against fascism.

Confronted with the 1940 Selective Service Act, DiGia moved from an antiwar to a pacifist position. During the 1930s, while a student at City College of New York, he participated in anti-ROTC demonstrations and the Oxford Pledge movement. Despite his peace activism, DiGia did not consider himself a pacifist. Initially, he opposed World War II from an antiwar position. He applied for conscientious objection status, but the draft board denied his request on the grounds that he was a political objector, not a religious one.

Refusing to be inducted, DiGia sought help from the U.S. Attorney's office, which suggested he contact Julian Cornell, a Quaker lawyer who handled CO cases for the WRL. DiGia visited WRL headquarters, discussed his situation with other objectors, and gradually completed his conversion to absolute pacifism. Despite Cornell's assistance, the courts rejected DiGia's appeal and sentenced him to prison.

At Danbury and Lewisburg, DiGia participated in many protests, including the Danbury Jim Crow strike and work and hunger strikes to challenge parole practices. At Danbury, DiGia and other COs developed the one-a-week strike to protest parole policies that discriminated against pacifists. Every Wednesday for fifteen weeks another CO joined the strike; authorities knew neither who would strike next nor how long the strike would last. Several weeks into the strike, the Bureau of Prisons tried to break the protest and the Danbury CO cohort by transferring some of them to other institutions. DiGia, Albon Man, and John Mecartney—all WRL members—were shipped to Lewisburg, a tough penitentiary that housed violent criminals. At Lewisburg they continued the one-a-week strike for two months. The strike failed to change parole policies, however.

In September 1944, James Bennett issued a decree denying "good time" for the period that inmates were on strike. Lewisburg officials then withheld forty-eight days of "good time" from John Mecartney for his involvement in the Danbury Jim Crow strike. DiGia and six other COs started a two-week hunger strike; six others went on a work strike to support Mecartney and to protest the Justice Department's refusal to recognize conscience.

DiGia had a good relationship with nonpacifist inmates. Several days after arriving at Lewisburg, an inmate asked DiGia if he was a friend of David Dellinger, then also at Lewisburg. DiGia had never met Dellinger, who had a reputation for supporting non-CO inmates, but he knew about him. Thinking quickly, he replied that he was a friend of Dellinger. "If anybody bothers you . . . just let me know," the inmate responded. "Any friend of Dave Dellinger is a friend of mine." After the COs abandoned the parole strike, DiGia was moved from segregation to the general population. Assigned to a dorm without other COs, on the first night he was doused with water and his bed was pushed across the floor while cellmates yelled: "You fucking CO. You yellow bastard." Ignoring the ambush and the taunts, DiGia returned his bed to its proper position. A guard appeared and asked what had happened. Nothing, DiGia replied. After the guard left, someone offered DiGia dry clothes, and the word spread that he was "OK" and did not "rat." By supporting and demonstrating loyalty to other prisoners, DiGia, Dellinger, and most other radical pacifist COs won the respect and friendship of nonpacifist criminals.[118]

The prison experience was pivotal to DiGia's radical pacifist activism. At Danbury he joined a community of COs. After the war he did volunteer work for the WRL before joining its staff in 1955. DiGia, who retired in 1995 but continues part-time volunteer work, has been a League staffer longer than any other CO of the World War II cohort. For over half a century the League has provided him with a "home" as well as the opportunity to "live" his beliefs. Prison changed his life forever, just as it did for other COs.[119]

WRL members who were CPS and prison COs refused to submit passively to "good war" sentiments, the Selective Service System, unfair parole procedures, prison censorship, and racial discrimination. Collective struggles in CPS and prison enabled resistant COs to share common experiences, forge personal relationships and pacifist networks, and experiment with the nonviolent direct action techniques that would mark postwar radical pacifist activism and nonpacifist social movements. Like the workers and slaves who have been studied by historians such as Herbert Gutman and Eugene Genovese, the WRL's CO members relied on culture and community to oppose and resist the overwhelming power of the prison system and to construct an autonomous and alternative political and ideological culture. To link the arguments of Gutman and pacifist author Richard Gregg, resistant CO "culture and power" in CPS and prison demonstrated "the power of nonviolence" to envisage and promote nonviolent social justice and civil rights.[120]

The CO rebellion had two important consequences for the WRL. First, the postwar League moved beyond its traditional reliance on political and educational methods and adopted the nonviolent direct action techniques that marked the wartime CPS and prison protests. In principle, the prewar League endorsed direct action, most notably the general strike against war. But in practice, it eschewed direct action until after World War II, when the influence of the CO revolts made itself felt. The change happened in large part because most of the League's new leaders were veterans of CPS and prison. Second, the CO rebellion radicalized the League and spurred it to broaden its traditional single-issue program of war resistance to embrace a multi-issue agenda for advancing social justice—most notably in the postwar civil rights movement.

World War II COs themselves expressed the connection between their wartime revolts and their postwar pacifist activism, as well as the links between the peace and justice movements. In March 1945, George Kingsley, a socialist WRL member and a CO who had been active in prison protests, voiced this connection: "Looking back I would evaluate the [Danbury] jimcrow strike as more important than a work strike against my imprisonment, because segregation is one of the causes of war whose abolition will not be realized until we eliminate the causes. If we are thorough-going social radicals, we will attack both [war and social injustice] with equal vigor."[121] Roy Finch recalled that COs left CPS with "a wonderful sort of new discovery"—the belief that Gandhian nonviolent direct action could reform society along democratic and egalitarian lines.[122] Jim Peck, explaining postwar pacifist activism, observed that the "demonstrations constituted our attempts to apply effectively on the outside, the non-violent methods of protest which we had used in prison. . . . We discovered that a small number of COs totalling not more than 30 could get national and even international publicity for pacifism by means of well-timed public demonstrations of such an unusual nature that the press could not ignore them."[123] The postwar WRL and pacifist movement proved adept at generating publicity. The more difficult challenge would be to transform the League's revolutionary commitment, imaginative protest, and media publicity into a mass nonviolent movement with the power to advance peace and social justice.

# 6

# The Pacifist House Divided

The Debate over Nonviolent Direct Action, Civil
Disobedience, and the WRL Agenda, 1945–1955

WITH THE RETURN TO PEACE, two distinct currents—traditionalists and
radicals—vied for control of the WRL, locking horns in a debate that transformed the League's purpose, principles, and strategies. Six months after World
War II ended, Abraham Kaufman—the most insistent proponent of the
League's traditional agenda and methods—recommended that the WRL "limit"
its work to war resistance. He contended that European food relief, imperialism,
world government, conscription, and amnesty for COs were important issues
but were ancillary to the WRL's central purpose, and that the League should not
expend its scant resources on them.[1] Radicals, and even some traditionalists,
challenged this narrow vision. Over the next half-decade the WRL underwent
an acrimonious debate over its proper mission and tactics.

The traditionalist old guard, who had founded the League and controlled it
through World War II, wanted to maintain the WRL as a single-issue organization
devoted to war resistance. They valued the League's enrollment and fellowship
functions, and they tended to endorse education, political action, majoritarian
rule, and democratic socialism centered in the Socialist Party. Significantly, they
disapproved of civil disobedience except as a last resort in extreme circumstances.
The traditionalist leaders included Abraham Kaufman, Frieda L. Lazarus, and
Jessie Wallace Hughan.

The radicals, who were led by World War II COs, were more militant and
absolutist. Even after the war they continued their revolt to reform CPS and the
prisons (where some COs remained long after the war ended). They also sought
an end to social injustice and the other causes of war. They championed direct
action and civil disobedience and refused to subordinate individual liberty and
conscience to political majoritarianism. By challenging the traditionalists to *act*

134

on their pacifist principles, the radicals invigorated both the postwar WRL and the broader peace movement.

Because of the radicals penchant for direct action and civil disobedience, some traditionalists labeled them anarchists. While some radicals did harbor anarchistic impulses, most of them repudiated neither the state nor political socialism. But they did argue that electoral strategies alone were insufficient. Moreover, their experience as COs and their adversarial relationship with the Selective Service System, the Bureau of Prisons, and the Department of Justice led them to mistrust the state, which they considered a threat to freedom and liberty.

Even those radicals who belonged to or supported the SP tended to reject institutional socialism and the bureaucratic state (whether capitalist or socialist). They espoused instead a decentralized, egalitarian, and libertarian socialism in the political and economic spheres. When they advocated nonviolent direct action and civil disobedience, this was more a demand for militant action outside the electoral and political arena than a commitment to ideological anarchism.[2]

Between 1945 and 1953, the WRL transformed itself. Building on wartime developments, it moved from a single-issue to a multi-issue agenda; it also began to promote nonviolent direct action and civil disobedience. The consequences of this were far-reaching. Most of the radicals had been World War II COs; representing a new generation of leadership, they gained titular control of the League by 1953. Their more absolutist impulses and proclivity for direct action, active resistance, and a multi-issue agenda sparked keen debate and divisions within the WRL. As the League shifted its emphasis from opposing war to attacking the causes of war, its former preoccupation with war resistance and the single-issue separation of peace *from* justice (always blurred), changed to a demand for peace *and* justice.

This shift was evident in the WRL's leadership: by 1948, half the League's executive committee came from the radical wing. Included were former COs David Dellinger, James Peck, Igal Roodenko, Bayard Rustin, Roy Finch, George Houser, Albon Man, Stanley Murphy, George Reeves, and Bent Andresen, as well as *Politics* editor Dwight Macdonald and A. J. Muste, who displayed a reborn militancy. In January 1948, Roy Kepler, a CPS veteran and radical stalwart, became the League's executive secretary.[3] This transformation did not take place in a vacuum. Under the nuclear cloud of the Cold War, the WRL and radical pacifists were urgently debating the most effective means of challenging the Soviet-American rivalry that was fostering a garrison state at home and threatening nuclear apocalypse.

## War Resistance in the Atomic Age

"The Atomic Bomb," wrote Jessie Hughan to Abraham Kaufman on the day after the nuclear bomb was dropped on Nagasaki, "may mean the end of the world."[4] WRL chairman Evan Thomas agreed with her, asserting several months later: "Thanks to the atomic bomb, the very existence of civilized life now depends on the elimination of war."[5] Hughan feared that a "dictator or traitor"[6] who possessed the atomic bomb would be able to hold the world hostage; she also believed that the new weapon strengthened the pacifist argument and would increase the number of conscientious objectors. Similarly, Frieda Lazarus declared: "Perhaps pacifism will at last come into its own—pacifism on the tail of an atomic bomb!"[7]

The bombing of Hiroshima and Nagasaki prompted WRL members to take dramatic action. On 8 August, in a telegram to A. J. Muste posted from the CPS camp in Minersville, California, John Lewis raised the possibility of a mass walkout "to turn opinion against further use of the bomb."[8] After Nagasaki, Thomas declared that he "no longer want[ed] to be an American."[9] Bent Andresen walked out of Minersville and hitchhiked across the country distributing flyers that denounced Hiroshima and Nagasaki as "needless" and "hideous" "atrocities" and that compared the bombings to Nazi "murder camps." Explaining his walkout and continental trek, Andresen declared: "I . . . have felt the concussion of this bomb, [and] can no longer be quiet or acquiescent." After his arrest in New York and conviction on AWOL charges, Andresen waged an eight-month hunger strike to protest the bomb and his incarceration.[10]

In a letter dated 10 August, Frank Olmstead offered the WRL's first response to the atomic bomb. He suggested that despite the "shock of horror," the bomb might focus attention on the imperative for global disarmament. Furthermore, atomic energy could eliminate scarcity and "free the nations from economic rivalry."[11] In a radio interview six months later, he called the bomb the "most important event in man-made history" and suggested that cheap atomic energy might help eradicate poverty in underdeveloped nations.[12]

On 24 August, at its first post-Hiroshima meeting, the WRL's executive committee convened to formulate its response to the atomic bomb. The members shared a common horror over Hiroshima and Nagasaki, but they could not reach agreement about how the League should respond or the bomb's significance to war resistance. Unlike Olmstead, Hughan took an apocalyptic view of the atomic bomb, contending that international control would not be enough—only the destruction of its blueprint could prevent a nuclear "Armageddon." She feared that the Anglo-Saxon monopoly of the bomb would divide the nascent UN Security Council and lead to open or covert war with the Soviet Union. Because she distrusted Stalin, she was against sharing the bomb with the Soviets or entrusting it to the Security Council, which Stalin could influence. Anticipating the national security state, she predicted that an American "Gestapo" would be necessary to guard the "secret of the universe" against espionage. But even such draconian measures, she warned, would not be able to stop other nations from developing the bomb.[13]

Not all members of the executive committee shared Hughan's urgency over the atomic bomb. Rex Corfman (a World War II CO), William Jaffe (a Northwestern economics professor), and Max Kampelman (a CPS veteran)[14] all insisted that warfare remained the real problem. Jaffe, noting that poison gas had not been used during World War II, predicted that the atomic bomb would not be used in future conflicts. He also suggested that once several nations developed atomic arsenals, making possible mutual nuclear destruction, the atomic bomb would lose its military value and be discarded. Kaufman criticized Hughan's initial emphasis on destroying the atomic blueprint, since the knowledge and ability to produce atomic weapons could not be abolished now that it had been developed.[15]

The WRL did not adopt an official statement on the bomb until February 1946. Instead of denouncing specific weapons, the statement reaffirmed the League's opposition to war: "The atomic bomb is the logical development of mechanized war, and [the WRL] sees no effectual method for its control short of the total abolition of armed conflict." Till that day came, the League called for the abolition of atomic weapons and for international control of atomic energy for economic purposes. It opposed the American atomic monopoly; it was also against control of the bomb by the United Nations, which was dominated by the United States, Britain, and Russia. The League did, however, support sharing American atomic technology with an international committee of scientists, at least once a majority of industrial nations renounced the production and use of atomic energy for military purposes and opened all nuclear projects to inspection.[16]

The atomic bomb raised fundamental questions for radical pacifists. The role of conscientious objection and individual war resistance in the atomic age was intensely debated within the WRL. Atomic warfare—with its ability to obliterate humanity without armies or conscription—compelled the League to reevaluate the efficacy of individual war resistance. One League member considered war resistance in the atomic age an "idle gesture": "Even if 99% of the people were pacifists there could still be an atomic war. Armies are no longer needed." Frank Olmstead responded to this by restating the traditional WRL position. A pacifist "2%," who formed "the conscience of the peace movement," could still "make war impossible," he contended. "The WRL job is to discover, organize and create such persons."[17] Most League members agreed with Olmstead that COs would play a pivotal role as long as governments depended on mass support to wage war.

The debate over the relevance of conscientious objection in the atomic age was illustrated by the WRL literature committee's review of Hughan's pamphlet, *War Resistance in the Atomic Age,* which reaffirmed the League's reliance on war resistance. Hughan acknowledged that modern warfare emphasized "machines rather than men" and that armies could not defend against atomic bombs, but she also contended that since nations measured their power in men, COs continued "to hold the strategic position for blocking the war regime."[18] Within the committee, opinion divided over the "strategic position" of COs to thwart war in the atomic age. Though the committee approved the leaflet and similar literature, the capacity of COs to prevent atomic war would remain a troubling issue.[19]

The atomic bomb was not the only challenge to the WRL's traditional strategy and vision of war resistance. Radical members were also questioning the relevance and effectiveness of the League's single-issue agenda and political methods.

### The Committee for Amnesty vs. the WRL CO Problems Committee

On Sunday, 15 October 1945, a band of protestors picketed the White House and Justice Department in defense of COs. The demonstration was organized by the Families and Friends of Imprisoned COs, a small group led by radical pacifists Julius and Esther Eichel. This picketing was the prologue to a campaign lasting almost three years to win amnesty for the 6,000 American COs sentenced to prison for refusing military service in World War II. The picketers were former prison COs and the families and friends of still-imprisoned COs.[20] They carried placards invoking the Nazi horrors and linking amnesty to freedom—a compelling notion in 1945. The placards read: "Federal Prisons—American Concentration Camps," "Amnesty for War Objectors," and "Free American Political Prisoners."[21] The demonstration garnered considerable publicity. Prison COs and their friends and relatives had initiated the amnesty campaign; however, it was the WRL and the established peace movement that created and supported the Committee for Amnesty, which led this grassroots social movement to restore civil liberties and human rights to prison COs.

In December 1945, nearly twenty organizations met in New York City's Labor Temple to establish the Committee for Amnesty for All Objectors to War and Conscription. The WRL attended the meeting and remained closely involved with the Committee for Amnesty. The Labor Temple participants were motivated by the plight of the 6,000 prison COs who, as convicted felons, had forfeited important civil rights and civil liberties. Moreover, some were still in jail. The Committee for Amnesty dedicated itself to work for "the release of imprisoned conscientious objectors and for the restoration of full civil rights to them and to CO's already released from prison." [22]

The Committee for Amnesty was opposed to working for individual pardons on a case-by-case basis; it advocated instead a general amnesty for all COs.[23] It forged a broad coalition of pacifist and nonpacifist groups and individuals and built a social movement to pressure President Harry S. Truman to grant COs amnesty, or at a minimum to adopt a more liberal policy on pardons. The committee demonstrates the impact of World War II COs on the WRL and the postwar radical pacifist movement. These CO veterans—militant, absolutist orientated, and committed to direct action—shaped the methods and goals of the amnesty campaign, dividing the WRL in the process.

The WRL played a major role in establishing the Amnesty Committee and in its subsequent activities. At the initiative of WRL leader Frieda Lazarus, the Joint Peace Board asked the League's CO Problems Committee to organize the December meeting that led to the formation of the Committee for Amnesty. The League offered the fledgling organization the half-time services of Frances Ransom for three months and provided office space for its headquarters. Furthermore, League members comprised the Amnesty Committee's key leadership and controlled its executive committee.[24]

Albon Man, who had participated as a CO in wartime strikes to abolish Jim Crow and censorship at Danbury and Lewisburg prisons, directed the Amnesty Committee's work as secretary. Most of Man's staff were COs or members of their families; they included Vivien Roodenko, Jim Peck, and Agnes Burns Wieck, a militant labor activist whose son was a CO veteran of the Danbury strike against Jim Crow. Dorothy Canfield Fisher, a liberal author whose only son died in World War II, served as honorary chair.[25]

The WRL and the Committee for Amnesty influenced each other. The League did a great deal to establish the committee and keep it running; the amnesty campaign contributed to the League's postwar shift in ideology and techniques. The amnesty campaign, with its attendant debate over general amnesty versus individual pardons, was one of several issues that divided WRL traditionalists and militants.

Differences between the Amnesty Committee and the WRL's COPC provoked a divisive debate within the League over CO policy and led Lazarus to resign as the COPC's chair. A member of the League's executive committee since 1935, Lazarus had devoted most of her pre-World War II peace work to the Women's Peace Union. The single-issue Women's Peace Union drafted and championed the Frazier Amendment, a constitutional amendment to outlaw war. In October 1940, Lazarus resigned from the nearly defunct WPU and shifted her activism to the League.[26]

Lazarus chaired the COPC and served as the League's principal liaison with government officials on CO issues. While the Amnesty Committee campaigned exclusively for a general amnesty, Lazarus and the COPC quietly lobbied the Justice Department, Selective Service, the Bureau of Prisons, and the Parole Board to obtain amnesty and individual pardons, with an emphasis on the latter. In September 1945, Lazarus led a COPC-organized delegation to the Justice Department to discuss prison COs with Attorney General Tom Clark, who promised to review their recommendations and reply within a month.

In mid-October the pro-amnesty Families and Friends of Imprisoned COs picketed the White House. Lazarus denounced the demonstration, which was held at the same time as the Justice Department was considering the COPC delegation's suggestions. She later contended that because of the protest, the government delayed its new CO policy until January 1946. The liberalized policy authorized individual paroles to men twenty-six years and older, fathers under twenty-six, and imprisoned COs who had completed one-third of their sentences. Judging that remaining COs were increasingly unlikely to see the "magic-wand of amnesty," [27] Lazarus began concentrating most of the COPC's efforts on pardons—a decision that sparked conflict both within the COPC and between the COPC and the nascent Committee for Amnesty. Several COPC members condemned paroles, considering negotiation with the government "appeasement." [28]

Partly as a result of the sharp disagreement and subsequent impasse between advocates of pardons and advocates of amnesty, the independent Committee for Amnesty was formed. In January 1946, "object[ing] strongly to any organization which did not concern itself with the need for paroles and which endorsed coercive methods as superior to those of negotiation," Lazarus resigned as the COPC chair.[29] After her resignation she continued to assist COs independently and through the Metropolitan Board for Conscientious Objectors, a New York group that provided counseling on draft and CO matters.[30]

Igal Roodenko, a WRL member and militant CO, expressed the radicals' opposition to Lazarus and pardons. Writing from Sandstone prison while on a pro-amnesty hunger strike, he endorsed the Amnesty Committee and disputed Lazarus's analysis. For Roodenko, refusal to compromise freedom and civil liberties—the key issue for radical pacifist prison COs—was more important than his immediate release from prison. Unlike amnesty, parole included conditions and restrictions on one's freedom. For instance, pardon applications required COs to "promise . . . obedience to the laws of this country, national and State, and loyalty to the Constitution of the United States"[31]—a stipulation at odds with the radicals' turn toward Gandhian civil disobedience. "The bulk of CO inmates I know," Roodenko asserted, "consider the *how* of release as being at least as important as release itself."[32] He also disputed the claim that the government had liberalized its parole policy because Lazarus and the COPC had intervened. Other factors contributed to the government's decision, he argued, including the October picketing of the White House, the end of the war, and restlessness among COs in CPS and prison. He suggested that instead of delaying a new parole policy, the White House picketing had provided the government with a "pretext" to temporize.[33] This exchange between Roodenko and Lazarus over amnesty (Amnesty Committee) versus parole (COPC) illustrates one contentious issue in the League's internal struggle between radicals and traditionalists.

Like military GIs impatient with the slow pace of demobilization, the Amnesty Committee complained that too many of the 6,000 prison COs—the "forgotten men"—were still in jail long after the war ended. Some of their sentences weren't due to expire until 1951. According to the Truman Administration, in October 1946, 681 COs remained in prison. The Amnesty Committee, which constantly disputed the government's figures, claimed that 1,500 COs were still incarcerated in September 1946, and between 700 and 1,000 in December 1946. More important than that, as felons, prison COs were "second-class citizens" deprived of full civil rights. Although the penalties varied among states, prison COs were typically forbidden to vote, hold political office, qualify for the civil service, and practice medicine, law, or dentistry. Only a presidential amnesty, the Amnesty Committee contended, could free imprisoned COs and restore full citizenship to all convicted objectors.[34]

The Amnesty Committee argued that amnesty was a well-established principle in American history. Beginning with George Washington, nine presidents had granted some form of amnesty to Americans penalized by civil or military courts. After World War II, American occupation authorities had issued amnesties to COs and other political prisoners in Germany and Japan; many American wartime allies had taken similar action. The Amnesty Committee also pointed to the arbitrary nature of the Selective Service System. Local draft boards were inconsistent in determining who qualified as a "genuine" conscientious objector; those imprisoned by one board might have been recognized as COs and assigned to CPS by another; furthermore, jail sentences varied by judge and by region. Finally, the committee quoted Supreme Court Justice Frank Murphy in a decision that reversed the conviction of two Jehovah's Witnesses: "All of the mobilization and all of the war effort will have been in vain if, when all is finished, we discover that in the process we have destroyed the very freedom for which we fought."[35]

Amnesty became an important liberal issue in postwar America. Though its leaders were COs and pacifists, the Amnesty Committee solicited sponsors and supporters among both pacifists and nonpacifists. Scores of important organizations and hundreds of prominent clerics, politicians, intellectuals, labor leaders, civil rights activists, and journalists either were represented on the Amnesty Committee or advocated amnesty. Calling for amnesty were the ACLU, the CIO, the NAACP, Reinhold Niebuhr, Pearl Buck, W. E. B. DuBois, Albert Einstein, Henry Luce, Thurgood Marshall, and Bertrand Russell. Influential newspapers, including the *New York Times* and the *Washington Post,* supported amnesty in editorials. The Amnesty Committee orchestrated many of the endorsements, letters, petitions, statements, and editorials that gave the amnesty campaign respectability and political clout. For instance, on the committee's initiative, 139 American authors, 100 labor leaders, 85 African American actors and artists, 20 British authors, and 9 Irish writers coauthored a series of collective letters to Truman appealing for amnesty. The distinguished people who sponsored the Amnesty Committee, endorsed its public appeals, and signed pro-amnesty letters constituted a social and intellectual elite.[36] By mobilizing this broad, influential, liberal-radical coalition, the Amnesty Committee transformed pro-amnesty sentiment into a social movement.

Although prison COs provided the Amnesty Committee with its core leadership and cadre, imprisoned COs played an active role in the campaign. At Danbury, a hotbed of CO resistance against Jim Crow, censorship, and parole policies, COs repeatedly took direct action to promote amnesty. For instance, during an August 1946 lunchtime rally, Roger Axford, a CO punished with solitary confinement for participating in an earlier work strike, hung from his cell a four-by-four-foot sign fashioned from sixteen sheets of typewriter paper glued together with oatmeal that proclaimed: "Free All War Prisoners." Three weeks later, as Axford addressed over two hundred inmates from his cell, more than fifty COs staged a half-day work strike to protest the White House's failure to grant amnesty.[37]

The Amnesty Committee organized many imaginative protests. These often expropriated prison and funeral symbols to dramatize the need for amnesty, the "death" of liberty and justice, and the continued peacetime incarceration of COs. In Washington, New York, Philadelphia, Boston, Chicago, Los Angeles, and other cities, the committee staged mock funeral processions, sometimes picketing and marching in striped prison garb complete with balls and chains. On one occasion it presented a petition to White House aides from inside a cell-like wooden cage. In 1947 and 1948, while a seven-car-long red, white, and blue "Freedom Train" was transporting historic American flags and documents to audiences nationwide, committee members—sometimes dressed in prison stripes—repeatedly met the train with demonstrations and pickets calling for amnesty and criticizing the exhibition for excluding past presidential amnesty proclamations.[38]

The most significant Amnesty Committee protest, which involved both imprisoned COs and their outside supporters, occurred on 11 May 1946. On that day, in the first mass amnesty demonstration, more than one hundred protestors from eight states picketed the White House. Newspaper accounts highlighted three-year-old Ann Neubrand, who led the procession with her mother Edith, wife of an imprisoned CO. Little Ann cut a cute and compelling figure with her curly hair, matching beret and jacket, saddle shoes, and oversized sign proclaiming: "Let My Daddy Out Of Jail." Besides the families and friends of imprisoned COs, the picketers included prison COs from both world wars, war veterans, religious leaders, writers, professors, and labor leaders.

The marchers pressed Truman to release the 2,600 COs remaining in jail and to restore the civil rights of all prison COs. Mothers and wives carried signs demanding: "President Truman Free My Husband" and "Restore Civil Rights to My Son." Other placards declared: "Free US Political Prisoners" and "Conscience Is No Crime." A delegation entered the White House and presented a letter urging presidential amnesty. As a result of careful planning, a calculated appeal to family reunification, and astute manipulation of the image of protective motherhood and domesticity, the demonstration received sympathetic newspaper coverage nationwide, as well as public support. Similar demonstrations took place in Chicago, Rochester, and Los Angeles.[39]

In a dramatic show of resistance timed to coincide with this mass picketing, COs in six federal prisons launched a collective hunger strike. Among them was Igal Roodenko. On the morning of 11 May, he and four other COs at Sandstone began a hunger strike to publicize the peacetime imprisonment of COs and to win unconditional release. Over the next several weeks, three more Sandstone COs joined the hunger strike. In a public statement the five original Sandstone strikers declared: "The undersigned are among the 3000 political prisoners confined by the Federal Government because of their conscientious opposition to war and conscription. Such imprisonment violates American ideals and traditions of liberty and freedom of conscience."[40]

During their hunger strike, Roodenko and the other Sandstone COs conducted an impressive letter-writing campaign to promote amnesty. They wrote to influential citizens and to more than two hundred members of Congress. In a letter to Rep. Clare Booth Luce, to buttress his argument Roodenko used patriotic, republican language that emphasized the obligation of active citizenship: "Countless men have given their lives for freedom and democracy; shall we hesitate to remain in prison for another year or two, if need be, for the same cause?" Writing to a senator, he pointed out that although the hunger strikers could have avoided prison by accepting CPS, "Freedom and democracy are not merely Fourth-of-July phrases for us . . . This has led us . . . to fasting for freedom . . . in an attempt to touch the public conscience and sense of justice." In a letter to Senator Pepper he also invoked the Nuremberg trials—then in progress—to explain the amnesty campaign: "If the American people wanted the Germans to conscientiously rise against the Nazis—even at the cost of their lives—let them stop punishing their own conscientious objectors."[41]

Refusing to compromise political freedom and civil liberties, Roodenko declined to seek or accept parole under Executive Order 8641. Unlike amnesty, parole restricted one's freedom: "I mean to remain in prison, a source of embarrassment for a freedom-preaching government, if my only alternative is return to society as a second-class citizen, a felon."[42] In January 1947—after he waged a 248-day hunger strike—prison authorities released him without condition.[43]

The Truman Administration rejected amnesty; however, it did respond to the political pressure mobilized by the Amnesty Committee. Truman had contempt for conscientious objection, and he wanted to take a tough stand toward COs in order to promote a muscular Cold War image; moreover, the veterans' groups that were opposed to amnesty had political clout. Even so, on 23 December 1946 he responded to the growing public pressure for a Christmas amnesty by appointing a three-member Amnesty Board to review each CO case individually and make recommendations.

One year later, on 23 December 1947, the Amnesty Board issued its report. The board endorsed "selective" rather than general amnesty,[44] and it recommended (and Truman issued) pardons for 1,523 of the 6,000 prison COs and 15,805 convictions under the Selective Training and Service Act of 1940. The board rejected the claims of religious Jehovah's Witnesses and secular/political, WRL-type COs; in effect, it limited pardons to men who were eligible for CO status under a narrow reading of the law's religious requirement. While only a handful of COs were still in jail in December 1947, most World War II prison COs never regained their full civil and political rights.[45]

The Amnesty Committee and the WRL denounced the Amnesty Board's report and Truman's Amnesty Proclamation, which endorsed the board's recommendations. In a letter to President Truman, WRL chair Evan Thomas condemned the report as "ludicrously inadequate" and repudiated the notion that secular prison COs were "less worthy" than religious ones.[46]

Even so, the amnesty campaign ebbed. In January 1948, Albon Man resigned as executive secretary to commit more time to his law school studies. After graduating from Columbia University Law School in 1950, the New York Bar refused to admit Man on the grounds that he was a convicted felon. In an ironic twist, President Dwight Eisenhower issued Man an individual pardon in 1957, and he joined the bar. The Central Committee for Conscientious Objectors (CCCO) was established in August 1948 and assumed primary responsibility for counseling prospective (especially secular) COs; at that point the Committee for Amnesty and the WRL's COPC disbanded. The League, though it pledged to cooperate with the CCCO, wanted to focus its efforts on pacifist fellowship, education, and action projects rather than on CO work.[47]

Although Truman never granted a general amnesty for COs, the Committee for Amnesty is important for several reasons. First, the political pressure orchestrated by the Amnesty Committee did spur the administration to liberalize its policy on pardons.[48] Second, the Amnesty Committee illustrates the postwar social activism of radical COs, who besides playing a role in the amnesty campaign, provided leadership to a number of peace and justice movements. Third, the Amnesty Committee continued the leadership role that radical pacifists had always played in championing civil liberties, human rights, and religious and secular conscientious objection. Like the World War I pacifists who did so much to establish the ACLU (1920), COs and pacifists took the lead in preserving and extending civil liberties after World War II. Indeed, during and after the war, radical pacifist COs both honored their own political and philosophical convictions and strengthened the civil liberties and human rights tradition in America.

Finally, the CO-led amnesty campaign influenced the postwar pacifist movement by popularizing nonviolent direct action and radicalizing the WRL. Indeed, the debate over general amnesty versus individual pardons divided radicals and traditionalists within the League; this contributed to its postwar factionalism, which ended in a triumph for the radicals.

### Civil Disobedience: The Committee for Nonviolent Revolution, Peacemakers, and the WRL Debate over Tax Resistance and Nonregistration

Both the Committee for Nonviolent Revolution (CNVR) and Peacemakers—comprising the militant Young Turks of the pacifist movement, who embodied

the postwar impulse toward direct action, civil disobedience, and multi-issue organization—moved the League toward a more radical position. In 1945 those
COs who believed strongly that pacifism offered the potential for revolutionary
social change, and who were dissatisfied with the WRL, the FOR, and the SP,
began communicating with one another about how to promote effective nonviolent political action. Late in that year, continuing the radical activism that
marked the wartime CO revolt, a number of League members, including Dave
Dellinger, Roy Finch, Ralph DiGia, George Houser, Albon Man, and Lew Hill,
called a Conference of Non-Violent Revolutionary Socialism, to be held in
Chicago from 6 to 9 February 1946. The "time has come for radical elements
from the groups devoted to war resistance, socialism, militant labor unionism,
consumer cooperation, and racial equality to attempt to come together in a common program of revolutionary action," their call proclaimed. The CNVR's program would attempt to fuse pacifism, socialism, and anarcho-syndicalism—an
ideological mix that offered fresh thinking but that also made common aims and
united action difficult.[49]

The ninety-five pacifists who attended the Chicago conference debated war
resistance, nonviolence, decentralized socialism, the process of revolutionary
change, international revolution and government, and organization and action.
The participants divided over democratic socialism versus anarcho-syndicalism,
economic versus cultural-psychological transformation, and theoretical discussion versus immediate action. But they all advocated democratic, egalitarian,
and decentralized ownership and control of the economy by workers through
(socialist) planning councils or (anarchist) direct action and worker occupation
of factories. The conference affirmed individual war resistance and the general
strike against war. In other resolutions, it rejected the fledgling United Nations
and endorsed world government. Perhaps most important, the CNVR conference offered hope of vigorous direct action for peace, justice, and socialism.
Roodenko wrote from Sandstone on the day the conference opened: "For one
like myself, who isn't quite ready to give up in despair & retire to Tahiti or southern Mexico, the outcome of the meeting carries a potential justification of my
activities these past few years & an arrow pointing the way ahead."[50]

The following year CNVR issued irregular bulletins, held a follow-up conference at a Catholic Worker farm, formed several local groups, and organized a
series of action projects in New York. Members of CNVR-New York picketed a
Waldorf-Astoria luncheon that was being held to honor delegates attending the
opening session of the UN General Assembly; they also picketed a reception at
the Hotel Savoy Plaza that Secretary of State Stettinius was hosting for UN delegations. They also supported a seamen's strike, demonstrated against CPS, and

participated in a mass draft-card burning as an act of civil disobedience. In addition, CNVR-New York members joined in demonstrations sponsored by the WRL and by other pacifist groups; these included actions to close CPS camps and to win amnesty for World War II prison COs.[51]

The CNVR's literature endorsed direct action, civil disobedience, a general strike against war, the abolition of Soviet and Anglo-American imperialism, egalitarian socialist revolution, and a multi-issue peace and justice agenda. One leaflet declared: "We know that *Revolution* means using the general strike, the sit-down strike, mass civil disobedience, to seize control from private owners, state bureaucrats, and fake labor czars."[52] Another flyer proclaimed: "This Is The Era of One World and Two Classes: We Must Attack War and Inequality Directly!" It then urged "workers to take control of the factories, mines, shops, and farms in which they work." The same flyer advocated decentralized socialism, arguing that "we should elect our own foreman, management committees, and representatives on planning committees."[53] Still another flyer, this one supporting the seamen's strike, resorted to revolutionary republican language, asserting: "The right of every working man to a voice in the management of his job is as fundamental a right as was the right of the early American Revolutionists to a voice in the government. Employment Without Representation is as great an evil as Taxation Without Representation."[54] Over a sketch of an exploding bomb, yet another flyer implored readers to "Resist conscription, sit-down to prevent a blow-up," and "Work in your union for a general strike against production of armaments."[55] Attacking imperialism, armaments, militarism, conscription, and capitalism, another flyer declared: "The UNO [United Nations] cannot prevent war because it protects these causes of war."[56]

Internal CNVR politics echoed debates between, on the one hand, the orthodox Marxist preoccupation with political economy and with the working class as the historic agent for radical social change and, on the other, the new postwar social movements that emphasized culture and community and that preferred anarchist, nonviolent direct action and civil disobedience outside electoral politics.[57] Both currents existed within CNVR, operating within a shared CO consensus. The resistant, social action, and absolutist COs (and others) had been shaped by their wartime experiences in CPS and prison, and they perceived the state as a threat to freedom and liberty. Although they disagreed about the role of organization and electoral politics, both socialists and anarchists within CNVR rejected institutional socialism and the bureaucratic state (socialist and capitalist) and supported direct action and some form of decentralized and egalitarian "socialism." Ideological divisions, however, limited CNVR's effectiveness. One CNVR founder explained that CNVR's reliance on Marxism had proved disappointing: "When one is looking for the proletariat one looks for chains; but in the industrial class in America what one sees is bathtubs and credit-plan refrigerators, with a heavy sprinkling of life-insurance investments."[58]

The CNVR and the WRL strongly influenced each other. Comparing WRL and CNVR principles, one CNVR bulletin quoted WRI founder Fenner Brockway on the socialist and anarchist membership and its support for nonviolent revolution, the WRI's abolition of capitalism, and the general strike against war. Albon Man, a leader in both the League and CNVR, later summarized CNVR's impact on the League: "CNVR had a profound impact on the WRL. It helped change the WRL from a largely single-issue organization and from an organization acting as a quiet registry of people (many nonreligious) subscribing to the motto, 'Wars will cease when men refuse to fight,' and campaigning for disarmament in a rather dignified way, to one concerned with other social issues, including economic injustice, racism, and related forms of violence."[59]

During 1946 and 1947 CNVR moved the WRL toward direct action, civil disobedience, and a broader social program. The CNVR formed the cutting edge of the pacifist movement, yet it accomplished little, and by 1948 it had been absorbed into a new group, Peacemakers. The latter would influence the WRL even more and prompt a spirited debate within the League over pacifist means and ends.[60]

In April 1948, 250 militant pacifists met in Chicago for a Conference on More Disciplined and Revolutionary Pacifism, and formed Peacemakers. The impetus for this conference was provided by radical pacifists who were dissatisfied with American militarism and with the moderate response of pacifist groups to the Cold War. In particular, the radicals demanded forceful action to block or overturn the 1948 peacetime draft. The conference brought together two groups of war resisters. One group, which included A. J. Muste, Dwight Macdonald, and Milton Mayer, comprised militant pacifists who had "compromised"[61] during World War II and were now prepared for more radical action. The second group, radicalized CPS and prison CO veterans, included half the CNVR membership. For the next several years Peacemakers was the most radical and creative pacifist group in the United States.

Peacemakers advocated radical pacifist action to reform society and the development of pacifist cells to promote communal life and personal "inner transformation."[62] They extolled absolutism, moral responsibility, commitment, and civil disobedience. They reflected the postwar pacifist desire to transcend individual protest and build a collective nonviolent movement that could resist war and abolish its causes. But they also argued that the "transformation of individuals" must precede social and political revolution, since imposed revolutions were usually tyrannical and tenuous. To eliminate the causes of war, they proposed a social and economic revolution to replace capitalism and to abolish the coercion, exploitation, and injustice that led to conflict and war. They relied on a network of local pacifist cells to provide mutual support, to advance unified pacifist action, and to promote communal social and economic living arrangements. These egalitarian cells, practicing participatory democracy and consensus, could challenge and eventually replace centralized, hierarchal institutions. The core of Peacemakers' program, however, was war resistance and civil disobedience—in particular, nonregistration and tax refusal.[63]

Like CNVR, Peacemakers had a profound impact on the WRL and prompted the League to reevaluate its program and broaden its agenda. League members helped to establish Peacemakers and provided much of its membership. In addition, members of the League's executive committee and staff, including Dellinger, Muste, Macdonald, Houser, Rustin, and Roy Kepler (the new executive secretary of the League), comprised half of Peacemakers' first executive committee.[64] Most significantly, Peacemakers' challenge spurred the League to tentatively endorse direct action and civil disobedience—a shift that fomented divisive debate and resignations. By 1951 the League and its leadership had changed and the debate had "ended." The debate within the WRL over tax resistance and nonregistration proved central to its reorientation and the resignations of key members.

## Tax Resistance

In 1948 a small tax resistance movement emerged when several tax refusers learned about one another and began to correspond. Many of these early tax resisters were WRL members. Abraham Kaufman, the League's executive secretary, facilitated many of these contacts. At its founding conference in April 1948, Peacemakers established a Tax Refusal Committee. League members formed a majority on this committee, which was chaired by Ernest Bromley, a Methodist minister and the nation's leading proponent of tax resistance.[65]

For the next two decades, Bromley championed tax resistance and publicized examples from three continents to demonstrate its power. American examples included Quaker tax resistance during both the French and Indian War and the American Revolution, the popular tax protests by colonists during the American Revolution, and Henry David Thoreau's refusal to pay the Massachusetts poll tax to protest the Mexican War. He also cited England's Wat Tyler (fourteenth century) and John Hampden (seventeenth century). Finally, he invoked Gandhi and the Indian independence movement; both resorted to tax resistance in the struggle against British rule.[66]

For both moral and pragmatic reasons, tax resistance appealed to Peacemakers and to radical pacifists. Most important, it enabled absolutists to express their total commitment against militarism and war. The Peacemakers' literature underscored this uncompromising position. One publication explained that tax resistance "is not merely a protest. It is an *act*."[67] Aware that modern, technological warfare required huge expenditures, tax resisters were seeking to cripple war preparation—and war—through nonpayment of taxes. Other literature asserted that nearly 35 percent of the national budget was earmarked for the military and that 80 percent paid for past, present, and future wars. The "new push-button type warfare," Bromley declared, would require "more drafted dollars than drafted men."[68] Tax resisters were hoping to influence American policy by publicly repudiating military preparedness and weapon stockpiling before conflict broke out again. Unlike COs and nonregistration, tax resistance was both age and gender neutral. By enabling men and women of all ages and occupations to participate, tax refusal expanded the sphere of war resistance and promoted solidarity with draft-eligible men.[69]

Ernest and Marion Bromley, whose Wilmington, Ohio, home served as unofficial headquarters of the Tax Refusal Committee, embodied the spirit of tax resistance. "The time has now come," Ernest exclaimed in his 1948 IRS tax statement, "when men ought no longer to depend solely upon their spoken witness against war or preparation for it. They ought to prepare themselves for an outright resistance by a thorough-going dissociation with the war-making system."[70] In her March 1948 letter to the tax collector, Marion charged that "this country did not turn to peace at the end of World War II, but instead sought to protect and expand an American Empire," declaring "I want to dissociate myself as completely as possible from these tragic, suicidal and evil policies . . . and to do all I can to convince my fellow citizens that we must completely renounce the way of war and violence."[71] The Bromleys believed that radical pacifist individuals and organizations must assume risks for war resistance. Anticipating the New Left, Ernest asserted: "Pacifists believe . . . that there is a . . . time and place where they as individuals must simply come to a stop, and 'clog [the system] with their whole weight.' Perhaps that time and place have come."[72]

Four months after its formation, Peacemakers' Tax Refusal Committee published the statements of active tax resisters. Many of these people were WRL members. These statements illustrate the total commitment and absolutist nature of Peacemakers and of a section of the League. Writing in a different venue, Caroline Urie similarly declared:

In a time of crisis like the present it is our duty as sovereign citizens to defend our country not only with protest but with our lives, if necessary, against military en-slavement and the possible annihilation implicit in atomic and bacterial warfare. In the brief time at our disposal, protest is not enough; if we are to assume real re-sponsibility, we must *act* in a manner simple enough and clear enough to be un-derstood and to arouse public conscience.[73]

As justification for tax resistance, several WRL members pointed to the Nurem-berg War Crimes Tribunal, which had established the principle of individual re-sponsibility for wartime actions, even in the face of wartime orders. In his 1948 letter to the IRS, Walter Gormley declared that he was "refusing to make any federal income tax payment, because the money would be used mostly for 'crimes against peace.' " "The U.S. is preparing for a shooting war of aggression by maintaining bases, subservient governments and military forces from Korea to Turkey, by intensive research on methods of mass slaughter and by maintain-ing a huge military organization," he charged. "I must refrain from supporting such a government."[74] Likewise, Valerie Riggs explained that "if our government . . . at Nuremberg could hold individuals responsible to stand against crime . . . I feel thoroughly justified by my own government in not paying this part of my tax."[75]

Perhaps A. J. Muste best expressed the compelling logic of tax resistance. "World War III has already started," he exclaimed in May 1948:

I cannot support a government in these war-measures, which I deem insane, wicked and suicidal. I must withdraw support from such war-measures in every possible way. The two decisive powers of government . . . are the power to con-script and the power to tax. Pacifists recognize that to be consistent they must re-fuse to be conscripted for military service or training. I have come . . . to the conviction that I at least am in conscience bound . . . to challenge the right of the government to tax me for waging war, and in particular for the production of atomic and bacterial weapons. . . . The need for getting our pacifist teaching off the level of talk and writing and onto the level of action is, I believe, imperative.[76]

Peacemakers was highly critical of pacifist organizations—the WRL included—that collected withholding taxes from their employees. By withholding taxes these pacifist groups were effectively barring tax refusers from working for them, or forcing them to resign. Both the WRL and the FOR paid a lot of attention to this issue. A special committee of the FOR examined the problem for a year be-fore recommending that the FOR withhold taxes, even though most FOR em-ployees had indicated that they wanted to make individual decisions about tax refusal. Staff member Marion Coddington (Bromley) resigned over the policy. The WRL also decided to withhold taxes. In justifying this policy, a member of the League's executive committee declared: "The life of the organization is at stake."[77] The Peacemakers' Tax Refusal Committee, which characterized the WRL and other pacifist groups as "tax collectors for the government,"[78] was scathing in its denunciation. "If pacifist organizations, whose business is to create a warless world, are not ready to risk something for war resistance *now*," the committee asked, "when will they be ready?"[79]

Tax resistance took various forms. Total refusers paid no tax. Since most workers could not avoid the withholding tax, total refusers were often self-employed. Miriam Keeler and Marion Coddington Bromley resigned from the Labor Department and the FOR staff in order to avoid the withholding taxes. Percentage refusers withheld that portion of taxes corresponding to the percentage the federal government would spend on war preparation and the military (calculations ranged from 35 to 80 percent). Finally, some tax resisters chose to live on an income below the taxable level or to work at several part-time, low-income jobs to preclude employers from withholding taxes. Some tax resisters refused to submit tax returns; others explained their action in letters to local tax collectors and the Bureau of Internal Revenue. Some tax resisters, instead of remitting taxes to the government, contributed the money to the WRL and other peace and justice organizations.[80]

As a result of Peacemakers' activism, tax resistance became a major issue for the WRL. The League sold stickers that tax resisters could attach to their tax forms: "This tax goes chiefly for war purposes, as a pacifist I pay under protest." In the spring of 1948 the League passed several resolutions commending those, members or not, who practiced tax resistance. Beginning in 1948, several tax resisters began donating a portion of their unpaid income tax to the League, an act consistent with their willingness to pay taxes for nonmilitary social programs. The League established a special literature fund for these donations to ensure that they did not go to pay staff salaries, which were subject to withholding taxes.[81]

Ammon Hennacy, a WRL member most often associated with the Catholic Worker movement, was a pioneer tax refuser praised by the League. A "Christian anarchist," he first practiced tax refusal in 1943, when the tax withholding system was implemented. Each year at tax time he prepared a statement and mailed it to the IRS. Hennacy's 1945 tax statement reflected the direct action and civil disobedience impulse that would shake the League over the next half-decade. "We can refuse to put our trust in Princes and Presidents," he declared. "With Thoreau and Gandhi we can start our own campaign of Civil Disobedience by refusal to buy war bonds . . . and . . . pay taxes for war or conscription."[82] In 1950, Hennacy began expanding his protest; each year, on 6 August, he fasted and picketed the local IRS office for as many days as years had passed since Hiroshima. While picketing, he distributed tax statements and leaflets that repudiated war, advocated anarchism, and declared his tax resistance. When threatened with arrest for disturbing the peace while picketing, he retorted: "I'm disturbing the war."[83]

In a letter to Hennacy, Kaufman expressed his disagreement with tax resistance. But then he added: "I admire your guts and want you to know that I am with you, for each of us must use the methods he feels to be effective in bringing the world out of its present insanity. Your method may prove most effective in the long run."[84] Although he did not delude himself that his "One Man Revolution"[85] would change government policy or transform the world, Hennacy insisted on the moral imperative of individual resistance to the militaristic state.

By mid-1949, radicals had succeeded in raising the issue of the WRL's payment of withholding taxes, especially for members like Roy Kepler who supported tax refusal. In October the WRL endorsed CCCO assistance for tax resisters and authorized a review of the issue. Although they extended moral support to tax refusers and publicized their actions, most League members did not support tax resistance, and the WRL did not officially endorse it. Kaufman, in particular, insisted that it would be "unethical" for a small minority to "coerce" the League into accepting such a policy. With minor revisions, the League accepted its subcommittee's Withholding Tax Report. Concluding that its survival as an organization took priority over tax refusal, the League decided to continue to withhold income taxes from its employees.[86]

### Nonregistration

Peacemakers and the Resist Conscription Committee also championed nonregistration, a policy that had a strong impact on the League. In March 1948 Truman requested—and Congress passed—the Selective Service Act of 1948, which limited conscientious objection to religious grounds; that is, COs would have to base their position on "religious training and belief." The act denied exemption to secular "political, sociological, or philosophical" objectors, which included many League members. It also narrowed the 1940 draft law by requiring that religious objectors base their convictions on a "Supreme Being."[87]

In response, the April 1948 Peacemakers conference asked the Resist Conscription Committee to organize a movement against draft registration. WRL members played an important role in the Resist Conscription Committee, an ad hoc group that promoted organized resistance and civil disobedience against the new peacetime draft. This committee, which George Houser led for a time, established close ties to Peacemakers and operated under its auspices.

At the April Peacemakers' conference, eighty-six delegates signed a Resist Conscription Committee pledge of nonregistration and resistance to conscription. Dave Dellinger and the other editors of *Alternative* urged readers to refuse conscription and join the American Gandhian civil disobedience movement. The Resist Conscription Committee circulated pledges of nonregistration and resistance, formed local groups, and sought to enlist prominent individuals and to rally support. Like the WRL, the Resist Conscription Committee tried to influence policy by notifying the government of its intention to resist the draft law.[88]

WRL members split over civil disobedience and over how much official support the League should offer the Resist Conscription Committee. In March 1948, over the opposition of Kaufman, Frieda Lazarus, and Winston Dancis, the League passed a resolution extending "support in principle" to the Resist Conscription Committee. To placate members who opposed illegal acts, the League limited its assistance to "moral support" and to informing its members of committee activities. In addition, the WRL's executive committee assured opponents of the measure that it had no intention of committing League members to Resist Conscription Committee actions.[89]

Mid-July saw a sharpening of the WRL debate over the Resist Conscription Committee. After robust discussion, the League's executive committee authorized the chairman to assign staff to assist Resist Conscription Committee projects. When Kaufman threatened to resign as acting executive secretary rather than implement such a policy, the executive committee tabled its decision.[90]

The debate over civil disobedience to resist conscription generated huge controversy within the WRL and drove several members—both radical proponents and traditionalist opponents—to resign from the League. In mid-July, Julien Cornell, a conservative Quaker attorney, resigned from the League and its executive committee over two flyers that the League had distributed in Washington, D.C., shortly before Congress passed the draft law: "Stop the Draft Now" and "Stop World War 3 Now." The text advocated civil disobedience and included the phrases "Refuse to be Drafted" and "Refuse to be drafted and encourage others to do likewise."[91] Cornell noted that because the League was an unincorporated association, its members were legally liable for the actions of the organization. Although he sympathized with those who resisted conscription, he also stated: "I am unable myself as a lawyer and a citizen to urge other people to commit crimes."[92]

The WRL's moderate policy on civil disobedience also alienated its radical faction. At the next executive committee meeting on 9 August, Jim Peck endorsed direct action and civil disobedience, condemned the League for its "weasel stand" and "remain-legal policy," [93] and resigned from the executive committee. His resignation letter forcefully presented the radical position:

> The only real stand of opposition to the draft is to urge defiance of it. To merely adopt a motion condemning it, as the WRL did, and to resolve to work for its repeal, is in effect no opposition at all. If the WRL should adopt a defiance [sic] stand and were prosecuted for it, the publicity and other resulting effects would be the greatest shot in the arm the League [sic] has ever had. . . .
>
> If the national executive committee takes such a weasel stand on an all important issue in this period of relative calm, what position will it take in a period of war hysteria? The function of the War Resisters League should be to resist war. But resisting war is incompatible with remaining legal. Every step in the struggle against war is illegal and the more militant and effective is the struggle, the more illegal it becomes. It seems to me that members of the national executive committee should realize this after their experiences in world war 2 [sic]. [94]

The resignations of Cornell and Peck demonstrate the dilemma over means (political/educational versus civil disobedience) and ends (single-issue versus multi-issue) that confronted radical pacifists during the Cold War. By decade's end there would be more resignations and the WRL would be turning more clearly toward civil disobedience. The League did not officially endorse tax resistance or nonregistration; however, it did flirt with civil disobedience, and a significant number of its radical members advocated or practiced nonresistance, tax refusal, and other forms of direct action and civil disobedience. [95]

Radicals viewed nonregistration and tax resistance as heroic and logical extensions of war resistance. However, traditionalists criticized such protests as counterproductive departures from the League's long-standing goals. The debate over the proper relationship with CNVR and Peacemakers radicalized the League and moved it toward civil disobedience and a broader program. The same debate created a chasm between radicals and traditionalists.

### Nonviolent Direct Action and the Journey of Reconciliation

Another example of the WRL's shift in programs and methods, and of its sharper focus on the causes of war and violence, was its role in the early postwar civil rights movement. In April 1947, in one of the earliest postwar applications of nonviolent direct action to the civil rights movement, sixteen men embarked on a Journey of Reconciliation, a two-week interracial bus trip through the upper South to test compliance with the Supreme Court's recent *Morgan v. Virginia* decision, which prohibited segregation in interstate transportation. The challenge precipitated twelve arrests for challenging seat assignments.

CORE's leading historians have contended that the journey, which was planned and led by George Houser and Bayard Rustin and jointly sponsored by the FOR and CORE, "depended on the initiative and idealism of a small group of pacifists."[96] Yet past accounts of the journey ignore the role of League members in what the *WRL News* termed "an experiment in a non-violent approach to racial segregation." Of the sixteen participants in the journey—half of them black, the other half white—eight were League members (three blacks and five whites). Women were excluded from the journey on the grounds that their involvement would trigger greater resistance among Southerners, especially among those who were obsessed with social mixing between white women and black men.[97] The League's involvement was indirect, being limited to fact that its members participated; even so, the Journey of Reconciliation is a splendid example of a nonviolent direct action project designed to advance social justice. It was projects like this that radical members wanted the League to sponsor and organize.

Leaving Washington on 9 April 1947, the participants split into two groups and boarded Greyhound and Trailways buses. Before leaving the capital they engaged in sociodramas, strategy sessions, and discussions on nonviolence. Over the next two weeks the participants, who were housed and fed in local black homes, addressed thirty church, college, and NAACP groups, most of them black. They made twenty-six tests of bus company policies and incurred twelve arrests. Their most harrowing confrontation and the most significant arrests took place in Chapel Hill, North Carolina. Joe Felmet and Andrew Johnson took seats in the front of the bus and were asked by the driver to move. When they refused, they were arrested. Rustin and Igal Roodenko moved up to the seat vacated by Johnson and Felmet; this prompted "much discussion"—and their arrest.[98]

The bus was delayed for two hours. During that time, a taxi driver at the station slugged Jim Peck in the head, accusing him of "coming down here to stir up the niggers." The activists were threatened further. Fearing that more violence would follow, they left town before nightfall.[99]

After the journey, Houser and Rustin offered "general observations" to support the thesis that nonviolent direct action might promote Southern civil rights. They wrote that most Southerners lacked knowledge and understanding of the *Morgan* decision and as a result responded to the "tests" with "confusion." Generally speaking, white passengers were "apathetic." Most blacks reacted first with fear and then with caution and "follow[ed] the dominant reaction of the bus." It seemed that Southern opinion on race relations was neither monolithic nor extreme; rather, it seemed to be in flux and amenable to change through education and nonviolent resistance. As the trip progressed, news of the project preceded the activists. This prompted discussion among police and local bus drivers, who in the process learned about the *Morgan* decision. Moreover, the power of example shaped behavior. "When cautious Negroes saw resistant Negroes sitting in the front unmolested," the authors reported, "many moved forward, too." In addition, Houser and Rustin argued that the interracial composition of the project reduced tensions by casting the issue in terms of "progressives and democrats, white and black" rather than white versus black.[100]

Houser and Rustin emphasized the important role that authority figures such as police and bus drivers played in advancing or blocking peaceful social change. They reported that the police, in response to the courteous, nonviolent behavior of the participants, were "polite and calm"[101] during the twelve arrests. Realizing that nonviolent direct action offered the most effective means for a powerless minority to resist the dominant power system, the authors argued:

> Without exception those arrested behaved in a nonviolent fashion. They acted without fear, spoke quietly and firmly, showing great consideration for the police and bus drivers, and repeatedly pointed to the fact that they expected the police to do their duty as they saw it. We cannot overemphasize the necessity for this courteous and intelligent conduct while breaking with the caste system. We believe that the reason the police behaved politely was that there was not the slightest provocation in the attitude of the resisters. On the contrary, we tried at all times to understand *their* attitude and position first. . . .
>
> It is our belief that without direct action on the part of groups and individuals, the Jim Crow pattern in the South cannot be broken down. We are equally certain that such direct action must be nonviolent.[102]

In the most significant trial, in June 1947, Rustin, Roodenko, Johnson, and Felmet were convicted of violating North Carolina's Jim Crow laws. Expressing the most contempt for the white defendants, the judge sentenced Roodenko and Felmet to thirty days on the road gang; he then let Rustin and Johnson off with a small fine and costs. The four appealed, but an all-white jury confirmed the conviction and the judge increased the sentences of the two black defendants, requiring all four men to serve thirty days. The North Carolina Supreme Court upheld the decision. To avoid prejudicing another case that had stronger constitutional merits, the FOR and CORE decided not to appeal the case to the U.S. Supreme

Court. In March 1949, Rustin, Roodenko, and Felmet returned to North Carolina and served twenty-two days of hard labor; Johnson declined to return. While the three were serving their sentences, Ted Walser, leader of FOR-New York and a member of the WRL's executive committee, wrote Roodenko: "We honor you for being willing to run risks and employ non-violence in the great struggle that is being waged and must be waged against racial discrimination." [103]

The Journey of Reconciliation did not stimulate CORE's growth, nor did it help the organization raise funds, nor did it force bus companies to end their Jim Crow policies to comply with *Morgan*. However, it did generate publicity and stimulate interest in nonviolent techniques and civil rights, and thus it provided the foundation for more successful protests in the 1960s. For instance, the better-known Freedom Rides of 1961 were modeled on the Journey of Reconciliation. "More important," the historians of CORE argue, "the Journey, by placing a spotlight on nonviolent direct action, functioned as one of the many events that gradually were to make this type of protest respectable, even fashionable." [104] It also made nonviolent direct action attractive and compelling to young militants in the peace and civil rights movements. The WRL did not contribute to the project financially or organizationally. That being said, the involvement of its leaders in the journey is more evidence that the League was moving toward nonviolent direct action and a broader agenda of social justice. [105]

As it turned out, the WRL's ambivalence toward civil disobedience as a means of advancing civil rights was short-lived. In April 1948, one year after the journey, the WRL applauded A. Philip Randolph and Grant Reynolds, leaders of the Committee Against Jimcrow in Military Service and Training, when they told the Senate Armed Services Committee they would urge draft-age whites and blacks both not to register and to join a national civil disobedience movement unless Congress abolished racial discrimination in the proposed Selective Service and Universal Military Training programs. "Greatly impressed" by the Randolph-Reynolds project, the League offered its "fullest moral support," declaring that "we are convinced that nonviolent resistance is the most effective tactic for combating injustices in our present-day world." [106] During the next major civil rights test—Montgomery 1955—the League again offered explicit support for nonviolent social protest, which would achieve a new level of legitimacy in America.

### Barometers of Radicalization: The WRL Annual Conferences

The WRL's annual weekend conferences provided a venue for the important debate over pacifist means and ends. They also offered a valuable forum for charting the League's growing commitment to direct action and civil disobedience. They were held in the wooded New Jersey hills outside New York City. Participants engaged in singing, softball, hiking, bird watching, and many informal exchanges; they also shared experiences that helped build a vibrant radical pacifist community. In June 1946, at its first postwar conference, the League debated its future direction and the most effective means of war resistance. Nearly half the one hundred participants were World War II COs. Bayard Rustin, released from Lewisburg prison that week, captivated the assembly with his singing. Abraham Kaufman, who championed the League's traditional enrollment and fellowship functions, opened the conference by comparing the organization "to a sharp pebble in the shoe of society, a small but bothersome conscience to the body politic." [107]

Most participants supported the idea of a socialist-pacifist third party, and agreed that an international pacifist movement needed to be established. But there was a lot of disagreement over the means for attaining peace. One group pointed to the experience of CNVR and Peacemakers and stressed the importance of changing society's political and economic structure; another group emphasized the need to transform the spiritual life of individuals. Not all participants supported moves to adopt "a more definite philosophy" for the League. Evan Thomas and Jessie Hughan rejected proposals that the League embrace a collective philosophy beyond simple war resistance. In their view, such a measure would prove "impossible," as well as detrimental to the diversity of views expressed in the League. [108]

The more radical 1947 conference demonstrated the shift toward direct action, civil disobedience, and a multi-issue agenda. With the endorsement of the WRL's executive committee, the 1947 conference resolved that "the WRL adapt its literature and activities to the promotion of political, economic, and social revolution by non-violent means." [109] The same executive committee, in a tie vote, rejected a more radical resolution that conference participants had overwhelmingly endorsed:

BE IT RESOLVED, that in addition to promoting individual conscientious objection the WRL work for the three following aims:

    1—To develop organized resistance to war, including a general strike against war, refusal to perform military or allied service, and refusal to engage in the manufacture of armaments;

    2—To promote the study and practice of non-violent revolutionary activities, seeking to accomplish by non-violent, democratic means the transfer of economic and political power from small groups of business and political leaders to the people themselves;

3—To promote the study and practice of effective political, educational and cooperative action for the elimination of the cause of war;

Specifically, we urge that power should be decentralized by the development of workers' control of factories, mines, shops and farms and we urge that the WRL oppose all the causes of war.[110]

This motion, which aimed to eliminate the economic causes of war and to "develop organized resistance to war," implied civil disobedience. The League's executive committee, which was still divided over civil disobedience, objected to the clauses on "workers' control" and the "general strike against war."[111] The opposition to a general strike is inexplicable in view of the League's history, philosophy, and postwar orientation. The resolution, which was defeated, nonetheless provides an accurate indication of the growing militancy within the League.

Other actions taken at the conference displayed a militant impulse. A. J. Muste advocated nonregistration, tax resistance, and picketing munitions plants. Also, the conference urged the League to extend "moral support and take action" to abolish racial segregation and discrimination.[112] This was two months after League members participated in the Journey of Reconciliation, and several weeks after a North Carolina court sentenced Rustin and Roodenko to thirty days on a chain gang for their part in this historic project.[113]

In 1948 the WRL considered its response to the new conscription legislation. During sessions on world government, political action, and direct action, the League's contending currents put forward alternative strategies for confronting conscription and war. Clearly, there was significant support within the League for direct action rather than traditional political activities. After Roy Kepler reported on the Resist Conscription Committee, most participants expressed support for a program of civil disobedience. Examples of direct action were offered that might guide League policy. One was the 1943 Danish general strike, which forced the German occupying forces to modify their demands.

After this discussion of direct action, the forum debated the League's response to the 1948 conscription law. Kaufman championed political action and opposed civil disobedience; however, most speakers endorsed the Resist Conscription Committee's statement, which called for young men to refuse to comply with the draft. Perhaps Dave Dellinger best expressed the sentiments of those radicals within the League who championed the Resist Conscription Committee, direct action, and civil disobedience: "People need hints as to what they should do. Advice is needed. We shouldn't be cautious. If enough people register smoothly, war *will* be upon us. We must use DA [direct action] and propaganda right away. We mustn't solace ourselves that the government will allow us to circularize a few leaflets during the war." [114]

Before the conference adjourned, the WRL affirmed its 1944 statement on conscription. Though there clearly was support for even more radical resistance, the resolution was silent on direct action and civil disobedience. The conference did, however, pass several resolutions that demonstrated the League's shift toward direct action and civil disobedience. In a resolution later adopted by the League's executive committee, the conference "commend[ed] the Committee to Oppose a Jim Crow Army for use of non-violent techniques in their work in the Civil Disobedience Campaign." [115] Other resolutions extended "moral support" [116] to League members practicing tax refusal and recommended that League members utilize both political action and direct action. [117]

The 1949 conference continued this militant spirit. Dellinger, the most forceful proponent of direct action, proclaimed that "all war resistance should start with people and not from congressional representatives." Furthermore, he declared, "pacifism is a revolutionary ideal; it calls for economic and political change. There is a need for a Karl Marx of pacifism, need for a leadership group, need for a basic pacifist literature." [118] Albon Man recalls that Dellinger, who recommended Leon Trotsky's *History of the Russian Revolution,* was "strongly influenced by the histories of past revolutions." [119] But Dellinger did more than read and talk: he also helped lead radical pacifist projects that endorsed egalitarian political and economic power projects such as CNVR, Peacemakers, the Glen Gardner intentional community, and *Alternative.* And while his rhetoric often did not resonate with American political culture, Dellinger did try to fuse radical pacifism with decentralized socialism and make both relevant to the broader working class and masses.

The 1950 conference devoted itself to exploring the strengths and weaknesses of the pacifist movement and to "molding the new WRL program." [120] League members were challenged to reexamine "dearly-held assumptions" and "old dogmas." [121] Radical members were impatient with the continued reliance on education and the enrollment of individual war resisters; they viewed both as tepid and anachronistic responses to the atomic age. Although the WRL Declaration committed League members "to strive for the removal of the causes of war," [122] radicals criticized the League for not developing a realistic "program of action" [123] to transform intentions into realities.

Charles Bloomstein, an ex-CPSer, opened the 1950 conference with an incisive survey of the League's history. Then he posed the central question confronting the League: Should it "continue as an enrollment agency "or" become an organization of tightly knit, committed individuals who are well disciplined in non-violent direct action techniques?" He contended that the League's traditional program of education and enrollment was premised on nineteenth-century values of rationalism and individualism and was "not adequate" in the present era of atomic warfare, authoritarianism, and sharp ideology.[124]

The conference submitted several recommendations to the executive committee. Without repudiating the WRL's traditional functions, two major proposals sought to move the League in a more radical direction. Dellinger, who had consistently championed a multi-issue, nonviolent direct action movement with the power to address social ills and resist war, presented the most radical proposal: "The WRL should include among its various functions an attempt to develop a Gandhi-like movement of non-violent civil disobedience within this country and devote staff-time and money to that end. This does not mean that all of the members are expected to participate in such a program, nor does it exclude other non-violent functions and activities." [125]

Bloomstein replied that the League was too diverse to adopt "a one-purpose program," and he suggested a compromise between the traditionalist and radical positions. He proposed that the League adopt a "service relationship" toward both radical "groupings" within the WRL and outside "direct action groups" [126] that it supported. Under this plan, the League would provide funds, staff, and publicity to assist such groups while retaining its own pluralistic identity.

Frieda Lazarus, who represented the League's traditionalist wing, offered a third proposal to counter the more radical resolutions presented by Bloomstein and Dellinger: "Any major issue which will commit the League should be submitted to the membership in the form of a referendum." [127] Existing records do not indicate whether the WRL's executive committee approved these proposals; clearly, though, advocates of an organized, nonviolent direct action movement—committed to direct action and civil disobedience to promote a multi-issue peace and justice program—were on the ascendancy.

It is difficult to judge how much support there actually was within the League for direct action and civil disobedience. Neither conference participants nor resolutions necessarily represented the views of the League as a whole. Those who attended the League conferences were activists and so were more likely to endorse radical positions than the general membership. Most League members probably opposed civil disobedience, and while these members extended support to pacifists who participated in civil disobedience as individuals, on moral and practical grounds they did not want the League as an organization to endorse civil disobedience. Most members considered it morally wrong for the League to commit its members to controversial, illegal positions without a consensus or referendum. They also contended that civil disobedience would alienate League members and potential supporters alike and invite prosecution by the government and persecution by conservative groups. The League's democratic heritage and the individualistic ethos of its members made it highly unlikely that the executive committee would commit members to illegal actions in the absence of a clear consensus. But at the same time, more and more League members—especially CO veterans—were advocating and practicing direct action and civil disobedience, though some hesitated to commit the League to this position out of concern that government prosecution might destroy the League.

## Traditionalist Demise and Radical Consolidation

In September 1947, after nineteen years as the WRL's executive secretary, Abraham Kaufman announced his decision to resign effective 1 January 1948. He was stepping down for various personal and political reasons. After World War II ended he felt "restless," "irritable," "tired," and "persecuted." [128] These things made him more egotistical and less efficient. Also, he wanted to devote more time to his family and other interests, such as the Socialist Party and the Brooklyn Ethical Culture Society. In the summer of 1946 he took a three-month leave of absence to escape the demands and politics of the League office. This leave failed to rejuvenate him. Now that the war was over, he felt less needed. He was thirty-nine and he did not want his livelihood dependent on the political vagaries of the League. [129]

There is no question that the League's ideological divisions, political in-fighting, and new orientation had taken their toll on Kaufman. According to Frieda Lazarus, his friend and ally, he was chaffing at his "secondary position" [130] and loss of control in the postwar League. Kaufman himself acknowledged that he had a proprietary interest in the League that "made it difficult for me to share responsibility." In sum, he resented the radical shift in the League and his own loss of authority and prestige. [131]

Kaufman's letter of resignation also revealed an ambiguity in his thinking on war resistance. He still accepted the importance of pacifist witness, educational work, and an association of war resisters that could unite and provide fellowship to radical pacifists; yet at the same time he was beginning to question the League's relevance in the atomic age. "I do not have the conviction that I once did that the work which the League is doing is relevant to the solution of the problem of war prevention," he confessed. "Whether World War III comes, will, I feel, be a matter of accident." Despite these doubts and his resignation as executive secretary, Kaufman stood for and was elected to the League's 1948 executive committee.[132]

During July and August 1948, Kaufman returned to serve as acting executive secretary.[133] The political and ideological divisions that marked his postwar relationship with the radicals and led to his resignation remained. These divisions were visible in his exchanges with Frances Witherspoon, James Peck, and David Dellinger. In mid-1948, Kaufman and Witherspoon—who were old friends—corresponded on the issue of civil disobedience and the Peacemakers/Resist Conscription Committee program. Witherspoon expressed "very great sympathy" with the Resist Conscription Committee perspective[134] and with radicals in the League who were advocating civil disobedience to combat conscription. She also suggested that such a course was preferable to the League's tepid response to World War II:

> I'm not sure that our very legal behavior in the past has netted us anything more than a certain amount of aid and comfort to C.O.s and the preservation of an organization which seems now to be devoted to "resisting" itself quite as much as to the big job of resisting war. I was shocked, you will recall, at the statement issued at the beginning of World War II, by the Executive Committee—(of which I was not then a member)—that "we are going to be good and not do anything you'd object to" statement. Also you will remember that I was a decidedly dissenting pacifist in World War I to the "Now, boys, you must register and make your protest later" dictum of [John Haynes] Holmes, Thomas (Norman), Hughan, etc. How much better had the World War I C.O.'s not registered—the straighter course morally, in my opinion, as well as much better physically, as things worked out. (one year in jail instead of 20 years after court martial).[135]

In his reply, Kaufman commented on both his own and the membership's "sense of dispiritedness, fatigue and futility." He added, however, that "a few souls" still had the "consuming fire and sense of mission and sense of importance of the work which is necessary for a movement of the future." Though he disagreed with the radicals, he credited "some" members of Peacemakers with displaying this passion. He still rejected civil disobedience, but he also recognized that Peacemakers had made an important contribution to the peace movement. However, he insisted that it and similar groups, such as the Resist Conscription Committee, should remain independent from the League:

> I consider the question of approval of the idea of there being a PEACEMAKERS group and the identifying the League with it are two different issues. And, that

one can be for the first and vigorously opposed to the second. That's my view. I am glad they have the courage and faith to undertake this move. I do not believe the (potential) risk and cost involved is commensurate with its effect on our fellow men. You cannot hope more than I that this is a mistaken estimate.[136]

With the younger, more confrontational radicals such as Peck and Dellinger, Kaufman's relationship was less cordial. Several observers believed that personality differences rather than ideological principles motivated Kaufman's (and Lazarus's) opposition to the radicals and to the League's new orientation.[137]

In an attack on Peck, Kaufman injected the explosive issue of communism into League politics. During a May 1950 discussion within the executive committee on whether to appoint Peck as interim executive secretary, Kaufman accused him of following "the 'soviet line' on issues other than militarism."[138] This irresponsible charge triggered a bitter exchange. Replying to Kaufman a week later, Peck deplored his resort to "McCartheyite [sic] hysteria":

The fact is that I am opposed to the Soviet setup—in particular to its complete denial of civil rights, to its censorship of the arts and to its government-company union structure under which unions have been transformed into organizations for speeding up production instead of for improving the workers' conditions. . . . Of course, I am also opposed to the Wall Street-dominated U.S. setup and, since I happen to live in the U.S., most of my actions have been directed primarily against social injustices here rather than those in Russia.

I consider the charge you made against me a dangerous symptom of the hysteria of our times.[139]

This exchange grew even more bitter. Kaufman criticized Peck's support for civil disobedience and repeated his red charge, accusing Peck of criticizing American but not Soviet policy in League discussions: "I felt it unwise to have at the center of things a person who places a premium upon illegality in choice of projects, and one who, except that he rejected militarism, followed the soviet line in foreign policy matters."[140] In a follow-up letter, Peck claimed that his greater criticism of America was justified since the press blindly depicted American foreign policy as a "peace policy" and Soviet foreign policy as "evil." Peck then attacked Kaufman for using as "exhibit A" a matchbook cover that Peck had designed criticizing "Wall Street imperialism without mentioning Russian imperialism." "I admit that the slogan should have been better," Peck confessed, "but, after all, how much can you say on a matchbook?"[141]

As leaders of the League's traditionalist and radical factions, Kaufman and Dellinger had an especially tense relationship. Both were ideological and strong-willed, and they clashed over the direction the WRL should take. Dellinger lived in Glen Gardner, a New Jersey intentional community, where he codirected the Liberation Press printing cooperative. Because of his work there, he spent little time in New York. Even so, he and Kaufman were personal and political rivals. Kaufman considered Dellinger a sanctimonious newcomer who had little respect for the League's original function—or for traditionalists like himself, who had built the League, valued its institutional survival, and opposed its turn toward civil disobedience and a multi-issue agenda.[142] And Dellinger no doubt viewed Kaufman as a timid peace bureaucrat.

The internecine struggle that had plagued the WRL for more than half a decade came to a head on 9 November 1950 during a meeting of the executive committee. The issue at hand was the League's policy toward the Metropolitan Board for Conscientious Objectors and a peace conference in Sheffield, England. The Metropolitan Board had been established in August 1940 by the United Pacifist Committee to provide counseling for COs from New York, New Jersey, and Connecticut, and became an independent agency in 1942. Its founders included Kaufman and Lazarus. The League referred draftees to the Metropolitan Board, which included many League members and operated from League headquarters.[143]

At the 9 November meeting, the executive committee considered a motion to refer area residents who contacted the WRL for draft information "immediately and solely"[144] to the Metropolitan Board. This motion would have transformed an informal working practice into official League policy and endorsed the board's moderate philosophy. Albon Man, a radical, challenged the motion, criticizing the absence of absolutists on the Metropolitan Board. He also denounced the agency for distinguishing between COs and draft evaders and for working with Selective Service on the basis of these distinctions—a practice that, he asserted, legitimized the subjective Selective Service policy of conditioning CO status on "sincerity."[145]

Kaufman and Lazarus vigorously rebutted these charges. Kaufman argued that the distinction between genuine COs and draft evaders was valid. Furthermore, if the Metropolitan Board was unrepresentative it was because of an absence of a "right wing"[146] that supported CPS and NSBRO, not because of a lack of absolutists. After debate, the executive committee formed a committee to investigate the policies of the Metropolitan Board, thus deferring a decision. In December 1950 a League committee recommended that the Metropolitan Board maintain its policy on representation (which had included absolutists before they resigned). However, the same committee offered no guidance on two contentious issues: whether conscientious objectors should be distinguished from draft dodgers; and whether such judgments should be shared with government officials. After the report was issued, the executive committee voted to ask the Metropolitan Board to add absolutists to its ranks.[147]

The communist-sponsored Second Congress of the World Congress of Defenders of Peace had invited the WRL to send an observer to its November conference in Sheffield, England. At its meeting of 9 November, the executive committee considered its response to this invitation. Supported by Lazarus, Kaufman—a staunch anticommunist socialist—strongly opposed sending an observer to Sheffield. The decision was made not to send a delegate, on the grounds that the one-sided Sheffield appeal endorsed the procommunist Stockholm Pledge and supported Soviet foreign policy. However, the executive committee did vote to ask either the Peace Pledge Union—the League's British counterpart—or the War Resisters' International to send an observer. Hughan broke with Kaufman on this issue, urging the League not "to prejudge" the communist-organized conference or "to fall for the current propaganda."[148]

At this point Kaufman sprang the news that he was resigning from the executive committee *and* the League, declaring that he "did not care to be in a group which wishes to send an observer to a communist-dominated group." In his resignation letter, which he submitted the following day, he criticized the decision to participate in the Sheffield conference and charged that "the group in control of the executive committee has destroyed the League's usefulness as a genuine antiwar group, clearly opposed to *all* totalitarians." He then lectured the League on the consequences of its postwar shift: "As long as the League continues its present effort to be more than an educational organization and tries to enter the area of politics, it will find itself torn forever between support of anarchistic impossibilists and alliance with Leninist communists. In either case, its main purpose has been destroyed."[149]

Clearly, Kaufman's disillusionment with the WRL's postwar direction had only grown since his resignation as executive secretary in 1947. Several months after quitting the League entirely, he explained why in more detail:

> In the three years which followed, I have regretted the trend in the executive committee toward a "purist" or "absolutist" frame of reference which seemed to me would, at *best,* narrow the League, to a small sect of self-satisfied persons, isolated from the "sinners" of society, and having no effect upon society. At *worst,* it seemed, this absolutism would, bit by bit, drive away the less absolutist League members; it would unnecessarily make the League and its members vulnerable

(with justification) to charges of pro-communism, support of draft dodgers and conducting a conspiracy against the government. I had become quite discouraged in dealing with people who place a premium upon illegality of action.[150]

He then turned his attention to the Metropolitan Board:

> The investigation of the Metropolitan CO Board by the WRL—its very basis is so shocking that I would not wish to be in a group whose executive committee members work on the assumption that pacifists may not distinguish between COs and draft dodgers; and that it is wrong to use the channels of government agencies for securing proper treatment for CO's. . . . I am often led to believe that some of the executive committee are objectors to government almost more than to militarism.[151]

At its next meeting, in December 1950, the executive committee formed a committee to meet with Kaufman with the goal of finding an accommodation that would allow him to return. This effort failed. In other business, Lazarus accused the League of adopting direct action projects without a membership referendum. Furthermore, she disapproved of the radicals' "tendency to create a superior group of absolutists within the League." [152] In response to these complaints by Kaufman and Lazarus, the executive committee scheduled a special meeting to review the issues that had led to Kaufman's resignation and the present imbroglio. Before this 11 January 1951 meeting took place, however, Lazarus and Evan Thomas also resigned from the League.[153]

After two decades of active involvement in the WRL, Lazarus resigned over its new absolutist leadership and changed orientation. She resented the "anarchistic" and Peacemakers' elements, accusing them of controlling and disrupting the League with their absolutist and controversial agenda of civil disobedience. She also lamented the emergence of a moral hierarchy which assumed that "only former [CO] prison men know what sacrifice for a cause means," [154] and expressed her dislike of Peacemakers' cavalier treatment of Kaufman, one of her closest allies. Finally, as an active member of the Metropolitan Board, she condemned the hostile policy of the WRL's executive committee toward the agency.

Thomas, the former WRL chairman, submitted his resignation in mid-December. Kaufman and Lazarus had acted for political and ideological reasons; in contrast, Thomas resigned over his doubts about pacifism's relevance in an age dominated by the atom bomb and communist expansionism. While professing that organized "non-violent resistance is the only rational solution to war and to tyranny," he concluded sadly that pacifists were "too divided in policies and motives to work together effectively." "Nothing that we war resisters have done or can do now brings peace," he lamented. "This is far and away the greatest disappointment of my life, but it is a fact."[155] Confronted with the dual threats of atomic warfare and communist aggression, pacifism's apparent impotence tormented Thomas and corroded his faith in its efficacy.

The resignations of Kaufman, Lazarus, and Thomas, and the WRL "Working Program" marked the triumph of the radicals and the end of the first phase of the League's history.[156]

A special session of the executive committee held on 11 January 1951 focused on Peacemakers' role in the WRL and the subsequent division of the League into radical and traditionalist factions. During this marathon session there were expressions of both support and criticism for Peacemakers; there was also unanimous agreement that "internecine warfare" had damaged the League and would have to stop. Most members, including Hughan, argued that the League should accommodate both currents.[157]

The executive committee appointed a subcommittee to formulate a program that would be acceptable to both traditionalists and radicals. Most of the committee members were centrists. In April 1951 the executive committee issued that subcommittee's report, "WRL Working Program for the Immediate Future." This report functioned as a discussion paper, and League members were invited to submit comments and request referenda on specific items. The four-page program addressed the immediate issues confronting the League. It was a compromise document, and the program it outlined was more radical than the League's traditional enrollment function but less radical than Peacemakers' absolutist alternative. It was also a transitional document that departed from past policies but did not repudiate the League's longstanding principles.

Under "Individual War Resistance," the program restated the League's traditional commitment to support all war resisters whether or not the League favored their specific course of action. In a departure from the League's World War II policy, the program stated that in the future the WRL would endorse only total exemption from conscription for conscientious objectors, and would not seek other government provisions. Mindful of the disillusionment with CPS, the League also would not help administer any alternative program under conscription.

The most controversial section was the one devoted to "Possible Legal Restriction of WRL Activity." It adopted an ambivalent, compromise position on civil disobedience. The executive committee did not advocate civil disobedience, but it did note that government legislation might some day prohibit the League's normal activities, at which point civil disobedience would be necessary. For instance, the 1949 Larry Gara case, which involved the bogus charge of counseling nonregistration, had made it plain that the government was ready to prosecute pacifists who extended even moral support to nonregistrants. However, the executive committee promised that members would be polled before the League committed itself to civil disobedience that might risk its legal existence.

The section on "Relations With Stalinists and Stalinist Groups" condemned "Stalinist Communists" [158] and declared the Soviet Union the most powerful authoritarian force threatening freedom and world peace. The WRL would refuse to cooperate with Stalinist groups; however, it would be willing to send representatives to Stalinist-dominated events to express its position. The League would continue to exclude Stalinists who were willing to fight for the Soviet Union; it would also refuse to support their claims for conscientious objector status. Significantly, however, the report advocated civil rights for communists.

The proposals on "membership," "pacifist education," and "civil defense" prompted little controversy. The WRL would continue to enroll COs in a common registry, publish and distribute literature, and educate the public about pacifism, nonviolence, and CO concerns through projects and other means. In a departure from its World War II policy, the League pledged that in the future it would not permit the government to review its membership list. Finally, the League vowed that while it would support those aspects of civil defense that provided humanitarian relief, it would dissociate itself from all psychological measures designed to prepare the nation for war.[159]

The *WRL News* printed select comments that readers submitted regarding the Working Program. Charles Mackintosh, a California WRL member who admired Peacemakers but supported a limited, traditional role for the League, offered the most trenchant criticism. He charged that the new program represented an "essential departure" from WRL principles."[160] Before engaging in illegal action, he argued, the League's staff should obtain the consent of every member. His central charge, however, was that the Working Program would transform the WRL from a loose league of individual war resisters into a centralized organization:

> The report proposes a league which is a solid personality or entity of itself which opposes, demands, recommends, campaigns, takes no part, advises, supports, fosters, will resist, strives, sponsors, tries, carries, recognizes, makes its own factual investigation, does not support or cooperate, recognizes the need to demonstrate, takes advantage of every opportunity, etc. This language is possible only in a tight organization where the members see eye to eye on a very wide area and

is I believe not suitable for the WRL. . . . If the League were to officially become such an actionist organization as this Working Program would make possible, I, too, would resign.[161]

On behalf of the executive committee, Frances Ransom replied to Mackintosh that the WRL had often presented a collective position. For years, in meetings with Congress, Selective Service authorities, and the Justice Department, the League had been authorizing delegates to "recommend," "request," "urge," "support," and "condemn" various actions on its behalf.[162] Clearly, the expression of a collective League position represented a continuation of rather than a departure from policy. Traditionalists could be reassured that the League had no plans to engage in illegal projects. The provision that committed the executive committee to poll the members before compromising the League's legal status had been inserted precisely to control Peacemakers' penchant for civil disobedience. The "present Executive Committee does not intend to make the League illegal," Ransom assured Mackintosh, "but it can conceive that the government might do so."[163]

Despite Mackintosh's concerns, Peacemakers did not seize control of the WRL, nor did the League impose collective discipline. In fact, only one member of the Peacemakers faction took part in the final meeting that drafted the Working Program. Moreover, in 1951 no Peacemakers were elected to the WRL's executive committee, no Peacemakers were officers, and Dellinger was no longer the League's vice chairman. Whatever the traditionalists' fears had been, the WRL executive committee and the Working Program were centrist, not radical.

The WRI and at least one member of the WRL executive committee criticized the draft Working Program for using the term communist without distinguishing between individual, independent communists and organized communist groups. In her reply to the WRI, Ransom explained "that by 'communists' the WRL means the Stalinists and the policy statement will state it so." The Working Program, however, remained silent on the League's relationship with non-Stalinist communists.[164]

The shift in direction toward civil disobedience, direct action, and a multi-issue agenda was cemented in 1953 with two key appointments; the WRL named Roy Finch chairman and Bayard Rustin to the staff. In addition, Ralph DiGia signed on in 1955 as the League's administrative secretary. These men constituted a new generation of leaders. All three were World War II COs, and all were committed to a more radical direction for the League.[165]

Rustin's appointment also raised issues of sexual bias and freedom. In January 1953, police in Pasadena, California, discovered Rustin engaged in oral sex with two men in a parked car and arrested him on a "morals charge."[166] Rustin pleaded guilty and served sixty days in jail. A. J. Muste, arguing that Rustin had compromised the FOR, offered him the option of resignation or dismissal. Rustin resigned as the FOR's field secretary, thus ending a distinguished career with the FOR as well as his father-son relationship with Muste. Within the FOR Rustin's sexual preference had long been common knowledge. Muste had countenanced his homosexuality but worried that Rustin's open promiscuity might embarrass the FOR or enable opponents to smear it. Rustin also offered his resignation to the WRL's executive committee. It was rejected.[167]

In August 1953 the WRL sought a new executive secretary to replace Sidney Aberman, who had replaced Kaufman and now wanted to resign. A month later the League made a dual appointment, hiring Arlo Tatum as executive secretary and Rustin as program director and office secretary—a new position that allowed him to develop nonviolent projects. The hiring of Rustin presented the League with both opportunities and potential liabilities. Dellinger contended that Rustin offered the best opportunity to "revitalize the League"[168] and spread pacifism. However, several members expressed concern that Rustin's sexual activities would embarrass the WRL. Muste even resigned in protest from the executive committee. "I am glad the vote was for keeping (Bayard)," Hughan wrote, "even if we have to lose A. J. from the Executive Committee. We have decided to take a risk, knowing that there is a risk."[169] In an era of routine sexual discrimination against gays, the League by appointing Rustin was challenging prejudice within and outside its ranks and allowing merit to determine its actions. Rustin proved to be an extraordinary leader; until his resignation in 1965 he used his position to advance the role and influence of the League and nonviolence in postwar America.[170]

On Easter Day, 10 April 1955, Jessie Wallace Hughan, the WRL's founder and its dominant voice throughout World War II, died suddenly from a stroke.[171] Though the League for several years had been controlled by CO radicals of the World War II generation, Hughan's death represented the symbolic transfer of power from the traditionalists to the radicals, from the League's founding generation to those who would extend the original vision of war resistance to broader nonviolent direct action on behalf of both peace and justice.

# 7

# Nonaligned International Pacifism

The WRL and the Cold War, 1945–1955

THE WRL DISSENTED from the Cold War, McCarthyism, and the era's dominant Cold War liberal consensus. As part of a nonaligned, international peace movement, it advocated an independent "Third Camp" position that repudiated both Soviet and American Cold War blocs. It also articulated an alternative vision for a new world order—one that renounced armed force to settle international disputes and that substituted a world government and "one world community"[1] for the existing nation-state system. Finally, it condemned conscription, militarism, nationalism, imperialism, power politics, spheres of influence, and the division of the world into antagonistic political-economic-military blocs. It also rejected the United Nations on grounds that it represented an alliance of the big powers.[2]

Lawrence Wittner has demonstrated that Hiroshima and Nagasaki spawned separate communist and nonaligned peace movements that challenged the atomic bomb and the Cold War. The communist-led peace movement relied on the Communist bloc and on communists in other countries, and supported Soviet foreign policy. In contrast, the independent, nonaligned peace movement drew its core support from atomic scientists, world federalists, and international pacifist organizations such as the War Resisters' International, the International Fellowship of Reconciliation, and the Women's International League for Peace and Freedom. The WRL was part of this nonaligned peace movement, which challenged both the "realist" view of the Cold War and the one-sided communist peace movement.[3]

Historians now recognize that the fifties was an activist decade that provided a seedtime for the sixties. The WRL and radical pacifism were only two of the oppositional currents resisting the dominant culture and providing a foundation for later social change.[4] In *New York in the 50s,* Dan Wakefield profiled Ammon

Hennacy as a symbol of the decade to rebut the "Silent Generation" thesis. Wakefield admired Hennacy, a WRL member and Catholic Worker, for "his willingness to go against the grain, to challenge the conformity of the fifties."[5] David Dellinger recalled that "during the Fifties I was involved in as many activities as at any time during the Sixties, and so were at least a few hundred people whom I knew personally and thousands whom I didn't know."[6] Similarly, in late 1949 the WRL summoned its members to action. "In these dark days of the cold war," it declared, "our job is that of nurture and propagation in order to bring about an atmosphere in which pacifism can grow."[7]

The Cold War and McCarthyism encouraged conformity, suppressed radicalism, and fostered a national security crisis mentality. In opposition to this, the WRL, operating in a loose coalition with FOR-NY, Peacemakers, and the Catholic Worker, nourished an alternative vision. During the fifties the League was part of a vibrant radical pacifist community, centered in New York City, that used nonviolent direct action and civil disobedience to challenge the Cold War, McCarthyism, and Cold War liberalism. The League warned of the domestic perils of the national security state and the anticommunist crusade, arguing that while tyranny needed to be resisted, it must be done through nonviolent means that preserved freedom. The League also maintained that reform must come from within American and Soviet societies and could not be imposed from outside.[8] In addition, although the League opposed cooperation with communists and maintained its distance from them, it advocated civil liberties for them and other radicals. The League was too marginal a group to reverse Cold War policies but it did help keep the possibilities open for change, and it did sow the seeds for the nonviolent social movements of the sixties and seventies.

### International Pacifist Humanitarianism and Solidarity

Between November 1945 and October 1946 the Nuremberg war crimes tribunal tried senior Nazis for war crimes. The WRL opposed the Nuremberg trials, arguing that the Allies and the Axis had both waged murderous war and committed war crimes. Criticizing Nuremberg as selective justice, the League declared that the tribunal should punish all aggressive war and war crimes,[9] regardless of national origin and regardless of whether the judges represented victor or vanquished nations. By punishing Nazis while ignoring the Allies' actions the tribunal was fostering the illusion that there were good and bad acts of killing. The League urged the tribunal "to indict U.S. officials responsible for preparing and waging aggressive war and for perpetrating war crimes."[10] More specifically, it suggested that President Harry Truman, Secretary of War Robert

Patterson, Secretary of the Navy James Forrestal, and other officials had committed war crimes in the way they had waged war in China and Indonesia, starved inhabitants in occupied Europe, and dropped the atomic bomb. The WRL announced that it planned to ask British, French, and Dutch pacifists to take similar action against guilty officials in their own countries. All of this aside, the League's immediate postwar task was to organize humanitarian relief and support for European pacifists and COs.[11]

In the fall of 1945, under WRI auspices, the WRL started a Food Packet Plan to provide food and clothing to European and Japanese war resisters struggling to rebuild their lives amidst the physical destruction and economic dislocation of the immediate postwar years. The program, which lasted through 1951, urged WRL members and friends to "adopt" overseas war resisters and provide support for them through monthly food packets.[12] The League could not provide sponsors for every European pacifist in need, but it did offer assistance to nearly five hundred WRI members and war resisters, and it also organized special Christmas parcels. The League's plan resembled the *Politics*-sponsored Packages Abroad program that Dwight and Nancy Macdonald operated between 1945 and 1948. Like Packages Abroad, the WRL initiative was an example of citizen participation in relief efforts and small-scale "personal" politics aimed at fostering international "fraternity and solidarity."[13]

The WRL adopted war resisters from allied and "enemy" nations alike. Indeed, the League made special efforts to find sponsors for German, Austrian, and Japanese pacifists. In a related move, it recommended that church and social groups furnish food packages to support the work of Theodor Michaltscheff, a Bulgarian pacifist who had lived in Germany for fifteen years before and during World War II. After the war, Michaltscheff led a pacifist group in Hamburg that sought to promote peace through relief work with disabled ex-soldiers and refugee orphans. Michaltscheff contended that the democratic reconstruction of Europe required not military occupation but "thousands of peace-workers . . . who are not prejudiced against their former enemies."[14]

The WRL made valiant private efforts to assist pacifists in postwar Europe; at the same time, it realized that relief and reconstruction required a vast public program. "Sending food packages," the *WRL News* declared in October 1945, "is *not a substitute* for urgent messages to Congress for large-scale relief."[15] Similarly, in mid-1947 the League urged the United States to provide adequate humanitarian and reconstruction aid to Europe and Asia. "We view this as an individual as well as a public responsibility."[16]

The WRL emphasized the political importance of food policy. In September 1945 it urged members to write elected officials and newspaper editors to promote a policy of " 'NO' for *militarism* and 'YES' for *food*."[17] The League praised Dwight Macdonald's *Politics* essay, "Shall Europe Starve,"[18] a biting indictment of postwar American food policy by an influential public intellectual and editor who joined the WRL's executive committee in 1947. The League asserted that providing a "prompt and adequate" food supply would nurture good will; this in turn would shorten military occupations in Europe and Asia, foster good international relations, and provide "our best defense."[19] The League objected to the initial American policy that forbade relatives and humanitarian groups from shipping food to Germany and Japan. Arguing that the United States had sufficient food to satisfy domestic consumption and relieve global hunger, the League advocated allocating "adequate amounts"[20] of food for overseas relief, as well as rationing to avert hoarding.[21]

The League financially supported the WRI's humanitarian and relief work in limited but important ways. Beginning in 1946 it backed a WRI program that sold used postage stamps to collectors to raise money for the WRI's relief fund. The League also solicited contributions for its International Fund, which subsidized WRI humanitarian projects. This fund's activities included supporting the families of war resisters, purchasing medical supplies for European pacifists, helping war resisters obtain conscientious objector status, and assisting men who were seeking to escape nations that executed pacifists. An Italian prison CO expressed in clear but grammatically shaky English the impact of the League's humanitarian program: "Unexpectedly, it arrives to me your package,—tangible demonstration of solidarity. The fact that from beyond the Atlantic, one could know my name and consequently my situation . . . does persuade me ever more that it has been useful to attack face to face the monster, 'War.' "[22] The League also served as a clearinghouse for American pacifists who wished to correspond with Japanese, Germans, and other Europeans.[23]

The WRL also bolstered the WRI's nascent German section. Under Michaltsheff's leadership, the first postwar meeting of German pacifists took place in 1947 in Hamburg. During its first three years the German WRI sponsored public forums, published pamphlets and a monthly newspaper, and formed local chapters. By 1952, in one year, the Hamburg section had increased its membership from 95 to more than 1,000.[24]

To support the emerging pacifist movement in Germany, in mid-1952 the WRL launched a campaign that raised over $1,000 for the German WRI. George Hartmann, the League's honorary chairman, identified aid to the German WRI as "probably the most outstanding single pacifist opportunity in the world today." Reporting on his recent trip to Germany, Roy Kepler told a WRL audience that the defeated nation "is psychologically right for pacifism and war resistance." [25] The League's donations financed posters, pamphlets, and 500,000 leaflets to assist the German WRI campaign against German rearmament and inclusion in NATO.[26] Although modest, this effort nourished the embryonic peace movement in postwar Germany.

Besides providing material relief, the WRL promoted a liberal American immigration policy and helped European pacifists and displaced persons (DPs) visit and resettle in the United States. League members helped DPs enter the United States by providing them with the required affidavits of support. In early 1947 the League called for the United States to admit 400,000 people over the next four years through the use of unfilled quotas; this would have doubled the number of DPs permitted to enter. In 1950, when the United States barred Jehovah's Witnesses and "extreme pacifists," [27] the League complained to the Attorney General and the Commissioner of Immigration and Naturalization.[28]

The WRL condemned the McCarran-Walter Immigration Act (1952) for its "racist immigration barriers and exclusion of C.O.s from citizenship," [29] and it urged Truman to veto the measure. The act's repressive character was illustrated in 1952 when Stuart Morris, the leader of the English Peace Pledge Union and a member of the WRI international council, arrived in New York for a nationwide lecture tour sponsored by the WRL and the American Friends Service Committee. As a pacifist, Morris was ruled an "inadmissible alien" under the McCarran Act,[30] denied entry, and interned on Ellis Island. After two weeks he won release on appeal. For the next six weeks he addressed crowds, appeared on radio and television, and articulated a pacifist message that included criticism of American and Soviet policies. Two days before his departure the League organized a dramatic public meeting in New York, where Morris used his recent experience to link the "fight against war with [the] fight to preserve civil liberties." [31]

## The Campaign Against Cold War Conscription

The WRL participated in the postwar campaign to resist peacetime conscription and universal military training. To buttress American military power and replace the 1940 conscription law, which expired in March 1947, President Truman proposed universal military training beginning in October 1945. Congress enacted the Selective Service Act of 1948; however, opposition from congressmen, educators, religious groups, and pacifists prevented passage of the more intrusive universal military training.[32]

Between 1945 and 1948 the WRL urged its members to carry out a program of public education and political pressure to block peacetime conscription and universal military training. It asked members to write and visit their local editors, newspapers, and congressmen; write key Washington officials; dramatize the issue through radio debates, interviews, and skits; conduct mock CO tribunals; form local committees and hold public rallies; distribute literature; fast; and forward to WRL headquarters the names of local leaders who might be sympathetic to the League. It would send these people anticonscription materials. In Chicago, WRL members distributed more than 10,000 matchbooks with covers exhorting citizens to "STRIKE A LIGHT FOR FREEDOM! DEFEAT UNIVERSAL MILITARY TRAINING (Peacetime Conscription)."[33]

The League warned that peacetime military conscription was an unprecedented departure from the American civilian tradition and that such a policy threatened to militarize the nation, erode individual freedom, subvert democratic society, encourage totalitarianism, create a permanent military bureaucracy, and foster international conflict. Roy Kepler told the House Armed Services Committee that conscription was a cause rather than a result of war, warning that the "logic of war is the logic of conscription—as it is the logic which leads to the concentration camps, to the incinerators, to the Hiroshimas, and to hydrogen bombs."[34] In the nuclear age, survival dictated that humankind combat tyranny through nonviolent resistance. Finally, the WRL challenged the policies of militarization and conscription, the intent of which was to thwart communist expansion. The League argued that the Soviet threat was not military but social, political, and economic, and that to counter it the United States must promote economic development, decolonialization, and conciliatory diplomacy to assist the world's impoverished people.

WRL members involved in the Break With Conscription group proposed returning their draft cards to protest the continuation of conscription. In September 1946 the WRL's executive committee declared its readiness "to support any conscientious objector in his actions of non-cooperation with conscription."[35] Six months later, however, the executive committee qualified its position. While reiterating its policy of supporting members who chose to destroy or return their draft cards to "break with conscription," the League refused officially either to endorse or participate in the civil disobedience action that was conducted on Lincoln's Day, 1947.[36]

During the nationwide Lincoln's Day demonstration more than 135 WRL members joined 1,000 protestors from twenty communities. Two hundred men either destroyed their draft cards or returned them to the president. The largest demonstration took place in New York City and was chaired by Bayard Rustin. A. J. Muste, David Dellinger, and Dwight Macdonald addressed two hundred sympathizers, who witnessed sixty-three men destroy their draft cards in the presence of police, reporters, and the FBI. Dellinger, representing the Committee for Nonviolent Revolution, declared the protest "the first significant antiwar demonstration since before Pearl Harbor" and a "good start" toward building an antiwar movement. Defending the action, Macdonald added that "pacifism to me is primarily a way of actively struggling against injustice and inhumanity; . . . My kind of pacifism may be called 'non-violent resistance.'"[37]

In 1948 the WRL and its members—some of whom also acted through Peacemakers—organized a number of actions against Selective Service and universal military training. To protest the enactment of the 1948 draft, Kepler organized a WRL White House demonstration on 5 June. Warning that the draft meant a "goosestepping" America, the protest featured eight men dressed as Uncle Sam in red, white, and blue suits. On 30 August, to mark the first day of registration under the new draft law, thirty League members joined Peacemakers and the Campaign to Resist Military Segregation and picketed two New York City high schools that were serving as registration sites. Pickets also marched in Boston, Cincinnati, Philadelphia, San Juan (Puerto Rico), and other cities. In mid-September two hundred clergy, some of whom were WRL members, issued a statement condemning war and conscription and urging men of draft age to refuse to register.[38]

With the support of WRL comrades, Jim Peck staged a unique protest. Max Kauten, a close friend and anarchist CO who had done time with Peck in Danbury, painted "Veto the Draft" on a white shirt. On the morning of 23 June, Peck and Kepler took a train to Washington, where Peck entered the White House with a group of tourists. Underneath his coat and tie he wore the white shirt emblazoned with the message that identified his mission. His coat and long-sleeved shirt also concealed a chain and padlock. Inside, he chained himself to a staircase bannister, removed his coat to expose the slogan, and passed out antidraft leaflets for five minutes before guards broke the chain and took him to Secret Service headquarters. There, an agent questioned Peck, demanding that he produce his Communist Party card. To deny Peck publicity, the Secret Service did not arrest him. However, while Peck was carrying out his protest inside the White House, Kepler was outside distributing a statement explaining the deed and notifying the press, which publicized the daring protest.[39]

For the WRL the most significant event to arise from the 1948 Selective Service Act was the conviction of Larry Gara, a League member, World War II prison CO, and history professor at Bluffton College. In 1949, Gara was convicted of having "counseled, aided, and abetted" a student's refusal to register. Even though he had told the student that he must make his own decision, Gara was convicted and sentenced to eighteen months in prison.[40]

To protest Gara's conviction, the WRL urged members to write the president, the attorney general, and Congress and to raise the issue of free speech and conscience in their churches and union halls. The League also cosponsored a demonstration in Washington. In July 1949, while Truman was performing the "warlike act" of signing the NATO treaty, sixty protestors picketed the White House, demanding the release of Gara and forty-six other jailed nonregistrants. When the U.S. Circuit Court of Appeals refused to overturn Gara's conviction, the *WRL News* called its ruling "completely contrary to the principles laid down . . . at the Nuremberg trials" and a blunt warning that "a person may not decide for himself whether a law is good or bad and if bad, that he is free to disobey it." After an unsuccessful appeal to the Supreme Court and seven months in prison, Gara was paroled in December 1949. To the League, the battles over conscription and the right of Gara and others to exercise free speech and conscience were local actions in a global struggle to win, protect, and expand the right of conscientious objection.[41]

Although the WRL focused on American conscription, its efforts to abolish conscription, promote conscientious objection, and support COs were also international. In 1947 the WRI initiated and the League took part in a campaign to persuade the UN Commission on Human Rights to include the right of conscientious objection in a draft International Declaration of Human Rights. While unsuccessful, this effort presaged future UN action on the issue.[42]

In the late 1940s the WRI and WRL organized a similar publicity campaign on behalf of imprisoned European COs. This effort, which focused on France, Italy, and Greece, emphasized the need for national laws codifying the right of conscientious objection. The League appealed to prominent Americans to write officials in these countries urging them to recognize conscientious objection and to cease persecuting and jailing COs. It also sent funds to the WRI to secure the release of COs attempting to emigrate, forwarded League literature, and mailed Christmas cards to imprisoned European COs and their families. Besides this, it picketed the French consulate in New York as a show of popular support for a conscientious objection law that was scheduled for debate in the French National Assembly. The League also urged Israel to include the right of conscientious objection in its constitution.[43]

Greek COs faced especially harsh conditions. Repressive government policies and savage civil war, both sustained by the Truman administration's military and economic aid to Greece, had lowered an iron curtain of oppression over Greece. When the Greek government reportedly executed a Jehovah's Witness who refused military service, five Danbury COs fasted and prayed in his memory. In late 1949, Evan Thomas coauthored letters to Secretary of State Dean Acheson and the Greek minister of war. He linked American foreign policy to the Greeks oppressive policy toward COs, and he appealed to the Greek government to end its imprisonment and threatened execution of COs. "The United States through the Truman Doctrine," he charged, "has been the chief protector and counselor of the present Greek Government."[44]

## The One World Movement

Throughout the Cold War the WRL stayed true to its radical pacifist vision and Third Camp position. Its members were nonaligned internationalists who rejected the UN and advocated the transfer of power from nation-states to the world community. They repudiated the American and Soviet blocs and articulated an internationalist challenge to national sovereignty. They supported both world government and the World Citizens movement of Garry Davis.

The WRL considered the UN an imperial "alliance of victor nations."[45] In a telegram to the Senate Committee on Foreign Relations, the League condemned the UN Security Council's antidemocratic composition and all-powerful role. Comparing the UN to the nineteenth-century Triple Alliance, it rejected the authority of the Security Council because it was controlled by the five military powers, which had been entrusted with permanent status and veto power and could protect their own national interests at the expense of global justice. It also repudiated the UN's willingness to use military force to administer international relations and enforce its decisions. Furthermore, the League charged that the UN was neither reducing armaments, nor abolishing conscription, nor addressing the root social, economic, and political causes of war.[46]

The WRL acknowledged that the UN Charter had provided a "welcome armistice" among rival Big Three imperialists, but it went on to warn that this "temporary compromise" was "not a step toward peace." The UN, the League concluded, was a merely nominal organization that "misleads people who are anxious for a genuine world government."[47] A year later, the 1946 WRL conference resolved that the UN was "powerless to prevent World War III because it is guided by reactionary, imperialist ideas." Rather than the UN, the conference endorsed a "true World Federation in which every person would be a citizen of the world."[48] In accordance with these sentiments, the League supported the World Federalist and World Citizens movements.

The World Federalist movement was a mass though short-lived movement. Catalyzed by the threat of nuclear holocaust, it challenged the world order of sovereign nation-states. In September 1946 a delegation representing more than three dozen organizations from fourteen countries met in Luxembourg and founded the World Movement for World Federal Government (WMWFG). A year later, three hundred delegates from twenty-four nations, including members of the legislatures of Britain, France, and Italy, attended a second WMWFG conference in Switzerland. By mid-1950 the WMWFG boasted fifty-two member groups and twenty-one affiliated groups from two dozen countries. The WMWFG argued that in the nuclear age, national rivalries were suicidal; then it posed a stark choice—"one world or none."[49]

In February 1947 the six largest world federalist groups in the United States merged to form the United World Federalists (UWF), the American section of the WMWFG. Within two years the UWF had won considerable support. By mid-1949 it had nearly 47,000 members and 720 chapters. Forty-five major national organizations endorsed transforming the UN into a world federation, and twenty state legislatures adopted resolutions supporting world government. In June 1949, ninety-one members of the House of Representatives introduced a resolution to make world federation a "fundamental objective" of American foreign policy. Despite concern that a world government might embrace armed force, the WRL endorsed the nonpacifist WMWFG movement.[50]

Like the WMWFG, the WRL repudiated autonomous national power and endorsed a "one world" vision. Capturing the growing mood for an alternative to the UN, Orlie Pell urged pacifists to stop debating blueprints and start building either "One World, or a world order or a world community or world citizenship." Tracy Mygatt, long-time officer of the Campaign for World Government, asserted that "the root of war lies primarily in *unlimited national sovereignty.*" Likewise, Frances Witherspoon championed the creation of "a *truly federal world government of peoples,* with all that that implies of the surrender of national war-breeding rivalries." In 1947 the League declared that it intended "to promote the *abolition* of national sovereignty in favor of one world community." The 1948 WRL conference resolved to "favor non-military World Government to supersede national sovereignty, as a necessary instrument toward establishing world unity." Finally, in September 1948 the League decided to affiliate itself with the WMWFG.[51]

The WRL also supported Garry Davis and his World Citizens movement. Unlike the United World Federalists, the World Citizens movement emphasized the role of individual citizens rather than nations in building a democratic world government. Davis, the son of bandleader Meyer Davis, had been a combat pilot during World War II and a Broadway comedy actor. In May 1948, disillusioned with war and with the "naked anarchy" of sovereign nation-states, he flew to Paris, entered the U.S. Embassy, renounced his American citizenship, and declared himself "a citizen of the world." In mid-September, as his French visa expired, the stateless Davis sought refuge on international soil, camping on the steps of the Palais de Chaillot, the provisional UN headquarters. In his search for UN recognition as the "first citizen of the world," Davis became an instant cause celebre.[52]

Davis found an ally in Robert Sarrazac, a prominent "one world" champion and former officer in the French resistance. In November 1948, Davis interrupted a plenary session of the UN General Assembly and issued a dramatic appeal for world government. The police quickly seized him, but Sarrazac completed his speech: "We, the people, long for the peace which only a world order can give. The sovereign states you represent here are dividing us and bringing us to the abyss of War."[53] Newsreels and newspapers lionized the stirring existential act, the press dubbed Davis "World Citizen No. 1," and the World Citizens movement burgeoned throughout Europe and the world.[54]

During his two years in Europe, Davis pursued several other pacifist and world citizenship projects. In Paris in January 1949, he established a World Citizen Registry, with the idea that World Citizens would elect delegates to a Peoples Constituent Assembly in 1950 to draft a World Constitution. The convention was never held; even so, by 1950 the World Citizen Registry had signed up nearly half a million people. Then, in the fall of 1949, Davis maintained a vigil at the Cherche-Midi military prison in Paris to protest the imprisonment of CO Jean Moreau and to promote the passage of a French law establishing the right of conscientious objection. This action sparked solidarity demonstrations in the United States. Also, Davis promoted Sarrazac's "mondialization" movement, a scheme that reflected his own ideas. A community became mondialized (world territory) when a majority of its people registered as world citizens and pledged themselves to vote in a Peoples Constituent Assembly. Mondialization was in effect world citizenship. It was meant to supplement national citizenship rather than to replace it. By mid-1951, four hundred communities, most of them in Western Europe, had adopted the Charter of Mondialization and become "world territory."

Davis returned to the United States in March 1950 as a "French non-quota immigrant." He spent four days on Ellis Island before being admitted as a "resident alien."[55] The WRL planned to greet Davis at the pier, but his unexpected detention upset this gesture of support.[56]

The WRL's radical members were especially excited by Davis's dramatic direct action. In *Alternative,* Dave Dellinger and Roy Finch editorialized that "it is only those rebels who act alone, as Davis did, who succeed . . . in . . . capturing the imagination and support of large numbers. . . . One person who *becomes* a world citizen is worth a hundred who talk and write about how nice it will be when everyone does so."[57] Kepler expressed similar sentiments in *Peace News*

(London). In mid-1950, Peck proposed that the League serve as a World Citizens Registry. However, by September of that year Davis had applied to have his U.S. citizenship reinstated. Dellinger and his copublishers at Liberation Press expressed their disappointment at this: "At a time when two giant nationalisms are struggling ruthlessly for world domination it is hard to see how the ideal of world peace and world citizenship can be advanced by taking any step that can be interpreted as giving support to either of the contending powers." [58]

In October 1949 the WRL cosponsored a poster walk and sit-down at the French Embassy in Washington, D.C., to protest Davis's arrest, trial, and threatened deportation from France for championing the cause of French CO Jean Moreau. Gaining admittance to the chancery, five demonstrators began a sit-down strike and announced their intention to remain for "24 hours on French soil to protest Garry Davis' trial." Eleven participants were arrested, including George Houser, A. J. Muste, and Dellinger. In Paris, Davis read about the demonstration. On his return to the United States he contacted Dellinger and the Glen Gardner cooperative and asked it to become the first American "world community." [59]

In June 1950, to commemorate its first anniversary as a world community, Glen Gardner telegrammed greetings to Cahors, France, the first European community to declare itself mondialized. "Today with Garry Davis present," the message proclaimed, "Glen Gardner Cooperative Community[,] comprising thirteen adults and six children[, was] recognized [as] World Territory . . . [the] beginning of [a] campaign to mondialize American Communities." [60] Several months later, Dellinger explained Davis's significance to the American peace and world government/citizens movements: "Garry Davis shook the tottering foundations of nationalism because he was not content just to *declare* himself for World Peace, World Brotherhood, and World Citizenship. He renounced his oath of allegiance to the United States and took simple, non-violent direct action as a World Citizen." [61]

Even before Peck proposed making the League a World Citizenship Registry center, the WRL had expressed interest in the idea. It aborted the project after it learned that World Citizen Registry policy precluded formal association with other groups; however, it did distribute world citizenship registration forms to its members. The League also stocked and advertised Davis's pamphlet, *From War Pilot to World Citizen.*[62] Like the World Citizens movement, the League endorsed the role of individual citizens in the formation of a democratic world government and community.

The WRL's alternative radical pacifist vision is illustrated by its support for the World Federalist and the World Citizens movements and by its rejection of the UN. At a time of intense, rival nationalisms, the League repudiated the sovereignty of nation-states and advocated supranational institutions.

In December 1949, Indian pacifists sponsored a month-long World Pacifist Meeting. Here, the notion of an alternative international pacifist organization received further impetus. This meeting had been conceived before Gandhi's death; the idea was that pacifists from West and East would be able to meet him. (After Gandhi was assassinated in February 1948, organizers postponed the conference.) Invited to send a delegate, the WRL chose Igal Roodenko, who joined nearly one hundred delegates from thirty-five countries.[63]

Through the WRI, the League had always cultivated international contacts. That said, the World Pacifist Meeting was a unique chance for it to connect with the twentieth century's most influential pacifist leader. Gandhi had been a powerful influence on the World War II COs who now controlled the League. The League sent Roodenko as its representative because of his CO experience, his record of nonviolent direct action, and his willingness to make a long-term commitment to serve on the WRL staff. Its desire to "organize a non-violent social movement," led the WRL to instruct him to explore "the ultimate establishment of a world pacifist movement."[64]

Though Roodenko attended the meeting mainly to link the WRL with Indian Gandhians, the League also wanted him to contact European and Israeli pacifists. To that end, he spent more than two months in Europe and Israel, visiting the WRI's London headquarters, WRI locals, antiwar groups, and individual pacifists. He met Garry Davis in Paris and dispatched a damning report to the League depicting him as sincere but also confused and naïve. Satisfying a personal desire to visit Israel, Roodenko conferred with WRI members who were working to have the right of conscientious objection included in the Israeli constitution.[65]

Roodenko's participation in the World Pacifist Meeting and his travels in Europe and Israel demonstrate the WRL's links with the international pacifist movement, its concern for European COs and the right of conscientious objection worldwide, its interest in the Davis phenomenon, and the special role that pacifists conferred on independent India—the nation of Gandhi and Nehru.

## The WRL and the Militarization of American Foreign Policy

The WRL denounced the militaristic turn in American foreign policy represented by the Truman Doctrine, NATO, and the rearmament of West Germany. The League also repudiated a Europe divided into armed, mutually hostile camps linked to political/economic/military alliances controlled by the United States and Soviet Union.

The WRL and its members denounced American military intervention in Greece's civil war and in Turkey. For instance, the WRL-NY cosponsored an Easter Day poster walk in New York City that publicized the dangers posed by the Truman Doctrine. The League also expressed its position in a letter to Truman drafted by the Consultative Peace Council (a federation of pacifist groups) and signed by many League members. The League later submitted this letter to the House Foreign Affairs Committee to register its disapproval of American military aid to Greece and Turkey:

> The Administration's proposed course with respect to Greece and Turkey accepts the division of the world into American and Russian spheres of influence and proposes to stop the expansion of Russia and the spread of Communism by force of arms.
>
> By its failure to deal with the needs of the Russian people and by intensifying their fears of being surrounded by hostile military force, this policy will actually help to bolster up the Stalin dictatorship in Russia. And since Communism thrives on war, civil disturbances and poverty, American dollars devoted to bolstering the military forces of dubious regimes in Europe and Asia will serve to multiply the grievances which make people outside Russia also a prey to Communism. American resources will be drained as the nation is thus drawn into the conflict against Russia and mounting chaos throughout the world. In the end, our own country will be militarized and dragged into an atomic war with no prospect for the survival of democracy anywhere.[66]

Rejecting both American isolationism and appeasement of the Soviet Union, which would only postpone the "inevitable clash of power against power," the WRL offered a general program to break the Cold War "deadlock." The letter called on the United States to reduce Soviet fears and create the mutual confidence and security necessary for peace. It could do this by renouncing military intervention; abandoning the atomic arms race and promoting universal disarmament; establishing a global relief and reconstruction effort; and expediting international control of atomic power and vital geostrategic points such as the Dardanelles and the Suez and Panama canals.[67] The following year, in another letter to the president, the League continued its attack on the Truman Doctrine: "We cannot insist on maintaining bases all over the world without expecting that other nations would try by one means or another to accomplish the same result."[68]

Individual WRL members also criticized the Truman Doctrine, articulating a revisionist perspective on Soviet behavior. Addressing the House Foreign Affairs Committee, Frank Olmstead noted that Soviets were faced with the British

Empire and a hostile UN; he then contended that Soviet foreign policy was based on the assumption that war with the West was likely. It followed that Soviet actions in the Baltic, the Balkans, China, and Korea were largely defensive. He asserted that the Truman Doctrine represented "the first step in the encirclement of Russia, and that is the route of empire." This American containment strategy to thwart communism relied on military force to impose United States control over nations that supported the Soviets. In short, it would create an American empire. As in Greece, the result would be to "support a fascist puppet regime under America." Instead of the Truman Doctrine, he called for Soviet-American cooperation.[69]

Writing in *Politics,* Dwight Macdonald contended that the Truman Doctrine had both foreign and domestic components. As foreign policy, the Truman Doctrine threatened the Soviet Union with "economic and ideological war" and "changed the face of postwar world politics." It also buttressed the repressive Greek "monarchist oligarchy" and the Turkish "military-police state."[70] Less than two weeks after announcing military support for Greece and Turkey, Truman had turned to the domestic element of his anticommunist policy. With Executive Order 9835 he had established the Federal Employee Loyalty Program, the purpose of which was to discover and remove federal employees suspected of "treason." This sort of political "purge," Macdonald declared, was "the essence of Nazi-Stalinist jurisprudence."[71] Macdonald, along with Jim Peck, also linked the "political-economic" Marshall Plan with the "militarist" Truman Doctrine, in that both policies were directed at the Soviets and neither promoted peace.[72]

The WRL also denounced NATO on various military, political, and economic grounds. In a letter to President Truman, George Hartmann depicted the treaty as "nothing more than an ominous, old-fashioned military alliance." A month later, testifying before the Senate Foreign Relations Committee, WRL representative Edward C. M. Richards dubbed NATO a "war measure."[73] Noting that NATO was a military alliance aimed at the Soviet Union and its satellites, he argued on the League's behalf that the pact contradicted the UN's aims and constituted a direct military threat to the Soviet bloc. Moreover, NATO perpetuated the dangerous division of Europe between two armed and hostile imperial camps, increased the atmosphere of fear and mistrust, stoked Soviet concerns for security, and "accelerate[d] the alarming drift towards war."[74] NATO would also retard European economic recovery and impose a steep tax burden to support a sustained arms race. The United States, Richards argued, should not "finance Operation Rathole via military lend-lease to Europe." The League also feared that collective defense would transfer the decision to declare war from the U.S. Congress to foreign governments. Finally, it warned that

NATO would militarize America and strengthen the influence of military forces worldwide. NATO, Richards told the Senate, was "just another in the age-long list of futile, costly, provocative, military alliances which during the past 50 years have repeatedly led Europe and the world into ever-increasingly destructive wars."[75]

The WRL also condemned West Germany's remilitarization and integration into NATO. Because of Germany's Nazi history, geostrategic importance, and potential to restore itself as a key player in Europe, American Cold War policy often focused on postwar Germany's role in western defense strategy. American containment policy demanded a pro-Western rather than a neutral Germany. After World War II the United States took steps to integrate West Germany into the Atlantic security framework, the goal being a rearmed and unified Western Europe that would serve as a bulwark against the Soviet Union. In May 1952 the United States, Britain, and France established the Federal Republic of Germany and placed it under the NATO umbrella.

The WRL opposed the remilitarization of West Germany and its inclusion in the Western security alliance. Appearing before the Senate Foreign Relations Committee, A. J. Muste rejected the Allies' wartime German settlements (at Yalta and Potsdam) that had divided Germany, as well as the Soviet proposal for an armed, united, independent, and neutralized Germany. Instead, he advocated a disarmed, united, and neutralized Germany. He contended that making West Germany part of NATO would create two armed and hostile German nations that would be mutually suspicious of each other. This would only exacerbate the contest between East and West. Comparing Germany to Korea, Muste warned that partition would require a militarized frontier guarded by hostile armies which eventually "by accident or design . . . are unleashed and . . . annihilate each other. This is not peace—this is war."[76] Although NATO and the Warsaw Pact avoided open war, between the Berlin Crisis in 1948 and the demolition of the Berlin Wall in 1989, perilous Cold War existed along the Iron Curtain. Paradoxically, Muste proved both wrong and prescient.

### The WRL and Nuclear Arms

The WRL condsidered the development, stockpiling, and use of atomic and hydrogen bombs immoral and suicidal. Its 1945 statement on the atomic bomb called for the abolition of atomic weapons and the international control of atomic energy. In 1946 the League contacted atomic scientists in an attempt to mobilize scientific opposition against the bomb. Although an atomic scientists movement was emerging that supported international control of atomic energy, most scientists were not pacifists, and the initiative fizzled.[77]

The WRL also monitored the debate over nuclear weapons among atomic scientists. In late 1948 the *WRL News* recommended to its readers two articles in the *Bulletin of the Atomic Scientists* that discussed nonviolent resistance and that challenged atomic scientists to refuse to participate in weapons projects. In 1949 the *WRL News* reported on the Society for Social Responsibility in Science, a nonpacifist association. The League approved of the group's efforts to foster among scientists "personal moral responsibility" for the consequences of their work. The organization also encouraged scientists to refuse jobs that violated their "moral judgement."[78]

In February 1950 the WRL cosponsored a public meeting to protest the hydrogen "Hell-Bomb." Victor Paschkis, the leader of the Society for Social Responsibility in Science, and Donald Harrington, a member of the WRL's executive committee who headed the Community Church, addressed an audience of four hundred. "Scientists should refuse to work on the [hydrogen] bomb, Congress should refuse to appropriate funds for it, [and] people should refuse to pay for it," Harrington declared. Paschkis reported that the group's scientists had already refused to produce armaments.[79]

Meanwhile, the Truman administration's January 1950 decision to develop the hydrogen bomb prompted renewed WRL protests. In an official statement on the hydrogen bomb, the League called atomic warfare a "crime against humanity" and compared it to the "genocide of Hitler." There were some who justified the hydrogen bomb on the basis of "necessity"; in contrast, the League argued that such a weapon could neither contain communism nor protect Americans. It noted that the atomic bomb had not prevented a communist victory in China, and then contended that the expansion of communism was the result of "discontent and desperation" rather than superior "force of arms." To stop communism, it argued, the West must provide a social and economic program that addressed the roots of human distress. Finally, the League disputed the functional value of the hydrogen bomb, asserting that no strategy could shield Americans from the devastation of nuclear warfare: "Public protest may not halt the development of the bomb," the League admitted, but it might prevent its use, since civilization confronted "the alternative of peace or probable annihilation."[80]

Individual WRL members also damned the hydrogen bomb. In early 1950, Roy Kepler advised war resisters to invoke the hydrogen bomb to radicalize and recruit apathetic citizens. Dave Dellinger, James Otsuka, and other WRL members acted along these lines, operating independently of Kepler. Emphasizing the power of heroic action and moral dissent to transform individual consciousness and historical possibilities, Dellinger contended that once radicals defined alternative solutions and dramatized them through personal sacrifice, "we will find that there are countless examples where apparent apathy will turn into revolutionary action."[81] Citing successful hunger strikes by World War II COs, Irish political prisoners, and Gandhi, Dellinger called for a collective hunger strike lasting at least ten days to stir individuals to renounce war and demand that the government halt plans for producing the hydrogen bomb.[82]

In February 1950 Peacemakers established an *ad hoc* Fast For Peace Committee. The following Easter Week more than forty men and women staged a seven-day fast in Washington, D.C., to protest the manufacture of the hydrogen bomb and to make a moral appeal for humankind to renounce war and embrace nonviolent conflict resolution. Many League members participated in parallel actions at seventy locations in the United States and abroad. In the capitol, protestors wrote Truman, picketed the White House, and visited the Soviet Embassy, Tass, the Voice of America, the Atomic Energy Commission (AEC), and the Pentagon. In New York, the Community Church hosted a simultaneous vigil.[83]

In March 1950, Jim Otsuka, a member of the WRL and Peacemakers, conducted a dramatic demonstration at the atomic bomb plant in Oak Ridge, Tennessee. This action linked tax refusal and civil disobedience with protest against the hydrogen bomb, militarism, and the Cold War. Early on the morning of 15 March, Otsuka boarded an employee bus and entered the restricted atomic complex. By 7:30 he was distributing leaflets to curious workers. The flyer read:

> I have come to Oak Ridge . . . to dramatize to my fellow citizens that our tax money is being used in large part for the destruction of the world.
>
> At 10:45 on an August morning in 1945 the first atomic bomb was used for human destruction. I came today to burn, at that hour, 70% of a dollar bill, symbolizing the percentage of taxes that, according to our President, Harry Truman, is being used for military preparation and for fighting the "Cold War."[84]

At 10:45, while being questioned by security guards, Otsuka took a dollar bill from his wallet. "Pardon me, George Washington," he said, and then he tore the bill at the 70 percent line and set fire to it with a match—a criminal act. The protest attracted national publicity.[85]

In 1954 the WRL coauthored a letter to the citizens of Hiroshima and Nagasaki to mark Hiroshima Day. Stating that "there are Americans who are deeply filled with shame and horror by these acts," the WRL went on to express regret and repentance over the atomic bombing of Japan, the subsequent atomic buildup, and the development of the hydrogen bomb. Although it condemned the bomb's use, the League did not charge America with atomic exceptionalism: "We know that had it not been our country that first developed these weapons and used them, it would have been another."[86] Members of Japanese FOR expressed their appreciation for this act of citizens' diplomacy and offered their own repentance for Japan's wartime "deeds."[87] Significantly, the WRL and Japanese FOR were among the first to attempt a postwar reconciliation—to express repentance for the war and to extend forgiveness both ways.

## The Korean War

In late August of 1950 the WRL warned that the Korean War "has brought the world a long step closer to the ultimate catastrophe of World War III."[88] Despite these urgent words, the League failed to organize a militant campaign against the Korean War, although it did support the vigorous actions of its members. In part, the WRL's belated response was a result of internal disagreements over whom to blame: the United States or the Soviet Union. In August, Jim Peck strongly criticized the League's inaction. Despite two months of warfare in Korea, he charged, the League had failed to issue a statement, publish a leaflet, or participate in several pacifist initiatives that had garnered antiwar publicity. For instance, in early July the Glen Gardner cooperative community, led by Dave Dellinger, had embarked on a two-week fast to protest the war. Around the same time, four WRL members, including Peck and Igal Roodenko, had traveled to UN headquarters at Lake Success, New York, and distributed leaflets urging immediate mediation.[89]

Notwithstanding Peck's criticism, the WRL did support several antiwar protests. It endorsed a Peacemakers initiative to mark Hiroshima Day (6 August) with public actions ranging from leaflet distribution to more militant direct action. On that day, League members picketed the atomic installation at Oak Ridge, Tennessee. Three days later, on Nagasaki Day, twenty-eight pacifists in Washington, D.C., visited the State Department and the Russian Embassy to present a statement declaring themselves World Citizens; League members participated in the latter action, and the League publicized it.[90]

Dellinger and the other Glen Gardner hunger strikers, who dubbed themselves the "Glen Gardner World Citizens' Community," illustrate the links between nonviolence, world citizenship, and the Korean War. Three days before the war erupted in Korea, Glen Gardner declared itself world territory. Less than two weeks later, its members began their collective fast. They compared their nonviolent direct action to Gandhi's resistance to British rule. In a statement explaining their fast, the hunger strikers combined a pacifist critique of the Korean War and the Cold War with a plea for an immediate ceasefire, mediation, and internationalism. The statement depicted the Korean conflict as an "artificial civil war" in the Cold War between the United States and the Soviet Union. Furthermore, sending American troops to Korea "transfers the United Nations into an agency of war on the side of the United States." Situating their critique of the Korean War within a radical internationalism, the fasters issued an urgent plea: "We call upon all people everywhere to withdraw their primary allegiance from their present governments and to declare themselves World Citizens whose loyalty is to the World and who are unwilling to take part in the conflicts of nations. . . . As World Citizens, we pledge ourselves to seek for non-violent solutions to all problems."[91]

In the fall of 1951, impatient over the absence of militant action by the League and other pacifist organizations, four WRL members launched a dramatic, Peacemakers-sponsored world citizens project to protest the Korean War and promote world citizenship. The four radicals—Dave Dellinger, Ralph DiGia, Bill Sutherland, and Arthur Emery—sailed to France and embarked on a Paris-to-Moscow bicycle trip in order to speak directly to citizens on both sides of the Iron Curtain. They distributed bilingual leaflets printed in English and either French, German, or Russian. Except for Emery, the activists were old friends who had shared prison together as World War II COs. Moreover, Dellinger and DiGia were members of Glen Gardner. The European press gave their mission front page coverage; in contrast, press coverage in the United States was limited.

In Europe, the cyclists advocated nonviolent resistance to militarism, totalitarianism, and social injustice in the form of strikes, boycotts, demonstrations, and civil disobedience. Their leaflet stated: "The United States you hear of most often is the United States of far-flung military bases, of atom bombs, of American dollars to bribe Europe into rearmament. We are from another United States, a United States of persons who want peace and friendship and economic equality throughout the world. . . . LET US REACH ACROSS THE ARTIFICIAL BOUNDARIES AND MAKE PEACE."[92]

For two months the group remained in Paris, awaiting visas, making plans, and studying Russian. In September 1950, after American occupation authorities refused them visas to enter West Germany and the Soviets ignored their requests for visas to visit Moscow, the four men left Paris amidst much publicity. They cycled to the French-German frontier, where they established camp at the Strasbourg-Kehl bridge, staged a one-week fast to protest "this Western Iron

Curtain,"[93] and espoused their nonaligned pacifist message. On the first night, police pulled down their tents, hauled the four to police headquarters, and threatened them with deportation from France; then they expelled them from the city, dumping them outside the municipal boundaries. The next evening, the police ignored the repitched tents but seized their leaflets. Publicity spread, however, and over the following week, Strasbourg citizens visited the camp with blankets, food, clothes, books, and flowers.

Leaving Strasbourg and still hoping to reach Moscow, the activists cycled to occupied Vienna to seek visas from Soviet officials. Rejecting the strict conditions the Soviets wanted to impose on them, but determined to contact Soviet citizens, they refused visas. Instead they illegally entered Russian occupation headquarters at Baden, just outside Vienna. There they passed out leaflets and spoke with friendly Soviet citizens and soldiers. Though they failed to reach Moscow, they were pleased to establish contact with Soviets. "We have seen for ourselves," the four declared, "that cold war propaganda cannot destroy the natural human warmth expressed when Americans meet Russians without governmental interference." In a November press release, they reported: "We presented the case for a Non-Violent Resistance which would combine the militancy of the war-time resistance movements with the total refusal to hate or kill exemplified by Gandhi."[94]

Meanwhile, in late August 1950, the WRL enunciated its position on the Korean War in a statement titled "War Can Be Stopped." Authored by Roy Finch, this statement charged both the Soviet Union and United States with responsibility for the conflict and contended that real peace required an armistice, disarmament, and open exchanges between nations:

The Cold War policies of distrust and tension, ruthless unbridled propaganda and interference with the affairs of smaller countries, which both sides have pursued in varying degrees for the past five years, have shown that they will lead only to open warfare. If these policies which are dividing the world are continued, Korea will only be the first of a series of ever more disastrous wars. . . .

This Civil War of Mankind must be stopped. Nobody will win if Russia and America in their fanaticism and blindness set the world on fire. . . .

The Korean War revealed the belief in violence of the Communists. . . . But it also showed that the United States knew of no other way to reply than by mobilization and an intensification of the war. . . .

We oppose all oppression and totalitarianism and we believe that those evils can be fought effectively only by non-violent methods.[95]

In its Korea statement and elsewhere, the WRL promoted immediate mediation of the conflict and encouraged India's prime minister, Jawaharlal Nehru, to assume this task. The League's efforts to initiate a mediation conference and petition met with little success in the Cold War climate, however.[96]

In October 1950, while UN troops were reversing early territorial losses and it was being debated whether General McArthur should cross the 38th parallel, the WRL renewed its call for mediation. The League supported Korean unification, and it called on the UN to promote a mediation plan that rejected the military occupation of North Korea. According to the WRL's proposal, once fighting ceased, Korean armies would be disbanded and UN forces withdrawn. Korea would then be unified under an Indian-led UN trusteeship, and free elections scheduled.[97]

In response to Truman's announcement in late November of 1950 that the United States was considering using the atomic bomb in Korea, the WRL dispatched urgent telegrams to the White House and the UN protesting the threat and urging mediation to bring peace and avoid war with China. The League also asked its members to protest Truman's statement in order to "PREVENT WORLD WAR III."[98]

Although it took little significant action during the Korean War, the WRL did maintain a nonaligned pacifist view of the conflict and of the Cold War generally. Two months after the July 1953 armistice that ended the Korean War, the League offered a bleak assessment of both that conflict and the future prospects for peace:

> Is there anything on the positive side? We contend that there is not—that the Korean war, perhaps more than any other, has demonstrated the complete futility of war. The armed conflict has solved none of the basic problems involved and has created an even deeper bitterness on both sides which makes a solution more difficult than in 1950. . . .
>
> While the hot war is over, fortunately, in Korea, the Cold War policies of both the U.S. and Russia camps will be a constant threat to a new outbreak of hostilities. . . . [In Korea,] the mounting sense of futility and frustration has failed to lead to disillusionment with the whole militarist power-bloc approach. It is for this reason that the forthcoming "peace" conference between former enemies cannot bring peace.[99]

Both this evaluation and the WRL's overall response to the Korean War illustrate the League's pacifist, third camp position. During the deadliest conflict of the Cold War, the League continued to speak and act for an alternative radical pacifist vision. However marginal, the WRL offered an important dissent of U.S. foreign policy and American Cold War orthodoxy.

## WRL-NY and Radical Pacifist Community

The WRL-NY conducted street meetings, public forums, poster walks, and protest actions to promote nonviolence, challenge Cold War militarism and McCarthyism, and nurture a pacifist community. These activities, which were often cosponsored with FOR-NY, Peacemakers, and the Catholic Worker, indicate that an alternative radical pacifist community existed in New York City, which was the center of the radical pacifist movement in the United States. By preserving autonomous spheres of dissent against Cold War liberalism, radical pacifists—especially those in the WRL, the FOR, Peacemakers, and the Catholic Worker Movement—provided the seed bed for the social movements that would emerge in the 1960s and 1970s.

WRL-NY was the most active WRL local. It conducted lunchtime street meetings on Wall Street and evening meetings outside Columbia University. During the 1948 anticonscription campaign it staged public simulated CO trials, which sparked lively discussion that benefited COs and "embryo COs." [100] After Gandhi's assassination in 1948, the League regularly honored his birthday and death. In 1949, to mark Armistice Day, WRL-NY leafleted Madison Square's military ceremony, as well as at the Astor Theater to protest its production of *Battleground*. In the early 1950s, WRL-NY sponsored a pacifist institute and weekly forums that explored pacifist critiques of the Cold War and nonviolent alternatives. When League member Ruth Reynolds was imprisoned for supporting the Puerto Rican independence movement, the WRL cosponsored a poster walk to publicize her plight and to raise funds for her appeal. Besides distributing anti-ROTC leaflets on campuses, WRL-NY hired Dave Dellinger to promote pacifism in area colleges. In 1952 it picketed visits by Winston Churchill, the British prime minister, and Dwight Eisenhower, the Republican presidential candidate. The League associated both of them with militarism. The WRL-NY and its members also organized picnics, parties, dinners, and social events to raise money and to cement personal and political bonds among members and friends. [101]

In 1947, WRL-NY began conducting annual demonstrations with FOR-NY and Peacemakers during the popular New York City Easter parade. Marching single file down crowded Fifth Avenue sidewalks, the protestors picketed, distributed literature, and wore colorful cardboard hats decorated with antiwar slogans. To declare their opposition to the Truman Doctrine, the 1947 demonstrators carried placards: "No Military Intervention in Greece and Turkey"—"Fascism and Communism Feed On Hunger"—"Would Jesus Send the Navy to the Dardanelles?" Pink leaflets asked whether America would risk atomic war "to protect oil interests and the capitalist system in the Near East." In 1948 the "Easter bonnet" slogans included "Stop Conscription," "Oppose UMT," and "President Truman, Stop War In Greece and China." In 1950, slogans included "Stop World War 3 Now." The WRL hats attracted considerable attention from parade watchers. Ignoring promises to respect civil liberties, the police harassed, repressed, and arrested the Easter Day protesters, charging them with obstruction of traffic and disorderly conduct.[102]

Besides all this, WRL-NY endorsed a "dynamic program," including an ambitious Africa Project that departed from traditional League policy and assisted West African independence movements.[103]

### The WRL and Global Nonviolent Liberation

The Africa Project was a milestone in the WRL's history. In 1953 the League helped the Africa Project promote nonviolent African independence movements and social change through Bill Sutherland's work on the Gold Coast. During Peacemakers' 1951 Paris-to-Moscow bicycle trip, Sutherland spoke to African nationalists in Paris, London, and Birmingham, and they sparked his interest in the anticolonial "winds of change" on the continent. In Birmingham, Sutherland met Jacob Mahlapo, a South African editor who told him the African National Congress was planning to lead a mass, nonviolent, antiapartheid campaign the following year. On his return to New York, Sutherland told Bayard Rustin and George Houser about the plan. He also tried to enlist the FOR's support for the campaign. When this did not succeed, he, Rustin, and Houser founded Americans for South African Resistance. Sutherland stayed in contact with African National Congress leaders, mailed them CORE literature, and put them in touch with CORE and FOR members. These African contacts spurred Sutherland to live and work on the continent, with support from the WRL and other groups. In 1953, prior commitments forced Rustin to decline an invitation from Nigerian leaders to assist a nonviolent civil disobedience campaign to win independence from Britain. Sutherland accepted the job in his place.[104]

Sutherland had personal and political reasons to leave America for Africa. In Paris during the 1951 bike trip, he had felt for the first time that he was being treated as a full member of the human race. According to Dave Dellinger, Sutherland vowed: "I shall never live in the United States again." When the opportunity arose, "I jumped at the chance of going to Africa," Sutherland later re-

called. "I wanted to be part of this movement for the independence of the continent," he explained. "It was also the time of the height of the McCarthy period
and I had pretty much given up on the United States . . . I was looking to Africa
as a place where some of my dreams of the kind of society we wanted might
come true." [105]

The WRL subsidized Sutherland's travel to and work on the continent to "advance war resistance in Africa" and "encourag[e] nonviolence among the existing
revolutionary movements." [106] This reflected the League's broader, postwar view
of war resistance. En route to Africa, Sutherland worked in London as press secretary to Nnamdi Azikewi, a publisher and leader of the Nigerian delegation that
was negotiating independence with the British. In December 1953, after British
officials denied him a Nigerian visa, Sutherland went to the Gold Coast (now
Ghana) to support Kwame Nkrumah's successful nonviolent independence campaign. In Ghana, Sutherland founded a WRI chapter, married a Ghanaian
teacher, and became the personal secretary of Ghana's finance minister, Komola
Agbeki Gbedema. He also promoted Gandhian principles on the continent and
facilitated contacts among African leaders interested in nonviolence, and between third camp forces and the dominant Convention People's Party.

By 1961, government corruption was increasing in Ghana and Nkrumah
was beginning to embrace authoritarianism. At the same time, Sutherland's mar-
riage was breaking up. All of this led him to take a job in Israel at the Center for
Asian-African Cooperation. In 1962 he moved to Tanzania to work with Julius
Nyerere. He still lives there. For five decades he has worked closely with many
African liberation leaders and on many campaigns to advance African independ-
ence, Pan-Africanism, and Gandhian nonviolence throughout the continent.
He has also provided a bridge between American peace and justice groups and
African liberation movements.[107]

A desire to bring about nonviolent and genuine decolonization led to calls
for an alternative third camp association. During the early 1950s some American pacifists started to formulate a "third position" as an alternative to the power
blocs led by the United States and Soviet Union and to the "neutralism" that was
popular in the colonialized world. The third camp movement sought independence from rival powers; it also offered a pacifist alternative to the nonaligned
movement, which found expression at the Bandung Conference of 1955 and in
various national liberation movements that were demanding freedom from European rule. The WRL considered the third camp movement an "important extension" of its pacifist convictions, its domestic activism, and its involvement in
the nonaligned, international peace movement.[108]

In September 1955 the WRL's decade-long support for a nonaligned third camp position culminated in the First International Third Way Conference. Thirty-one groups attended this conference, held in London. The WRL sent Bayard Rustin as its representative, though several other League members attended. The conference elected A. J. Muste chairman and Ralph DiGia cotreasurer of an interim Third Way Committee, which was charged with planning a worldwide conference in 1956.

The London conference issued a statement of its principles and goals: "The purpose of the Third Way Movement is to bring together all those who oppose and reject both the capitalist and totalitarian communist social systems and who refuse to give support—'critical' or otherwise—to the war preparations and activities of either side in the contemporary power struggle, or to any alternative military struggle." The same statement endorsed nonviolent liberation from colonialism, capitalism, and communism; advocated civil liberties and the democratic ownership and administration of the economy; and repudiated militarism, power blocs, and political tyranny. Significantly, the conference reflected a kindred example of the WRL's independent radical pacifism.[109]

### Communism and the Anticommunist Crusade

The WRL condemned the international communist peace movement and the domestic anticommunist crusade known as McCarthyism. Both shaped its response to the Cold War. Consistent with its libertarian radical pacifism, the League championed the freedom of radical (including communist) dissent and criticized the Smith Act (1940), the Internal Security Act (1950), and other repressive measures. The League had long sought to innoculate itself against the communist stigma. At one point its executive committee vetoed a proposal to decorate its 1954 peace calendar with a dove after two committee members warned that the bird had become a "Communist, rather than a peace symbol." Even so, the WRL suffered under the anticommunist crusade that marginalized radical dissent during the Cold War.[110]

The WRL, which, like other socialist, pacifist, and liberal groups, was burned by communist duplicity in the 1920s and 1930s, practiced both principled and functional anticommunism. The League repudiated the Communist Party and the international communist peace movement on the following principled grounds: communists advocated and often resorted to organized violence to advance or defend social justice and socialist revolution (for instance, during the Spanish Civil War and World War II and in postwar national liberation movements); communist movements and regimes were totalitarian; and communists were nonpacifist, hypocritical, partisan, and aligned with the Soviet

Union. The League's functional anticommunism stemmed from different concerns. Based on tactical, political, and organizational calculations, it rejected cooperation with communists to avoid being smeared by anticommunists and to protect its credibility and effectiveness.[111]

Similarly, the WRL opposed the communist peace movement that the Soviets launched in the late 1940s. Between 1948 and 1950 the communist peace campaign held a series of international meetings to organize a pro-Soviet alternative to the independent peace movement. Unlike the nonaligned peace movement, which remained critical of both Cold War camps, the communist peace movement aligned itself with Soviet foreign policy and praised communist nations as peace-loving; at the same time, it blistered the U.S.-led Western bloc as imperialist, war-mongering fascists bent on world domination.

Meeting in Poland in 1948, the World Congress of Intellectuals for Peace inaugurated the communist peace movement. Renamed the World Congress of the Partisans of Peace, this organization met again in Paris the following spring, with more than two thousand communist peace activists attending. The conference was organized by Frederick Joliot-Curie, a French communist and prominent scientist. He depicted the congress as the people's rebellious response to NATO. Participants skewered the United States and praised the communist camp.

In March 1950 in Stockholm, Joliot-Curie convened the Permanent Committee of the Partisans of Peace. In his opening remarks he declared that the Soviet atomic bomb, the communist victory in China, and the creation of East Germany had strengthened the "Peace Front." The Stockholm conference entertained procommunist and anti-American speeches, denounced Truman's decision to develop the hydrogen bomb, demanded the prohibition of atomic weapons, and drafted a petition—the Stockholm Peace Appeal—to support its procommunist peace program. By December 1950 the Stockholm appeal had secured 500 million signatures from seventy-nine nations, though 400 million of these were from communist countries.

The Partisans of Peace scheduled a second conference in Sheffield, England, for late 1950. When the British denied visas to half the delegates, it met in Warsaw instead. The congress renamed itself the World Peace Council, made Joliot-Curie its president, and adopted a program that condemned American aggression in Korea and China, demanded an end to the Korean War, and called for a ban on atomic and bacteriological weapons of mass destruction. In the United States the international communist peace movement operated through the Communist Party. The Peace Information Center in New York City, chaired by W. E. B. Du Bois, circulated the Stockholm Pledge and claimed 2,500,000 signatures.[112]

The WRL repudiated the communist peace offensive and the Stockholm appeal, declaring, "The CP use of the term 'peace' is not peace at all." [113] The League declined Joliot-Curie's invitation to attend the Warsaw Congress, charging that the Warsaw appeal was "inadequate and one-sided, endorses the Stockholm pledge and follows the foreign policy of a dominant world power." [114] The League contended that the appeal, "while expressing many noble sentiments, is in our opinion so inadequately worded and so partial to one side in the present big power struggle, that little hope exists that genuine strides towards lasting peace can be made on that basis." [115] However, the League asked the Peace Pledge Union or the WRI to send an observer—a decision that prompted Abraham Kaufman's resignation in November 1950. [116]

Meanwhile, the 1948 presidential campaign of Henry Wallace and the Progressive Party prompted keen debate within the WRL. Most League members criticized Wallace's excuses for Soviet foreign policy, his antipacifist record, and the role the communists were playing in his campaign. League members noted that Wallace had lionized World War II as "the people's War," [117] that he had supported Selective Service and unconditional surrender, and that he had helped plan the Manhattan Project. Moreover, he endorsed a postwar million-man volunteer army, the Morgenthau Plan, the division of Europe into spheres of influence and, if necessary, military action to thwart Soviet threats to "American" oil in Saudi Arabia. Finally, he sneered at "namby-pamby pacifism" and remained silent on the issue of COs. [118] Even without the communist issue, there was much about Wallace for radical pacifists to criticize.

The Progressive Party's relationship with the Communist Party and the perception that Wallace was an apologist for Soviet foreign policy prompted much alarm and some disagreement within the WRL. Most League members condemned Wallace for appeasing Soviet expansionism and for being an unwitting puppet of the Communist Party. Donald Harrington, who succeeded John Haynes Holmes at the Community Church, called Wallace "the outstanding American champion of appeasement of expansionist Russia." Wallace, Harrington concluded, "is rapidly becoming Stalin's American Benes, and it is a pitiful sight to behold—a man who pictures himself as liberalism's Gideon becomes its Judas." [119] Similarly, A. J. Muste cautioned that "in the realm of objective political reality, a vote for Wallace is a vote for the Communist Party." [120] Wallace's "double standard in evaluating American and Russian policies" was condemned by Dwight Macdonald, a League member and editor of *Politics*. "It is not true that Henry Wallace is an agent of Moscow," Macdonald observed. "But it is true that he behaves like one." [121]

Jim Peck was the most prominent WRL member to support Wallace. He argued that Wallace was the strongest antiwar candidate. He also hoped the Progressive Party would initiate a "people's third party which will oppose the policies of two tweedle-dum-and-tweedle-dee parties." Peck viewed the Truman Doctrine and Marshall Plan as "inseparable" attempts to "divide Europe into two warring camps," and he praised Wallace for attacking these policies, especially the more subtle Marshall Plan.[122]

In response to charges that communists were influencing the Wallace campaign, Peck countered: "If you were against everything the Communists endorse . . . you would have to be against unionism, racial equality and civil liberties as well as against anything antiwar." He also contended that a large Wallace vote would demonstrate opposition to "the bi-partisan reactionary war policy which is dividing the world into two armed camps and making inevitable the day when American soldiers will be lying in their Arctic suits in the Russian snow."[123]

From its independent third camp perspective, the WRL's opposition to Wallace on foreign policy illustrates its principled anticommunism and radical pacifism. Most League members probably voted for Norman Thomas and the Socialist Party in 1948—an election that both reflected and advanced the national anticommunist climate.[124]

The political intolerance that stamped Cold War America and stifled the WRL is illustrated by two letters written by nonpacifists and published in the mainstream New York press. In a May 1950 letter printed in the *New York Herald Tribune,* an eye witness described how two legionnaires, yelling "dirty communist," assaulted Peck as he distributed leaflets during a parade.[125] Several months later, the *New York Times* published a letter that posed a key question: "Shall it remain the exclusive prerogative of the Communist Party to cry for peace?" Although most Americans desire peace, the letter continued, they "are being drummed into silence by the current newspaper practice of placing the phrase 'peace rally' between quotation marks and emphasizing that all such are suspect of being Communist-sponsored. . . . Who wishes for peace must speak for peace."[126] These letters express the League's dilemma during the Cold War. It sought to promote radical pacifism and to prevent communists from co-opting the peace issue; at the same time, it feared that public opinion—which often associated peace activism with communism—would condemn the League as subversive, procommunist, and un-American.

In October 1949, after eleven Communist Party leaders were convicted under the Smith Act, the WRL adopted a statement on civil rights. It denounced the Smith Act, deplored the trial, and defended civil liberties—in particular the freedom of expression for all radicals, communists included. This political liberty was also important to radical pacifists. Lamenting the "departure from historic American principles," the League noted that the Smith Act made "it un-lawful to 'advise or counsel disloyalty or mutiny in the armed forces,' which in a period of war hysteria might be easily stretched to apply to any who advocated, encouraged or practiced conscientious objection to military service."[127] Signifi-cantly, draft resistance and tax refusal—which many League members em-braced—could be prosecuted under the Smith Act.

Besides defending the First Amendment, the WRL offered a strategy for de-feating communism without compromising freedom, one that relied on social reform rather than repression. "Limiting freedom of expression," the League as-serted, "is not, however, an effective way to combat Communism." To prevent communism without resorting to "anti-Communist dictatorship," America needed to eliminate the "poverty, insecurity, discrimination and repression which breed social unrest and make Communism seem an attractive way out to substantial numbers of people. . . . Democracy will not be saved by abandoning or diluting it under pressure, nor by the attempt to 'contain' Communism be-hind certain geographical barriers by threat of armed force."[128]

Finally, the WRL reiterated its opposition to communism and emphasized the differences between pacifist and communist ideology and methods. The League restated its philosophical disagreement with the Communist Party: "As people who are committed to the rejection of all violence and war, we certainly do not advocate, indeed we oppose, any violent measures against government, as we oppose violence and war when perpetrated by governments." This statement summarized the League's principled opposition to communism and to anticom-munist repression alike. Undoubtedly, the League also calculated that the state-ment's staunch anticommunism would serve as a functional shield to deflect McCarthyite attacks.[129]

The WRL practiced functional anticommunism in many other ways. For in-stance, the League often emphasized in its literature that it was noncommunist, and it acted quickly when the press portrayed it as a communist organization. During the first half of 1950 the League paid sustained attention to an article in the *Putnam County News* (NY) that labeled it a communist group. That a minor newspaper article commanded the WRL's attention for months suggests how preoccupied the League was with establishing its anticommunism and defend-ing itself against potentially ruinous charges. Similarly, in August 1950, when press accounts erroneously linked a World Citizens delegation (which included League members) visiting Washington, D.C., to the communist Peace Informa-tion Center, Peck quickly dispatched a letter correcting the mistake.[130]

Addressing the difficult dilemma of "what is to be done with groups which say they are for peace, but which may be manipulated by communists," the

WRL advised its members on the "dangers and opportunities" of working with nonpacifist peace groups.[131] In July 1950 the League counseled that "pacifists can avoid being identified with Communist-front organizations by emphasizing their opposition to Russian militarism as well as to U.S. militarism."[132]

In 1954—the same year that Senator McCarthy departed from the national stage after the Senate censured him—the WRL linked its "challenge to mc-carthyism" to its broader mission. Invoking its "service to freedom," the League contended that "the current national mood of repression is an inevitable by-product of the cold war." To resist the widespread "fear and hysteria," it pledged "to extend its message of non-violence, to hold street meetings, to protest 'civil defense' drills, to pass out leaflets, to picket, to oppose wire tapping, to practice racial equality, and to protect the constitutional rights and civil liberties of *all,* including Communists and others with whom we disagree."[133]

During the Cold War the WRL continued its pre–World War II policy of excluding communists while supporting their civil liberties. Consistent with its pacifist principles, and disillusioned by prewar attempts (both its own and those of other radicals and liberals) to work with communists, the League shunned political cooperation with the Communist Party, individual communists, and the communist peace movement. At the same time, it championed the right of all citizens to dissent, and it repudiated measures that would restrict the liberties of communists. In the context of the Cold War and McCarthyism, the League found it difficult to avoid being smeared as communist while advancing radical pacifism and defending the civil liberties of communists.

The WRL was too marginal to influence the Cold War. Even so, it was a voice of cogent dissent—and it articulated a critique of dominant Cold War liberalism. In concert with the international nonaligned peace movement, the League repudiated both Cold War blocs, offering in their place an alternative, third camp vision that endorsed some form of world government. Domestically, the League opposed McCarthyism, promoted civil liberties, and defended radical dissent, including the rights of communists. Finally, the League built a radical pacifist community that later would sustain vibrant peace and justice movements.

# 8

# Present at the Creation

The WRL, Direct Action, Civil Disobedience,
and the Rebirth of the Peace
and Justice Movements, 1955–1963

JESSIE WALLACE HUGHAN'S sudden death on Easter Sunday of 1955 can
be seen as a powerful historical symbol. Easter Sunday signifies for Christians the
resurrection of Jesus; in the same way, 1955 marked the rebirth of the peace and
social justice movements in the United States. Throughout the McCarthy era
and the often repressive post-1945 decade, the WRL and radical pacifists challenged the Cold War and nourished pockets of dissent. Beginning in 1955, the
peace movement experienced a renaissance during which nonviolent activism
became broad-based and Gandhian techniques of resistance and protest were
popularized and Americanized.[1]

Furthermore, in the mid-1950s the WRL's new orientation became apparent. Following the radicals' ascension to power, the League discarded its single-
issue program, its aversion to direct action, and its opposition to civil
disobedience. For the first time it unambiguously endorsed, practiced, and promoted militant direct action, civil disobedience, and a multi-issue program for
social justice. Between 1955 and 1963 the League demonstrated this radical
shift through its tax resistance, its founding of *Liberation* magazine (1956), and
its pivotal role in the civil defense protests in New York City (1955–61), the civil
rights movement (1955–63), and the antinuclear Committee for Nonviolent
Action (1957–67).

Between 1955 and 1957, after a decade of Cold War retreat, the peace and
justice movements underwent a revival. Outside developments contributed to
this rebirth. In 1953, Josef Stalin died and the fighting ended in Korea. These
things and the decline of McCarthyism led to a "thaw" in the Cold War;[2] they
also prompted renewed interest among the scientific community in the interna-

tional control of nuclear weapons. In July 1955, eleven scientists signed the international Bertrand Russell-Albert Einstein appeal urging governments to move beyond the Cold War to prevent a conflict certain to destroy humanity. One week later, fifty-two Nobel laureates, meeting in Switzerland, called on all nations to renounce force. In April 1957, in response to the hazards of nuclear fallout, Albert Schweitzer broadcast an appeal to end nuclear weapons testing. That same month, eighteen West German physicists pledged to refuse to participate "in the production, the testing or the use in warfare of atomic weapons."[3] Two months later, Linus Pauling released a petition signed by 11,000 scientists requesting a global ban on testing nuclear weapons.

The WRL did much to catalyze the post-1955 peace and justice movements. At its 1950 conference, Charles Bloomstein recommended that the League develop a "service relationship" with radical "groupings" within the WRL and with "direct action groups which it thinks it can support"—for example, by providing publicity and staff and by helping raise funds for them.[4] Between 1955 and 1963 the League adopted this policy toward the peace, antinuclear, civil rights, and student movements. In 1955 the League had 1,136 active members and a mailing list double that number.[5] Despite its small size it had a disproportionate influence on the rebirth of the peace and social justice movements: it took on a multi-issue program, sponsored direct action and civil disobedience projects, supported reform groups, and subsidized *Liberation,* a well-produced movement journal that transcended the pacifist community.

In his cultural study of America's response to the atomic bomb, Paul Boyer identified "cycles of activism and apathy."[6] The initial American alarm (1945–46) about the atomic bomb diminished until the mid-1950s. Between 1955 and 1963, their alarm over nuclear weapons, testing, and radioactive fallout surged again. In 1952 the United States renewed its atmospheric nuclear testing program. The 1954 tests caused illness and death among Japanese fishermen eighty miles away, prompting much comment and anxiety in the United States. In 1955, radioactive rain fell on Chicago; in 1959, scientists began detecting strontium-90 in milk. After the 1963 test ban treaty between the United States, Great Britain, and the Soviet Union, which prohibited atmospheric nuclear testing, fears of the atomic bomb declined again. To use Boyer's apt phrase, between 1963 and the late 1970s, Americans entered a "Big Sleep," during which they exhibited indifference toward the nuclear threat.[7]

The WRL did a great deal to foster a resurgence of antinuclear activism between 1955 and the 1963. It protested the annual civil defense drills in New York City; it also supported the antinuclear protests conducted by the Committee for Nonviolent Action. In both campaigns the League embraced direct action and civil disobedience. Consistent with its independent, nonaligned, pacifist third camp position, it denounced the nuclear arsenals, testing, and proliferation of both the U. S. and Soviet blocs.

The WRL also influenced Martin Luther King, Jr., and the civil rights movement. From *Brown v. Board of Education* (1954) and the Montgomery bus boycott (1955–56) to the March on Washington (1963), the civil rights movement was the most significant social justice movement in America. Although many leaders, grassroots activists, and organizations contributed to this civil rights revolution, most observers consider King the most important leader in this struggle for racial integration and legal equality. Between 1955 and 1963, King and the civil rights movement relied on nonviolent techniques and benefited from the advice of pacifists from the WRL, the FOR, and CORE. The League influenced King and the nonviolent civil rights movement, largely through Bayard Rustin, whom it often released to advise the civil rights movement, The League's involvement in the civil rights movement represented a commitment to a multi-issue peace and justice agenda, as well as to direct action and civil disobedience to promote racial equality.

In addition to the WRL's leadership in the civil rights and antinuclear movements, the founding of *Liberation* in 1956 under WRL auspices provided the radical pacifist movement with a publication of unusual intellectual quality and influence. *Liberation* was independent; that said, it was conceived, established, subsidized—and staffed—by the League. Originally coedited by David Dellinger, Roy Finch, A. J. Muste, Bayard Rustin, and Charles Walker, the journal sought to catalyze revolutionary nonviolent action, liberate individuals from all forms of domination, and build a radical pacifist movement based on the heritage and values of "the libertarian, democratic, antiwar, socialist, anarchist and labor movements in Europe and the United States in the latter half of the nineteenth century and the early years of the twentieth." [8]

The editors mourned the "decline of independent radicalism and the gradual falling into silence of prophetic and rebellious voices," and declared their commitment to a "third camp" between liberalism and Marxism.[9] They promised to publicize third camp groups and projects involving nonviolent, democratic, and libertarian socialist alternatives to communism and capitalism. Neither a WRL nor pacifist "house organ," *Liberation* reached a broad pacifist-radical-civil rights audience. It also provided the later 1950s with a voice of radical dissent and contributed to the New Left. Consistent with the League's post-1955 orientation, *Liberation* published articles promoting direct action, civil disobedience, and a broad agenda of social reform.[10]

In the mid-1950s, the League moved beyond moral support for tax resisters by reversing its 1949 decision to withhold payroll taxes from staff members who wished to practice tax resistance. In 1956, at his request, the League stopped withholding Ralph DiGia's income taxes. Despite IRS harassment the WRL has followed a policy of illegal tax resistance ever since. However, this did not become a major issue for the League until the Vietnam War.[11]

## The New York City Civil Defense Protest Movement, 1955–61

On 15 June 1955, in a civil disobedience demonstration cosponsored by the WRL, a band of twenty-eight radical pacifists in New York City initiated the first meaningful protest against Operation Alert, the nationwide civil defense drill. Some held signs proclaiming: "End War—The Only Defense Against Atomic Weapons."[12] When they remained on their benches in City Hall Park and refused police orders to take shelter at the sound of the sirens, they were arrested. "For the first time since the air raid drills began," one newspaper reported, "there was an organized resistance movement here during today's theoretical H-Bomb drill."[13] Operation Alert and the pacifist counterdemonstrations became an annual ritual that allowed the League to criticize civil defense and other Cold War policies. The protests mobilized nonpacifists and evolved into a successful antinuclear movement.

Since World War II the federal government has coordinated a national civil defense program. In January 1951, President Truman and Congress created the Federal Civil Defense Administration (FCDA) to direct national civil defense policy. Between 1954 and 1961 the FCDA organized annual rehearsals for World War III—named Operation Alert—that simulated a nuclear attack against as many as a hundred American cities. Operation Alert 1955, which targeted fifty cities, assumed the destruction of Washington, D.C. Its aim was to demonstrate the government's capacity to survive a nuclear strike. The exercise transferred the president, the cabinet, key federal agencies, and 15,000 employees to undisclosed sites outside the capital. Casualties were estimated at 8.2 million dead, with an additional 6.5 million injured, and 24 million homeless. In later years the drills offered similar scenarios of simulated nuclear holocaust.[14]

Political scientist Guy Oakes has argued that civil defense—which included Operation Alert—was critical to Cold War planners. Civil defense authorities were trying to persuade both Americans and their potential adversaries that the United States could survive a nuclear war with its institutions intact. They were also encouraging citizens to consider the hitherto unthinkable notion that civilization might survive nuclear war. Significantly, the willingness of Americans to risk nuclear war—which relied in part on the public believing that civil defense could protect them—made nuclear deterrence credible to the Soviets.[15] Oakes has shown that defense policy depended on public acquiescence; this affirms the WRL's premise that citizens could prevent war by withholding support for the material and psychological preparations for war. The League worked to erode public support for civil defense and the militaristic Cold War policies that it buttressed.

The WRL operation was a key part of New York City's civil defense protest movement. The League helped form it and helped run it. Though this movement usually has been associated with the Catholic Workers, the 1955 demonstration was cosponsored by the League, the FOR, and Peacemakers. Of the twenty-eight pacifists arrested, more belonged to the League than to any other group. Ammon Hennacy, a League member and prominent Catholic Worker, has claimed that it was he who initiated the idea of a protest. He shared his plan with Catholic Worker leader Dorothy Day; he then contacted WRL staffer Ralph DiGia, who notified the other participants.[16]

The demonstrators planned to walk across the park during the drill and deliver a protest letter to the mayor; this action was precluded by their arrest. The letter charged: "The promotion of such public and publicized civil defense tests as the one now taking place, whatever the intentions may be, helps to create the illusion that the nation can thus devote its major resources to catastrophic war and at the same time shield people from its effects. We can have no part in helping to create his illusion."[17]

The protestors dismissed the notion that civil defense and bomb shelters could protect Americans from nuclear attack. They asserted that civil defense drills were a form of "war preparation" that "condition[ed] the public to accept and expect war, instead of demanding peace and working for it."[18] They argued the 15 June drill had "no realistic connection with saving life under the conditions simulated, viz. an H-bomb attack."[19] Quoting a prominent nonpacifist supporter, they also argued that in the age of intercontinental missiles, civil defense was "as dated as a moat and portcullis."[20] Finally, invoking the right of conscientious objection, they argued that participation in quasi-military civil defense drills violated their conscience.

After the June arrests, pacifists established the Provisional Defense Committee (PDC) to coordinate and raise funds for the defense of those charged. The WRL provided the PDC with office space at its Beekman Street headquarters. League members dominated the PDC and its executive committee; PDC officers included Bayard Rustin (secretary), A. J. Muste (treasurer), and DiGia (assistant treasurer).[21]

The WRL and its members would remain central to the subsequent annual civil defense demonstrations. "We believe that the H-bomb is an issue through which the pacifist position can be dramatized and placed before the American people," the League declared shortly after the demonstration of 15 June.[22] It pledged "wholehearted support" to the PDC and "the crucial pacifist and civil liberties issues of the case in the belief that it holds promise of being the key pacifist endeavor of this post-war period."[23]

During the trial and appeal, the PDC emphasized the issues of "conscience and civil liberties,"[24] including the right of religious and secular conscientious objection to mandatory participation in civil defense drills. The PDC claimed that their arrests and the New York Emergency Act (on which the arrests were based) violated the constitutional rights of free speech, press, and assembly; the freedom of conscience and religion; the right to petition the government; and the right to equal protection under the law, since authorities had not arrested the 20,000 baseball fans in Yankee Stadium or the many others who did not seek shelter. Also, they maintained that the U.S. Supreme Court's "clear and present danger" test (1917), which defined the conditions under which the state could curtail civil liberties, had not been met.[25]

Finally, the case raised the issue of whether conscience should be defined in secular as well as religious terms—a matter of particular concern to the secular WRL. Muste (who represented Peacemakers during the trial) invoked religious principles to explain his pacifism; in contrast, League spokesman DiGia explicitly based his peace activism on secular grounds. The PDC declared: "Should it prove possible in appealing this case to obtain a clear definition of conscience to include religious, moral, ethical and humanitarian grounds, then a precedent of immense importance for Constitutional law will have been established."[26]

The hostile and intemperate judge, who red-baited the defendants, further underscored the secular component of their challenge to the Cold War consensus. He asked the lead defense attorney whether he would call Soviet Foreign Minister Molotov as a witness. In the same vein, he asked Muste if he had read Karl Marx. During their November 1955 trial, twenty protestors pleaded not guilty; most of the arrested Catholic Workers had already pleaded guilty. Expressing his "abhor[rence]" that "not all the defendants were motivated by religious scruples," the judge found all of the defendants guilty but suspended their sentences. The PDC appealed the verdict. The New York Court of Appeal narrowly affirmed their convictions (1959), and the U.S. Supreme Court refused to review the case (1961).[27]

Meanwhile, every year from 1956 to 1959, the WRL and a band of radical pacifists demonstrated against the drills, refusing to take shelter during the re-

hearsals. These demonstrations attracted sympathetic media attention, generated publicity for the pacifist critique of civil defense and nuclear testing, led
nonpacifists to join the protests and the emerging antinuclear peace movement,
and conformed to a ritualized pattern. The annual protest ritual included educational leafleting to protest civil defense, nuclear bombs, and war; committing
civil disobedience in a New York City park by refusing to take shelter; arrest;
picketing the Women's House of Detention, where convicted female activists
were jailed; and mounting legal challenges to the civil defense law.[28]

WRL literature linked its opposition to civil defense to its historical aim of
abolishing war. "THE ONLY REAL DEFENSE . . . is to ABOLISH WAR," the League's
1956 civil defense leaflet proclaimed.[29] The leaflet reprinted a *New York Post* editorial attributing popular indifference toward the drills not to public apathy but
rather to increasing awareness that "ALL BLUEPRINTS FOR DEFENSE are utterly
obsolete."[30] In 1959 the League distributed thousands of leaflets that counseled:
"End War—The Only Real Civil Defense."[31] The same year, in an editorial that
affirmed the WRL's position, the *New York Post* opined: "We feel a certain kin-
ship with those behind bars. For the notion that modern man can snugly protect
himself against the hydrogen bomb by conducting such fire drills is a form of self
delusion almost indistinguishable from madness."[32]

Between 1956 and 1959, two developments took place that popularized the
pacifist perspective, linked it to nonpacifist concerns, and laid the groundwork
for mass demonstrations in 1960 and 1961. First, the participation of mothers
and their young children in the picketing of the Women's House of Detention legitimized the protests by wrapping peace activism in motherhood; it also connected peace action to ordinary families and infused the peace movement with a
new dynamism, which became even more pronounced in the 1960 and 1961
demonstrations.[33] Second, the WRL and the PDC began seeking broader participation by offering both legal and illegal opportunities to challenge civil defense.[34]

The 1960 protest, conducted on 3 May in City Hall Park, was a mass
demonstration. This watershed event was organized by the Civil Defense Protest
Committee (CDPC), an *ad hoc* New York City-wide citizens committee built
around the PDC. The WRL provided the major impulse for the creation of the
CDPC and the 1960 protest. WRL members comprised nearly half the CDPC's
executive committee, and the group operated out of the WRL's office. On 3
May, a thousand protestors jammed City Hall Park. While half of them left
when the drill alarm sounded, the rest remained in the park and refused to take
shelter in a demonstration of civil disobedience. For the first time, nonpacifists
had joined the civil defense protest. The demonstration received considerable
media coverage, most of it favorable.[35]

The 1960 demonstration provided evidence of broad public rejection of civil defense. The protest was sponsored by prominent New Yorkers, including Kenneth Clark, Nat Hentoff, and Paul Goodman. Literary celebrities Norman Mailer, Dwight Macdonald, and Kay Boyle joined the demonstration. Avoiding CDPC leaders and celebrities, the police arrested twenty-six protestors. After five years of tiny but determined civil defense protests, the 1960 action transformed the small, pacifist-led civil defense protests of past years into a popular liberal-radical movement. Columnist Murray Kempton observed: "We seem to be approaching a condition of sanity where within a year or so there'll be more people defying than complying with the Civil Defense drill."[36] Once prophetic, the WRL's critique and rejection of the drills had become widely accepted among important liberal elites.

The crowd that jammed City Hall Park showed the power of organized, nonviolent civil disobedience. "War is not possible if we all say 'No,'" the nonpacifist Boyle declared, echoing the WRL slogan that "wars will end when men refuse to fight."[37] Following postwar radical pacifists and anticipating the New Left, the always quotable Mailer proclaimed that "politics is like sex: you got to go all the way."[38] Ann Morrissett, a member of the WRL's executive committee and one of those arrested, told the court: "There comes a time when a direct act of conscience in protest against an anti-social law may be the only way of calling attention to that law and eventually changing it through the democratic processes we believe in."[39] More humorously, Macdonald confessed: "I don't know whether I'll stay out or not. I wouldn't mind going to jail if they let me out in time to speak on anarchism at Yale tomorrow."[40] Defying police orders to leave and take shelter, the demonstrators underscored their patriotism by singing "The Battle Hymn of the Republic," "America the Beautiful," and "We Have Not Been Moved!" When the drill ended, David McReynolds, a socialist pacifist and *Liberation* staffer, climbed on a park bench and declared: "The law is dead. The token arrests prove it."[41]

McReynolds was born in 1929 and reared in Los Angeles by a military family. He graduated from UCLA in 1953 with a degree in political science. His father was a World War II veteran and a lieutenant-colonel in the air force. His grandfather, an army colonel and Commodore George Dewey's secretary in Manila, watched his boss dictate the terms of surrender to the Spanish in the Spanish-American War.

McReynolds had been involved since high school in radical causes. When he was sixteen he joined the Prohibition Party. In 1947 he delivered a pacifist message in his valedictorian address. The following year he joined the FOR. In 1949 he heard Bayard Rustin speak, a formative experience. "Bayard had a decisive

impact on my life," he recalled. "He was the one who really convinced me to become a pacifist."[42] As a radical student activist at UCLA, he opposed loyalty
oaths, participated in battles over the right of students to distribute political literature on campus, and chaired the Student Committee Against Compulsory
R.O.T.C. In 1951 he left the Prohibition Party and joined the Socialist Party,
where he quickly rose to leadership positions. Perhaps more than any WRL
leader since Jessie Wallace Hughan, Devere Allen, and the League's founding
generation, McReynolds immersed himself in SP affairs.

Although McReynolds's major contribution to the WRL has been that of a
socialist pacifist intellectual and organizer, he has also acted on his convictions.
Though he was prepared to go to prison rather than enlist in the military, his
draft board granted him conscientious objection status. In 1952 his draft board
required him to reapply. Refusing to affirm that he believed in a supreme being
on the grounds that it was a "privileged exemption"[43] denied to his atheist
friends, McReynolds lost his conscientious objector classification. In 1954 he refused to be inducted into the armed services and was arrested and brought to
trial. The case was dismissed when the FBI refused a defense request to review his
FBI file.

By the time he moved to New York City in 1956, McReynolds was already
involved in the FOR through its youth group, but not the WRL. Yet even before
relocating to New York and connecting with the League, McReynolds—a Marxist—had developed a third camp, socialist pacifist position consistent with that
of the League. Like the League's post-World War II radicals, he supported a
multi-issue social reform program and advocated a vigorous, radical pacifism
that acted to solve social problems: "[W]e have a line to sell our own people—
Gandhian pacifism as opposed to Quaker pacifism. We must get people to realize that non-violence is a weapon, and that pacifists use it in the social struggle.
We must broaden the front on which pacifists work—to include race, economic,
community relations, etc. That is our first job."[44]

Like other independent socialists, McReynolds followed the Eastern European revolts that followed Soviet leader Nikita Khrushchev's de-Stalinization
speech at the twentieth Communist Party congress in 1956. Several days after
Polish factory workers in Poznan organized a demonstration that led to deadly
clashes with police, McReynolds wrote:

> It is now obvious that a real worker's [*sic*] underground exists in Eastern Europe.
> The uprising was beautifully timed and expertly carried off—clear evidence of
> organization. And as in East Berlin it was the working class which carried the

thing through. Unrest continues. Let the others talk about co-existence—I want to see revolution behind the Iron Curtain. Tragically enough I realize it isn't likely to happen when the only support such a revolution could have would come from the reactionary West—God (or Marx) grant a Socialist Third Force to stimulate more Poznan's [*sic*] and Montgomery's [*sic*].[45]

McReynolds moved to New York in 1956 and became editorial secretary of *Liberation* the following year. In the interim he worked for Rustin at In Friendship, a New York group providing support to Martin Luther King. In 1957 he practiced tax refusal.[46] By 1958 he was a member of the WRL's executive committee, the board of FOR-NY, and the SP national committee. Around this time he was also instrumental in organizing the Student Committee for a Sane Nuclear Policy. In 1958 the SP nominated him to run for the 19th congressional seat; later, in 1980 and 2000, he ran for president on the SP ticket.

In August 1960 McReynolds became the WRL's field secretary. As part of that work he served as a bridge between the Old Left and New Left, and between the League and student activists. He also was a key participant in the 1960 civil defense protest, serving as staff coordinator and a major leader.[47] Writing in the *Village Voice,* he condemned civil defense as a "deadly farce" that provided a false psychological shield from the realities of nuclear war.[48] Regarding the potential of pacifists to break the American-Soviet deadlock, he observed: "If we cannot do great things we can at least do little things." "You and I have not got the power to solve the Berlin crisis," he acknowledged, "but we still have the power to sit on a park bench, and that is a power that we dare not underestimate."[49]

In a leaflet distributed before and during the demonstration, the CDPC summarized its arguments against civil defense and outlined both legal and illegal protest options. "CIVIL DEFENSE IS NO DEFENSE," the leaflet proclaimed. The fire, shock waves, and radiation produced by one hydrogen bomb would "wipe out any city" and turn fallout shelters into death traps. The same leaflet urged citizens to distribute copies in shelters during the drill, or remain in City Hall Park until police ordered them to seek shelter, or refuse to take shelter as an act of civil disobedience. Emphasizing mainstream political opposition to civil defense, the leaflet emblazoned New Jersey governor Frank Meyner's dissent across the top: "We are fostering a cruel deception on the American people if we try to persuade them that they can have Civil Defense through underground shelters . . . there is only one defense against a nuclear war—and that is peace." The leaflet concluded with an appeal to the tradition of nonviolent social change in America, a tradition that included the labor, women's suffrage, and civil rights movements.[50]

Besides radical pacifists, both students and mothers—most of whom were nuclear pacifists—made an important contribution to the 1960 civil defense demonstration. Throughout New York, 1,000 students protested civil defense drills or conducted civil disobedience by refusing to take shelter at high school and college campuses.[51]

Led by Mary Sharmat and Janice Smith, a militant committee of mothers cooperating with the CDPC mobilized support. As it turned out, they were vital to the demonstration's success. Historian Dee Garrison has shown that these women astutely manipulated the image of domesticity and protective motherhood to attract public support. The *Village Voice* reported that eighty mothers brought a "squeaking brigade of children" to the event.[52] Correctly anticipating that the police would be reluctant to arrest parents (with their children, playpens, and toys), the mothers' committee loaned out babies to single male demonstrators.[53]

Mothers and babies were among the three to four thousand people who picketed in front of the Women's House of Detention. The *New York Times* noted the bright sunshine, the festive atmosphere, the baby carriages, and the mothers chatting and sipping coffee under a tree, and compared the picket line to a "Saturday family outing." One mother had in tow her three-year-old son carrying a sign announcing, "I am a boy, not a mole."[54] Commenting on the demonstration's unprecedented success, the *Nation* predicted that in 1961 the police would need more than three paddy wagons.[55]

The 1961 demonstration, held on 28 April, was even larger than the previous year's. The CDPC distributed fifty thousand leaflets entitled "BRAVE MEN DO NOT HIDE," which also outlined protest opportunities short of civil disobedience. To highlight the legitimacy and widespread appeal of the protest, the leaflet quoted prominent critics of civil defense and listed two dozen eminent sponsors, including David Riesman, Lewis Mumford, and supporters from the previous year.[56] When the 733 civil defense sirens "wailed like a king-size banshee,"[57] two thousand protestors assembled in City Hall Park to challenge civil defense. As in 1960, many of the protesters were mothers or students. Female peace activists, many of whom were mothers, had helped plan the demonstration. The police arrested fifty-two, including WRL/CDPC leaders McReynolds, DiGia, and Robert Gilmore.[58]

The WRL had assigned McReynolds to organize the 1961 protest, for which he served as staff coordinator. In speeches, memos, and articles he argued that civil defense drills promoted the arms race and war and must be opposed to preserve peace—the sole guarantor of security in the nuclear age. He also asserted that the protest offered citizens the opportunity to "vote" against war and a nuclear weapons-based foreign policy; to repudiate the dangerous illusion that shelters could protect men and women in the event of a nuclear war; to warn the government to expect sustained "resistance" to civil defense; and to overcome public apathy, itself a result of the "false sense of security" fostered by civil defense.[59] "Those who take shelter—whether here or in the Soviet Union . . . are acquiescing in the nuclear-arms race," he declared.[60] "Neither Run Nor Hide," his two-part *Village Voice* article, reached a broad New York audience and promoted interest in and support for the demonstration.

In "Neither Run Nor Hide," McReynolds addressed the dilemma of how "responsible citizens should respond to an immoral law when it has been enacted democratically." To build a case for civil disobedience, he cited northern defiance of the Fugitive Slave Act (1850) and Europeans who, in response to Hitler's order that Jews wear the Star of David, *also put on yellow stars, to identify with the Jews and thus destroy so evil a law.* Writing at the time of captured Nazi leader Adolf Eichmann's trial in Jerusalem on charges of war crimes, he declared that civil defense protests aimed to shatter the public "apathy" that had allowed the "extermination of the Jews" and now permitted American and Soviet war preparations to continue, threatening the "extermination of the human race."[61]

In his statement to the court during his trial, McReynolds emphasized the imperative of individual resistance to immoral acts. He also invoked the Nuremberg precedent and American revolutionary and antislavery traditions: "Today this courtroom is haunted by the Nuremberg Tribunal, for those of us who have broken the state Civil Defense Act have done so in the name of that higher law which our government invoked against the Germans at Nuremberg." Citing Peter Zenger, the Boston Tea Party, the Underground Railway, and the emergent civil rights sit-in movement in the South, he observed, "[O]ur democracy has in large part been created and sustained by individual men and women who defied state authority." The magistrate sentenced him to twenty-five days in prison or a $50 fine. McReynolds chose jail.[62]

Nearly six months after the 1961 protest, the WRL released its executive secretary, Bayard Rustin, on a half-time basis to coordinate a national CDPC campaign. In February 1962, McReynolds, the League's field secretary, replaced Rustin as CDPC coordinator. McReynolds maintained that civil defense protests would channel activists into existing peace groups and provide a bridge between the peace and social justice movements, asserting that "right now the C.D. protest is to the pacifists what CORE was once in its history." He contended that pacifists could link their critique of nuclear arms policy to the concerns of nonpacifists by emphasizing civil defense, since it was "more personal, more direct, and more immediate to people than missiles or war work or taxes or draft." In justifying the League's leadership of a national civil defense campaign, he offered this judgment of the League's significance to the civil defense movement: "In one sense the League has an historic claim [on] the C.D. protest movement, since it really turned it from a small witness into a mass movement in New York (with much work from many others)—but the point is the League was able to create an atmosphere within which this work and the effort of others took place."[63]

In a major victory for the WRL, for the pacifist-led CDPC, and for the power of mass, nonviolent social protest, civil defense authorities canceled the 1962 Operation Alert drill. From a small band of radical pacifist dissenters in 1955 to the mass protests of 1960 and 1961, the WRL had been instrumental in constructing a popular campaign against civil defense and nuclear weapons. In doing so, it contributed to the rebirth of the American peace movement. The Catholic Worker had initiated the civil defense protests, and the mothers' committee had brought a powerful vitality to the demonstrations, but it was the WRL that had provided the foundation for the movement's success. Significantly, the New York City civil defense protests illustrate the WRL's support for and embrace of civil disobedience.

### The WRL and Civil Rights in the Martin Luther King Era

"I salute the War Resisters League," Martin Luther King, Jr., declared at the organization's annual dinner in 1959. "You have been prophetic and you may yet help lead mankind from self-destruction."[64] Echoing the League's call for peace and justice, King asserted that "no sane person can afford to work for social justice within the nation unless he simultaneously resists war and clearly declares himself for non-violence in international relations." "What will be the ultimate value" he asked, "of having established social justice in a context where all people, Negro and white, are merely free to face destruction by strontium 90 or atomic war?"[65] Two months earlier, King had joined the FOR.[66] While he never joined the secular, more radical WRL, both the WRL and the FOR influenced King's pilgrimage to nonviolence and the civil rights movement.

The Montgomery bus boycott (1955–56) galvanized the civil rights movement and propelled King to the forefront of the national movement for racial justice. While King was the most prominent champion of the nonviolent civil rights revolution from 1955 until his assassination in 1968, WRL activists had made significant contributions to the civil rights movement from the 1940s to the 1960s. In the 1940s, League members cofounded CORE and participated in the Journey of Reconciliation. Jim Peck edited CORE's publication, the *Core-*

*later,* from 1949 until 1965, when black power advocates removed him because he was white. Most importantly, Bayard Rustin, the WRL's executive secretary, played a critical role in King's pilgrimage to pacifism and his adoption—and subsequent popularization—of Gandhian nonviolent protest techniques. Rustin and the League offered important advice and support to the King-led Montgomery bus boycott and the Southern Christian Leadership Conference (SCLC). Finally, the League's role in advancing civil rights between 1955 and 1963 demonstrates its shift from a single-issue to a multi-issue program.

Rosa Parks's refusal to surrender her seat to a white male bus passenger on 1 December 1955 sparked the Montgomery bus boycott. The boycott, which originated in local black activism and was initiated by local black leaders, had already started when King became involved. The boycott began on 5 December and lasted until the following December, when activists won their demand for integrated buses. Local black leaders established the Montgomery Improvement Association (MIA) to direct the boycott, and they elected King, a newcomer to the city, as its president. With help from the local black leadership and outside support, King led the boycott with great ability. The League was one of the first outside groups to offer advice and assistance to the MIA and its new leader.[67]

The Montgomery bus boycott electrified the pacifist movement. Writing to his SP comrades, David McReynolds suggested that the civil rights movement offered the nonpacifist Left an instructive example of nonviolent social revolution: "WHAT IS HAPPENING IN MONTGOMERY IS NON-VIOLENT, DIRECT, MASS ACTION. WHAT WE SEE IN MONTGOMERY IS ESSENTIALLY AND FUNDAMENTALLY A REVOLUTIONARY ATTACK CARRIED ON IN THE MOST DIRECT MANNER AGAINST JIM-CROW. ALL OF US HAVE A LESSON TO LEARN, BOTH IN TECHNIQUE AND IN SPIRIT, FROM THE NEGROES OF MONTGOMERY."[68]

Rustin remained the key link between the WRL, King, and the civil rights movement. He was influential—perhaps instrumental—in King's conversion to a full Gandhian position in early 1956. For the next decade he would be a close confidant and influential advisor to King. During the Montgomery bus boycott he served as the liaison between King and the northern noncommunist Left. He also helped found the Southern Christian Leadership Conference (1957) and served it as a key adviser. And he was pivotal to organizing the March on Washington (1963). He also wrote articles that appeared under King's name, including "Our Struggle," an April 1956 piece in *Liberation* that generated northern support for the boycott. Consistent with its "service agency" role, the League provided critical advice and support to King—a role largely ignored by historians. It did so mainly through Rustin but through other venues as well.

At the beginning of the Montgomery boycott, King was not a pacifist, nor was he committed to Gandhian nonviolence. For instance, he and other MIA leaders initially carried guns, and King relied on armed bodyguards for protection.[69] During his decade-long "pilgrimage to nonviolence"[70] he was greatly influenced by WRL members (who also belonged to the FOR). As a Morehouse College undergraduate (1944–48), he read Henry David Thoreau's "Essay on Civil Disobedience," his "first intellectual contact" with nonviolent resistance.[71] While at Crozer Theological Seminary (1948–51), two pacifist speakers prompted him to consider nonviolence more seriously. A campus lecture by A. J. Muste was his initial direct exposure to pacifism; while "deeply moved," he remained skeptical of pacifism's "practicability."[72] King also heard Mordecai Johnson, the president of Howard University, speak about Gandhi at a forum in Philadelphia sponsored by the FOR. Excited, he bought half a dozen books on Gandhi. This intellectual encounter transformed King's views on the power of nonviolence to advance social reform. At Boston University (1951–55) he met many pacifists, and was influenced in particular by Allan Knight Chalmers, a leader of the Theological School and a long-serving member of the WRL's executive committee. King then repudiated his sympathy for the antipacifist views of Reinhold Niebuhr, who, he argued, mistakenly confused "passive nonresistance" with active "nonviolent resistance."[73]

In 1954, King moved to Montgomery to accept a pastorship at Ebenezer Baptist Church. On the eve of the Montgomery boycott he believed that "nonviolent resistance was one of the most potent weapons available to oppressed people"; however, he also acknowledged that he "had merely an intellectual understanding and appreciation of the position, with no firm determination to organize it in a socially effective situation."[74]

The Montgomery bus boycott completed King's pilgrimage to nonviolence. He later explained: "Living through the actual experience of the protest, nonviolence became more than a method to which I gave intellectual assent; it became a commitment to a way of life."[75] Though he sympathized with nonviolence, there was no assurance that King—in the middle of a volatile social protest campaign—would in practice honor his intellectual leanings toward nonviolence.

Bayard Rustin and Glenn Smiley—the FOR's white, Texas-born, southern secretary—were the men most responsible for King's full commitment to Gandhian nonviolence. Alfred Hassler, the FOR's executive secretary, worked with Smiley and King in Montgomery, and later recalled that they "were the two most important factors by far in bringing nonviolence into the situation." In February 1956, Smiley noted that "Bayard has had a very good influence on King, wrote the much quoted speech of last week, and was in on all the strategy." Following his March visit to Montgomery, Homer Jack, a cofounder of CORE, reported that Rustin's "contribution to interpreting the Gandhian approach to the leadership cannot be overestimated." For example, Rustin was alarmed when he saw a gun during a visit to King's home, and discussed with King the incompatibility of weapons with a Gandhian strategy. King soon removed all guns from his house. Rustin and Smiley provided their expertise in nonviolent protest strategies to King, and through him to the growing civil rights movement.[76]

In February 1956 an anonymous WRL member donated funds to send Rustin to Montgomery to consult with the boycott leaders and "to explore the possibilities of setting up a workshop in [the] principles and tactics of non-violence." Viewing the situation as "not only a question of race relations but also of violence and non-violence," the League released Rustin for the project. Roy Finch, the WRL's chairman, declared that "the League should do all in its power to help strengthen those forces in the Negro community which are exploring non-violence." Advocating the expansion of Montgomery into a regional bus boycott, Rustin arrived in Montgomery on 21 February and remained there for two weeks before returning to New York on 8 March.[77]

Not all MIA activists and sympathizers supported Rustin's trip to Montgomery. Opponents of Rustin's involvement worried that the overt involvement of outside individuals and groups—especially those perceived as radical—would harm the boycott movement. The FOR could present its program in familiar Christian language; the secular, politically more radical WRL lacked such a cultural shield. Rustin's opponents were even more concerned that his personal history might have a negative impact on the MIA movement. His brief membership in the Young Communist League, his World War II draft refusal, and his 1953 conviction on a homosexual charge offered conservative southern segregationists an opportunity to smear the boycott. One FOR leader cautioned: "It would be easy for the police to frame [Rustin] . . . and set back the whole cause there."[78]

During a February meeting in A. Philip Randolph's New York office, leaders from the pacifist, civil rights, and labor movements concluded that Rustin should return home because Alabamans saw him as a northern communist.[79] Several days earlier, Rustin himself had told the League that a Montgomery reporter was spreading rumors that he was a "communist NAACP organizer" planning "a violent uprising." "I have been followed by police cars, and never go out after dark alone," he added.[80] Motivated by concerns like these, the FOR decided not to cooperate with Rustin. Realizing that his background might harm the boycott, Rustin moved to Birmingham, where he continued to advise King.[81]

Shortly after his first trip to Montgomery, the WRL published Rustin's report on the boycott, which attracted international attention. Rustin reported that although MIA leaders rejected the first use of violence, there existed "considerable confusion on the question as to whether violence is justified in retaliation to violence directed against the Negro community." The MIA leadership had not yet developed a "careful, non-violent preparation for any such extreme situation," he wrote; however, King is developing a decidedly Gandhi-like view and . . . is eagerly learning all that he can about non-violence and evidence indicates that he is emerging as a regional symbol of non-violent resistance in the deep South." Rustin claimed that the Montgomery boycott was advancing world peace and civil rights, offering blacks "a new direct-action method that is bound 'to spread over the deep South,'" and "reveal to a world sick with violence that non-violent resistance has relevance today in the United States against forces that are prepared to use extreme measures to crush it." He concluded by asking advocates of nonviolent protest to send donations to the WRL earmarked Montgomery.[82]

Besides releasing Rustin, the WRL supported King and the Montgomery protest by raising funds for the MIA and by publicizing the boycott and his non-violent strategy. In part, the League promoted the protest through its subsidy of *Liberation,* which publicized King and the boycott. The WRL financed *Liberation*'s reprint of King's April 1956 article to encourage "a non-violent response in other parts of the south where terror exists."[83] In March 1956, E. D. Nixon, who initiated the boycott, told his story at a WRL-sponsored New York meeting. In May 1956 the League promoted a civil rights rally at Madison Square Garden organized by In Friendship, a New York group formed to provide northern support for King, in which the WRL and Rustin played important roles.[84]

Citing their two special issues on Montgomery (April and December), *Liberation*'s editors declared that the magazine and the WRL had made "a crucial contribution to *nonviolent action* in the South." On several occasions the League released Rustin to assist In Friendship and to advise King and other Southern civil rights leaders on nonviolent principles and techniques. The League and Rustin played a leading role in organizing the Committee for Nonviolent Integration, a pacifist-liberal group that donated cars and bicycles to the MIA, organized southern workshops on nonviolence, and distributed King's *Liberation* essay.[85]

Following his return from Alabama, Rustin contended that Montgomery demonstrated the efficacy of nonviolence under dangerous and inhospitable conditions: "Many people have been amazed that southern Negroes, faced with bombing, police brutality and murder could take so successfully to nonviolence. People like to excuse themselves from examining the power of such a technique by convincing themselves that it can be effective only against the 'gentlemanly and civilized' British." [86]

Several months later, Roy Finch asserted that the South constituted a laboratory for demonstrating the effectiveness of nonviolence in the struggle to achieve social justice. To members who questioned whether the League (rather than groups such as CORE) should assume civil rights work, he explained why the League had recently committed itself to help abolish southern racial segregation. It was advancing nonviolence in the South, Finch argued, "by placing before Negro leaders our philosophy and by aiding them to employ pacifist tactics . . . [which might lead them] to adopt the whole pacifist philosophy." [87] He contended that the South was a showcase for radical pacifist methods:

> One of the principal arguments used against war resistance is that we do not offer any alternatives to war. . . . Our answer must be to show in practice that there *are* ways of gaining justice and settling disputes without war and violence. By encouraging effective concrete demonstrations of pacifist methods in conflict situations we create a powerful argument for war resistance.
>
> The South today is a miniature war situation. Our interest is to show that pacifism will work there. At the same time in doing this we believe that we are helping to relieve one of the tensions from which violence and war spring on a national scale. We are attacking a sore spot that in every part of the world today breeds war. [88]

To sustain the Southern civil rights protest following the MIA's triumph in Montgomery, in 1957 Rustin helped organize the Southern Christian Leadership Conference. From the beginning of the Montgomery boycott, Rustin had lobbied to expand the nonviolent protest across the South through a mass-based southern movement led by black clergy and directed by King. The SCLC, formed in January 1957, performed this role. King endorsed the venture after Rustin assured him that "I can show you how to do it." [89] Addressing the SCLC's significance to American pacifism, the *WRL News* predicted that nonviolent resistance would infuse the southern civil rights movement and increase the awareness of nonviolence's relevance to war and other issues. [90]

The WRL continued to endorse Rustin's civil rights work, releasing him for SCLC and King projects such as the Pilgrimage of Prayer, the Youth Movement for Integrated Schools, the Crusade for Citizenship, and the 1960 Election Protests. In February 1957, King and other SCLC leaders urged President Dwight Eisenhower to denounce segregation. In response to the White House's silence, Rustin helped organize the Pilgrimage of Prayer. The demonstration took place on 17 May 1957, the third anniversary of *Brown v. Board of Education,* the historic ruling widely resisted in the South. As many as 25,000 people gathered at the Lincoln Memorial to protest white violence and legal obstruction and to urge the passage of federal civil rights legislation. In a keynote speech influenced by Rustin, King promised: *"Give us the ballot,* and we will quickly and nonviolently . . . implement" the *Brown* decision.[91]

Rustin also played a key role in planning the Crusade for Citizenship, a 1957–58 SCLC voter registration campaign that aimed to double the 1,250,000 southern blacks then registered. Rustin helped King organize the registration drive, and King asked him to coordinate the crusade's rallies. However, Stanley Levison and other New York activists persuaded King not to allow Rustin to work on the crusade in the South, arguing that his homosexuality and his radical background would enable segregationists to smear King. Because of inadequate resources, lack of cooperation from the NAACP, and King's chauvinistic attitude toward Ella Baker, who replaced Rustin, the crusade faltered and never registered significant numbers of new black voters. Perhaps Rustin would not have made an appreciable difference to the crusade. The point is that once again, the WRL had demonstrated its commitment to black voting rights by releasing him to help organize the Crusade for Citizenship.[92]

In 1958 and 1959, Rustin directed and the WRL endorsed two Youth Marches for Integrated Schools. The goal of both was to mobilize public support for compliance with *Brown v. Board of Education.* The League also provided a loan to support the first march. Randolph announced the 1958 march, which was organized by an *ad hoc* committee close to King—who served as an honorary chairman—after Eisenhower showed no inclination to convene a White House conference on school integration. Prominent people endorsed the Youth March, and League members made important contributions to it. Ralph DiGia helped with the organizing; Jim Peck served on the publicity committee; and Edward Gottlieb, Robert Gilmore, and Michael Harrington advised students. Explaining its decision to release Rustin to work on the project, the League pointed out that the march aimed "to relieve the frustration on the Negro community that could easily lead to violence."[93]

On 24 October 1958, ten thousand people, most of them young, walked down Constitution Avenue to the Lincoln Memorial. Shortly after the integrated march, Randolph thanked the WRL for promoting racial harmony: "Your contribution cannot be overestimated. Bayard Rustin coordinated an historic non-violent demonstration."[94]

The following April, the 1959 Youth March for Integration brought 26,000 people to Washington. According to Jervis Anderson, the Prayer Pilgrimage and

Youth Marches, which Rustin helped organize, nurtured the post-Montgomery consciousness of and support for civil rights and attracted talented young leaders to the burgeoning civil rights movement.[95] The following year, King again sought assistance from Rustin.

At the request of King and Randolph, in February 1960 the WRL released Rustin to work with the SCLC as a special assistant to King. Rustin—who continued to serve as the WRL's executive secretary—headed the SCLC's New York City office, raising money to support black registration and voting rights, the southern student sit-in movement, and other direct action projects. "The WRL is making a great service to the cause of freedom and justice by making Bayard Rustin available to us at this crucial period in our struggle," King wrote Edward Gottlieb, the League's new chairman. "We can only continue our resistance to evil in the south if Negroes can remain nonviolent."[96]

Regrettably, King succumbed to political blackmail by Congressman Adam Clayton Powell, Jr., a black Democrat who represented Harlem. For the SCLC, Rustin began organizing civil rights demonstrations as well as picketing at the July 1960 national Democratic and Republican conventions. The moderate 1960 Civil Rights Act had been passed one month earlier; even so, the SCLC wanted both political parties to denounce race discrimination and segregation, endorse the student sit-it movement, and enforce *Brown.* To advance either John F. Kennedy's candidacy or his own position in Congress, Powell blocked the demonstration at the Democratic convention. In early July, soon after charging that Rustin exercised an undue radical influence on King, Powell informed King that unless he dismissed Rustin and canceled the protest, he would announce that King and Rustin were involved in a homosexual relationship—a patently false charge. Rustin resigned as King's assistant and from the SCLC to protect the movement. Instead of submitting a personal report to the WRL, Rustin forwarded Nat Hentoff's *Village Voice* article on the incident. Hentoff, a League member, portrayed Rustin as "the most brilliant tactician in the civil rights field with no interest in publicity or power. . . . Powell gets the headlines, but it has always been men like Bayard Rustin who get results."[97]

Between 1960 and 1963 the WRL continued to show its commitment to civil rights, a multi-issue agenda, and nonviolent direct action and civil disobedience. During the 1960 campaign the League rejected both the Democrats and the Republicans. Instead, it formed a new committee, the Committee for Protest Action in the 1960 Election. Working out of WRL headquarters and comprised of prominent citizens, this committee "urge[d] people to work for, not merely vote for, peace and civil rights." On election day the League sponsored a civil rights rally led by Fred Shuttlesworth, who counseled blacks to use mass nonviolent action to advance and obtain equality. In all this the League was endorsing direct action and making civil rights as important an issue as peace.[98]

In mid-November of 1960 the WRL sponsored a two-day Student Institute on Nonviolence and Social Change. Sixty students heard prominent pacifists and social reformers speak about nonviolent direct action and its relevance to the civil rights—and to the peace and anticolonial—movements. Youth groups, including the Students for a Democratic Society, the Student Peace Union, and the Young People's Socialist League, helped organize the event. This is evidence of links between the WRL and the emergent student movement.[99]

The WRL also promoted the student civil rights movement in the South. Ecstatic over the dramatic nonviolent resistance offered by students who led a sit-in demanding service at a lunch counter in Greensboro, North Carolina, and over the southern sit-in movement that this action inspired, the League dedicated its 1961 Peace Calendar to "the Southern students who . . . participated in the heroic 'sit-in movement' which deeply stirred this nation, and who by their dignity and their willingness to accept insult, physical injury, and prison without bitterness and retaliation, have given millions throughout the world an example of the power of non-violent action as a positive method for creative social change."[100] The League donated over one thousand of its annotated calendars to CORE locals, the FOR, the Student Nonviolent Coordinating Committee (SNCC), the Student Peace Union, and the American Friends Service Committee.[101]

The WRL supported CORE, SNCC, and the nonviolent civil rights movement in other ways besides this. In May 1961, CORE organized the Freedom Rides to integrate interstate buses in the deep South—a project modeled on the 1947 Journey of Reconciliation. Jim Peck, the only participant on both rides, joined an interracial group of men and women and was beaten so badly by a Birmingham mob that he required fifty-three stitches to his face. When authorities in Mississippi arrested more than three hundred Freedom Riders, the League appealed to its membership and friends to offer CORE interest-free loans to provide bail bonds. Furthermore, Rustin advised the fledgling SNCC on its program and fundraising. In 1962 and 1963, SNCC maintained its northern headquarters in the WRL offices.[102]

In November 1963 the WRL provided a grant to promote the Fast for School Integration, a project initiated and led by Edward Gottlieb. An innovative New York elementary school principal, Gottlieb staged weekend fasts at the Community Church "to break the Harlem school ghetto." This action did not persuade white parents to enroll their children in black Harlem schools; even so, the League claimed that it led people to promote other school integration plans.[103]

The WRL also released Rustin to organize the largest civil rights demonstration of the 1960s, the 1963 March on Washington for Jobs and Freedom.[104] On 28 August 1963, to mark the centenary of the Emancipation Proclamation, the March on Washington convened 250,000 people—black and white—at the Lincoln Memorial. Under Randolph's leadership the march had adopted a nonviolent strategy to advance a civil rights and labor agenda. At Randolph's request, Rustin had codrafted a blueprint emphasizing economic goals and recommending direct action and civil disobedience. Randolph had dropped plans for civil disobedience in order to obtain the support of the conservative NAACP and National Urban League; however, he had rejected Roy Wilkins's demand to drop Rustin as the march's organizer because of his controversial past.

It was at the March on Washington that King delivered his famous "I Have A Dream" speech. Following King to the podium, Rustin listed the goals of the march: passage of the Kennedy administration's civil rights bill, a $2 hourly minimum wage, a federal public works program, and federal action to prohibit racial discrimination in employment. The March on Washington helped win passage of the Civil Rights Act of 1964 and the Voting Rights Act of 1965. WRL member Charles Bloomstein observed: "Dr. King will go down in history as Lincoln did after the Gettysburg address. . . . Bayard's masterful planning of the march made King's speech both possible and meaningful." Rustin contended that the protest showed "that nonviolence had been accepted as a method and symbol of Negro and White unity." [105] One week after the demonstration, *Life* featured Rustin and Randolph on its cover, with Lincoln enthroned on his marble chair in the background.[106]

After 1963, Rustin remained active in the civil rights movement but moved to the right politically. In 1965 he resigned as the WRL's executive secretary, assumed leadership of the A. Philip Randolph Institute—a service agency for labor and civil rights—and became a leading advocate of coalition politics. That same year, he explained his new position in an important *Commentary* article, "From Protest to Politics." According to Rustin, the civil rights movement had won legal integration and equality. In order to solve the social and economic problems that remained, the civil rights movement should drop street protest and enter into an alliance with labor, liberals, and the Democratic Party. Consistent with his break with the League, Rustin opposed the radical pacifist stand on the Vietnam War (an immediate and unconditional American withdrawal from

Vietnam) and supported the moderate pacifist stance (an immediate negotiated settlement). Undeterred, the WRL continued League maintained its commitment to radical pacifism.[107]

## The Committee for Nonviolent Action

In the spring of 1957, in response to the fears and anxieties over nuclear war, the established peace movement and several antiwar liberals created two *ad hoc* groups to spearhead an American campaign to abolish nuclear testing and nuclear weapons. Despite different memberships and methods, the National Committee for a Sane Nuclear Policy (SANE) and the Committee for Nonviolent Action (CNVA)—"the pragmatists and visionaries" of the antinuclear movement—shared the same goals and often cooperated.[108] SANE appealed to nuclear pacifists and antiwar activists; it was a broad-based, liberal organization devoted to political education and action. In contrast, the CNVA was a small, disciplined vanguard of sixty to seventy radical pacifists who championed Gandhian techniques of direct action and civil disobedience.

The League and its leaders played a key role in establishing both SANE and CNVR. The League cooperated with SANE, and its members were active in both SANE and CNVA; that said, the League was most closely involved with CNVA, and most of that group's members were also League members. Lawrence Wittner contends that SANE and CNVA contributed to a "breakthrough" in the postwar peace movement.[109] By helping to midwife the rebirth of the SANE and CNVR, the League helped the peace movement achieve a rebirth.

Lawrence Scott, a WRL member from the Midwest, was the person most responsible for establishing SANE and CNVA. During World War II, Scott had worked on civil rights projects with A. J. Muste and James Farmer. In 1948 he broke with Henry Wallace, became a Quaker, joined Peacemakers, and practiced tax refusal. In 1957 he resigned as peace education director of the Chicago AFSC. Dissatisfied with "effete, middle class Friends," opposed to the deduction of payroll taxes from his salary, and convinced that "words are not enough" to create a social and economic revolution or to abolish radiation poisoning and nuclear arsenals, he embarked on a program of nonviolent civil disobedience.[110]

Scott went to New York and persuaded pacifist leaders to launch an antinuclear campaign. With Robert Gilmore, another WRL member and secretary of the New York Friends, Scott invited some twenty radical pacifist, nuclear pacifist, and liberal antiwar leaders to a meeting in Philadelphia on 22 April 1957. The meeting was convened to discuss his proposal for a campaign to abolish nuclear testing and nuclear weapons. The WRL was represented by Muste. Both

SANE and CNVA emerged from this Philadelphia meeting. Gilmore led SANE, while Scott headed the more radical CNVA.[111]

At Scott's initiative, on 17 May twenty representatives from various peace organizations met in the Washington, D.C., office of the Women's International League for Peace and Freedom to discuss an antinuclear test campaign. That same afternoon, in a link—both symbolic and concrete—between the pacifist and civil rights movements, the SCLC's Pilgrimage of Prayer brought 25,000 people to the Lincoln Memorial to promote equal rights for African Americans. Meanwhile, pacifists decided to organize a civil disobedience project to protest the upcoming Nevada nuclear tests. Nearly two weeks later, on 29 May 1957, representatives of the WRL, the FOR, the AFSC, the Catholic Worker, and the WILPF met in New York City to form Nonviolent Action Against Nuclear Weapons (NVAANW, which in 1959 was renamed CNVR), an *ad hoc* committee that championed Gandhian nonviolent direct action and civil disobedience. After naming Scott coordinator and George Willoughby chairman, NVAANW began planning a direct action, civil disobedience project to protest the Nevada tests. The League, which had started to explore similar protests, played a key role in the CNVA's Nevada project.[112]

In its first action, NVAANW organized a series of events in Nevada between 3 and 9 August 1957 to protest the Atomic Energy Commission's (AEC) decision to conduct a nuclear test explosion on 6 August, the twelfth anniversary of the Hiroshima bombing. Scott, who organized the NVAANW project, argued that civil disobedience—not traditional political action or education—was the most effective nonviolent technique for challenging the Nevada test: "Civil disobedience against immoral and irrational laws by a few people does not constitute a non-violent revolution. But it is a beginning." [113]

On 3 August, more than thirty NVAANW members and supporters met in Las Vegas. To commemorate Hiroshima Day they held a twenty-four-hour Prayer and Conscience Vigil two hundred yards from the entrance to Camp Mercury, the test site sixty-five miles northwest of Las Vegas. On the morning of 6 August, as the climax of a week-long peace action, eleven of them entered Camp Mercury. This act of civil disobedience was observed by armed guards and also by reporters from the major networks. After Muste explained NVAANW's nonviolent plans, one official sounded relieved: "You mean, then, that there really isn't going to be a riot?" [114]

The eleven trespassers were transported sixty miles to Beatty, Nevada, where a Justice of the Peace gave them suspended sentences. The trespassers caught a ride back to Camp Mercury with newspaper reporters and continued to stand watch for the test explosion, which had been postponed one day because of heavy winds. According to Jim Peck, who later wrote several first-hand accounts of the protest and explosion, the next morning at 5:30 "the early dawn light was suddenly obliterated with a blinding flash." Several pacifists turned their backs in symbolic protest; others observed sideways; others looked directly into the light "to come a little closer to realizing how the people of Hiroshima had felt." Meanwhile, the WRL and CNVA sponsored "black sash" demonstrations in New York and Chicago to coincide with the Nevada protest.[115]

Another CNVA project captured even more attention. On 10 February 1958 the *Golden Rule,* a thirty-foot ketch with a crew of four, set sail from California to protest American nuclear weapons tests scheduled off Eniwetok Island, located in the Pacific Ocean nearly two thousand miles from Hawaii. Captained by Albert Bigelow, the crew included William Huntington, David Gale, and George Willoughby (a World War II CO and executive secretary of the Central Committee for Conscientious Objectors). All except Gale were WRL members.

The WRL endorsed this civil disobedience project and supported it in various ways. Its office served as publicity headquarters for the project; League staffers Rustin, DiGia, and Peck helped plan and publicize it; the League released Rustin to assist it on a part-time basis; and the 1959 WRL Peace Calendar publicized the *Golden Rule* and other antinuclear projects.[116] Meanwhile, consistent with its third camp position, the NVAANW attempted to send a pacifist delegation to the Soviet Union to appeal for an end to Soviet nuclear testing.

Bigelow turned out to be a dashing and intriguing media figure. A Harvard graduate and a former Eisenhower precinct captain, he had served as a naval officer in World War II. Shocked by the devastating effects of the atomic bomb, his family had hosted two Hiroshima maidens—survivors of the blast of 6 August—bringing them to America for cosmetic surgery. This experience drew Bigelow further toward pacifism. A month before qualifying for a pension, he resigned his commission in the Naval Reserve. Within a few years he had joined the Quakers and become a committed pacifist. Like other members of the *Golden Rule*'s crew, he had participated in NVAANW's Camp Mercury project the summer before; the sight of the test flash confirmed his belief "that nuclear war must go." Six months later, certain "that *all* nuclear explosions are monstrous, evil, unworthy of human beings,"[117] he announced that he would skipper the *Golden Rule* into the Pacific testing zone. "I am going because it is time to do something about peace, not just talk about peace," he declared. "I am going because I have to—if I am to call myself a human being."[118]

In Gandhian fashion, he and NVAANW wrote President Eisenhower in January informing him of their intention to block the "monstrous delinquency" of nuclear testing: "For years we have spoken and written of the suicidal military preparations of the Great Powers, but our voices have been lost in the massive effort of those responsible for preparing this country for war. We mean now to speak with the weight of our whole lives."[119]

Seven hundred miles from California, after being battered by a storm, the *Golden Rule* returned to San Pedro to make repairs and replace Gale, who was suffering terribly from seasickness. The ketch departed again on 25 March and reached Honolulu in mid-April. Ignoring a federal injunction, the crew set sail for the Eniwetok testing area on 1 May. The Coast Guard stopped the ketch and towed it back to Honolulu. After a week in jail, each crew member received a sixty-day suspended sentence. On 4 June, with Peck replacing Huntington, the crew made another attempt to reach the test site. Again they were halted, arrested, and convicted. This time they were sentenced to thirty days in Honolulu City Jail.[120]

The first arrest of the *Golden Rule*'s crew sparked a nationwide protest. Shortly after the arrest on 1 May, Robert Gilmore, a NVAANW member and director of SANE-NY, prepared a memo documenting one week of coast-to-coast picketing at AEC offices, the Honolulu federal prison, and other federal buildings. "Our drive for nuclear sanity has now reached the proportions of a genuine, nationwide grass-roots movement," he observed, noting the widespread press, television, and radio coverage of the many antinuclear actions. The WRL authorized DiGia to participate in one such protest, a week-long fast and sit-down in the Maryland offices of the AEC.[121]

While the *Golden Rule* crew was awaiting trial, the *Phoenix of Hiroshima* arrived in Honolulu. On board was Earle Reynolds, an anthropologist who had spent three years in Japan studying the effects of radiation; with him were his wife Barbara, their two teenage children, and a Japanese sailor. The Reynolds decided to continue the protest of the *Golden Rule* and sail into the nuclear test zone. On 2 July 1958 the *Phoenix* entered the test area and notified the authorities. Earle was arrested and sentenced to six months in jail. "The Phoenix, in its trip, *was* the *Golden Rule*," Reynolds later told Bigelow. The WRL and its leaders publicized the Reynolds saga and raised contributions for the Phoenix Defense Fund.[122]

Plans to send an NVAANW delegation to Moscow at the same time as the *Golden Rule* protest were thwarted by Soviet officials, who refused to grant visas to the five people in the group. The Soviets had assured them that visas would be waiting for them in Helsinki. On this basis, the delegation, which included WRL members Bayard Rustin, Lawrence Scott, and Morton Ryweck, left for Russia in April. After waiting fruitlessly for several weeks in Helsinki, the five issued a statement denouncing Russia's refusal to grant them visas and returned to the United States.[123] In November 1958, assisted by a loan from the League, NVAANW sent the *Golden Rule* and *Phoenix* crews to the Geneva Conference to urge American, British, and Soviet negotiators to sign a test ban treaty. The trip generated modest publicity.[124]

In the summer of 1958 the WRL linked the spirit of the *Golden Rule* to the political awakening that was taking place among college students: "For the first time since World War II, it has become possible to present the pacifist point of view on the campus." Notwithstanding "the prosperity and fatalism" of the 1950s, the League detected a "residue of conscience and idealism" in students who responded to the pacifist style: "What impresses the student today is the kind of concrete personal action exemplified by the Golden Rule . . . This speaks a language which everybody can understand, free from political manipulations and double-talk. Somebody has believed enough in something to put their reputations and their lives on the line." [125]

The voyage of the *Golden Rule* was an important milestone in the rebirth of the peace movement. Since World War II the WRL and radical pacifists had been engaging in peace projects to dramatize the perils of warfare and nuclear holocaust. But, as Lawrence Wittner has observed, "in contrast to pacifist activities of the preceding decade," the *Golden Rule* and the Phoenix "caused an immediate furor." [126]

Omaha Action, the next CNVA project, was land-based. Its purpose was to focus attention on the Atlas ICBM base near Mead, Nebraska, southwest of Omaha. The Mead base was being constructed to house Intercontinental Ballistic Missiles (ICBMs), which were tipped with nuclear warheads. The goals of Omaha Action were to promote disarmament and block construction of the Mead ICBM site. Initiated by CNVA in 1959, the project was later sponsored by an independent *ad hoc* committee, Omaha Action—Nonviolence Against Nuclear Missiles. Homer Jack served as chairman; A. J. Muste and Brad Lyttle were coordinators. The FOR did not endorse the project because it was going to involve civil disobedience; the WRL did support it, permitting the organizers to use its mailing list, publicizing the protest through *WRL News,* and authorizing Bayard Rustin to visit Omaha to help plan and direct the protest. Other League members also participated.[127]

Between 18 and 22 June, Omaha Action participants conducted public meetings in Lincoln and Omaha, organized training sessions, held conferences with public officials and opinion makers, and distributed literature. On 22 June the participants divided into two groups of five and seven and began the two-day walk from Omaha and Lincoln to the Mead missile base. They arrived at the base gate from different directions on 24 June, retired to a wooded knoll 150 feet from the base entrance, and made camp. In the week that followed they maintained a vigil and established contact with base workers and officials.

Civil disobedience and nonviolent obstruction began on 1 July and continued until 21 July. On 1 July, Muste committed civil disobedience by climbing over a wooden fence and entering the base. Guards escorted him back out. He repeated his action and was arrested. Over the next three weeks, fifteen protesters were arrested, most of them for repeating Muste's act of trespass. More controversial, two pacifists conducted nonviolent obstruction by lying down on the road to stop trucks from carrying construction materials onto the base.[128] Most of those convicted for trespassing were given the maximum sentence: six months in jail and a $500 fine. However, the judge suspended the sentences on condition that the pacifists did not interfere with any military operations or construction anywhere in the United States over the following year. Most Omaha Action veterans elected to serve the prison time, and all of them refused on principle to pay the fines.[129]

Omaha Action generated much local publicity and some national and international attention. The local press offered detailed reports on the protest but also red-baited the dissidents. Members of the American Legion picketed the pacifists. In response to their criticism, Dr. Herbert Jehle, a German immigrant and WRL member—and perhaps Omaha Action's only local backer—declared: "I spent more than a year in a Nazi concentration camp because I refused to build bombers [to bomb the Allies] in World War II."[130] Besides local media, publications such as the *New York Times* and *Peace News* (London) covered the protest.[131]

A few months after Omaha Action, CNVA sponsored its first international civil disobedience action, the Sahara Protest Project. The French were seeking to develop an atomic bomb to bolster their military power and political prestige. In response to French plans to conduct a nuclear test at Reggan in the Algerian Sahara in January 1960, CNVA agreed to cosponsor the Sahara Protest Project. This international project was initiated by the British-based Direct Action Committee Against Nuclear War, a group with views similar to those of CNVA. The goal was to place a team of pacifists inside or near the test site to either prevent or challenge the French test. The protesters risked deportation, imprisonment, and death.

The project also offered a "direct link" between the campaign to abolish nuclear weapons and the African struggle for independence. African nations, mindful of radioactive fallout, were urging the French to cancel the test, which threatened to contaminate the air, water, and food supply of the region and nearby countries.[132]

Many Ghanian organizations supported the project. The most important of these was the Ghana Council for Nuclear Disarmament (GCD), an umbrella group that included independent associations of women, lawyers, veterans, trade unions, Christians, and—most significantly—the ruling Convention People's Party. Ghana's prime minister, Kwame Nkrumah, supported the protest. So did his country's chiefs and the Committee of African Organisations, which represented various groups throughout the continent. Finally, prominent individuals supported the Sahara Project, including Martin Luther King, Linus Pauling, Bertrand Russell, Philip Toynbee, and Jayaprakash Narayan.[133]

Although the League supported the Sahara protest team, the project highlighted the WRL dilemma of balancing its traditional focus on peace action with its more recent emphasis on civil rights. On request from CNVA, the League dispatched Rustin to Ghana to assist the project. While the League continued to assign priority to peace activism, Rustin was increasingly making civil rights his major concern. The Sahara Project forced Rustin (and the League) to confront the competing demands of the peace and civil rights movements. Bill Sutherland, the black League member who lived in Ghana and worked for the Ghanaian government, provided a bridge between Ghanaian and British activists and did much to persuade CNVA and the WRL to endorse the project.[134]

In October 1959, Rustin traveled to Ghana to help plan the Sahara Project. Comprising a half-dozen pacifists from Europe and the United States and a dozen African volunteers, the Sahara protest team included Sutherland, who, with WRL financial support, had moved to Ghana in 1953 to assist the Ghanian and African independence movements. Once Rustin arrived in Africa, it became clear to the team that it was "imperative" for him to participate fully in the project. Rustin himself agreed. As a veteran Gandhian and African American, he would be able to offer tested advice on "tactics and strategy"; furthermore, because he was black he would be able to gain the confidence and support of African leaders. So the team asked the League to grant Rustin an extension.[135]

Shortly after he arrived in Ghana, Rustin learned that A. Philip Randolph opposed his participation in the Sahara Project and wanted him to return to the United States to organize civil rights protests (including civil disobedience) at the 1960 Democratic and Republican conventions. Rustin replied that he thought planning for the civil rights demonstrations had been delayed until February. He also outlined his role in and the enormous significance of the African peace action, and asked his friends in the WRL and in New York pacifist and civil rights circles to advise him on whether he should join the Sahara protest team. If the French arrested him, he was looking at three years in jail, which would jeopardize his American civil rights work. He wanted to remain in Africa, but he did not want to "be placed in a position where I can be accused of irresponsibility or shirking in duty to the Civil Rights struggle."[136]

In mid-November, several pacifist and civil rights leaders met in Randolph's New York office to discuss Rustin's situation. They failed to reach a consensus. Nearly a week later, Rustin received a telegram indicating that they could not agree on what action he should take. This led him to conclude that the choice must be his own.[137]

In addition, DiGia and Peck wrote Rustin to report on the meeting. They offered no instructions but did make clear their own preference and that of the WRL. DiGia wrote:

> I imagine you are pretty essential to the [Sahara] project and that the Africans . . . would feel very let down . . . for you to pull out. . . . Randolph and [Stanley Levison] state that you are essential [over here], that the civil rights movement is the greatest thing for peace [and] the worldwide struggle for equality. They want you back. Meanwhile we [in the pacifist movement] want you to stay. From the pacifist viewpoint, this Sahara Project has much more potential than the civil rights stuff. Which will turn out more important I don't know, [but] from the WRL viewpoint the Sahara Project should take precedence.[138]

In his report to Rustin, Peck seconded the preference of DiGia and the WRL that he remain in Africa. He also saluted the project's fusion of peace and decolonization, and combined an assessment of Rustin's importance to the peace and justice movements with a warning against social movements relying on particular individuals:

> The main theme music throughout the meeting was your indispensability for ALL non-violent action projects. While this is a merited and genuine tribute to you, it certainly does not speak well for Randolph, King or the civil rights movement in the U.S. It is a sad situation when non-violent action on such an issue depends on a single individual in order to take place. And such is the case because Randolph said as much.[139]

Since Randolph had not directed him to return, Rustin continued to work with the Sahara Project, though he left Africa after the first stage of the protest to initiate the Election Project. Ironically, the Election Project prompted Congressman Powell to blackmail King into firing Rustin, who instead resigned.[140]

Amidst a rousing sendoff, on 6 December 1959 the Sahara protest team left Accra on a two-thousand-mile overland trip to the nuclear test site. There were eighteen men and a woman on the team, including Rustin and Sutherland, three Britons, a Frenchwoman, eleven Ghanaians, and various other Africans, among them the president of the Basutoland National Congress (and later the president of Lesotho). On 9 December they crossed into French Upper Volta (now Burkina Faso). Sixteen miles beyond the border, French officials detained them. Four days later, they returned to Ghana to regroup. On 17 December seven members of the team again crossed into Upper Volta, only to be stopped again by armed guards eleven miles from the border. The team refused orders to move their vehicles off the road; instead they distributed leaflets and produced tape recordings of the leaflet's text in two local languages. Having been deported, the team members returned to Accra. They explored alternative routes to the test site, but they never did reach Reggan, and the French conducted the nuclear test.[141]

The Sahara protest team distributed forty thousand leaflets printed in four languages. "PEOPLE OF AFRICA! AFRICA IS IN DANGER!" these proclaimed. "For the Government of France to use the soil of Africa as a base for nuclear war means that NUCLEAR IMPERIALISM now threatens you, an imperialism more menacing than anything you have ever known." The leaflet appealed to nationalist sentiments but disavowed the revolutionary violence common to independence struggles, including the Algerian war for independence then being fought against the French. "TO MEET VIOLENCE WITH VIOLENCE WOULD ONLY INCREASE THE DANGERS WE MUST AT ALL COST AVOID," the leaflet cautioned. "We, the International Sahara Protest Team, are trying another way to stop this test—the way of Gandhi—NON-VIOLENT POSITIVE ACTION, which was born on the soil of South Africa." By identifying nonviolent resistance with South Africa and the Sahara protest with African nationalism, the leaflet was adroitly fusing nonviolent revolution and decolonization with nuclear disarmament.[142]

Although it failed to reach El Hammoudia, the team generated publicity for antinuclear groups and inspired solidarity demonstrations in Europe, Africa, and the United States. In New York City on 9 December—the day the protest team entered French-controlled territory—the WRL led a poster walk from the United Nations to the French Mission to show solidarity with the Sahara team. The League also appealed to France not to violate the moratorium on nuclear tests and not to join the "nuclear club." Such action, the League warned, would cripple disarmament efforts by encouraging other nations to develop atomic arsenals.[143]

Radical pacifists believed their movement had benefited from the aborted Sahara Project. A French sympathizer suggested that the International Sahara Protest Team could "be considered as the embryo of a world peace army."[144] After visiting Ghana, Muste observed that the project had produced "an immense propaganda job for the idea of nonviolence . . . among the masses" and had trained African volunteers in nonviolent philosophy and strategy.[145] "No matter what the future may bring," he proclaimed after the first attempt to reach El Hammoudia was thwarted, "this project has now unquestionably developed into the most significant in the series of direct-action civil-disobedience projects in which radical nonpacifists have been involved in recent years."[146] By participating in the Sahara Project, the WRL demonstrated that it endorsed civil disobedience and a multi-issue agenda—one that included decolonization. Sutherland recalled: "It was so exciting because we felt that this joining up of the European anti-nuclear forces, the African liberation forces, the U.S. civil rights movements could help each group feed and reinforce the other. Then, to be sponsored by a majority political party in government clearly marked a unique moment in progressive history."[147]

Between 1960 and 1 January 1968, when it merged with the WRL, CNVA continued to organize dramatic peace projects involving direct action and civil disobedience. These included Polaris Action (1961), the San Francisco-Moscow Walk for Peace (1960–61), Everyman I/II/II (1962), the Quebec-Washington-Guantanamo Walk (1963–64), and the Saigon Project (1967). WRL members continued to dominate CNVA's leadership, and the WRL often provided support for these projects. By the mid-1960s, however, CNVA was losing its relevance. David McReynolds, a sympathetic critic of CNVA and the League's strongest proponent of a merger with CNVA, explained why in a 1964 memo and later in a 1968 *WRL News* article. He argued that CNVA had transformed itself from an *ad hoc* committee that coordinated civil disobedience projects for radical pacifist groups into a permanent organization with its own headquarters, staff, budget, bulletin, and literature. All of this, he maintained, amounted to an expensive duplication of CNVA-WRL efforts, especially since both groups relied on much the same people for membership and contributions. When CNVA began running into financial difficulties in the mid-1960s, the issue of duplication became critical.

McReynolds criticized CNVA for shifting, after the Sahara Project, toward a narrow expression of direct action in the form of "'witness'—without much regard for strategic or tactical considerations." He commended both the use of "mass witness" by the March on Washington (which did not involve civil disobedience) and the use of "mass [direct] action" by the Sahara Project and the New York City civil defense protest movement (which did involve civil disobedience). In McReynolds's view, the *Golden Rule,* "which combine[d] direct action and 'witness' on a small scale, but [was] so planned as to attract a very large degree of public attention, [was] the most brilliant of all CNVA projects." He acknowledged that CNVA had "pricked" the "public conscience," but he also contended that its exclusive emphasis on direct action was reaping diminishing returns and that CNVA should merge with the WRL, whose "political" pacifism and tactical flexibility offered a more realistic program for permanent change.[148]

McReynolds and CNVA's historian Neil Katz concur that by 1968, direct action within both the New Left and the peace and justice movements had become commonplace. This meant there was less and less point in having two separate organizations. When CNVA stopped playing a "unique" role in the pacifist movement, it merged with the WRL; after all, their programs were similar, their memberships overlapped, and they had a close working relationship.[149] In 1968, McReynolds praised CNVA members, who had produced "one of the most exciting and courageous experiments in the history of American pacifism":

> For ten years CNVA provided the "shock troops" of the pacifist movement, working on projects that seemed impossible, taking risks that older groups would not have taken.
> . . . What was so daring in 1957 had become commonplace in the mid-1960's and the debate was no longer between "legal" versus "illegal" pacifist actions, but between nonviolent and violent methods of resistance. CNVA's unique contribution was not in the area of ideology or organization but in the area of nonviolent direct action. Once that technique had become part of the movement the special function of CNVA was at an end.[150]

In 1959 and 1961 the WRL reviewed its program and its role as a "service agency" to the broader peace and social justice movements. During two reevaluation conferences, the League considered whether it should go back to being a single-issue organization focused on war resistance only or continue to embrace a multi-issue program that sought to remove the "causes of war." "In this period of grave tension," the League asked in late 1961, "should the WRL limit its action program solely to resisting war and forego for the present any program directed toward removal of the causes of war?"[151] The League affirmed its earlier shift toward a multi-issue program and its endorsement of direct action and civil disobedience. The 1961 conference recommended that the League continue to support the Student Peace Union ("the most creative and positive force for peace amongst young people today") through financial aid, office space in League headquarters, and McReynolds's mentoring. As yet more evidence of support for a broad program, the 1961 conference contended that the emergent "Women's Protest Movement and the growth of the 'nuclear pacifist' forces create a new opportunity for the League."[152]

In 1961 the WRL decided to keep participating in the nonviolent civil rights movement, encourage civil rights leaders to adopt nonviolence and pacifism, and "make every effort to broaden the concept of nonviolence by those who accept strategic nonviolence for specific goals." [153] It would also try to reach those outside the peace movement who held antiwar sentiments by working with them on various peace and justice projects. Roy Finch summed up the WRL's significance: "The importance of permanent organizations like the WRL is that they can provide continuity leadership and growth, enabling persons ready for a permanent commitment to take such a step." [154]

During the late 1950s and early 1960s, the WRL regularly publicized its "service role" of assisting peace and justice groups. In particular, the League pointed to its contributions to the CDPC and the New York City civil defense protest movement; to Martin Luther King, the SCLC, CORE, SNCC, and the nonviolent civil rights movement; to CNVA and its direct action and civil disobedience campaign to abolish nuclear testing and nuclear weapons; to the Student Peace Union and student movement through educational and organizational work with youth and student groups in high schools and colleges; and to *Liberation* for promoting nonviolent social movements. [155]

During an April 1964 WRL fundraising campaign, Bayard Rustin reviewed the League's contribution to important peace and justice movements over the past decade, especially those involving civil rights, civil defense, and nuclear weapons and testing. Shortly before this appeal, Ralph DiGia was released from an Albany, Georgia, jail after serving four weeks with participants of the CNVA-sponsored Quebec-Washington-Guantanamo Peace Walk, a project designed to protest U.S. policy toward Cuba. The racially integrated team had challenged Albany's segregationist ordinances, thereby sparking a major civil rights struggle. DiGia's presence symbolized the League's continued commitment to nonviolence, civil rights, civil disobedience, and an anti-imperial American foreign policy. Concluding his appeal, Rustin offered a fitting portrait of the WRL four decades after its birth: "Organizations that work on the frontier of social thought do not have mass support. . . . [or] tax exemptions. . . . [or] large memberships. But such organizations are essential if our society is to survive, if the words 'peace,' 'freedom,' 'justice' are to be given real content." [156]

A month before this, in a review of its program, the League had concluded that "there was general agreement that the WRL presented the radical position within the peace movement, though it tended to be a 'social radicalism' growing from anarchist and socialist roots, rather than the 'personal radicalism' of a group such as Peacemakers." [157] Maurice Isserman, a prominent historian of the American Left, has argued that in the 1960s pacifism appealed to the "new radical movements" and "newly radicalized young" in ways that socialism could not.

Furthermore, the pacifist emphasis on Gandhi, values, and individualism offered a more American message than the discredited "socialist" tradition of Stal-
inism, sectarianism, and rigid ideology.[158]

The WRL, however fused socialist *and* Gandhian traditions to advance a
radical pacifist analysis of—and solution to—war, violence, and social injustice.
Fashioned from the Socialist International's general strike against war, the socialist pacifism of the No-Conscription Fellowship, the Fellowship of Reconciliation, the women's peace movement, the War Resisters' International and its
socialist/anarchist pacifist currents, the example of Mohandas Gandhi, and the
influence of its own radical (chiefly socialist) leadership, between 1923 and 1963
the War Resisters League pioneered, popularized, and Americanized a secular,
socialist-oriented, Gandhian, radical pacifism in the United States.

# Epilogue and Conclusion

## Epilogue

SINCE 1963 THE WAR RESISTERS LEAGUE has continued to advocate Gandhian nonviolent direct action and civil disobedience to advance a multi-issue peace and justice program. Consistent with its post-World War II "service relationship" orientation, the WRL has also continued to operate as a "movement halfway house"[1] and to assist other nonviolent reform groups. Despite its multi-issue social justice agenda, the League has remained rooted in the peace movement. Charles DeBenedetti and Charles Chatfield have observed that by 1963 the League was part of a broad peace movement that encompassed liberal and radical pacifists. Between 1955 and 1963 the peace movement had been preoccupied with the Cold War, disarmament, and a nuclear test ban treaty. In 1963 and 1964 it turned its attention to the Vietnam War.[2]

Vietnam marked a new phase in the WRL's history. From 1964 to 1975 the League focused on opposing, resisting, and ending American participation in the Vietnam War. In a continuation of its post-1955 shift toward direct action, it organized mass civil disobedience protests against the war in Indochina. Besides counseling confirmed and potential conscientious objectors, it advocated draft refusal and desertion, sponsored draft card burning protests, blocked induction centers with sit-ins, and organized a war tax resistance campaign that enlisted 200,000 citizens who refused to pay all or part of their federal income and/or telephone war taxes.[3]

The WRL was among the earliest critics of the Vietnam War. In October 1963, after leading smaller New York protests in July and September, it organized the first major antiwar demonstration at the Waldorf-Astoria hotel to coincide with the arrival there of Madame Nhu, sister-in-law of South Vietnam's premier, Ngo Dinh Diem. Madame Nhu's visit to the United States coincided with the Buddhist crisis, and she had mocked the Buddhist monks' self-immolation as a "barbecue."[4] In 1964, in a July "Memo on Vietnam," the WRL urged unconditional withdrawal of American troops. It also cosponsored an August vigil by four hundred protesters at the Democratic convention in Atlantic City. That December it organized the first international protest against the war.

Throughout the Vietnam War, the WRL and its members provided leadership to the broad, nonpacifist, antiwar coalition. League leaders A. J. Muste and Norma Becker led—and the League was active in—the New York Fifth Avenue Peace Parade Committee, the nation's largest local antiwar group. In April 1968, 100,000 protestors walked down Fifth Avenue led by the Fifth Avenue Parade Committee. The WRL banner was positioned behind two cars carrying aloft a huge poster of A. J. Muste and Martin Luther King, Jr. In addition, the Resistance and other antiwar groups operated from WRL offices.

The League and its members also helped organize the annual springtime mass mobilizations,which involved as many as 200,000 protesters. With several others, Dave Dellinger and Muste cochaired the Spring Committee to End the War in Vietnam. On 15 April 1967, 50,000 citizens in San Francisco and 200,000 in New York City protested the war, including 150 men who burned their draft cards in Central Park's Sheep Meadow in a ceremony that "christened the new draft resistance movement."[5] In May 1968 the *ad hoc* Spring Mobilization Committee became the permanent National Mobilization Committee to End the War in Vietnam (Mobe). Dellinger remained a key Mobe leader, and he did much to organize the antiwar protests in August 1968 at the Democratic Party convention in Chicago. Although violence marred Chicago, there and elsewhere the League advised the antiwar movement to reject violence and adopt nonviolent protest.[6]

In the early 1970s the WRL formed Campaign Freedom, a project that encouraged participants to "adopt" South Vietnamese political prisoners and write letters on their behalf. Following the 1973 Paris Peace Accords and America's military withdrawal from Vietnam, the League cofounded the United Campaign, which organized opposition to the war, which continued until reunification in 1975.[7]

Like previous wars, the Vietnam war raised controversial issues and alternative policies that prompted debate within the WRL. Two questions were especially contentious. First, should the United States immediately withdraw from Vietnam or should it seek a negotiated peace aimed at installing an independent South Vietnamese government based on the Buddhist movement? Second, should the WRL exclude antiwar communists from the pacifist-organized peace movement? On these issues the League advocated nonexclusion (i.e., the inclusion of communists) and the immediate withdrawal of American troops and military aid from Vietnam (i.e., an immediate decision to withdraw as expeditiously as possible and to negotiate on that basis). Not all WRL members agreed with these decisions, and several resigned from leadership positions or from the League.[8]

Besides participating in the anti-Vietnam War movement, the WRL influenced the 1960s New Left. Radical pacifist tax resistance, nonregistration, direct action, and civil disobedience during the 1940s and 1950s inspired the New Left. Like the League members and radical pacifists who preceded them, the New Left rejected the atomic bomb-dominated Cold War culture; played a leadership role in myriad reform movements; honored moral dissent; advocated participatory democracy; and emphasized individual, existential action and total, uncompromising commitment—by putting one's body on the line and practicing civil disobedience.[9]

The sixties also influenced the WRL. Galvanized by the Vietnam War and by the New Left and other social movements, the League's active membership rose from 3,000 to 14,000 between 1964 and 1973. The New Left, the women's movement, Third Worldism, and the counterculture (the latter shown by the League's sponsorship of *WIN* magazine— "*Workshop In Nonviolence*") all had an impact on the League. The women's movement in particular had a lasting effect on the WRL.[10]

In the early 1970s, female members raised a feminist critique of their role in the WRL and the peace movement. Writing in the *WRL News,* Wendy Schwartz declared that "the time has come for us women within WRL to assert our rights as equals of the men who, for all practical purposes, control the organization."[11] Though the League had "not stooped to Stokely Carmichael's level by suggesting that the best position for women is prone," it kept women "chained to desks." "How odd," she observed, "that there was never a reluctance to give staff or advisory positions to black (or homosexuals or other minority) people, while women unabashedly have been allowed to remain in the background."[12]

In response to gender inequality and in tune with the emergent women's movement, women began to caucus during League meetings. Responding to this feminist challenge, the League expanded its program to include women's concerns. The 1972 WRL Peace Calendar honored female contributions to the peace and justice movements. More significantly, in 1973, fifty years after Jessie Wallace Hughan founded the League, Irma Zigas became the first female WRL chair.[13]

After the Vietnam War, the WRL turned its attention to disarmament, nuclear power, and social justice. In 1976 it sponsored the Continental Walk for Disarmament and Social Justice to emphasize the link between the arms race and social injustice—in particular, racism, sexism, and classism. The Continental Walk highlighted the League's concern with the social causes of organized violence. To this end it harnessed the idealism of a new generation of activists who had been radicalized by Vietnam. Starting in Canada and Washington state on 1 January 1976, the Continental Walk ended in Washington, D.C., on 19 October 1976.[14]

Reversing its initial post-Hiroshima support for atomic power to promote economic development, the WRL joined the growing movement against nuclear power plants and the dangers posed by radiation. In the later 1970s the League provided training in Gandhian civil disobedience, as well as organizational support for nuclear power plant occupations. It also cooperated with antinuclear, nonviolent direct action groups such as the Clamshell Alliance, the Shad Alliance, and the Abalone Alliance. It made a significant contribution to the Clamshell Alliance, which began a Gandhian civil disobedience campaign that led to 1,400 arrests and shut down New Hampshire's Seabrook nuclear power plant in 1977. This protest spurred similar ones across the nation. Through Seabrook and the issue of nuclear power, the League became involved in the ecological movement. In 1978, to link the issues of nuclear armament and nuclear power, League members simultaneously raised banners on Moscow's Red Square and the White House lawn proclaiming: "No Nuclear Weapons, No Nuclear Power—USA or USSR".[15]

Since the 1970s, from a nonaligned, radical pacifist perspective, the WRL has continued to oppose American and Soviet defense spending, military policies, and armed interventions. In 1977 it helped establish Mobilization for Survival, a coalition to promote the abolition of nuclear weapons, a ban on nuclear power, and an end to the arms race. In May 1978 this group brought ten thousand people to the United Nations during its Special Session on Disarmament. In June, at the U.S. Mission to the UN, four hundred protesters were arrested while committing civil disobedience during the Sit-In for Survival, which the League led. Four years later, during the second UN Special Session on Disarmament, the League helped organize a peace crowd of one million people. In a related Blockade the Bombmakers action led by the League, 1,650 protestors were arrested for staging sit-ins at the U.S., Soviet, British, French, and Chinese missions to the UN. In the 1980s and 1990s the League organized resistance to American policy in Central America, the invasions of Grenada and Panama, the Gulf War, and armed UN peacekeeping in Somalia, Haiti, and Bosnia. Finally, the League denounced Al Qaeda's 11 September 2001 attack on the World Trade Center and the subsequent American "war on terrorism."[16]

## Conclusion

In its first four decades the WRL and its members made significant contributions to the United States. First, the WRL helped to transform pacifism from its original focus on the repudiation of war to an often nonpacifist tactical emphasis on Gandhian techniques to abolish the causes of war and to advance social change. This represented a shift from radical pacifism's original concern with organized killing to a focus on the "violence of the status quo," a broader construct concerned with the structural "violence" inherent in classism, racism, patriarchy, and, to some, even eating meat. Popularized in part by the League, notably in the civil rights and antinuclear movements, the reliance on Gandhian methods to bring about social change now characterizes numerous reform movements. In summary, the WRL has promoted, legitimized, and popularized Gandhian nonviolence in America.

Second, the WRL has advanced the right of conscientious objection and the right to base conscientious objection on secular rather than religious principles. In part as a result of pressure from pacifists, the Selective Training and Service Act of 1940 extended the right of conscientious objection. Unlike the Selective Service Act of 1917, the 1940 law made provision for civilian service and broadened the religious test for conscientious objection beyond membership in the historic peace churches to include objections based on "religious training and belief," whatever one's church affiliation.

Not until the Vietnam War did the U.S. Supreme Court establish the right of secular objection to war. In a landmark case, *United States v. Seeger* (1965), the Court declared that conscientious objectors need only demonstrate a "sincere or meaningful belief" that occupied a place "parallel to that filled by God."[17] Five years later, in *Welsh v. United States* (1970), the Court reaffirmed *Seeger* and further ruled that strongly held atheistic "moral" or "ethical" beliefs met the test for conscientious objection.[18] These two cases extended conscientious objection and validated the WRL's long-held contention that secular principles constituted a legitimate source of nonviolence and pacifism. The Court's rulings were partly a response to militant citizen peace activism and to demands by the antiwar movement—the WRL included—that conscientious objection be granted on the basis of constitutional principles such as the Nuremberg precedent.[19]

Third, the WRL and its members have championed civil liberties and in doing so strengthened the American libertarian tradition. During and after World War I, this activism included Anti-Enlistment League and (future) WRL members Frances Witherspoon, Tracy D. Mygatt, and John Haynes Holmes, who cofounded the New York Bureau of Legal Advice and the American Civil Liberties Union. Later on, the League established its CO Problems Committee and cofounded the Metropolitan Board for Conscientious Objectors and the Central Committee for Conscientious Objectors to provide counseling, assistance, and legal aid to COs.

The WRL's support for prison COs and amnesty also raised civil liberties issues. During World War II the League supported COs who agitated to improve prison conditions and to abolish prison censorship. In 1945 the Committee for Amnesty—a group led by WRL members and supported by the League—led an impressive though ultimately unsuccessful campaign to win amnesty and the restoration of full citizenship for COs who went to prison to honor conscience and principle.

In addition, the WRL has championed the right of free speech and dissent. From World War I to the Vietnam War, League members risked persecution by speaking and acting in accordance with their radical pacifist principles. Most League leaders rejected capitalism, nationalism, imperialism, and reliance on military power; instead, they advocated some form of democratic "socialism," internationalism, restrictions on national sovereignty, a more equitable global distribution of natural resources, and the repudiation of armed force in international relations. Persecuted for their pacifism and for their radical dissent on social, economic, and political issues, League members have espoused freedom of expression and condemned recurring antiradical campaigns. During and after World War I, Jessie Wallace Hughan denounced the red scares that harassed her and other pacifists. John Haynes Holmes, another red-baited League leader, was a charter member and leader of the ACLU. Similarly, the League later condemned McCarthyism. Finally, the League-sponsored Civil Defense Protest Committee appealed its 1955 convictions in part on free speech grounds.

Fourth, from World War II to 1963 the WRL and its members helped lead the civil rights movement. Historians often date the modern civil rights movement from *Brown* and Montgomery; actually, the League and its members— sometimes working under the auspices of the FOR and CORE—were pioneering nonviolent civil rights activism for nearly fifteen years before these landmark events. During World War II, COs who were League members waged strikes and protests to abolish Jim Crow in Civilian Public Service and prison. Furthermore, League members participated in A. Philip Randolph's nonviolent March on Washington Movement and helped found CORE. League members also participated in the 1947 Journey of Reconciliation, which was the model for the Freedom Rides of 1961.

The WRL supported and influenced the mass, nonviolent civil rights movement that abolished legal segregation in America. Through Bayard Rustin, the WRL forged an important link to Martin Luther King, Jr., and the southern civil rights movement. During the Montgomery bus boycott, Rustin played an influential—perhaps instrumental—role in transforming King's philosophical pacifist orientation into a Gandhian social movement of nonviolent direct action. In addition, the League publicized and raised money for the Montgomery campaign. After Montgomery, Rustin served as a key adviser to the King-led Southern Christian Leadership Conference. Besides all this, Rustin conducted workshops to train younger civil rights leaders in Gandhian nonviolence, organized the 1963 March on Washington, and advised the Student Nonviolent Coordinating Committee, whose northern office operated from WRL headquarters. In all these ways the League played a vital role in the postwar nonviolent civil rights movement. The civil rights revolution offers compelling evidence of the efficacy of Gandhian techniques even under adverse conditions.

Fifth, the WRL espoused an alternative, radical pacifist analysis, program, and vision. Unlike the "realists" who dominated international relations, the League rejected the idea that military power was necessary to defend national interests and maintain world peace. Similarly, it repudiated armed social revolution to abolish the structural causes of war and promoted its own vision of a socialist-oriented society. The League contended that armed warfare and revolution were ineffective and counterproductive. Military strategies perpetuated violence, seldom settled disputes permanently, and often failed to achieve their objectives. Moreover, armed revolution was usually futile in the modern world since governments almost always commanded more armed force than their opponents. In summary, the League repudiated organized violence on the grounds that it was both unethical and ineffective.

Despite repeated wars and American military intervention around the world, the WRL's central premise and strategy remain valid. Clearly, citizens mobilized for collective nonviolent action can influence government decisions on war; this is a valid strategy for nonviolent social reform and revolution. Historical examples demonstrate that nonviolent resistance can be effective: the 1905 Russian Revolution, the defeat of Kapp Putsch, the Ruhrkampf, Gandhi's many campaigns for Indian independence and social justice, and more recently, the "people power" that has toppled repressive regimes in Iran, Poland, the Philippines, the Soviet Union, Yugoslavia, Indonesia, and elsewhere.[20] According to Lawrence Wittner, the world nuclear disarmament movement—"the largest grassroots struggle in modern history" (and one in which the League participated)—galvanized public pressure to abolish nuclear testing and weapons and reduced the likelihood of nuclear war.[21] All movements and ideas have a history, however. To borrow Charles Chatfield's apt phrase, from the perspective of contemporary "people power," the League's vision has proved "prophetic" and has contributed to the development of nonviolent realism.[22]

But too often, advocates of nonviolence have failed to mobilize enough public pressure and collective action to thwart war, armed rebellion, and murderous repression. This does not invalidate the WRL's premise, but it does suggest how difficult it is to forge united protest against military solutions and war, especially when the dominant political culture teaches that armed force is essential to defend national interests and promote global peace and justice. It also underscores the challenge of transforming small-scale (often symbolic) peace action into mass resistance to war and organized violence. Indeed, in the age of nuclear weapons and weapons of mass destruction, peace remains the "necessary" reform.[23]

The WRL's radical pacifist analysis and program sought to explain and abolish the causes of war and to advance social justice. Although it did not articulate an explicitly socialist platform, the League advocated a radical pacifist ideology and program, one with a pronounced socialist orientation. Rooted in the pre-1914 Second International with its revisionist socialism and proposals for a general strike against war, the League mirrored the socialist pacifist No-Conscription Fellowship and joined the socialist-anarchist-pacifist War Resisters' International. During the 1930s, WRL (and FOR) members formed a socialist pacifist current within the Socialist Party. By World War II the WRL was combining its socialist pacifist orientation with techniques of Gandhian nonviolent direct action and civil disobedience to create a distinctive, secular pacifist socialist-anarchist-Gandhian fusion. After 1945 the League sponsored *Liberation* (with its socialist-anarchist-pacifist editorial position), supported the Committee for Nonviolent Revolution (whose ideology resembled and preceded that of *Liberation*), and broadcast its conviction that capitalism and economic imperialism were among the main causes of war. All of this illustrates the socialist bent of the League's radical pacifism.

Finally, the WRL articulated a cogent dissent from, and a radical pacifist alternative to, the mainstream consensus and the Left. It rejected attempts by the Left to advance social revolution through armed violence; even so, it opposed aggressive American foreign policy abroad and capitalism and social injustice at home. Since 1923, the WRL has been the most important mixed-gender, secular, absolute pacifist organization in the United States. It has also been the most important expression of the secular, radical pacifist democratic Left in America. Insisting that nonviolent techniques constitute an effective political strategy for creating a more just and peaceful world, the War Resisters League has promoted radical pacifism, not quietistic passivism.

# Notes

The documentation for key figures in this book relies heavily on archival sources, including their unpublished papers (e.g., the Jessie Wallace Hughan Papers and the Abraham Kaufman Papers) in the Swarthmore College Peace Collection and other depositories. To enhance the readability and clarity of multiple reference notes, full citations for these documents are provided only at first appearance; subsequent references simply cite the author's surname instead of complete name.

## Introduction

1. A. J. Muste Memorial Institute, *1983 Annual Report,* Roy Kepler Papers, DG-185 (unprocessed), Swarthmore College Peace Collection (hereafter SCPC).

2. Ibid.

3. Aldon D. Morris, *The Origins of the Civil Rights Movement: Black Communities Organizing for Change* (New York: Free Press, 1984), 139–73. According to Morris, in its role as a "movement halfway house," the WRL assisted the post–World War II civil rights movement. See ibid., 57, 140, 159.

4. Charles DeBenedetti, *The Peace Reform in American History* (Bloomington: Indiana Univ. Press, 1980), 108; see also pages 108–37. In addition to DeBenedetti's work, general studies that survey the American peace movement from the colonial era to the twentieth century include Peter Brock, *Pacifism in the United States: From the Colonial Era to the First World War* (Princeton: Princeton Univ. Press, 1968); Arthur A. Ekirch, *The Civilian and the Military* (New York: Oxford Univ. Press, 1956); Merle E. Curti, *Peace or War: The American Struggle, 1636–1936* (New York: W. W. Norton, 1936, reprint, New York: Garland, 1971); and John W. Chambers II, "Conscientious Objectors and the American State from Colonial Times to the Present," in *The New Conscientious Objection: From Sacred to Secular,* by Charles C. Moskos and John W. Chambers II (New York: Oxford Univ. Press, 1993), 23–46. See also Charles Chatfield, *The American Peace Movement: Ideals and Activism* (New York: Twayne, 1992), which begins in 1815.

5. For a general introduction and access to the literature on the women's peace movement, see Harriet H. Alonso, *Peace as a Women's Issue: A History of the U.S. Movement for World Peace and Women's Rights* (Syracuse: Syracuse Univ. Press, 1993). The major women's peace groups that emerged from World War I include the Woman's Peace Party (WPP), founded in 1915 and renamed the Women's International League for Peace and Freedom (WILPF) in 1919; the Women's Peace Society (WPS), founded in 1919; and the Women's Peace Union (WPU), founded in 1921. Both the WPS and WPU originated in the WILPF.

6. Here I depart somewhat from the standard categorization that divides the postwar peace

movement into liberal internationalist and liberal pacifist wings. For an introduction to the modern American peace movement, see DeBenedetti, *Peace Reform*; Chatfield, *American Peace Movement*; and Peter Brock and Nigel Young, *Pacifism in the Twentieth Century* (Syracuse: Syracuse Univ. Press, 1999). See also the bibliographies in John W. Chambers II, ed., *The Eagle and the Dove: The American Peace Movement and United States Foreign Policy, 1900–1922*, 2d ed. (Syracuse: Syracuse Univ. Press, 1991), xv–lxxxvii; Charles F. Howlett, *The American Peace Movement: References and Resources* (Boston: G. K. Hall & Co., 1991); and Charles F. Howlett and Glenn Zeitzer, *The American Peace Movement: History and Historiography* (Washington, D.C.: American Historical Association, 1985).

7. Jessie Wallace Hughan, *What Is War Resistance?* (New York: WRL, 1930s), copy in Jessie Wallace Hughan Papers (hereafter, Hughan Papers), CDG-A, SCPC.

8. Moskos and Chambers, *New Conscientious Objection*, 3, passim, especially 3–46 and 196–208.

9. Barbara Epstein, *Political Protest and Cultural Revolution: Nonviolent Direct Action in the 1970s and 1980s* (Berkeley: Univ. of California Press, 1991), especially 1–57 and 227–78. See also Carl Boggs, *Social Movements and Political Power: Emerging Forms of Radicalism in the West* (Philadelphia: Temple Univ. Press, 1986).

10. Charles DeBenedetti, introduction to *Peace Heroes in Twentieth-Century America,* ed. Charles DeBenedetti (Bloomington: Indiana Univ. Press, 1988), 1, 24.

11. Ibid., 2.

12. Chatfield, *American Peace Movement,* 170, 180.

13. Gene Sharp's books include *The Politics of Nonviolent Action,* 3 vols. (Boston: Porter Sargent, 1973); *Gandhi as a Political Strategist* (Boston: Porter Sargent, 1979); *Social Power and Political Freedom* (Boston: Porter Sargent, 1980); *Making Europe Unconquerable: The Potential of Civilian-Based Deterrence and Defense* (Cambridge, Mass.: Ballinger, 1985); and *Civilian-Based Defense: A Post-Military Weapons System* (Princeton: Princeton Univ. Press, 1990). Building on Sharp's work, Peter Ackerman and Christopher Kreugler have developed twelve principles of strategic nonviolent action and analyzed six cases of twentieth-century "people power." The case studies include the Russian Revolution (1904–6), the *Ruhrkampf* (1923), the Indian Independence Movement (1930–31), the civic strife in El Salvador against the military dictatorship (1944), and the Solidarity movement (1980–81). See Peter Ackerman and Christopher Kreugler, *Strategic Nonviolent Conflict: The Dynamics of People Power in the Twentieth Century* (Westport, Conn.: Praeger, 1994); and Ackerman and Jack Duvall, *A Force More Powerful: A Century of Nonviolent Conflict* (New York: St. Martin's Press, 2000).

### Chapter 1. Jessie Wallace Hughan and the WRL

1. For Hughan, see Frances H. Early, "Revolutionary Pacifism and War Resistance: Jessie Wallace Hughan's 'War Against War,' " *Peace and Change* 20 (July 1995): 307–28; Scott H. Bennett, "Radical Pacifism and the General Strike Against War: Jessie Wallace Hughan, the Founder of the War Resisters League, and the Socialist Origins of Secular Radical Pacifism in America," *Peace and Change* 26 (July 2001): 352–73. An unpublished rough draft of a biography of Hughan, written by her grandniece, Annie Ridley Crane Finch, quotes from Hughan's diaries and letters. See A. R. C. Finch, "Resister for Peace: A Life of Jessie Wallace Hughan," Hughan Papers. Annie Finch borrows generously from Michael D. Young, "Wars Will Cease When Men Refuse to Fight: The War

Resisters League, 1925–1950" (B.A. honors thesis, Brown Univ., 1975), the only previous scholarly study of the WRL. See also Stephen Siteman, "Jessie Wallace Hughan," *East Villager* (New York), 15 and 31 Oct. 1984.

2. John H. Lathrop, quoted in Hester Donaldson Jenkins, "War Resisters League Annual Dinner," [Dec. 1937], Devere Allen Papers (unprocessed; hereafter, Allen Papers), DG-53, SCPC.

3. *WRL News,* May-June 1955.

4. This portrait is drawn from A. R. C. Finch, "Resister for Peace," 8–12, 15; Margaret Rockwell Finch, introduction to "Resister for Peace," by A. R. C. Finch; and Abraham Kaufman, interview in "Resister for Peace," by A. R. C. Finch, all in Hughan Papers; Kaufman, "Manuscript," Abraham Kaufman Papers (hereafter, Kaufman Papers), at his home in Minneapolis, Minnesota, and SCPC; Margaret Finch and Roy Finch, interview by author, 13 Nov. 1993; Kaufman, interviews by author, 1993 and 1994; and Edward P. Gottlieb, interviews by author, 6 Nov. and 5 Dec. 1993.

5. Hughan, "Autobiography of Jessie Wallace Hughan," 21 Nov. 1926, courtesy of Margaret Rockwell Finch.

6. A. R. C. Finch, "Resister for Peace," 17, Hughan Papers.

7. For her diaries, see A. R. C. Finch, "Resisters for Peace," 17, Hughan Papers. For the Vera Cruz incident and its impact on U.S. opinion, see Robert E. Quirk, *An Affair of Honor: Woodrow Wilson and the Occupation of Veracruz* (New York: W. W. Norton, 1962); and John S. D. Eisenhower, *Intervention! The United States and the Mexican Revolution, 1913–1917* (New York: W. W. Norton, 1995), 109–38.

8. A. R. C. Finch, "Resister for Peace," 3, Hughan Papers.

9. Ibid., 5.

10. For the influence of her parents on Hughan, see Hughan, "Autobiography"; A. R. C. Finch, "Resister for Peace," 1–9, 13, 16–17, 33, 36, 41, Hughan Papers; Hughan, interviews by Mercedes M. Randall, May 1950, 20 Feb. 1951, and 12 Dec. 1951, Mercedes M. Randall Papers (hereafter, Randall Papers), Box 7, DG-110, SCPC; Siteman, "Jessie Wallace Hughan"; M. Finch and R. Finch, interview by author, 13 Nov. 1993; Kaufman, interviews by author, 1993 and 1994. Hughan's Barnard thesis is in the Jessie Wallace Hughan Papers, Barnard College. Hughan traveled to Europe on several occasions and once to Asia and the Middle East.

11. Hughan, "Autobiography."

12. See Hughan, "Autobiography"; and A. R. C. Finch, "Resister for Peace," 4–7, 20, Hughan Papers.

13. All quotes in this paragraph from Hughan, review of *Good Friday: A Passion Play of Now,* by Tracy D. Mygatt, 7 June 1919, Hughan Papers.

14. Hughan, "Some Words and Symbols: A Bit of Interpretation," Aug. 1940, Hughan Papers.

15. Hughan, "Revolutionary Pacifism," Dec. 1919, Hughan Papers.

16. WRL, *The Use of Force and the Conscientious Objector* (New York: WRL, 1939), 1, copy in War Resisters League Papers, Series A, Box 3, DG-40 (hereafter, WRL Papers, Series letter/Box number), SCPC.

17. Ibid.

18. Hughan, "For the Symposium on Conscience, Pacifism, and the Commonwealth," 29 Oct. 1944, 2, Hughan Papers.

19. Hughan, "What Is Pacifism?—Again," *Pacifica Views,* 29 Dec. 1944.

20. M. Finch and R. Finch, interview by author, 13 Nov. 1993.

21. Ibid.

22. Hughan, interview by Randall, May 1950, Randall Papers.

23. Hughan, quoted in M. Young, "Wars Will Cease When Men Refuse To Fight," 5.

24. Kaufman, interview in "Resister for Peace," by A. R. C. Finch, Hughan Papers; David A. Shannon, *The Socialist Party of America* (Chicago: Quadrangle Books, 1955), 9, 56. Hughan's books on socialism and international relations include *American Socialism of the Present Day* (New York: John Lane Co., 1911); *A Study of International Government* (New York: Thomas Y. Cromwell Co., 1923); and *What Is Socialism?* (New York: Vanguard Press, 1928).

25. Hughan, *International Government,* 125–33, 255–60; and Hughan, *What Is Socialism?* 19–21, 93–95.

26. Hughan, *International Government,* 281–82, 298–356, 378; and Hughan, *Pacifism and Invasion* (New York: A. J. Muste Memorial Institute, 1980s), 7, 14–17, 36–37, 43–45. This pamphlet was initially serialized as "Defense Without Armament" in *Friends Intelligencer,* 4, 11, and 18 Mar. 1939. In July 1941 the WRL published a revised 3rd. edition under the title *If We Should Be Invaded: Facing a Fantastic Hypothesis* (New York: WRL, 1941), a copy of which is in the Hughan Papers. In Feb. 1942, it reissued the pamphlet as *Pacifism and Invasion,* and in the mid-1980s, the A. J. Muste Memorial Institute reissued the pamphlet under this name. Unless otherwise noted, all references are to this latest edition.

27. Hughan, "Has International Socialism Collapsed?" [1914], Hughan Papers; and Hughan, *Three Decades of War Resistance* (New York: WRL, 1942), 5–6, copy in Hughan Papers.

28. Hughan, "Has International Socialism Collapsed?"; Hughan, [untitled draft], [1915], Hughan Papers; Hughan, *International Government,* 140–41; William E. Walling, ed., *The Socialists and the War* (New York: Garland, 1972), iii, a collection of socialist documents, including those central to the socialist debate over the general strike against war, which Hughan reviewed in draft (probably in late 1914) prior to the book's May 1915 publication. These sources demonstrate that in 1914 Hughan was aware of the Hardie-Vaillant proposal and the Socialist International's debate over the measure.

29. George Haupt, *Socialism and the Great War: The Collapse of the Second International* (Oxford: Oxford Univ. Press, 1972), 27.

30. For the SI's debate over the general strike, see Haupt, *Socialism and the Great War*; G. D. H. Cole, *A History of Socialist Thought: The Second International, 1889–1914* (London: Macmillan & Co., 1956), 44, 59–70, 75, 82–87, 90–103, 364–65, 370, 506; James Joll, *The Second International, 1889–1914* (New York: Praeger, 1956), 126–83, 196–98; Alexander Trachtenberg, ed., *The American Socialists and the War* and *Socialists and the Problems of War* (New York: Garland, 1973); and Walling, *Socialists and the War,* 27, 30–37, 42–60, 114–21, 133, 201–2, 318, 472.

31. Hughan, [untitled draft], 22 Oct. 1916; and Hughan, "Has International Socialism Collapsed?" both in Hughan Papers; Hughan, *Three Decades of War Resistance,* 5.

32. Hughan, [untitled draft], [1915], Hughan Papers.

33. Chambers, *Eagle and the Dove,* 116.

34. Hughan, "Has International Socialism Collapsed?"; and Hughan, [untitled draft], [1915], both in Hughan Papers; Hughan, *Three Decades of War Resistance,* 10–11; and Chambers, *Eagle and the Dove,* 114–16.

35. Haupt, *Socialism and the Great War,* 237.

36. Ibid., 183–249.

37. Ibid.

38. For instance, see Alonso, *Peace as a Women's Issue.*

39. Ibid; and Margaret Hope Bacon, "By Moral Force Alone: The Anti-Slavery Women and Nonresistance," in *The American Sisterhood: Women's Political Culture in Antebellum America,* ed. Jean Fagen Yellin and John C. Van Horne (Ithaca: Cornell Univ. Press, 1994), 46–65, 67–88, 275–97.

40. A. R. C. Finch, "Resister for Peace," 9, 15, Hughan Papers; and Barbara J. Steinson, *American Women's Activism in World War I* (Ph.D. diss., Univ. of Michigan, 1977; publ. ed., New York, Garland, 1982), 365–67, 397.

41. WPP Preamble, *Addresses Given at the Organization Conference of the Woman's Peace Party, Washington, D.C., Jan. 10, 1915,* presented by Anna Garlin Spencer, quoted in Chambers, *Eagle and the Dove,* 51.

42. Jane Addams, quoted in Chambers, *Eagle and the Dove,* 55–56.

43. WPP Preamble, 51. Hughan, "Autobiography"; A. R. C. Finch, "Resister for Peace," 22, Hughan Papers; WPP letterhead in Margaret Lane to Louis F. Post, 25 Apr. 1918, Woman's Peace Party Papers (microfilm; hereafter, WPP Papers), Reel 12.3, SCPC; "Shall We Change the Name?" n.d., WPP Papers, Reel 12.4; and Alonso, *Peace as a Women's Issue,* 60, 63–68, 74, 80–83, 86–87.

44. Letterhead, Fanny Garrison Villard to Dear Fellow Member, 5 June 1922, Women's Peace Society Papers (hereafter, WPS Papers), DG-106, SCPC.

45. Ibid.

46. Hughan, "Women Pacifists in 1920," *The Call Magazine,* 29 Feb. 1920, 8.

47. [Elinor Byrns] to Hughan, 28 Oct. 1921, WPS Papers.

48. Ibid.

49. Hughan, "Preparedness," *The Intercollegiate Socialist,* (Feb.-Mar. 1916), reprinted version in Hughan Papers; Hughan, "Has International Socialism Collapsed?"; Hughan, [untitled draft], 22 Oct. 1916; Hughan, "Revolutionary Pacifism"; and Hughan, "The Disarmament Parade," 29 Oct. 1921, all in Hughan Papers; Hughan, *International Government,* 139, 277–81; Hughan, *What Is Socialism?* 18–21; and Hughan, *American Socialism in the Present Day.* For the preparedness campaign, see John W. Chambers II, *To Raise an Army: The Draft Comes to Modern America* (New York: The Free Press, 1987).

50. For J. Fenner Brockway's perspective on pacifism and socialism, see his *Inside the Left: Thirty Years of Platform, Press, Prison and Parliament* (London: George Allen & Unwin, [1942] 1947).

51. Ibid., 43–119, 130–34; Thomas C. Kennedy, *The Hound of Conscience: A History of the No-Conscription Fellowship, 1914–1919* (Fayetteville: Univ. of Arkansas Press, 1981); *The No-Conscription Fellowship: A Souvenir of its Work During the Years 1914–1919,* n.d., copy in No-Conscription Fellowship Papers (hereafter, NCF Papers), CDG-B (Great Britain), SCPC; and Jo Vellacott Newberry, "Women and War in England: The Case of Catherine E. Marshall and World War I," *Peace and Change* 4 (Fall 1977): 13–17.

52. Kennedy, *Hound of Conscience,* 286–89; Martin Ceadel, *Pacifism in Britain, 1914–1945: The Defining of a Faith* (Oxford: Clarendon Press, 1980), 53, 70–79, 199–200, 318; Keith Robbins, *The Abolition of War: The "Peace Movement" in Britain, 1914–1919* (Cardiff: Univ. of Wales, 1976), 210; William J. Chamberlain, *Fighting for Peace: The Story of the War Resistance Movement* (New York: Garland, 1971, reprint, 1928), 115–29; and Brock and N. Young, *Pacifism in the Twentieth Century,* 101–2.

53. Hughan, "Autobiography."

54. Witherspoon, "Jessie Wallace Hughan" [Jan. 1962], John Nevin Sayre Papers (hereafter, Sayre Papers), Series A, Box 7, DG-117, SCPC.

55. "Anti-Enlistment League Statement," Anti-Enlistment League Papers (hereafter AEL Papers), CDG-A, SCPC.

56. Roosevelt-Hughan exchange quoted in Frances H. Early, "Jessie Wallace Hughan's 'War Against War,' " 316–17.

57. For the Anti-Enlistment League, see Hughan, "Autobiography"; A. R. C. Finch, "Resister for Peace," 17–20a, Hughan Papers; materials in AEL Papers; and Hughan, *Three Decades of War Resistance*, 8–9, 11.

58. For the wartime antiradical crusade, see Julian F. Jaffe, *Crusade Against Radicalism: New York During the Red Scare, 1914–1924* (Port Washington, N.Y.: Kennikat, 1972); H. C. Peterson and Gilbert C. Fite, *Opponents of War, 1917–1918* (Madison: Univ. of Wisconsin Press, 1957); Roy Talbert, Jr., *Negative Intelligence: The Army and the American Left, 1917–1941* (Jackson, Miss.: Univ. Press of Mississippi, 1991); Chambers, *To Raise an Army*, 109–12, 205–20; and Donald Johnson, *The Challenge to American Freedoms: World War I and the Rise of the American Civil Liberties Union* (Lexington: Univ. of Kentucky Press, 1963). For *Four Lights,* see Mary Alden Hopkins, "Woman's Way in War" and Editorial, *Four Lights,* 28 July 1917, WPP Papers, Reel 12.3.

59. A. R. C. Finch, "Resister for Peace," 19, Hughan Papers.

60. N.a. to Hughan, 26 Mar. [1915?], Hughan Papers.

61. Hughan to editor of [?], 7 Sept. 1917, Hughan Papers.

62. Hughan, *International Government,* 348–50, 363–65.

63. Hughan to editor of [?], 7 Sept. 1917, Hughan Papers.

64. Hughan, *International Government,* 348–50, 363–65.

65. Jaffe, *Crusade Against Radicalism,* 105.

66. Ibid., 104–18; Peterson and Fite, *Opponents of War,* 102–12; Charles F. Howlett, "Quaker Conscience in the Classroom: The Mary S. McDowell Case," *Quaker History* 83 (Fall 1994): 99–115; and Stephen J. Whitfield, *Scott Nearing: Apostle of American Radicalism* (New York: Columbia Univ. Press, 1974), 25, 35.

67. A. R. C. Finch, "Resister for Peace," 21–22, Hughan Papers.

68. Ibid., 15, 21–22; John L. Tildsley to Hughan, 2 July 1918, Hughan Papers; *Brooklyn Daily Eagle,* 1 July 1918, 3.

69. *New York Times* (hereafter, *NYT*), 25 Jan. 1919, 1.

70. Hughan, quoted and cited in *NYT,* 25 Jan. 1919, 1, 4; and 26 Jan. 1919, 8.

71. Hughan quoted in the *New York Call,* 9 June 1922, 1. See also Jaffe, *Crusade Against Radicalism,* 119–42; Talbert, *Negative Intelligence,* 175–81; Finch, "Resister for Peace," 30–31. For the postwar Red Scare, see Robert Murray, *Red Scare: A Study in National Hysteria* (Minneapolis: Univ. of Minnesota Press, 1955); Jaffe *Crusade Against Radicalism,* 119, 172–74; and Talbert, *Negative Intelligence,* 146–49.

72. Hughan, *The Challenge of Mars* (New York: Correlated Graphic Industries, 1932), 43–44.

73. Elizabeth Dilling, *The Red Network: A "Who's Who" and Handbook of Radicalism for Patriots* (Chicago: by author, 1934), 61–69, 237–39, 257–59, 292.

74. Hughan, quoted in A. R. C. Finch, "Resister for Peace," 15, Hughan Papers. See also Hughan, "Autobiography."

75. See, for instance, Hughan, "Revolutionary Pacifism," Dec. 1919, Hughan Papers.

76. Larry Gara, "WRL: The Early Years," *The Nonviolent Activist,* Oct.-Nov. 1987, 8–10; Kaufman, interview in "Resister for Peace," by A. R. C. Finch, Hughan Papers; Kaufman, interviews by author, 1993 and 1994; and Hughan, *What Is War Resistance?*

77. Hughan, "Has International Socialism Collapsed?" [1914], Hughan Papers.

78. Hughan, "Non-Cooperation in War," [1920], Hughan Papers.

79. Hughan, *What Is War Resistance?*; Hughan, "Direct Attack upon War," *The Social Preparation* [1923], 12–13; Hughan, "Revolutionary Pacifism," Dec. 1919; Hughan, "The Outlook for Aggressive Pacifism in 1920," [1920]; and Hughan, "Non-Cooperation in War," [1920], all in Hughan Papers; Hughan, "Socialists and War," n.d., WRL Scrapbook (c. 1923–45; hereafter, WRL Scrapbook), WRL Papers; Kaufman, interview by author, 18 Nov. 1993; Kaufman to Michael Young, 16 Dec. 1974, Kaufman Papers; Kaufman, interview in "Resister for Peace," by A. R. C. Finch, Hughan Papers. Hughan preferred "declaration" to "pledge," since it indicated intent and enabled a person to change his or her mind should conditions change.

80. Hughan, *On Dueling* (New York: A. J. Muste Memorial Institute, n.d.), 49.

81. Ibid.; Hughan, "Socialists and War"; Hughan, "Direct Attack Upon War," 13; and Hughan, "Revolutionary Pacifism," all in Hughan Papers; and Hughan, *What Is War Resistance?* See also chapter 3.

82. Hillquit, quoted in A. R. C. Finch, "Resister for Peace," 19, Hughan Papers.

83. Norman Thomas to Hughan, 5 Oct. 1920, Hughan Papers.

84. For instance, see Hughan, "How About Civil War?" n.d., Allen Papers.

85. N. Thomas to Hughan, 18 Feb. 1920, Hughan Papers.

86. Roger Baldwin to Hughan, 17 Feb. 1920, Hughan Papers.

87. Hughan, *Three Decades of War Resistance,* 14.

88. Hughan, "Some Suggestions for Work in Non-Resistant Pacifism," [1921?], Hughan Papers.

89. Hughan, "Non-Cooperation in War," Hughan Papers.

90. Hughan, "Some Suggestions for Work in Non-Resistant Pacifism"; Hughan, "Non-Cooperation in War"; and Hughan, "Revolutionary Pacifism," all in Hughan Papers; Frank Olmstead, *A Brief Biography of the War Resisters League* (New York: WRL, 1945), copy in WRL Papers, A/4; M. Finch and R. Finch, interview by author, 13 Nov. 1993; and Kaufman, interview by author, 18 Nov. 1993.

91. M. Young, "Wars Will Cease When Men Refuse to Fight," 14, 20; and Charles Chatfield, ed., *The Radical "No": The Correspondence and Writings of Evan Thomas on War* (New York: Garland, 1974).

92. This is suggested by [untitled draft], [1923?], WRL Papers, A/1; Elinor Byrns, "Federation of Passive-Resistants or Non—Resistants," 15 Nov. 1922, Fellowship of Reconciliation Papers/U.S. Section, Series A-1, Box 1, DG-13, SCPC (hereafter, FOR Papers, Series letter/Box number).

93. Hughan, *Three Decades of War Resistance,* 14–15; and Hughan, "Non-Cooperation in War," Hughan Papers. Both WRL literature and historians often erroneously claim that Tracy Mygatt and Frances Witherspoon *cofounded* the League with Hughan. For a discussion of this issue, see Scott H. Bennett, " 'Pacifism Not Passivism': The War Resisters League and Radical Pacifism, Nonviolent Direct Action, and the Americanization of Gandhi, 1915–1963" (Ph.D. diss., Rutgers Univ., 1998), 64–65, note 149.

94. [Eugenie] A. Reltinger to Dear Friends, 15 Sept. 1920, FOR Papers, A-1/5.

95. Byrne, "Federation of Passive-Resistants or Non-Resistants," 15 Nov. 1922, FOR Papers, A-1/1.

96. Ibid.; Hughan, *Three Decades of War Resistance,* 14; and A. R. C. Finch, "Resister for Peace," 25–27, Hughan Papers.

97. Brockway, *Inside the Left,* 131.

98. For the WRI, see Brockway, *Inside the Left,* 116, 130–31; Hughan, *Three Decades of War Resistance,* 14–15; Ceadel, *Pacifism in Britain,* 70–73, 318–19; Kennedy, *Hound of Conscience,* 286; Chamberlain, *Fighting for Peace,* 118; Brock and N. Young, *Pacifism in the Twentieth Century,* 102–3; and Robbins, *The Abolition of War,* 210–11.

99. Brockway, *Inside the Left,* 133–35; "Report-International No More War Demonstration, July 28–29, 1923," [1923]; Henrietta M. Heinzen, Paul Jones, and Caroline L. Babcock to Dear Friend, 6 July 1922; (Letterhead) International No More War Demonstration, [1923], all in Women's Peace Union Papers (hereafter, WPU Papers), Reel 88.3–22, SCPC; and *No More War* (WPU), Apr. 1923; and Minutes of Federation Committee, 4 Apr. 1923, WRL Papers, A/1.

100. Different versions of the NMWM declaration are quoted in Ceadel, *Pacifism in Britain,* 73–74; Hughan to [Devere] Allen, 26 Oct. 1929, Allen Papers; and documents in No More War Movement Papers, CDG-B, SCPC.

101. For the formation of the War Resisters League, see A. R. C. Finch, "Resister for Peace," 27–39, Hughan Papers; and "Memorandum," [1923]; and "Meeting of Peace Organizations of the United States at the Home of Mr. and Mrs. Sayre" (Draft minutes), 5 Mar. 1925, both in WRL Papers, A/1.

102. [Hughan] to H. Runham Brown, July [?], 1923, Hughan Papers.

103. Ibid.; "Memorandum," [1923], WRL Papers, A/1; and Hughan, *Three Decades of War Resistance,* 15.

104. Published accounts often erroneously state that the WRL was founded in 1924 or 1925. By 1924 the WRL had an executive committee comprised of Hughan, Elinor Byrns, Edith B. Cram, Paul Jones, Henry Neumann, Edward C. M. Richards, Kathleen W. Sayre, and Olivia D. Torrence. Regarding the confusion about the WRL's founding, and for information on executive committee members, see Bennett, "Pacifism Not Passivism," 44, 66–68nn. 164–72.

105. Minutes of Federation Committee, 4 Apr. 1923, WRL Papers, A/1.

106. Ibid., and 4 May 1923, WRL Papers, A/1.

107. Hughan, [untitled report], 21 Feb. 1924, WRL Papers, A/1.

108. "War Resisters' Conference" [press statement], [6 Mar. 1925?], WRL Papers, A/1.

109. "Peace Organizations at the Home of Mr. and Mrs. Sayre" (draft minutes), WRL Papers, A/1.

110. For information on the 1925 conference of absolute pacifist groups, see [H. R. Brown], "Manifesto Against Conscription," Feb. 1925, War Resisters' International Papers (hereafter, WRI Papers), Box 1, DG-39, SCPC; "Peace Organizations at the Home of Mr. and Mrs. Sayre" (revised and draft minutes), and attached No More War Movement, "Call on Governments to Disband Armies, Navies and Air Forces," *No More War,* n.d.; "War Resisters' Conference" (press statement), [6 Mar. 1925?]; and [WPU] to Hughan, 13 Feb. 1925, all in WRL Papers, A/1. Besides the WRL (temporarily renamed the No More War Group to avoid confusion with the American Section of the WRI), delegates from the FOR, WPS, WPU, and three other pacifist groups attended.

Hughan organized the WRL and WPS delegations, providing further evidence of her roots in the women's peace movement.

111. This reconstruction of the 15 Mar. 1925 meeting and related developments is based on minutes, letters, and statements that appear in folders marked "Organizational Conference, 1925" and "Minutes and Reports, 1925," WRL Papers, A/1; newspaper clippings dated Feb.-Mar. 1923, WPU Papers, Reel 88.22; Minutes, WPU Working Committee, 7 May 1925, WPU Papers, Reel 88.1; [Hughan] to H. R. Brown, 25 Sept. 1925, WRI Papers, Box 4; and 31 Oct. 1925, [Hughan] to H. R. Brown [Mar. 1925?], WRI Papers, Box 1; Minutes, FOR Executive Committee, 2 Apr. 1925, FOR Papers, A-2/1; and Hughan, *Three Decades of War Resistance,* 15.

112. H. R. Brown to Elinor Byrns, 10 Nov. 1925, WRI Papers, Box 4. For the discussion on gender, see [Elinor Byrns] to H. R. Brown, 20 Nov. 1925, and 13 Sept. 1926, WRI Papers, Box 4; and other correspondence among Brown, Byrns, and Hughan, Oct.-Nov. 1925, WRI Papers, Box 4; Minutes, WRI International Council, 21–22 May 1927, WRI, Archives of War Resisters' International, 1921–74, microfiche (Hassocks, England: Harvester Press, 1977).

113. *WRL News,* May-June 1955.

114. Kaufman, interviews by author, 11 Nov. and 9 Dec. 1993; M. Finch and R. Finch, interview by author, 13 Nov. 1993; Kaufman, interview in "Resister for Peace," by A. R. C. Finch, Hughan Papers; Kaufman, "Some Episodes in the Life and Works of Jessie Wallace Hughan," June 1973; and Kaufman to Dear Friends, 2 July 1973, both in Kaufman Papers.

115. [Hughan] to H. R. Brown, 25 Sept. 1925, WRI Papers, Box 4.

116. [Hughan] to H. R. Brown, 31 Oct. 1925, WRI Papers, Box 4.

117. WRL Declaration, quoted in Hughan, *Three Decades of War Resistance,* 17. For the late 1920s, see Hughan to Allen, 26 Oct. 1929, Allen Papers.

118. Different versions of the NMWM declaration are quoted in Ceadel, *Pacifism in Britain,* 73–74; Hughan to [Devere] Allen, 26 Oct. 1929, Allen Papers; documents in No More War Movement Papers; A. R. C. Finch, "Resister for Peace," 27–39, Hughan Papers; "Memorandum," [1923], WRL Papers, A/1; and "Peace Organizations at the Home of Mr. and Mrs. Sayre" (draft minutes), WRL Papers, A/1.

119. This discussion is based mainly on Kaufman, interviews by author, 18 Nov. and 22 Dec. 1993. The WRL and WRI Declarations are identical, but the WRI also provided an explication which expressly rejected class violence to liberate the proletariat. See H. R. Brown, "Principle Policy and Practice," in *International War Resistance Through World War II,* ed. Charles Chatfield (New York: Garland, 1975), 57–58.

## Chapter 2. Consolidation and Growth

1. Kaufman, interview by author, 4 Mar. 1997; and Kaufman, unrecorded conversation with author, 3 May 1995.

2. Liberal pacifist groups included the American Friends Service Committee (1917), the Women's International League for Peace and Freedom (1919), and the National Committee on the Cause and Cure of War (1924). Radical pacifism found expression in the Fellowship of Reconciliation (1915), the WRL (1923), the Women's Peace Society (1919), and the Women's Peace Union (1921), as well as (for the most part) the Catholic Worker movement (1933). Like the WRL, the Women's Peace Society (1919–34) and the Women's Peace Union (1921–42) repre-

sented the secular, radical pacifist Left and were affiliated with the WRI; both, however, had a dominant female orientation. The WPU, inactive during its last several years, did not survive World War II.

3. Hughan, *What Is War Resistance?*

4. Kaufman, interview in "Resister for Peace," by A. R. C. Finch, in Hughan Papers; and Hughan, *What Is War Resistance?*; Olmstead, *Brief Biography of the War Resisters League*; and Kaufman, interviews by author, 1993 and 1994.

5. WRL Declaration, quoted in Hughan, *Three Decades of War Resistance*, 17.

6. For an analysis of the WRL's 1938 membership by gender and occupation, see Kaufman, "Report of the Executive Secretary," 4 May 1938, in Minutes, WRL-EC, WRL Papers, A/2.

7. WRL Declaration, quoted in Hughan, *Three Decades of War Resistance*, 17.

8. [Kaufman] to Michael Young, 15 Sept. 1974, Kaufman Papers.

9. Kaufman to Michael Young, 16 Dec. 1974, Kaufman Papers.

10. Ibid.

11. For biographical information on Abraham Kaufman, see Kaufman, interviews by author, 1993 and 1994; Kaufman, "Manuscript"; and Kaufman-Michael Young correspondence, 1974–75, both in Kaufman Papers; Kaufman, interview in "Resister for Peace," by A. R. C. Finch, Hughan Papers; W. W., "He'd Prefer Jail to Conscription," *P.M.*, 17 July 1940, clipping; *Life* magazine, 29 Jan. 1925 (reprinted with WRL slogans), clipping, both in WRL Scrapbook; Kaufman to Scott H. Bennett, Dec. 1997.

12. Kaufman to [M. Young], 25 Jan. 1975, Kaufman Papers.

13. Ibid.; "War Resisters League Statement on Communists and United Fronts," [1939 or 1940], WRL Papers, A/5.

14. [Kaufman] to [M. Young], 9 Apr. 1975; Kaufman, "Manuscript"; and M[artin] Goldwasser, "History of Metropolitan Board for C.O.'s," 25 Oct. 1971, all in Kaufman Papers; Kaufman, "An Outline of Our Work During the First Ten Months of 1939—to Nov. 1st," 10 Nov. 1939, in Minutes, WRL-EC, WRL Papers, A/2; and "Pacifists Set Up Board to Advise War Objectors," [16 July 1940], clipping, WRL Scrapbook.

15. For biographical information on John H. Holmes, see Carl H. Voss, *Rabbi and Minister: The Friendship of Stephen S. Wise and John Haynes Holmes* (Cleveland: World Publishing Co., 1964); Charles Chatfield, *For Peace and Justice: Pacifism in America, 1914–1941* (Knoxville: Univ. of Tennessee Press, 1971), 63–67, passim; and C. Seshachari, *Gandhi and the American Scene: An Intellectual History and Inquiry* (Bombay: Nachiketa Publications, 1969), 103–24. Published works by Holmes include *I Speak for Myself: The Autobiography of John Haynes Holmes* (New York: Harper & Brothers, 1959); *My Gandhi* (New York: Harper, 1953); and *New Wars for Old* (1916; reprint, New York: Garland, 1971). His sermons are located in the John Haynes Holmes Papers (hereafter, Holmes Papers), CDG-A, SCPC.

16. Holmes, quoted in *NYT*, 4 Apr. 1964, 27.

17. Ibid.; see also, Holmes, *I Speak for Myself*, 72, 82–99, 110–11, 190–231, 282–83.

18. Holmes, *New Wars for Old*, 222.

19. Ibid.; Chatfield, introduction to *New Wars for Old*, by Holmes, 5–15; Holmes, *I Speak for Myself*, 115, 160–91; Voss, *Rabbi and Minister*, 138–50; and Chatfield, *For Peace and Justice*, 63–67.

20. Holmes, *I Speak for Myself*, 173–86, quotation at 178.

21. For Gandhi's impact in America and the role Holmes played in popularizing him, see

Charles Chatfield, introduction to his edited *The Americanization of Gandhi: Images of the Mahatma* (New York: Garland, 1976), 23–69; Seshachari, *Gandhi and the American Scene.*

22. Holmes, "Who Is the Greatest Man in the World Today?" in *Americanization of Gandhi,* ed. Chatfield, 610.

23. Ibid., 618.

24. Ibid.

25. Ibid., 599–621; Carl H. Voss, "John Haynes Holmes: Discoverer of Gandhi," in *Americanization of Gandhi,* ed. Chatfield, 589–91; Holmes, *My Gandhi,* 21–33; and Voss, *Rabbi and Minister,* 198–200.

26. Holmes, "Who Is the Greatest Man in the World Today?" 599, 610.

27. Holmes, "World Significance of Mahatma Gandhi," 12 Mar. 1922 ([New York]: Friends of Freedom for India, reprinted from *Unity* (6 Apr. 1922), copy in Holmes Papers, 11–14, quotation at 12.

28. Ibid., 11.

29. Holmes, "Who Is the Greatest Man in the World?" 620.

30. Holmes, "World Significance of Mahatma Gandhi," 16; see also Chatfield, introduction to *Americanization of Gandhi.*

31. Holmes and Reginald Lawrence, *If This Be Treason* (New York: Macmillan, 1935), 85.

32. Ibid., 47.

33. Holmes and Lawrence, *If This Be Treason*; Holmes, *I Speak for Myself,* 114–15, 219–21; and Kaufman to Scott H. Bennett, Dec. 1997.

34. Minutes, WRL-EC, 27 Jan. 1938, Allen Papers; Kaufman, "Report of the Executive Secretary," 4 May 1938, in Minutes, WRL-EC, WRL Papers, A/2.

35. This portrait of Devere Allen borrows generously from Charles Chatfield, "The Life of Devere Allen," in *Devere Allen: Life and Writings,* ed. Charles Chatfield (New York: Garland, 1976), 19–57. See also Barbara Addison, "Pragmatic Pacifist: Devere Allen and the Twentieth Century Peace Movement," unpublished essay in author's possession; [E. D. Chase, Manager, Devere Allen's Tours], "Devere Allen Information for Publicity," [1940?], Sayre Papers, A/1.

36. Allen to N. Thomas, 13 Aug. 1931, Allen Papers.

37. Allen [handwritten notes], Apr. [1931], 8–18, Allen Papers.

38. Chatfield, "Life of Devere Allen," 32.

39. Ibid., 33.

40. Allen to N. Thomas, 13 Aug. 1931.

41. Allen, *The Fight for Peace* (New York: Macmillan, 1930), 648.

42. Ibid., 395.

43. Ibid., 171.

44. Ibid., 613–19, 631–35.

45. Ibid., 548; for League of Brotherhood pledge, see 416–17. See also chapter 25 for his theses, which offer an excellent statement of the WRL's intellectual and ideological assumptions and its logic—its mentalité.

46. Minutes, WRL-EC, 12 Aug. 1940, WRL Papers, A/2.

47. For biographical information on Frances M. Witherspoon and Tracy D. Mygott, see Frances H. Early, *A World Without War: How U.S. Feminists and Pacifists Resisted World War I* (Syracuse: Syracuse Univ. Press, 1997); Ann M. Davidon, "The Lives of Tracy D. Mygatt and Frances Witherspoon," *WRL News,* Jan.-Feb. 1974; Nancy Manahan, "Future Old Maids and Pacifist Ag-

itators: The Story of Tracy Mygatt and Frances Witherspoon," *Women's Studies Quarterly* 10 (Spring 1982):10–13.

48. Frances H. Early, *World Without War,* xxi, 200.

49. For the Bureau of Legal Advice (BLA), see Early, *World Without War;* and Frances H. Early, "Feminism, Peace, and Civil Liberties: Women's Role in the Origins of the World War I Civil Liberties Movement," *Women's Studies* 18 (1990): 95–115.

50. Baldwin, quoted in Nat Hentoff, *Peace Agitator: The Story of A. J. Muste* (New York: A. J. Muste Memorial Institute, 1982), 54–55.

51. Foster, quoted in Hentoff, *Peace Agitator,* 77.

52. Jo Ann Ooiman Robinson, *Abraham Went Out: A Biography of A. J. Muste* (Philadelphia: Temple Univ. Press, 1981), 51.

53. Ibid., 56.

54. Quoted in ibid., [xiii]. For biographical information on A. J. Muste, see Nat Hentoff, ed., *The Essays of A. J. Muste* (New York: Bobbs-Merrill, 1967); A. J. Muste, "My Experience in Labor and Radical Struggles," in *As We Saw the Thirties,* ed. Rita A. Simon (Urbana: Univ. of Illinois Press, 1967), 123–50; Robinson, *Abraham Went Out;* and Hentoff, *Peace Agitator.*

55. Evan W. Thomas to [Mother], 16 May 1916, in *Radical "No,"* ed. Chatfield, 57.

56. Evan W. Thomas to [Mother], 30 June 1916; 3 Sept. 1916, in *Radical "No,"* ed. Chatfield, 64–70.

57. Chatfield, editorial note, in *Radical "No,"* ed. Chatfield, 79–81.

58. Ibid., 20.

59. Ibid., 81.

60. E. Thomas to [N. Thomas], 8 June 1918, in *Radical "No,"* ed. Chatfield, 147.

61. Chatfield, *For Peace and Justice,* 68–87. Actually, more than 20,000 conscientious objectors were inducted into the army, though 16,000 abandoned their objection during training camp.

62. E. Thomas, Erling H. Lunde, Harold S. Gray, and Howard W. Moore to Newton D. Baker, 21 Aug. 1918, in *Radical "No,"* ed. Chatfield, 173.

63. E. Thomas to [N. Thomas], 21 Aug. 1918, in *Radical "No,"* ed. Chatfield, 172.

64. For biographical information on Evan W. Thomas, see Chatfield, ed., *Radical "No,"* which contains his wartime and postwar letters and writings and insightful commentary by the editor. For a contemporary account of World War I COs, camps, and prison life by Evan's brother, see N. Thomas, *The Conscientious Objector in America* (New York: B. W. Huebsch, 1923).

65. Frieda L. Lazarus and Frances R. Ransom, "Report of Membership Secretary, 1942," 31 Dec. 1942, Minutes, WRL-EC, WRL Papers, A/2; H. R. Brown to Hughan, 21 Mar. 1936, WRI Papers, Box 4.

66. For WRL activities, see Hughan, *Three Decades of War Resistance,* 17; and A. R. C. Finch, "Resister for Peace," 35–39, 42, Hughan Papers; Gottlieb, interviews by author, 1993 and 1994; Kaufman, interviews by author, 1993 and 1994; Kaufman, "Manuscript," Kaufman Papers; [Kaufman] to Grace M. Beaton, 14 Mar. 1938, WRI Papers, Box 4; WRL, "Pacifist Team Organization," Jan. 1942; Minutes, WRL Sub-Committee on the Refugee Problem, 9 Feb. 1939, in Minutes, WRL-EC, WRL Papers, A/2; "WRL Summary of Activity: January 1st to December [31st], 1929," [31 Dec. 1929], Allen Papers; and folder marked "Refugee Committee, 1938–1940," WRL Papers, A/29. For WRL peace action in 1936 (a typical year), including participation in Emergency Peace Campaign coalition projects, see Kaufman, "WRL: Summary of Activities for the Year 1936" [Feb. 1937?], in Minutes, WRL-EC, WRL Papers, A/1.

67. William Floyd, *War Resistance: What Each Individual Can Do for War Prevention* (New York: The Arbitrator, [1931–32]), copy in WRL Papers, A/3.

68. Kaufman, "Manuscript," Kaufman Papers.

69. Quoted in "The Challenge of Mars and Other Verses" [/] " 'Guns' or 'Disarmament'— A New and Improved Edition," n.d., Allen Papers. For the games and poetry, see also "The Game of Guns or Disarmament," WRL Papers, A/5; "The New and Improved Edition of 'GUNS,' " Allen Papers; A. R. C. Finch, "Resister for Peace," 37; and Hughan, *The Challenge of Mars*.

70. Quoted in advertisements in *New Leader,* 1 Dec. 1934, clipping in WRL Scrapbook.

71. Kaufman, "Manuscript," Kaufman Papers; Sheba Strunsky to Edward P. Gottlieb, n.d., Edward P. Gottlieb Papers (unprocessed; hereafter, Gottlieb Papers), SCPC; Kaufman, interviews by author, 1993 and 1994; and Gottlieb, interviews by author, 1993 and 1994.

72. Albert Einstein, quoted in Otto Nathan and Heinz Norden, ed., *Einstein on Peace* (New York: Simon and Schuster, 1960), 117.

73. Hughan to Dear War Resister, n.d., WRL Papers, A/5.

74. Ibid.; Sidney E. Goldstein to Dear Friend, n.d., WRL Papers, A/5; "Einstein on War Resistance," [1930?], Albert Einstein Papers, GDC-A, SCPC; Gottlieb, unrecorded conversation with author, 10 Nov. 1996; Hughan, *What Is War Resistance?*; Hughan, "Disarmament and the Fight Against War," *The New Deal,* Mar. 1932, clipping, WRL Scrapbook; and A. R. C. Finch, "Resister for Peace," 36, 38, Hughan Papers.

75. "Peace Letter to the President of the United States,"[1927], WRL Papers, A/3; [Hughan] to President Herbert Hoover (Draft), [Nov. 1929], Allen Papers; Hughan to My Dear [?], n.d., Hughan Papers; and Kaufman, "Manuscript," Kaufman Papers.

76. Statement attached to Al Hamilton to Allen, 8 Nov. 1937, Allen Papers. For information on the Oxford Pledge, student strike for peace, and 1930s student antiwar movement, see Robert Cohen, *When the Old Left Was Young: Student Radicals and America's First Mass Student Movement, 1929–1941* (New York: Oxford Univ. Press, 1993); Joseph P. Lash and James A. Wechsler, *War Our Heritage* (New York: International Publishers, 1936); and Chatfield, *For Peace and Justice,* 259–61, 271–73, 295–96.

77. Lash and Wechsler, *War Our Heritage,* 147.

78. Kaufman, "Practical Pacifism: Out-door Celebration, 120 Years of the Unarmed Frontier Between the United States and Canada," WRL Papers, A/35.

79. Folder marked "Anti Air Maneuvers Protest Demonstration, May 1931," WRL Papers, A/35; *NYT,* 11 May 1931, 21; 23 May 1931, 1, 3; 24 May 1931, I-1, 26–28.

80. Tracy D. Mygatt and Frances M. Witherspoon, "An Office of Commemoration for the Dead Who Died in the Great War and of the War Resisters' Pledge of Brotherhood to All Mankind," *Pilgrim Highroad,* Nov. 1935, 1–2, clipping, Allen Papers.

81. For information on the WRL's Armistice Eve ceremony and the role of emotion in peace ceremonies, see Mygatt and Witherspoon, "Office of Commemoration for the Dead"; Tracy D. Mygatt and Frances M. Witherspoon, "Responses or People, Torchbearers and Nationals, Taking Part in 'An Office,' Armistice Day Service," [1935], Allen Papers; Gottlieb, interview in "Resister for Peace," by A. R. C. Finch; and A. R. C. Finch, "Resister for Peace," 35, Hughan Papers; "War Resisters to Renew Pledge" (flyer card), n.d., WRL Scrapbook; Allen, *Fight for Peace,* 348–57, 545–46; and Hughan, *International Government,* 310–65.

82. Hughan, quoted in A. R. C. Finch, "Resister for Peace," 39, Hughan Papers.

83. Committee on Decorations (No More War Parade) to Cooperating Groups [1934], WRL Papers, A/35.

84. *NYT,* 19 May 1935, Section 2, 1–2.

85. Ibid.

86. "New 'No More War' Songs," [1935], WRL Papers, A/35.

87. [Frank Olmstead] to Gareth Matthews, 17 Oct. 1946, WRL Papers, A/16. See also [*Evening State Journal* (Lincoln, Nebraska)], [25 Aug. 1942], clipping, WRL Scrapbook; Frank Olmstead, Testimony before House Committee on Foreign Affairs, Assistance to Greece and Turkey: Hearings on H.R. 2616, 80th Cong., 1st sess., 1947, 300–302.

88. Committee on Decorations (No More War Parade) to Cooperating Groups [1934], WRL Papers, A/35.

89. "The League's Relation to Other Peace Groups," 29 June 1936, in Minutes, WRL-EC, WRL Papers, A/1; and folder marked "No More War Parade, 1934–35," WRL Papers, A/35. For a view supportive of the exclusion of communists in the 1930s and critical of that policy's reversal in the 1960s, see Guenter Lewy, *Peace and Revolution: The Moral Crisis of American Pacifism* (Grand Rapids: Mich.: William B. Eerdmans, 1988).

90. Chatfield, *For Peace and Justice,* 256–86, quotation at 256. For information on the Emergency Peace Campaign, see also Hughan, "The War Resisters League and the Emergency Peace Campaign," 2 Nov. 1936, WRL Papers, A/3; "The League's Relations to Other Peace Groups," 29 June 1936, in Minutes, WRL-EC, WRL Papers, A/1; and Robert Kleidman, *Organizing for Peace: Neutrality, the Test Ban, and the Freeze* (Syracuse: Syracuse Univ. Press), 58–88.

91. For WRL opposition to collective security and the WRL debate over boycotts, see Hughan to Fellow War Resister, 17 July 1936, and attached Lord Ponsonby, "The League of Nations and Collective Security," 7 May 1936; WRL Press Release ("American War Resisters Support Ponsonby, Lansbury in Their Opposition to War Support in the Form of Government 'Sanctions' ") [1935]; Gottlieb, "Economic Sanctions and War," *New York War Resister,* 1 Mar. 1938; and Minutes, WRL-EC, 11 Oct. 1937, all in Allen Papers; Sidney E. Goldstein to Holmes, 13 Oct. 1937; "Proposed Statement of the War Resisters League on the Far Eastern Problem," [Oct. 1937]; and [Hughan] to Holmes, 29 Oct. 1937, all in WRL Papers, A/35; Tracy D. Mygatt, "War Resister Strategy" (WRL conference), 6–8 May 1938; and Hester D. Jenkins, "WRL Annual Dinner," [21 Dec. 1937], WRL Papers, A/9. Both questionnaires (from 1931 and 1937) are reprinted, with tabulations, in "A Study of Pacifist Social Thought as Exemplified by the War Resisters League," [1939?], by Sanford Klein, WRL Scrapbook. See also Kaufman, interview by author, 22 Dec. 1993; Kaufman, interview in "Resister for Peace," by A. R. C. Finch, Hughan Papers; and Kaufman, "Manuscript," Kaufman Papers.

92. For biographical information on Reinhold Niebuhr, see Reinhold Niebuhr, *Moral Man and Immoral Society* (New York: Charles Scribner's Sons, 1932); Chatfield, *For Peace and Justice,* 206–7, 212, 239; Lawrence S. Wittner, *Rebels Against War: The American Peace Movement, 1933–1983* (Philadelphia: Temple Univ. Press, 1984), 15–16; and Richard W. Fox, *Reinhold Niebuhr: A Biography* (New York: Pantheon, 1985).

93. Richard B. Gregg, *The Power of Nonviolence* (New York: Schocken Books, 1969), 43–51.

94. Bart de Ligt, *The Conquest of Violence* (New York: E. P. Dutton & Co., 1938), 162.

95. Krishnalal Shridharani, *War Without Violence: A Study of Gandhi's Method and Its Accomplishments* (New York: Harcourt, Brace & Co., 1939).

96. Hughan, *If We Should Be Invaded* (3d. ed.). See chap. 1, n. 26.

97. For all quotations in the last two paragraphs, see ibid., 3, 6, 8–9, 15, 21.

98. Ibid., 17.

99. For examples of this interwar literature, see Hughan, *International Government,* 348–50; Hughan, *What Is War Resistance?*; Hughan, *Pacifism and Invasion;* Allen, *Fight for Peace,* case studies at 624–42; Gregg, *Power of Nonviolence,* case studies at 15–42; Holmes and Lawrence, *If This Be Treason;* de Ligt, *Conquest of Violence;* Shridharani, *War Without Violence;* Donald Port, *The British People Stopped a War* (London: Peace News, 1944); and the pamphlets and articles by Hughan and Allen cited in chapter 3. For a discussion that situates Holmes, Allen, Gregg, and Shridharani within the debate in the FOR and SP over violence and coercion, see Chatfield, *For Peace and Justice,* 191–220. For a post-World War II study that extends the interwar literature, see Sharp, *The Politics of Nonviolent Action.* Hughan, Allen, and Gregg were members of the WRL and the FOR, though Gregg was primarily associated with the FOR.

### Chapter 3. Socialist Pacifism and Nonviolent Social Revolution

1. The literature on the Spanish Civil War is contentious and voluminous. For an introduction, see Gabriel Jackson, *The Spanish Republic and the Spanish Civil War, 1931–1939* (Princeton: Princeton Univ. Press, 1965); and Hugh Thomas, *The Spanish Civil War,* rev. ed. (New York: Harper & Row, 1971). More recent works include Burnett Bolloten, *The Spanish Civil War: Revolution and Counterrevolution* (Chapel Hill: Univ. of North Carolina Press, 1991); Michael Alpert, *A New International History of the Spanish Civil War* (New York: St. Martin's Press, 1994); and Stanley G. Payne, *The Franco Regime: 1936–1975* (Madison: Univ. of Wisconsin Press, 1987), 1–228.

2. *Socialist Call,* 25 July 1936, 4.

3. Allen Guttmann, *The Wound in the Heart* (New York: Free Press of Glencoe, 1962); and Robert A. Rosenstone, *Crusade of the Left: The Lincoln Battalion in the Spanish Civil War* (New York: Pegasus, 1969).

4. Hughan, *What about Spain?* (New York: WRL, 1937), 3, copy in Hughan Papers.

5. For an earlier version of this chapter, see Scott H. Bennett, "Socialist Pacifism and Nonviolent Social Revolution: The War Resisters League and the Spanish Civil War, 1936–1939," *Peace and Change* 25 (Jan. 2000): 102–28. For the SP and the Spanish Civil War, see Frank A. Warren, *An Alternative Vision: The Socialist Party in the 1930s* (Bloomington: Indiana Univ. Press, 1974), 41–44, 111–12, 134, 152–57, 176; Shannon, *Socialist Party of America,* 254, 260; Bernard Johnpoll, *Pacifist's Progress: Norman Thomas and the Decline of American Socialism* (Chicago: Quadrangle, 1970), 185–88; W. A. Swanberg, *Norman Thomas: The Last Idealist* (New York: Scribner's Sons, 1976), 210–16, 218, 227; Harry Fleischman, *Norman Thomas: A Biography* (New York: Norton, 1964), 174–79; Murray Seidler, *Norman Thomas: Respectable Rebel,* 2d ed. (New York: Syracuse Univ. Press, 1967), 175, 203–5, 308; and James C. Duram, *Norman Thomas* (New York: Twayne, 1974), 29–31, 125–28. The most detailed account is Scott H. Bennett, "Pragmatic Visionaries: The Socialist Party of America and Franklin D. Roosevelt's First Administration" (M.A. thesis, Florida State Univ., 1985), 112–60. The links among pacifism, the 1930s student left, and Spain are discussed in Cohen, *When the Old Left Was New,* 154–87.

6. For a discussion of the debate in the FOR and the SP, see Chatfield, *For Peace and Justice,* 191–220. Chatfield does not examine the WRL, but he does discuss Allen, who was active in the FOR, WRL, and SP. For the SP debate and subsequent factionalism, see also Johnpoll, *Pacifist's*

*Progress,* 120–91; Seidler, *Respectable Rebel,* 105–78; Fleischman, *Norman Thomas,* 163–81; War-ren, *Alternative Vision,* 3–20 and passim; Swanberg, *Last Idealist,* 166–73, 185–87, 191–96, 199–207; and Shannon, *Socialist Party of America,* 235–56.

7. See, for instance, Hughan to Fellow War Resister, 11 Nov. 1936, Allen Papers, A/3.

8. Brockway, *Inside the Left,* 294–322, 338–40; and J. Fenner Brockway, "Fenner Brockway's Resignation," *The War Resister,* Dec. 1936, 3.

9. Kaufman, interview by author, 22 Dec. 1993. For statements by WRL members on Spain that mirror Kaufman's, see James Peck, *Underdogs vs. Upperdogs* (New York: AMP&R, 1980), 32–33; and David Dellinger, *From Yale to Jail: The Life Story of a Moral Dissenter* (New York: Pan-theon, 1993), 85.

10. Devere Allen, "Pacifism and Its Critics," in *Devere Allen: Life and Writings,* ed. Charles Chatfield (New York: Garland, 1976), 601; and Allen, "Notes for War Resisters League—Fellow-ship of Reconciliation Meeting," 22 Dec. 1936 (hereafter, "Notes for WRL-FOR"), Allen Papers.

11. Allen to Hughan, 24 Dec. 1936, Allen Papers.

12. See WRI, *Principle, Policy and Practice,* in *International War Resistance Through World War II,* ed. Chatfield, 57–58. In a "Statement of Principles" that accompanied its declaration, the WRI stated that refusal to take up arms to liberate the proletariat remained the "most difficult" tempta-tion of force.

13. [Hughan], "How about Civil War?" Allen Papers; Hughan, *Revolution and Realism* (New York: WRL, n.d.), copy in WRL Papers, Series A/5; and Hughan, *War Resistance in the Class Strug-gle* (New York: WRL, [c. 1930]), copy in WRL Scrapbook.

14. Hughan, *War Resistance in the Class Struggle,* 4.

15. [Hughan], "How about Civil War?" Allen Papers.

16. Hughan, *War Resistance in the Class Struggle,* 7.

17. Chatfield, *For Peace and Justice,* 196.

18. Chatfield, *For Peace and Justice,* 191–97; and clippings in Sayre Papers, D/1.

19. For the dispute within the SP, see "Debate on Declaration of Principles" (Stenographic Report), *American Socialist Quarterly,* 3 (July 1934): 3–60; [Allen] to Editor of Bridgeport Post [George C. Waldo], 2 Dec. 1938, Allen Papers; Warren, *Alternative Vision,* 3–20, passim; Shan-non, *Socialist Party of America,* 235–56; Chatfield, *For Peace and Justice,* 197–202; Johnpoll, *Paci-fist's Progress,* 120–91; Seidler, *Respectable Rebel,* 105–78; Fleischman, *Norman Thomas,* 163–81; and Swanberg, *Last Idealist,* 166–73, 185–87, 191–96, 199–207.

20. SP, "Declaration of Principles," reprinted in Warren, *Alternative Vision,* 193.

21. Ibid.

22. Ibid., 194.

23. Ibid., 193; [Allen] to Editor of Bridgeport Post [George C. Waldo], 2 Dec. 1938, Allen Papers.

24. For U.S. diplomacy during the Spanish Civil War, see Douglas Little, *Malevolent Neutral-ity: The United States, Great Britain, and the Origins of the Spanish Civil War* (Ithaca: Cornell Univ. Press, 1985); Richard Traina, *American Diplomacy and the Spanish Civil War* (Bloomington: Indi-ana Univ. Press, 1968); and Robert A. Divine, *The Illusion of Neutrality* (Chicago: Univ. of Chicago Press, 1962).

25. See N. Thomas, "Memorandum on the Socialist Party and the Debs Column," n.d. [1936], Socialist Party Papers (microfilm; hereafter, SP Papers), Reel 35; [N. Thomas] to Hughan, 30 Dec. 1936, and his attached "Memorandum on the Spanish Situation in the Socialist Party"

[1936]; and N. Thomas to Emily and Horace A. Eaton, 21 Jan. 1937, both in Allen Papers; John-poll, *Pacifist's Progress,* 185–88; and Fleischman, *Norman Thomas,* 56–64, 174–78. Thomas opposed World War I as both a Christian pacifist and a socialist. He later broke with organized Christianity. The Spanish Civil War and the fascist threat led him to accept the Debs Column to stop Hitler and Mussolini and prevent another world war.

26. No study exists of the Eugene V. Debs Column, but the International Brigades have spawned a large, contentious literature. For American participation, see Peter N. Carroll, *The Odyssey of the Abraham Lincoln Brigade: Americans in the Spanish Civil War* (Stanford: Stanford Univ. Press, 1994); Danny Duncan Collum and Victor A. Berch, eds., *African Americans in the Spanish Civil War: 'This Ain't Ethiopia, But It'll Do* (New York: G. K. Hall, 1992); Robin D. G. Kelley, *Race Rebels: Culture, Politics, and the Black Working Class* (New York: Free Press, 1996), 123–58; and John Gerassi, *The Premature Antifascists: North American Volunteers in the Spanish Civil War, 1936–1939, An Oral History* (New York: Praeger, 1986). For a judicious overview, see Michael Jackson, *Fallen Sparrows: The International Brigades in the Spanish Civil War* (Philadelphia: American Philosophical Society, 1994). Some 36,000 foreign volunteers joined the International Brigades, including 2,800 Americans, of whom one-third died.

27. N. Thomas to Jack Altman, 24 Dec. 1936, SP Papers, Reel 35. See also *Socialist Call,* 26 Dec. 1936, 1; 2 Jan. 1937, 6; and "Statement by the National Action Committee, Socialist Party U.S.A., on Present Confusion in Party on Spanish Question," 11 Jan. 1937. Internal SP documents demonstrate that the SP controlled the Friends of the Debs Column, which recruited volunteers and raised funds to transport them to Spain. See Scott H. Bennett, "Pragmatic Visionaries," 137–45.

28. Gottlieb to *Socialist Call,* 26 Dec. 1936, 4.

29. *Socialist Call,* 9 Jan. 1937, 4; 23 Jan. 1937, 7; and Elisabeth Gilman to N. Thomas, 24 Dec. [1936], Norman Thomas Papers (microfilm; hereafter, Thomas Papers), Reel 7, New York Public Library (hereafter, NYPL).

30. Joseph M. Coldwell to Editor [of *Socialist Call*], [Jan. 1937, unpublished], Allen Papers.

31. Holmes to N. Thomas, *New Leader,* 2 Jan. 1937, 8.

32. Ibid. One work that does identify Holmes with the WRL is Guttmann, *Wound in the Heart,* 111–12.

33. Muste, Winston Dancis, and Hughan to Editor of *Socialist Call,* 23 Jan. 1937, 7; 13 Feb. 1937, 4.

34. "Excerpt from letter from [Ed Melnicoff to] Dave Felix," 17 Mar. 1937, Allen Papers; Fleischman, *Norman Thomas,* 177; Warren, *Alternative Vision,* 155; and Johnpoll, *Pacifist's Progress,* 187.

35. For WRL policy on signed articles, see Kaufman, interviews by author, 16 Oct. and 22 Dec. 1993. The four pamphlets were Hughan, *What about Spain?;* H. R. Brown, *Spain—A Challenge to Pacifism,* reprinted in *International War Resistance,* ed. Chatfield, 594–601; Holmes, *Spain! Is Armageddon Coming?* (New York: WRL, [1937?]); and Holmes, *A Statesmanship of Peace: If Not War, Then What? Spain—and the Next War!* (New York: WRL, 1937), copies in WRL Papers, A/3.

36. Hughan, *What about Spain?* 4.

37. Allen, "Pacifism and Its Critics," 604.

38. Allen, "Notes for WRL-FOR," Allen Papers.

39. Allen, "Pacifism and Its Critics," 604.

40. Ibid.

41. Hughan, *What about Spain?* 4–6; Allen, "Pacifism and Its Critics," 604–5; Allen, "Notes for WRL-FOR"; and [Allen] to N. Thomas, 25 Mar. 1938, both in Allen Papers; Allen to Amicus Most, 23 Mar. 1938, Thomas Papers; Holmes, *Armageddon,* 16–19; and Holmes, *Statesmanship,* 11.

42. Allen, "Notes for WRL-FOR," Allen Papers.

43. [Allen] to N. Thomas, 25 Mar. 1938.

44. For all preceding quotations in this paragraph, see Hughan, *What about Spain?* 7.

45. Ibid., 8.

46. Holmes, *Armageddon;* Holmes, *Statesmanship,* 11–13, 19–20. See also Hughan, *What about Spain?* 6–9; and Allen, "Pacifism and Its Critics," 602–3.

47. Hughan, *What about Spain?* 8.

48. Allen, "Pacifism and Its Critics," 605.

49. Ibid., 602, 605. See also Hughan, *What about Spain?* 5, 7–8, 10; and Hughan, *Pacifism and Invasion.*

50. Allen, "Notes for WRL-FOR," Allen Papers.

51. Hughan, "Mars and His Aliases," 27 Nov. 1937, WRL Papers, A/3.

52. Holmes, *Statesmanship,* 21–22. See also Hughan, *What about Spain?* 7.

53. Allen, "Notes for WRL-FOR," Allen Papers.

54. Brown, *Spain,* 598–600; Allen, "Notes for WRL-FOR"; [Allen] to H. R. Brown, 6 Oct. 1936; and Allen to Irving Barshop, 21 Dec. 1936, all in Allen Papers; Allen, "Pacifism and Its Critics," 601; and Hughan, *What about Spain?* 6–7.

55. Holmes, *Armageddon,* 17.

56. Hughan to Fellow War Resister, 15 Jan. 1937, Allen Papers.

57. Hughan to Editor of the *Nation,* 17 July 1937, 82.

58. Hughan, *What about Spain?* 5.

59. Ibid.

60. Hughan, ["Fascism: Its Cause and Cure"], [29–30 May 1937], in Minutes of 1937 WRL Conference Program, WRL Papers, A/9.

61. Hughan, *What about Spain?* 6.

62. Ibid., 5. Although disagreeing with Runham Brown's "compromise" with armed force, Hughan praised his pamphlet and quoted from it approvingly. See Hughan, *What about Spain?* 3, 5–6, 8; Hughan to H. R. Brown, 31 Dec. 1936, WRL Papers, A/3; and Hughan, ["Fascism: Its Cause and Cure"] [29–30 May 1937], WRL Papers, A/9.

63. *Yipsel Organizer,* 13 July 1936, Allen Papers.

64. Ibid.; Winston Dancis to Allen, 31 July 1936, Allen Papers. After declaring membership in the WRL incompatible with that in the SP and YPSL, YPSL-NY submitted the issue to the SP-NYC Central Committee for resolution.

65. Gottlieb, interview by author, 5 Dec. 1993; Kaufman, interviews by author, 16 Oct. and 15 Dec. 1993; and 3 Mar. 1997; Gottlieb, "Pacifists and [the] Spanish Civil War," [mid-1990s], Gottlieb Papers; [Winston Dancis] to Devere [Allen], 30 Nov. 1937, Allen Papers; and [Winston] Dancis to Devere [Allen], 6 Dec. 1937, Allen Papers. Both Saul Parker and James Burnham (a Trotskyite member of the SP and a future conservative political theorist) brought complaints or formal charges against Gottlieb.

66. Irving Barshop to Clarence Senior, 11 Nov. 1936, Allen Papers.

67. All preceding quotations in this paragraph are from Allen to Irving Barshop, 21 Dec.

1936, Allen Papers. The list of WRL-FOR members belonging to the SP was prepared hurriedly by Kaufman and did not purport to be complete. Besides Allen, this list included prominent socialists Harry W. Laidler, Clarence Senior, George Hartmann, Holmes, Hughan, Muste, Dancis, and Gilman.

68. Irving Barshop to Allen, 20 Jan. 1937, Allen Papers.

69. James Burnham, "Socialists and the Coming War," *American Socialist Monthly* (hereafter, *ASM*) 5 (Aug. 1936): 25–26.

70. Ibid., 27.

71. Caroline F. Urie, "Socialism and Pacifism," *ASM* 5 (December 1936): 57.

72. Ibid.

73. Ibid., 55–57. See also James Burnham, reply to Caroline Urie, *ASM* 5 (Dec. 1936): 55–59; and the exchange between Amicus Most and Allen in *ASM* 5 (Feb. 1937).

74. "Brief History of the New York Socialist War Resister Group," [Feb. 1937?]; Winston Dancis and Kaufman to Dear Comrade, 7 Aug. 1936; and Winston Dancis and Kaufman, "Some Thoughts on the Present Spanish Situation," 6 Aug. 1936, all in WRL Papers, A/3.

75. N. Thomas, "Memorandum on the Spanish Situation in the Socialist Party," [1936], Allen Papers.

76. "Brief History of the New York Socialist War Resister Group." See also Allen to Kaufman, 30 Dec. 1936, Thomas Papers, Reel 7; N. [Thomas] to Hughan, 30 Dec. 1936; and attached Thomas, "Memorandum on the Spanish Situation in the Socialist Party," [1936], both in Allen Papers.

77. Allen, "American Radicals and the Spanish Conflict," n.d., Allen Papers.

78. Allen, "Notes for WRL-FOR," Allen Papers.

79. Ibid. See also Allen to Kaufman, 30 Dec. 1936, Thomas Papers, Reel 7.

80. See [Allen] to Roy [Burt], 11 Jan. 1937; [Allen] to Lawrence Van Camp, 14 Jan. 1937; Allen to Alfred Baker Lewis, 16 Mar. 1937; Allen to N. Thomas, 5 Jan. 1937; Allen to Glen Trimble, 26 Aug. 1936; and Roy E. Burt to Allen, 18 Mar. 1937, all in Allen Papers; Fleischman, *Norman Thomas,* 175; and Warren, *Alternative Vision,* 154–55.

81. For Kaufman's report to the WRI, see Kaufman to H. R. Brown, 26 May 1937, WRI Papers, Box 4; for concern over Devere Allen's "logic," see [Kaufman] to [Allen], 13 July 1937, Allen Papers.

82. [Allen] to H. R. Brown, 20 May 1937, Allen Papers.

83. Ibid.

84. [Allen] to Kaufman, 9 July 1937, Allen Papers.

85. Hughan to Allen, 12 July 1937, Allen Papers.

86. For information on the rift between Allen and the WRL and its resolution, see also Hughan to Allen, 30 Dec. 1936; [Allen] to Hughan, 15 July 1937; Hughan to Allen, 21 Aug. 1937; and N. Thomas to Allen, 29 Mar. 1938, all in Allen Papers.

87. For information on WRI/WRL support for Jose Brocca and humanitarian aid in Spain, see material on Spain in WRI Papers, WRL Papers, and Allen Papers; citations in Bennett, " 'Pacifism Not Passivism,' " 161–62. For WRL financial support, see Hughan to Fellow War Resister, 11 May 1937, Allen Papers; excerpt from [Kaufman?] letter to H. R. Brown, 2 June 1937, WRI Papers, Box 4; Hughan to Fellow War Resister, 11 Nov. 1936, WRL Papers, A/3; and *WRL News,* 8 Dec. 1947.

## Chapter 4. Dissent from the "Good War"

1. Most studies on the World War II home front either ignore pacifism and conscientious objection, or mention them in passing, offering only a cursory discussion of them and treating both as issues of civil liberty. Richard Polenberg offers the most extended treatment of COs in *War and Society: The United States, 1941–1945* (Westport, Conn.: Greenwood, 1972), 54–60. For a brief discussion of the literature, see Bennett, " 'Pacifism Not Passivism,' " 232nn. 1 and 3.

2. The major study of World War II COs remains *Conscription of Conscience: The American State and the Conscientious Objector, 1940–1947,* by Mulford Q. Sibley and Philip E. Jacob (Ithaca: Cornell Univ. Press, 1952). More general works that examine CO wartime activism and resistance in CPS and prison include Lawrence S. Wittner's pioneering work, *Rebels Against War: The American Peace Movement, 1941–1960* (rev. ed.; Philadelphia: Temple Univ. Press, 1984); James R. Tracy, *Direct Action: Radical Pacifism from the Union Eight to the Chicago Seven* (Chicago: Univ. of Chicago Press, 1996); and Maurice Isserman, *If I Had a Hammer: The Death of the Old Left and the Birth of the New Left* (Urbana: Univ. of Illinois Press, 1987). For informaton on CPS, see also Albert N. Keim, *The CPS Story: An Illustrated History of Civilian Public Service* (Intercourse, PA: Good Books, 1990); Heather T. Frazer and John O'Sullivan, *"We Have Just Begun to Not Fight": An Oral History of Conscientious Objectors in Civilian Public Service During World War II* (New York: Twayne Publishers, 1996); and Rachel Waltner Goossen, *Women Against the Good War: Conscientious Objection and Gender on the American Home Front, 1941–1947.* For prison COs, see also Holley Cantine and Dachine Rainer, eds., *Prison Etiquette: The Convict's Compendium of Useful Information* (Bearsville, New York: Retort Press, 1950); and Mulford Sibley and Ada Wardlaw, *Conscientious Objectors in Prison, 1940–1945* (Philadelphia: Pacifist Research Bureau, 1945). Several valuable memoirs and biographies recount the wartime resistance experiences of World War II COs belonging to the WRL. These include James Peck, *We Who Would Not Kill* (New York: Lyle Stuart, 1958) and *Underdogs vs. Upperdogs* (New York: AMP&R, 1980); Lowell Naeve, with David Wieck, *A Field of Broken Stones* (Glen Gardner, N.J.: Libertarian Press, 1950); Dellinger, *From Yale to Jail;* Jervis Anderson, *Bayard Rustin: Troubles I've Seen: A Biography* (New York: HarperCollins, 1997); Daniel Levine, *Bayard Rustin and the Civil Rights Movement* (New Brunswick, N.J.: Rutgers Univ. Press, 1999); and Larry Gara and Lenna Mae Gara, eds., *A Few Small Candles: War Resisters of World War II Tell Their Stories* (Kent, Ohio: Kent State Univ. Press, 1999). Peter Brock's *Pacifism since 1914: An Annotated Reading List* (Toronto: Peter Brock, 2000) includes an invaluable guide to the literature on World War II COs.

3. In addition to the studies listed in note 2, see Gretchen Lemke-Santangelo, "The Radical Conscientious Objectors of World War II: Wartime Experience and Postwar Activism," *Radical History Review* 45 (1989): 5–29.

4. Hughan, "Questions: Procedure of the War Resisters League in the Event of a More Serious Crisis Situation," 7 Sept. 1939 (revised May 1940), in Minutes, WRL-EC, May 27, 1940, WRL Papers, A/2.

5. *Conscientious Objector* (newspaper; hereafter, *CO*), June-July 1941, 6; W. W., "He'd Prefer Jail to Conscription," *P.M.,* 17 July 1940, clipping, WRL Scrapbook; Gottlieb and Kaufman, interviews and conversations with author, 1993–1995, 1997.

6. In addition to the WRL's explanation of war discussed in previous chapters, see remarks at the 1940 and 1941 WRL Dinners and the 1941 WRL Conference, WRL Papers, A/9; WRL flyers in folder marked "Literature Committee, 1944," WRL Papers, A/28; [Igal Roodenko], Form 47

[Nov. 1941], Igal Roodenko Papers (unprocessed; hereafter, Roodenko Papers), DG-161, SCPC; I. Roodenko, "Supplementary Statement" [to Form 47], [1941–42], Roodenko Papers; "Statement of David Dellinger [to Draft Board]," 18 July 1943, FOR Papers, A/17; David Dellinger, *Revolutionary Nonviolence* (New York: Bobbs-Merrill, 1970), xiii–xxiii, 8–16; Dellinger, *From Yale to Jail,* 73–78; Peck, *Underdogs vs. Upperdogs,* 33.

7. Campaign flyer [1940], WRL Papers, A/35.

8. Press release [1940], WRL Papers, A/35.

9. For information on Hughan's campaign, see folder marked "Hughan Anti-War Write-in Campaign, 1940," WRL Papers, A/35; "Write-in Jessie Hughan" [1940], Hughan Papers; and *NYT,* 6 Feb. 1940, 20, 23; and *NYT,* 7 Feb. 1940, 1, 12. For the anti-interventionists on the eve of World War II, see Justus D. Doenecke, *Storm on the Horizon: The Challenge to American Intervention, 1939–1941* (New York: Rowman & Littlefield, 2000).

10. Minutes of Pacifist Teachers League, 15 Dec. 1941, Kaufman Papers.

11. For information on the Pacifist Teachers League, see *CO,* Dec. 1941, 2, 7, Apr. 1942, 3; August Gold, interviews by author, 17 June, 30 July 1996; A. R. C. Finch, "Resister for Peace," 44a, 52, Hughan Papers; Gottlieb, interview in "Resister for Peace", by A. R. C. Finch; Gottlieb, interview by author, 6 Nov. 1993, and untaped conversations with author, 13 July, 8 Sept. 1995, 8 Sept. 1996; Kaufman, interview by author, 16 Oct. 1993; "Rules Set for Oct. 16 Draft," [1940], [*New York Telegram* and *Sun*], clipping, Gottlieb Papers. For the experience of August Gold, a member of the WRL and the Pacifist Teachers League, see Bennett, "Pacifism Not Passivism," 184–85.

12. For the Selective Training and Service Act of 1940 (including the passages quoted in this paragraph), see Sibley and Jacob, *Conscription of Conscience,* 45–52, 487; Chambers, "Conscientious Objectors and the American State," 33–37; Chatfield, *For Peace and Justice,* 305–6; and George Q. Flynn, *The Draft, 1940–1973* (Lawrence: Univ. Press of Kansas, 1993), 9–52.

13. Kaufman, Testimony Before House Committee on Military Affairs, Compulsory Military Training and Service: Hearings on H.R. 10132, 76th Cong., 3d sess., 1940, 451.

14. Ibid., 450–59; [Kaufman], "Report of the War Resisters League Delegation in Washington July 25 to Aug. 2, 1940" [Aug. 1940], in Minutes, WRL-EC, WRL Papers, A/2.

15. Frazer and O'Sullivan, *"We Have Just Begun to Not Fight,"* xvii.

16. For a list of the 151 CPS camps, with the group operating each camp, its location, and the dates it opened and closed, see Keim, *The CPS Story,* 106–10.

17. For CPS's origins, see Sibley and Jacob, *Conscription of Conscience,* 45–52, 110–23, 471–75; Frazer and O'Sullivan, *"We Have Just Begun to Not Fight,"* xiii–xxv; Keim, *The CPS Story,* 7–33; and Wittner, *Rebels Against War,* 70–72.

18. Hughan, quoted in A. R. C. Finch, "Resister for Peace," 45, Hughan Papers.

19. Hughan to Kaufman, 29 Aug. 1947, Kaufman Papers. See also Hughan, quoted in A. R. C. Finch, "Resister for Peace," 45, Hughan Papers; and Minutes, WRL-EC, 9 Dec. 1941, WRL Papers, A/2.

20. All quotes in this paragraph from "A Communication from the Executive Committee to the Membership," 19 Dec. 1941, WRL Papers, A/35.

21. Minutes, WRL-EC, 9 Dec. 1941, WRL Papers, A/2.

22. Ibid.

23. Hughan, "Our U.S.A. Movement Since Pearl Harbor: Dec. 7, 1941 to May, 1942," 27

May 1942, 5, in Minutes, WRL-EC, WRL Papers, A/2; and Minutes, WRL-EC, 9 Dec. 1941, WRL Papers, A/2.

24. [Kaufman], "Our Inventory of Morale," 23 Jan. 1942; "What Is the Work" (WRL Report) [1939 or 1940]; Kaufman, "Digest of Work in 1939 and the First Two Months of 1940" [Feb. or Mar. 1940]; Frieda L. Lazarus and Frances R. Ransom, "Report of Membership Secretary, 1942," 31 Dec. 1942; [Frances R. Ransom], "Report of Membership Secretary," 20 July 1943; Ransom, "Report of the Membership Secretary to the Executive Committee of the War Resisters League," 8 Dec. 1943; and Minutes, WRL-EC, 11 Nov. 1946, all in Minutes, WRL-EC, WRL Papers, A/2. See also Frank Olmstead to Mary Dwyer, 31 Oct. 1944, WRL Papers, A/13; and *CO,* Feb. 1943, 2. The decrease in enrolled members from 1941 to 1942 is explained by the WRL's decision to remove persons from its membership list who could not be located because of death or relocation.

25. Hughan, "Our U.S.A. Movement Since Pearl Harbor," 10, in Minutes, WRL-EC, WRL Papers, A/2. For information on the WRL-FBI relationship, see also Kaufman, "The Foreign Agents Registration Act of 1938, as Amended as It Applies to the Work of the War Resisters League," 10 July 1942; [Kaufman?], "Miscellaneous notes which Frank Olmstead may wish to include in his report," [1942], in Minutes, WRL-EC, WRL Papers, A/2; Kaufman, "Manuscript," Kaufman Papers; and Susan Dion, "Pacifism Treated as Subversion: The FBI and the War Resisters League," *Peace and Change* 9 (Spring 1983): 43–54. Kaufman contends that he only provided the FBI information that helped CO claimants.

26. Winston Dancis, "Peace Team Organization," Jan. 1942 (revised version of document written by Hughan in 1932), in Minutes, WRL-EC, WRL Papers, A/2; "[Peace Teams] Organizational Background," [1939–45], WRL Papers, A/4; and *CO,* Feb.-Mar. 1940, 3, and Oct.-Nov. 1940, 1, 4, 8.

27. Kaufman, "Digest of Work in 1939 and the First Two Months of 1940" [Feb. or Mar. 1940], in Minutes, WRL-EC, WRL Papers, A/2; *CO,* Aug.-Sept. 1940, 6, May 1942, 10, Apr. 1944, 4, Sept. 1944, 3; folders in WRL Papers, A/10.

28. "WRL Relationships With Other Groups: List of Individuals Representing the WRL," [15 Nov. 1941]; [Kaufman?], Miscellaneous Notes [Dec. 1942], in Minutes, WRL-EC, WRL Papers, A/2.

29. Minutes, WRL-EC, 28 Feb. 1945, WRL Papers, A/2.

30. For information on the *CO,* see Stephen Siteman, introduction to the *Conscientious Objector,* 2 vols. (New York: Greenwood Reprint Corp., 1968); folders marked "Minutes Before Incorporation" and "Article of Organization," WRL Papers, A/6; Lillian D. Mosesco, I. Roodenko, and Jay N. Tuck to C.O. Subscriber, June 1947, WRL Papers, A/4; and Kaufman, "Manuscript," Kaufman Papers.

31. Sibley and Jacob, *Conscription of Conscience,* 193.

32. Ibid., 153, 193, 257, 456, 566; *WRL News,* 22 June 1946; Blanche W. Cook, preface to, and William L. Neumann, introduction to *Pacifica Views: A Weekly Newspaper of Conscientious Objectors,* 7–15; *Pacifica Views,* 11 June 1943.

33. WRL Peace Aims Committee, "What's New on the Peace Front?" Mar.-Apr. [1943], in Minutes, WRL-EC, WRL Papers, A/2.

34. Ibid.; Draft WRL Statement on the Peace Now Movement, 28 Jan. 1944; Kaufman, Speech, 16 June 1942, Kaufman Papers; Hughan, "Is the Time Ripe for Peace?" 22 June 1943, and other flyers, WRL Papers, A/28.

35. George Hartmann, *A Plea for an Immediate Peace by Negotiation* (New York: WRL, 1942), 8.

36. Glen Zeitzer and Charles F. Howlett, "Political Versus Religious Pacifism: The Peace Now Movement of 1943," *The Historian* 48 (May 1986):375–93.

37. "Resolution Passed by the Executive Committee of WRL," 28 July 1941, in Minutes, WRL-EC, WRL Papers, A/2.

38. For the relationship between the WRL and the PNM, see ibid.; Kaufman, "Manuscript" (which provides a detailed critique of Zeitzer and Howlett, "The Peace Now Movement of 1943"), Kaufman Papers; "Memorandum from Executive Committee to Staff for Answering Inquiries," 18 Feb. 1944; and [Kaufman], draft statement on the Peace Now Movement, 28 Jan. 1944, all in Minutes, WRL-EC, WRL Papers, A/2; Kaufman, "Peace Now Movement," 13 Mar. 1944; Kaufman to [Hartmann], 18 Sept. 1943; Hughan to Hartmann, 4 Sept. 1945; and Muste to David Morgan, Jan. ? 1944, all in WRL Papers, A/24; Kaufman to Grace Beaton, 30 Aug. 1944, WRI Papers, Box 4; and Hughan to Dear Friend, 8 Feb. 1944, WRI Papers, Box 7. For support within the WRL for the PNM, see E. Thomas to David White, 17 Feb. 1944; Philip [Isely], "Concerning the Peace Now Movement," [Apr. 1944], both in WRL Papers, A/24; and Anna M. Graves to E. Thomas, 4 Jan. 1944, WRL Papers, A/14.

39. Dellinger, *From Yale to Jail,* 106, 113–15; Charlotte Bentley et al., "Statement of Purpose" (PPN), June 1943, Peace Now Movement Papers (hereafter PNM Papers), GDC-A, SCPC; PPNC, "Appeal for Uncommon Sense," [17 July 1943], Roodenko Papers.

40. Hughan, "What about the Jews in the Ghettoes?" *Pacifica Views,* 3 Sept. 1943.

41. Ibid.

42. Ibid.

43. Hughan to John N. Sayre, 27 Nov. 1942, WRL Papers, A/15.

44. Hughan to Editor of *NYT,* 27 Feb. 1943. See also Minutes, WRL Subcommittee on the Refugee Problem, 9 Feb. 1939, in Minutes, WRL-EC, WRL Papers, A/2; and Hughan, "Why Not Peace in 1944?" 15 Mar. 1944, Hughan Papers.

45. Minutes, WRL-EC, 25 Apr. and 14 May 1945; Theodore D. Walser, "An Immediate Settlement with Japan," 14 May 1945; WRL Papers, A/2, and Hughan, "Tentative Plans for Peace Offensive," 14 May 1945, in Minutes, WRL-EC, all in WRL Papers, A/2. For information on Walser (d. 1949), see *WRL News,* 26 Sept. 1949; *Fellowship,* Oct. 1942, 159–60 and Sept. 1949, 19; and *NYT,* 15 Aug. 1949, 17.

46. Quoted in "To Those Who Missed the Boat," 14 Sept. 1945, WRL Papers, A/17. See also Roy Finch, interview by author, 29 Jan. 1994; Ralph DiGia, interview by author, 9 May 1995. For both the Japanese Project and Hill, who founded Pacifica Radio after World War II, see Jeff Land, *Active Radio: Pacifica's Brash Experiment* (Minnesota: Univ. of Minnesota Press, 1999); Matthew Laser, *Pacifica Radio: The Rise of an Alternative Network* (Philadelphia: Temple Univ. Press, 2000).

47. For "the second mile," see Frank Olmstead, "The CO—An Ethical Barometer," [Aug. 1945], 5–6, WRL Papers, A/17.

48. WRL, "A Referendum on Alternative Service Camps," [Feb. 1941], WRL Papers, A/29; [Hughan] to National Service Board for Religious Objectors, 18 Mar. 1941, and attached WRL, "Referendum on Alternative Service," [17 Mar. 1941], WRL Papers, A/23.

49. Frank Olmstead, "$64 Question for the Quakers," [7 Aug. 1944], WRL Papers, A/17.

50. For the WRL's view on the WRL-NSBRO understanding, see Frank Olmstead, "Out of the Frying Pan," 28 May 1943; and Hughan to Members of the Executive Committee, 9 July

1941, both in WRL Papers, A/29; Olmstead, "$64 Question for the Quakers," [7 Aug. 1944]; and Olmstead, "The CO—An Ethical Barometer," [Aug. 1945], both in WRL Papers, A/17; E. Thomas to Nevin [Sayre] and [Muste], 27 Aug. 1942, WRL Papers, A/19; and E. [Thomas] to Paul French, 6 Nov. 1941, WRL Papers, A/23. For WRL criticism of NSBRO and Selective Service, see WRL, "Our Position on Alternative Service," 16 Nov. 1942; Kaufman, "Manuscript," Kaufman Papers; Harrison De Silver, Kaufman, and E. Thomas to Paul Comley French, 22 June 1942, Allen Papers; Hughan, "Our U.S.A. Movement since Pearl Harbor"; "Action Taken by Executive Committee on Maintenance, Pay, and Alternative Service for C.O.s," [Oct. 1942?], WRL Papers, A/33; Frank Olmstead, *C.P.S. After Eighteen Months* (New York: WRL, 1942), copy in WRL Papers, A/4; and *CO,* Apr.-May 1941, 1.

51. Kaufman, interviews by author, 1993 and 1994. The absolutist position can be sampled in the leading wartime absolutist publication, the *Weekly Prison News Letter,* (1943) and its successor, the *Absolutist* (1943–47), and in WRL et al., *Why We Refused to Register* (New York: WRL, n.d.).

52. Sibley and Jacob, *Conscription of Conscience,* 121; and "Statement of A. J. Muste," [1940–41?], WRL Papers, A/29.

53. For information on resignations, see E. Thomas to Members of the National Council of the F.O.R., 14 Sept. 1944, WRL Papers, A/19; Paton Price to Muste, 8 Jan. 1943, WRL Papers, A/33; and David Dellinger et al., "An Open Letter to the FOR," 3 June 1944, FOR Papers, A/18.

54. E. Thomas, quoted in Wittner, *Rebels Against War,* 71.

55. E. Thomas to Members of the Consultative Council of the National Service Board for Religious Objectors, 12 Nov. 1941, WRL Papers, A/23; and E. [Thomas] to Frank [Olmstead], 21 Nov. 1942, WRL Papers, A/19.

56. E. Thomas to Dear Friend, 16 Dec. 1941, WRL Papers, A/23. For information on Evan Thomas and CPS, see also Sibley and Jacob, *Conscription of Conscience,* 121; Evan Thomas to Members of the Consultative Council, 12 Nov. 1941, WRL Papers, A/23; and other letters and statements in folders marked "Evan Thomas, 1941–1947" and "NSBRO, 1940–1941, B: Corresp.," WRL Papers, A/19 and A/23.

57. E. Thomas, "The Status of Conscientious Objection in America," Nov. 1942, WRL Papers, 1/19.

58. E. Thomas to Clarence Pickett, 21 Nov. 1941, WRL Papers, A/23.

59.[E. Thomas] to [Muste], 11 Dec. 1941, WRL Papers, A/23; and E. Thomas to Nevin [Sayre] and [Muste], 27 Aug. 1942, WRL Papers, A/19.

60. For information on Evan W. Thomas and CPS, see also "Statement of Evan W. Thomas," [1940–41?], WRL Papers, A/29; [E. Thomas] to [Muste], 11 Dec. 1941; and E. Thomas to Clarence Pickett, 21 Nov. 1941, both in WRL Papers, A/23; E. Thomas to Nevin [Sayre] and [Muste], 27 Aug. 1942, WRL Papers, A/19; and E. Thomas, "Conscientious Objection in America." For information on Thomas's resignation, see Thomas to Members of the National Council of the F.O.R., 14 Sept. 1944, WRC Papers, A/29.

61. Olmstead, *C.P.S. after Eighteen Months,* WRL Papers, A/4, 3, 5.

62. Ibid., 11; Olmstead, "Out of the Frying Pan," WRL Papers, A/29, 3. See also Olmstead, [draft article submitted to *Fellowship*], Mar. 1943, WRL Papers, A/28.

63. Olmstead, "The CO—An Ethical Barometer," 3, WRL Papers, A/17.

64. Olmstead, "$64 Question for the Quakers," 5, WRL Papers, A/17.

65. Frank Olmstead, *They Asked for a Hard Job: CO's at Work in Mental Hospitals* (New York:

Plowshare Press, [1943–44]), 4, copy in WRL Papers, A/4.

66. Roy Finch, interview by author, 29 Jan. 1994.

67. Olmstead, *They Asked for a Hard Job,* 9, 12.

68. Alex Sareyan, *The Turning Point: How Men of Conscience Brought About Major Change in the Care of America's Mentally Ill* (Washington, D.C.: American Psychiatric Press, 1994), 266–67. See also Sibley and Jacob, *Conscription of Conscience,* 134–40. About two thousand women lived in or near CPS camps. Some were "camp followers" who chose to live and work near their husbands or fiances. Some 15 percent performed paid work in the camps; another three hundred women left college to work alongside CO men in psychiatric institutions. See Goossen, *Women Against the Good War,* 45, 69, 105.

69. Peck, *We Who Would Not Kill,* 154.

70. For information on COs' work in mental hospitals and medical experiments, see Sibley and Jacob, *Conscription of Conscience,* 143–49; Frazer and O'Sullivan, *We Have Just Begun to Not Fight,* xxiii–xxiv, 82–83, 115–17; Peck, *We Who Would Not Kill,* 152–55; *CO,* July 1943, 4; Oct. 1944, 7; Max M. Kampelman, *Entering New Worlds: The Memoirs of a Private Man in Public Life* (New York: HarperCollins, 1991), 48–52; Robert T. Dick, ed., *Guinea Pigs for Peace: The Story of C.P.S. 115-R, 1943–1946* (Windsor, Vt.: Annex Press, [1990]); and Charles Bloomstein, interviews by author, 15 May and 15 Nov. 1995. For WRL members in "hospital projects," see Lazarus and Ransom, "Report of Membership Secretary, 1942," 31 Dec. 1942, in Minutes, WRL-EC, WRL Papers, A/2.

71. Kaufman, "Manuscript," Kaufman Papers; Wittner, *Rebels Against War,* 56.

72. For WRL support of non-WRL member Corbett Bishop, a religious CO who waged a 144-day hunger strike in prison, see Bennett, "Pacifism Not Passivism," 247, note 144.

73. Hughan, "Our U.S.A. Movement since Pearl Harbor," May 27, 1942, 7; "Problems of WRL Administration," 30 Oct. 1943; [Ransom], "Report of Membership Secretary," 20 July 1943; Frank Olmstead and Frances R. Ransom, "War Resisters League Report of Field Work [in] 1943" [7 Feb. 1944?]; "Work of CO Problems Committee of War Resisters League—Jan. 1944: Report to Executive Committee," 7 Feb. 1944; COPC, "Proposed Outline of Problems and Activities" [7 Feb. 1944?], all in Minutes, WRL-EC, WRL Papers, A/2; Frances R. Ransom to Dear Friend, 28 July 1942, Civilian Public Service Papers (1940–46)(Series I, Box 2, DG-96, SCPC).

74. *CO,* Nov. 1945, 4; Kaufman to Paul C. French, 6 June 1941, WRL Papers, A/23; and Kaufman to James Stanley, 4 May 1945, WRL Papers, A/24. The leaflets, which were issued by the WRL and MBCO, are located in Metropolitan Board for Conscientious Objectors Papers, DG-60, SCPC, Box 1.

75. WRL, "Morale Situation in CPS," 20 Jan. 1944, in Minutes, WRL-EC, WRL Papers, A/2.

76. Corfman, Kampelman, and R. Finch, quoted in WRL, "Morale Situation in CPS," 20 Jan. 1944, in Minutes, WRL-EC, WRL Papers, A/2.

77. Bloomstein, quoted in WRL, "Morale Situation in CPS," 20 Jan. 1944, in Minutes, WRL-EC, WRL Papers, A/2.

78. WRL, "Morale Situation in CPS," 20 Jan. 1944, in Minutes, WRL-EC, WRL Papers, A/2.

79. *CO,* Apr. 1943, 1, 8.

80. Sibley and Jacob, *Conscription of Conscience,* 412.

81. Ibid.

82. Julius Eichel to [Kaufman], 12 Aug. 1941, WRL Papers, A/13; and Kaufman, interview by author, 14 May 1995.

83. Charlotte Bentley, David Dellinger, Julius Eichel, Philip Isely, Elizabeth Murphy, Frank Olmstead, Evan Thomas, "Exhibit A," [1943], in Minutes, WRL-EC, WRL Papers, A/2. See also *CO,* Apr. 1943, 1, 8.

84. Ibid.

85. Meredith Dallas, Willa Dallas, David Dellinger, Hugh Fitch, William Kuenning, Paton Price, and Caroline Schmidt, "Proposed Nationwide Call for Action" (draft), [Mar.-Apr. 1943], in Minutes, WRL-EC, WRL Papers, A/2.

86. Ibid.

87. For the April 6 Committee, see April Six Action Committee to Dear Friend, 1 Apr. 1943; David Dellinger et al., "April Six—Anniversary of U.S. Entry into World War I," [1943]; Sarah Cleghorn to Editor of *NYT,* 7 Apr. 1943 (draft), FOR Papers, C-4/18. For opposition to Dellinger's proposal by WRL members, see [Frances R. Ransom], Bulletin [to Frank Olmstead], 1 Apr. [1943], WRL Papers, A/7; and I. Roodenko et al. to April Six Action Committee, 26 Mar. 1943, FOR Papers, II, A-3/12 (who suggest that the 6 April protest was illegal, though I have not been able to determine the basis for their conclusion).

88. "Resolution Regarding the Murphy and Taylor Fast Adopted by the Chicago Conference on Social Action," 24 Apr. 1943.

89. I. Roodenko to Paul Furnas, 29 Apr. 1943, FOR Papers, A/18.

90. Hughan to Kaufman, 20 Mar. 1943, Kaufman Papers.

91. Ibid.

92. Hughan to Kaufman, 13 Mar. 1943, Kaufman Papers.

93. Hughan, *If We Should Be Invaded,* 10.

94. Kaufman to Dear Friend, 18 Mar. 1943, in Minutes, WRL-EC, WRL Papers, A/2.

95. Ibid.

96. "Statement in Opposition to War Resisters League Withdrawal from National Service Board for Religious Objectors," [May? 1943], in Minutes, WRL-EC, WRL Papers, A/2; and Kaufman to David Dellinger et al., 9 June 1944, FOR Papers, A/18.

97. Quotes from Frieda Lazarus, Frank Olmstead, E. Thomas, "Report of the Sub-Committee on C.O. Problems," 17 Mar. 1943, in Minutes, WRL-EC, WRL Papers, A/2. See also "Statement for Withdrawal," [May? 1943], in Minutes, WRL-EC, WRL Papers, A/2; Frieda L. Lazarus, "Resolution Submitted by the Committee on C.O. Problems, War Resisters League," 22 Mar. 1943, WRL Papers, A/29; Kaufman to Paul C. French, 16 June 1941, WRL Papers, A/23.

98. Minutes, WRL-EC, 22 Mar. 1943, WRL Papers, A/2.

99. Holmes to E. Thomas, 29 Mar. 1943, WRL Papers, A/15.

100. A. R. C. Finch, "Resister for Peace," 51, Hughan Papers.

101. Hughan to Holmes, 3 Apr. 1943, WRL Papers, A/15.

102. Minutes, WRL-EC, 1 May, 26 May 1943, WRL Papers, A/2; Holmes to E. Thomas, 29 Mar. 1943; Evan Thomas to Holmes, 1 Apr. 1943; Hughan to Holmes, 3 Apr. 1943, all in WRL Papers, A/15; A. R. C. Finch, "Resister for Peace," 51, Hughan Papers; and *CO,* June 1943, 1, 8.

103. For the Murphy-Taylor hunger strike, Springfield, and WRL support for the strikers, see Sibley and Jacob, *Conscription of Conscience,* 412–16; Frances R. Ransom, "COPC, Report to WRL Executive Committee," 3 Apr. 1944, WRL Papers, A/29; E. Thomas, "A Statement Regarding Mr. Palmer's Reports on Stanley Murphy," 22 Sept. 1943 (revised, 29 Sept. 1943), WRL Pa-

pers, A/19; the *Weekly Prison News Letter* and its successor, the *Absolutist*; the *CO* during the strike; and the *NYT,* 7 Mar. 1943, 14; 10 Mar. 1943, 19. For the view of prison officials, see Howard B. Gill to Alfred Schmalz, 1 Oct. 1943, WRL Papers, A/30.

104. For a sharp exchange between proponents of direct action and political/educational strategies, see materials on the Dellinger-Kaufman debate over a proposed WRL flyer on peace negotiations with Japan, WRL Papers, A/28.

105. Frances R. Ransom to WRL-EC, 15 Sept. 1943, in Minutes, WRL-EC; Minutes, WRL-EC, 20 Sept. 1943, WRL Papers, A/2.

106. Holmes to E. Thomas, 29 Mar. 1943, WRL Papers, A/15. For a similar view by Hoffman, see *CO,* June 1943, 8.

107. "This Must Not Be" (WRL Statement on Conscription), n.d., attached [at SCPC] to the *Absolutist,* 24 Oct. 1944; "Testimony of Edward C. M. Richards, the Representative of the WRL in Opposition to Peacetime Conscription Before the House Select Committee on Postwar Military Policy," 13 June 1945; "Statement by Dr. Evan W. Thomas, Chairman of the WRL for the House Select Committee on Postwar Military Policy," 6 June 1945, in Minutes, WRL-EC; and Minutes, WRL-EC, 19 Nov., 27 Nov. 1944, WRL Papers, A/2.

108. For Gandhi's influence on black civil rights activism during the war, see Sudarshan Kapur, *Raising Up a Prophet: The African-American Encounter with Gandhi* (Boston: Beacon Press, 1992), 101–23.

109. Frank Olmstead and Kaufman, [Report], 29 June 1943, in Minutes, WRL-EC, WRL Papers, A/2; and Minutes, WRL-EC, 22 June 1942, WRL Papers, A/2. For Smith and the NVDAC and WRL support for them, see Anderson, *Bayard Rustin,* 69–71; David Scott Cooney, "A Consistent Witness of Conscience: Methodist Nonviolent Activists, 1940–1970" (Ph.D. diss., Iliff School of Theology and the Univ. of Denver, 2000), 152–80; and *CO,* Feb.-Mar. 1941, 1, 3, 7, Apr.-May 1941, 8; Oct. 1942, 2; Mar. 1943, 6, June 1943, 3, July 1943, 2–3, and Aug. 1943, 1, 6.

110. *CO,* Feb. 1943, 1, 8.

111. Ibid.

112. *CO,* Feb. 1943, 1, 8, Aug. 1943: 2. For information on Randolph and the MOWM, see Jervis Anderson, *A. Philip Randolph: A Biographical Portrait* (Berkeley: Univ. of California Press, 1986); Anderson, *Bayard Rustin,* 83–86; and Herbert Garfinkel, *When Negroes March: The March on Washington Movement in the Organizational Politics for FECP* (New York: Atheneum, 1969).

113. For information on CORE, see George M. Houser, *CORE: A Brief History* (New York: CORE, 1949); James Farmer, *Lay Bare the Heart: An Autobiography of the Civil Rights Movement* (New York: New American Library, 1985); and August Meier and Elliot Rudwick, *CORE: A Study in the Civil Rights Movement, 1942–1968* (New York: Oxford Univ. Press, 1973). For biographical information on George M. Houser, see his "Reflections of a Religious War Objector (Half a Century Later)," in *A Few Small Candles,* ed. Larry Gara and Lenna Mae Gara, 130–51; and Cooney, "Methodist Nonviolent Activists," 181–93, passim.

114. George M. Houser to Muste, 11 June 1941, FOR Papers, A/17.

115. George M. [Houser] to Muste, 13 July 1942, FOR Papers, A/17.

116. [George M. Houser] to Muste, 28 Dec. 1943, FOR Papers, A/17. See also "Provisional Statement on Program for George Houser's Work," n.d., FOR Papers, A/8; George M. Houser, "A Statement for Non-Violent Actionists," 14–16 Mar. [1942–45], FOR Papers, A/13; and George M. Houser, interview by author, 18 May 1995.

117. For the influence of Gandhi and the WRL's wartime shift, see, for example, "Resolutions Adopted at the Close of the Thirteenth Annual Conference of the War Resisters League," 5–7 June 1942, WRL Papers, A/9; R. Finch to Paton Price, 26 Feb. 1943, WRL Papers, A/33; and *CO*, Aug. 1942 (Special India Section); and "Resolutions Adopted at the Fifteenth Annual Convention of the WRL," 26–28 May 1944, both in WRL Papers, A/9.

### Chapter 5. Toward Direct Action

1. For documentation, see Bennett, " 'Pacifism Not Passivism,' " 311–12, notes 1–2; and Hughan to Dear Friend, 8 Feb. 1944, WRL Papers, A/4. No comprehensive list of WRL members who served in CPS and in prison exists, but WRL and NSBRO reports suggest totals. Reported numbers should be viewed as minimum figures, since certainly there were unreported WRL members in CPS and in prison. For instance, NSBRO reports listed as WRL members only COs who designated the WRL and who were not financed by a religious church or agency. It is likely that some WRL members who also belonged to the FOR or the Friends did not appear on the list. At a minimum, 399 WRL members served in CPS in 1942 and 542 in 1943 (often the same men). In early 1944, Hughan claimed that there were 578 WRL members in CPS and 100 more in prison, in addition to those on appeal or awaiting trail. This revises the estimates of Mulford Sibley and Philip Jacob who, in *Conscription of Conscience,* state that "about fifty" WRL members entered CPS. It is even harder to calculate the number of WRL members who went to prison since, unlike CPS, the "assignment" was not for the duration. Once a CO completed his prison sentence he was released. At least 81 WRL members went to prison, with the number likely reaching about 100.

2. George B. Reeves to E. Thomas, 27 Nov. 1941, WRL Papers, A/23. See also Bent Andresen to M. H. Sawyer, 4 Dec. 1946, WRL Papers, A/18.

3. Sibley and Jacob, *Conscription of Conscience,* 354, 358. Of prison COs, 5.4 percent were classified as philosophical or political objectors; 237 prison COs were so classified by 30 June 1944. The Bureau of Prisons considered these COs the most difficult. For statements on philosophical objection to war and on the variety and thus subjective nature of religious beliefs, see WRL, *What Is Religious Training and Belief?* (New York: WRL, 1943); and "Pacifist Philosophies," *CO*, Feb. 1943. For the case of Carlos Cortez, an antiwar but nonpacifist Marxian socialist CO—who later became an anarchist and a Wobbly—see Scott H. Bennett, "Workers/Draftees of the World Unite! Carlos A. Cortez Red Cloud Koyokuikatl: Soapbox WW II CO, and IWW Artist/Bard," in *Carlos A. Cortez Koyokuikatl: Soapbox Rebel and Artist,* ed. Victor Sorell (Chicago: Mexican Fine Arts Museum, 2002), 12–56.

4. E. Thomas to George B. Krouse, William Hoskins, and Stanley McNail, 12 Apr. 1943; and E. Thomas to Stanley McNail, 19 Apr. 1943, both in WRL Papers, A/21.

5. This overview of the CO community is based mainly on Sibley and Jacob, *Conscription and Conscience,* 18–44, 152–54, passim. But see also Cynthia Eller, *Conscientious Objectors and the Second World War: Moral and Religious Arguments in Support of Pacifism* (New York: Praeger, 1991). For the Brethren and Mennonite experience and nonresistance position, see Guy F. Hershberger, *War, Peace, and Nonresistance* (Scottdale, Penn.: The Herald Press, 1944); and Perry Bush, *Two Kingdoms, Two Loyalties: Mennonite Pacifism in Modern America* (Baltimore: John Hopkins Univ. Press, 1998). For Jewish pacifism (which led some 250 Jewish COs to enlist in CPS or go to prison), see Michael Young, "Facing a Test of Faith: Jewish Pacifists During the Second World

War," *Peace and Change* 3 (Summer/Fall 1975): 34–40. For wartime CO resistance and activism, see chapter 4, note 2.

6. During 1943, Paton Price collected materials from other COs to prepare a detailed White Paper on CPS that would support the radical critique of CPS. Evan Thomas suggested the project, and other WRL members endorsed it. See folder marked "Paton Price White Paper," WRL Papers, A/33.

7. Unless otherwise noted, the COs discussed in this chapter were WRL members.

8. Charles Butcher, "The 'Absolutists' Were Right," 9 Feb. 1943, WRL Papers, A/33; Donald W. Rockwell to Charles Thomas, [Recd. 25 Feb. 1944]; and Wallace Hamilton to Dave Swift, [Recd. 3 Nov. 1942], both in WRL Papers, A/30.

9. Douglas Dobson to Hughan, 16 May 1943, WRL Papers, A/13,; R. Finch to Paton [Price], 16 Mar. 1943; and Paton Price, "Price to Leave Camp: Advocates Abolition of C.P.S." (Bulletin), [Dec. 1942], both in WRL Papers, A/33.

10. Philip Isely to All, Feb. 1943; Paton Price to Francis Biddle, 14 Dec. 1942; and Julian Jaynes to Francis Biddle, 14 Dec. 1942, all in WRL Papers, A/33; John H. Abbot, "Statement by John H. Abbot," [1943], WRL Papers, A/30; and Hughan to Polly Klein [Weil], 22 May 1947, WRL Papers, A/20.

11. [Report on Big Flats Strike], 8 Oct. 1942, WRL Papers, A/33. At least seven of the twelve strikers were WRL members, including Taylor, Murphy, George Kingsley, Ed Kalada, John Petrik, Marvin Penner, and Ralph Norton. The other strikers—Bill Brinton, John Kepler, Ed Moyer, Ed Roehrs, and Tom Richie—may have been members.

12. John Lewis, "Toward an Understanding of the CPS Slowdown," 1 Nov. 1944, quotes on 6, 9, and 10, Roodenko Papers.

13. Kepler, quoted in Deena Hurwitz and Craig Simpson, eds., *Against the Tide: Pacifist Resistance in the Second World War: An Oral History* (1984 WRL Calendar; New York: WRL, 1984), at 14–17 May 1984, copy in WRL Papers, B/7.

14. Ponch, quoted in Hurwitz and Simpson, eds., *Against the Tide,* at 23–29 Apr. 1984.

15. Henry Dyer, "Workers of the World Unite! You've Only Shirts to Lose," *CO,* Oct. 1941, 3.

16. Frank Olmstead, "New Pacifist Strategy Emerges at Germfask," 17 June 1944, WRL Papers, A/21. On government-run CPS camps, see Sibley and Jacob, *Conscription of Conscience,* 242–56.

17. Dyer, quoted in Sibley and Jacob, *Conscription of Conscience,* 268.

18. San Dimas "Declaration," 13 Oct. 1941, WRL Papers, A/23. WRL files designate the second petition, the Baird Petition; George Baird was a WRL member in CPS. For the petition and a tabulation of signatures by camp, see folder marked "Baird Petition: Correspondence," WRL Papers, A/29; Sibley and Jacob, *Conscription of Conscience,* 268–69; and Henry Dyer to Kaufman, 14 Feb. 1945, WRL Papers, A/24.

19. *CO,* Dec. 1942, 1, 5, Jan. 1943, 1–2, and Feb. 1943, 1, 4; and [Kaufman], "Miscellaneous notes which Frank Olmstead may wish to include in his report of our work during the last year," [Dec. 1942], in Minutes, WRL-EC, WRL Papers, A/2.

20. R. Boland Brooks, "Statement for the United States District Court for the Southern District of New York," 22 May 1944, in Minutes, WRL-EC, WRL Papers, A/2.

21. *CO,* June 1944, 2, 4.

22. "Towards Greater Opportunity in C.P.S.," [Aug. 1942], WRL Papers, A/33.

23. "Suggestions for an Inter-camp Educational Program," [Aug. 1942], WRP Papers, A/33.

24. Philip Isely to Members of the Socialist Party and to Others Who Are Sympathetic to the Enclosed Material, 12 Aug. 1942; "Towards Greater Opportunity in C.P.S.," [Aug. 1942]; and Philip Isely, "Progress Report," 5 Aug. 1942, all in WRL Papers, A/33.

25. E. Thomas to Philip Isely, 10 Aug. 1942, in intercamp correspondence, WRL Papers, A/33. See also "Summary of Letters Received on 'Towards Greater Opportunity,'" 22 Aug. 1942; Isely, "Progress Report," 5 Aug. 1942; Philip Isely to Dear Friends (Second Progress Report), [29 Aug. 1942]; Philip Isely et al. to Dear Friends (Third Progress Report), 22 Sept. 1942; Philip Isely et al. to Dear Friends (Fourth Progress Report), Nov. 1942; and Harold Guetzkow, Rudy Potochnik, and Nelson Underwood, "A Proposal for Civilian Public Service Specialized Training in Pacifist Living and Post-War Work," [3 Aug. 1942]; intercamp correspondence, all in WRL Papers, A/33; and Kaufman to Isely and Rex Corfman, 16 Apr. 1943, WRL Papers, A/23.

26. William G. Webb to Mark Y. Schrock, 7 Feb. 1943, WRL Papers, A/33.

27. Minutes, Cascade Locks, Oregon, CPS Camp CO Meeting, 6 Apr. 1942, WRL Papers, A/33.

28. Nelson Fuson to Dear Friends [Olmstead], 5 Feb. 1941, WRL Papers, A/23; and *CO,* Sept. 1942, 8, Nov. 1942, 8.

29. *CO,* Jan. 1943, 7, Feb. 1943, 6, Mar. 1943, 1, 8, Apr. 1943, 1, 4, May 1943, 1, 6; and Nov. 1944, 7.

30. Sibley and Jacob, *Conscription of Conscience,* 269. See also ibid. 269–70; and *CO,* July 1944, 1, 8, Aug. 1944, 1, Oct. 1944, 1, 7, Nov. 1944, 1, 7; and July 1945, 2.

31. Paul G. Voelker, quoted in *CO,* Apr. 1945, 1, 7; John H. Abbott to Olmstead, 10 Jan. 1944, WRL Papers, A/30.

32. [I. Roodenko], Form 47, [Nov. 1941], Roodenko Papers.

33. This account of Igal Roodenko is based primarily on written responses that he submitted to his draft board. See [I. Roodenko], Form 47, [Nov. 1941]; and I. Roodenko, "Supplementary Statement" [to Form 47], [1941–42], Roodenko Papers; I. [Roodenko] to Vivien [Roodenko], 29 Oct. 1942, Vivien (Roodenko) Lang Papers (hereafter, Lang Papers), at her home in Glenside, Pennsylvania; Igal Roodenko NSBRO File, American Friends Service Committee: Civilian Public Service Papers (1940–46), DG-02, SCPC (hereafter, AFSC Papers); and Vivien Lang, interviews by author, 21 Mar. and 20 Apr. 1995.

34. I. Roodenko to E. [Thomas], 6 May 1943, Roodenko Papers. See also I. [Roodenko] to V. [Roodenko], 20 Mar. 1943, Lang Papers; and Igal Roodenko File, AFSC Papers.

35. [I. Roodenko] to John [Marshall], 20 June 1943, Roodenko Papers.

36. I. [Roodenko] to V. [Roodenko], 4 June 1943, Lang Papers. For information about Powellsville, see also I. [Roodenko] to V. [Roodenko], 20 Mar. 1943; I. [Roodenko] to V. [Roodenko], 10 Apr. 1943, both in Lang Papers.

37. I. [Roodenko] to V. [Roodenko], 2 Aug. 1943, Lang Papers.

38. [I. Roodenko?], Press Release, 24 Aug. [1943], Roodenko Papers.

39. I. Roodenko et al. to Major-General Lewis B. Hershey, 23 Sept. 1943, Roodenko Papers.

40. Ibid.

41. I. [Roodenko] to V. [Roodenko], 6 Sept. 1943, Lang Papers.

42. I. [Roodenko] to V. [Roodenko], 22 Sept. 1943, Lang Papers.

43. I. [Roodenko] to Dave [?], 20 Oct. 1943, AFSC.

44. Ibid.

45. Ibid.

46. I. [Roodenko] to V. [Roodenko], 22 Oct. 1943, Lang Papers.

47. V. [Roodenko] to I. [Roodenko], 6 Sept. 1943, Roodenko Papers.

48. I. [Roodenko] to V. [Roodenko], 22 Sept. 1943, Lang Papers.

49. Ibid. For exceptions to this neglect of women, see Goossen, *Women Against the Good War*, Heather T. Frazer and John O'Sullivan, "Forgotten Women of World War II: Wives of Conscientious Objectors in Civilian Public Service," *Peace and Change* 5 (Sept. 1978): 46–51.

50. Paton Price to I. Roodenko, 9 July 1943, Roodenko Papers.

51. [I. Roodenko] to Paton Price, 22 Dec. 1943, Roodenko Papers.

52. WRL Press Release, 13 Nov. 1943, Roodenko Papers.

53. *Action,* 12 Nov. 1943. See also [I. Roodenko] to [Kaufman], 6 Nov. 1943, Roodenko Papers.

54. I. Roodenko, quoted in Hurwitz and Simpson, eds., *Against the Tide,* at 7–13 May 1984.

55. "Brief of Defendants (First Draft)," [1944], Roodenko Papers.

56. The other defendants were James Glenn Hutchinson, Donald West Rockwell, and Everett A. White. For the trial, appeal, and constitutional arguments raised, see "Brief of Defendants (First Draft)," [1944]; *Denver Post,* 16, 17 Mar.; 6 June 1944, clippings; I. Roodenko et al. to Editor of *The Christian Century* (draft), n.d., all in Roodenko Papers.

57. COPC Report to [WRL] Executive Committee, 7 Feb. 1944; *CO,* Feb. 1944, 3.

58. I. Roodenko et al. to Mr. Madigan (Associate Warden), 15 Aug. 1945 (Petition); [I. Roodenko] to Lew [Hill], 17 Aug. 1945; I. Roodenko to V. Roodenko, 9 Nov., 23 Nov. 1945, Roodenko Papers; Carlos Cortez (a Sandstone CO and petition signer), interview by author, 13 May 2000; and Cortez, untaped conversations with author. See also Bennett, "Workers/Draftees of the World Unite!" 23.

59. Kepler, quoted in Hurwitz and Simpson, eds., *Against the Tide,* at 24 Dec. 1984. See also Sibley and Jacob, *Conscription and Conscience,* 277–78.

60. "War Resisters League Attitude Towards Prison Problems," 15 Nov. 1943, in Minutes, WRL-EC, WRL Papers, A/2; Minutes, WRL-EC, 15 Nov. and 20 Dec. 1943, 27 June 1945, WRL Papers, A/2; "WRL Correspondents for Federal Prisoners," 24 Mar. 1945, WRL Papers, A/30; E. Thomas to James V. Bennett, 15 Nov. 1943, WRL Papers, A/29; Edward Burrows to Kaufman, 21 Sept. 1945, WRL Papers, A/11; *Absolutist,* 20 Feb. 1945; and Kaufman, interview by author, 14 May 1995. The WRL placed the following advertisement: "CO WIVES[:] Could your problems be solved through cooperation with other wives? The New York War Resisters League will serve as a clearing house to introduce those with common desires or difficulties." For the ad's first appearance, see *CO,* Apr. 1944: 8.

61. Slogan quoted in *CO,* May 1945, 6. See also Kaufman to Winston Dancis, 9 July 1943, WRL Papers, A/13; Kaufman to Howard [B.] Gill, 14 July 1941; Howard B. Gill to Kaufman, 21 July 1941, all in WRL Papers, A/23.

62. COs also took action to protest Jim Crow at other prisons. For instance, WRL member Milton Kramer smuggled out a letter denouncing Jim Crow blood banks at the Milan, Michigan, federal prison. See the *Absolutist,* 4 Nov. 1944.

63. For the Danbury strike, see Peck, *We Who Would Not Kill,* 98–133; Naeve, *Field of Broken Stones,* 133–48; folders marked "Danbury Hunger Strike, 1940–44" and "Danbury Strike Against Racial Segregation," FOR Papers, A/18; folder marked "Danbury Prison," WRL Papers, A/31;

*CO,* Sept. 1943-Feb. 1944; Albon Man, interview by author, 23 Apr. 1995; and Ralph DiGia, interview by author, 9 May 1995.

64. Naeve, *Field of Broken Stones,* 137.

65. Other WRL members participating in the strike included John Mecartney, Ernest Allyn Smith, George Kingsley, Max Kauten, Homer Nichols, and Nat Horwitz.

66. Albon Man, interview by author, 23 April 1995.

67. Peck, *Underdogs vs. Upperdogs,* 13.

68. Ibid., 15, 17.

69. Ibid., 34. For information on Peck, see Peck, *Underdogs vs. Upperdogs* and *We Who Would Not Kill.*

70. Peck, *We Who Would Not Kill,* 49–52, 139–41.

71. Ibid., 111.

72. Naeve, *Field of Broken Stones,* 139. Man recalls that Peck, though an atheist, got along well with religious COs and influenced Man to judge people by their actions rather than by whether they were religious or not; see Albon Man, interview by author, 23 Apr. 1995.

73. Peck, *We Who Would Not Kill,* 120–21.

74. Ibid., 122.

75. Albon Man, interview by author, 23 Apr. 1995.

76. Peck, *We Who Would Not Kill,* 125. See also "Partial List of Problems Brought to the Conscientious Objectors Committee," n.d., WRL Papers, A/29.

77. For McAdam's role, see Peck, *We Who Would Not Kill,* 126, 172–73; and Bennett, "Pacifism Not Passivism," 321n. 128.

78. *CO,* Jan. 1944, 4.

79. Naeve, *Field of Broken Stones,* 144; Peck, *We Who Would Not Kill,* 129–30. See also *CO,* Feb. 1944, 3.

80. Peck, *We Who Would Not Kill,* 160, 174.

81. For the Lewisburg strike, see Sibley and Jacob, *Conscription of Conscience,* 374–76; Sibley and Wardlaw, *Conscientious Objectors in Prison,* 45; Wittner, *Rebels Against War,* 88–89; Dellinger, *From Yale to Jail,* 119–32; *CO,* July-Nov. 1943; [Mrs. Harry Patton], "Visit to Harry Patton," 27 June 1943, WRL Papers, A/31; Caroline B. Lovett to E. Thomas, 25 June/3 July 1943, WRL Papers, A/30; Muste to James V. Bennett, 24 Sept. 1943, FOR Papers, A/18; and William Sutherland, interview by author, 12 Feb. 1994. For Sutherland, see Bill Sutherland and Matt Meyer, *Guns and Gandhi in Africa: Pan African Insights on Nonviolence, Armed Struggle and Liberation in Africa* (Trenton, N.J. and Asmara, Ethiopia: Africa World Press, 2000).

82. Sutherland, interview by author, 12 Feb. 1994.

83. Ibid.

84. [Patton], "Visit to Harry Patton," 27 June 1943, WRL Papers, A/31. According to Mrs. Patton, strikers included Bill Sutherland, Paton Price, Harry Patton, Jim Riddle, Harold Keene, and [?] Kelsey.

85. Caroline B. Lovett to E. Thomas, 25 June/3 July 1943, WRL Papers, A/30.

86. [E. Thomas] to Mrs. Harry Patton, 8 July 1943, WRL Papers, A/31.

87. For the Ashland strikes and CO activism against Jim Crow, see Anderson, *Bayard Rustin,* 100–101, 106–8; Sibley and Wardlaw, *Conscientious Objectors in Prison,* 47–48; *CO,* Aug. 1945-Apr. 1946; *Absolutist,* 12 July, 14 Aug. 1945; and John M. Mecartney to Dear Friend [Frieda Lazarus], 23 July 1945, WRL Papers, A/31. For previous action by Ashton Jones and Larry Gara,

see the *Absolutist,* 7 Mar., 24 Oct. 1944; and Larry Gara and Lenna Mae Gara, eds., *A Few Small Candles,* 12–15, 85–88.

88. Anderson, *Bayard Rustin,* 27.

89. Ibid., 74.

90. Irwin Stark, [Minutes]"Panel Discussion on C.P.S. Camps," 6 June [1942], WRL Papers, A/9.

91. F[rances] R[ansom] to [Olmstead], 16 Nov. 1943, WRL Papers, A/17. See also [Frances Ransom?], Bulletin, 1 Apr. [1943], WRL Papers, A/17.

92. *CO,* May 1944, 2.

93. Anderson, *Bayard Rustin,* 109. Except where noted, this sketch of Rustin is drawn from Anderson, *Bayard Rustin;* and Levine, *Bayard Rustin and the Civil Rights Movement.*

94. Bayard Rustin, quoted in Anderson, *Bayard Rustin,* 107. See also John M. Mecartney to Dear Friend [Lazarus], 23 July 1945, WRL Papers, A/31. The eight COs who first went on strike were Alfred Partridge, George Yamada, Morris Horowitz, Jason Hopkins, John Neubrand, Arden Bode, Rodney Owen, and Bjorn Eikrem. Several days later, they were joined by Rustin, Bill Fogerty, Bill Hefner, and Arnold Satterthwaite. The two black nonpacifists were Phillip Brooks and Charles Hall.

95. Rustin, quoted in Anderson, *Bayard Rustin,* 108.

96. Adam C. Powell to Tom Clark, in the *Absolutist,* 8 Oct. 1945.

97. [Lazarus] to Malcom Rose, 7 Aug. 1945, WRL Papers, A/31.

98. *CO,* Dec. 1945, 1, 8; *Absolutist,* 20 Nov. 1945.

99. James V. Bennett to Lowell Naeve, 1 Sept. 1943. See also James V. Bennett, "Racial Problems in Federal Prisons," 6 Dec. 1943, FOR Papers, A/18.

100. "A Pacifist Plan of Action," 26 June 1944, in Minutes, WRL-EC, WRL Papers, A/2. See also "Resolutions Adopted at the Close of the Thirteenth Annual Conference of the War Resisters League," 5–7 June 1942; and "Resolutions Adopted at the 15th Annual Conference of the WRL," 26–28 May 1944, both in WRL Papers, A/9; and "Proposals for Inclusion in Political Party Platforms," 5 June 1944, in Minutes, WRL-EC, WRL Papers, A/2.

101. Kaufman, interview by author, 4 Mar. 1997.

102. Dellinger, *From Yale to Jail,* 26.

103. For information on Dellinger, see ibid.; Dellinger, *Revolutionary Nonviolence;* and Dellinger, "Why I Refused to Register in the Oct. 1940 Draft and a Little of What It Led To," in *A Few Small Candles,* ed. Larry Gara and Lenna Mae Gara, 20–37. Almost every WRL member I interviewed commented on Dellinger's impressive charisma and abilities.

104. Dellinger, *From Yale to Jail,* 78.

105. Donald Benedict et al., "Why We Refused To Register," in Staughton Lynd, ed., *Nonviolence in America: A Documentary History* (New York: Bobbs-Merrill, 1966), 296–99, quotes on 297 and 299.

106. Dellinger, *From Yale to Jail,* 78.

107. *New York World-Telegram,* 15 Nov. 1940, clipping, FOR Papers, A/18. See also Benedict et al., "Why We Refused To Register"; Dellinger, *From Yale to Jail,* 73, 78–80; and clippings and other materials in folder marked "Union Theological Seminary COs," FOR Papers, A/18.

108. Besides Dellinger, *From Yale to Jail,* 91–93, the Benedict baseball strike is described in Howard Schoenfeld, "The Danbury Story," in *Prison Etiquette,* ed. Cantine and Rainer, 24–26.

109. James Bennett, quoted in Dellinger, *From Yale to Jail,* 93–94.

110. Dellinger, *From Yale to Jail*, 106.

111. Dellinger, quoted in *CO*, Nov. 1943, 2. See also *CO*, July 1943, 1, and Oct. 1943, 3, 5; Muste to Austin H. MacCormick, 12 Nov. 1943, FOR Papers, A/18; and WRL Press Release, 7 Nov. 1943, WRL Papers, A/31.

112. Paton [Price] to Mother, Father, Christine, and Marie, 10 Oct. 1943, WRL Papers, A/31.

113. Dellinger, *From Yale to Jail*, 121, 123, 125–26, quotes on 125–26. See also *CO*, Nov. 1943, 1–2, Dec. 1943, 1, 8.

114. Muste, "Thoughts on the CO Situation at Lewisburg," [1943], FOR Papers, A/18. See also WRL Press Release, 7 Nov. 1943; and "Letter to A. J. Muste from Lewisburg Hunger Strikers," 2 Dec. 1943 (reprinted by WRL), both in WRL Papers, A/31; and E. Thomas to James Bennett, 15 Nov. 1943, WRL Papers, A/29.

115. "Letter to A. J. Muste from Lewisburg Hunger Strikers," 2 Dec. 1943 (reprinted by WRL), WRL Papers, A/31.

116. *CO*, Jan. 1944, 4. For the Lewisburg hunger strike, see Sibley and Jacob, *Conscription of Conscience*, 375–76; Sibley and Wardlaw, *Conscientious Objectors in Prison*, 45–47; Wittner, *Rebels Against War*, 88; and Dellinger, *From Yale to Jail*, 119–31, 137.

117. James Bennett, quoted in *CO*, Dec. 1943: 1, 8.

118. DiGia, interview by author, 9 May 1995.

119. For both DiGia and the one-a-week strike, see ibid.; John M. Mecartney to Frances Ransom, 2 May 1944, WRL Papers, A/30; Ruth E. MacAdam, letters and statements in folder marked "Danbury Hunger Strike, 1943–1944," FOR Papers, A/18; Peck, *We Who Would Not Kill*, 134–37, 141–46, 155–57; Ralph DiGia, "My Resistance to World War II," in *A Few Small Candles*, ed. Larry Gara and Lenna Mae Gara, 38–52; Wendy Schwartz, ed., *The War Resisters League Honors Ralph DiGia on His 25th Anniversary as a Staff Member* (New York: Faculty Press, 1981); *Nonviolent Activist*, Sept.-Oct. 1994, 12–13.

120. Ira Berlin, ed., *Herbert G. Gutman, Power and Culture: Essays on the American Working Class* (New York: New Press, 1987); Richard B. Gregg, *The Power of Nonviolence* (New York: Schocken Books, 1969); and Eugene D. Genovese, *Roll, Jordan, Roll: The World the Slaves Made* (New York: Vintage, 1976).

121. Kingsley, quoted in the *Absolutist*, 3 Apr. 1945.

122. R. Finch, interview by author, 29 Jan. 1994.

123. Peck, *We Who Would Not Kill*, 174.

## Chapter 6. The Pacifist House Divided

1. Kaufman, "War Resisters League[:] The First Three Months of 1946—A Report in Summary Form," 1 Apr. 1946, in Minutes, WRL-EC, WRL Papers, A/2.

2. Lawrence Wittner also notes this anarchist impulse in the postwar pacifist movement in *Rebels Against War*, 153–56, 225–27.

3. *WRL News*, 25 Jan. 1949.

4. Hughan to Kaufman, 10 Aug. 1945, Kaufman Papers.

5. E. Thomas to Dear Friend, 7 Jan. 1946, WRL Papers, A/4.

6. Hughan to Kaufman, 10 Aug. 1945, Kaufman Papers. See also Hughan to Kaufman, 20 Aug. 1945, Kaufman Papers.

7. [Frieda Lazarus] to Roy Kepler, 8 Aug. [sic] 1945, WRL Papers, A/30.

8. John Lewis to Muste, 8 Aug. 1945.

9. [Frieda Lazarus] to Roy Kepler, 8 Aug. [sic] 1945, WRL Papers, A/30.

10. Bent Andresen, "A Message to People of Goodwill," [Aug. 1945], FOR Papers, A/12. For information on Bent Andresen (1908–91), who joined the WRL in 1932, see Bennett, " 'Pacifism Not Passivism,' " 407n. 16.

11. Frank Olmstead to Fellow Worker to End War, 10 Aug. 1945, WRL Papers, A/4.

12. Transcript, Frank Olmstead, interview on KGW radio station, 1 Jan. 1946, 3–4, WRL Papers, A/36.

13. "Excerpts of Comments Received from Members Unable to Attend Executive Committee Meeting of 24 Aug. 1945," in Minutes, WRL-EC, WRL Papers, A/2.

14. The atomic bomb led Kampelman to doubt pacifism's relevance. Under Presidents Carter and Reagan, he led the U.S. delegation in arms and security negotiations with the Soviet Union. See Kampelman, *Entering New Worlds,* 52–53.

15. "Excerpts of Comments Received from Members Unable to Attend Executive Committee Meeting of 24 Aug. 1945," in Minutes, WRL-EC, WRL Papers, A/2; Max Kampleman to Kaufman, 19 Aug. 1945, WRL Papers, A/15; and Kaufman to Hughan, 25 Aug. 1945, Kaufman Papers.

16. WRL, "The Atomic Bomb," 11 Feb. 1946, in Minutes, WRL-EC, WRL Papers, A/2.

17. Ed Qualye to Frank Olmstead, 24 May 1946, and Frank Olmstead to Ed Qualye, 1 June 1946, both in Kaufman Papers.

18. Hughan, "War Resistance in the Atomic Age" (Draft), 9 Apr. 1946, WRL Papers, A/28.

19. For the debate over the role of COs in the atomic age, see ibid.; and other materials in folder marked "Literature Committee, 1946–1947," WRL Papers, A/28. For other literature, including Hughan, *War Resistance in the Atomic Age* (New York: WRL, 1946), see folders marked "Literature, 1944–1945"; and "Literature, 1946–50," both in WRL Papers, A/4; and "War?" [1947–48], Kaufman Papers.

20. Depending on the context, I use the term *prison COs* to refer to all COs who had served or were serving time in jail, including those who had completed their jail terms or who were out on probation, parole, or conditional release. I use the term *imprisoned COs* to refer to COs in jail at that time. Thus, *imprisoned COs* are a subset of *prison COs*.

21. James Peck, "Amnesty Drive Seeks to Free American Political Prisoners," [1946?], Committee for Amnesty for All Objectors to War and Conscription Papers (hereafter, CFA Papers), Box 2, GDC-A, SCPC; *Amnesty Bulletin,* 18 Jan. 1946.

22. Committee for Amnesty for All Objectors to War and Conscription (hereafter CFA), "Of Amnesty: Concerning Proposals for a Presidential Pardon for Conscientious Objectors," Dec. 1946, CFA Papers, Box 2. See also "Report on Conference on a Campaign for Amnesty for Imprisoned Conscientious Objectors," in Minutes, CFA, 1 Dec. 1945, CFA Papers, Box 1. For the amnesty campaign, see Andrew J. Dunar, "Harry S. Truman and the Issue of Amnesty for Conscientious Objectors," *Peace and Change* 16 (July 1991): 285–301; Sibley and Jacob, *Conscription of Conscience,* 379–98; Scott H. Bennett, " 'Free American Political Prisoners': Pacifist Activism and Civil Liberties, 1945–48," *Journal of Peace Research* 40 (July 2003): 413–33.

23. *Amnesty Bulletin,* 18 Jan. 1946.

24. "Report on Conference on a Campaign for Amnesty for Imprisoned Conscientious Ob-

jectors," in Minutes, CFA, 1 Dec. 1945; and Minutes, CFA, 15 Dec. 1945, both in CFA Papers, Box 1; *WRL News,* 10 Apr. 1946; Albon Man, interview by author, 23 Apr. 1995.

25. Peck, "Amnesty Drive Seeks to Free American Political Prisoners," [1946?], 3–4, CFA Papers, Box 2; David Thoreau Wieck, *Woman from Spillertown: A Memoir of Agnes Burns Wieck* (Carbondale: Southern Illinois Univ. Press, 1992), 213–18; Albon Man, interview by author, 23 Apr. 1995; Vivien Roodenko Lang, interview by author, 20 Apr. 1995.

26. Alonso, *Peace as a Women's Issue,* 122–23; and Alonso, *The Women's Peace Union and the Outlawry of War, 1921–1942* (Knoxville: The Univ. of Tennessee Press, 1989), passim.

27. Frieda Lazarus to James Bennett, 13 Aug. 1946, Frieda L. Lazarus Papers (hereafter, Lazarus Papers), Box 2, Manuscript Division, NYPL.

28. Frieda Lazarus, "Resignation Explained," *CO,* Apr. 1946, 5. See also Sibley and Jacob, *Conscription of Conscience,* 387–88.

29. Frieda Lazarus, "Resignation Explained," *CO,* Apr. 1946, 5.

30. Ibid. See also Frieda Lazarus to Dear Friend, 11 Jan. 1946; and Frieda Lazarus to Grace Rhoades, 24 Jan. 1946, both in WRL Papers, A/30; and Kaufman to Hughan, 7 Sept. 1945, WRL Papers, A/15. For Lazarus's post-resignation CO work, see Lazarus Papers, Box 2.

31. "Petition for Pardon after Completion of Sentence" (with Luitweiler's annotations), attached to Frances R. Ransom to Bob Luitweiler, 3 Apr. 1948, WRL Papers, A/15.

32. I. Roodenko, "Discloses Error in Mrs. Lazarus' Letter," *CO,* June 1946, 3.

33. Ibid.

34. CFA, "Of Amnesty," 1–2. See also "Top Authors Call upon Truman to Grant Amnesty," 23 Sept. 1946, CFA Papers, Box 2; Dorothy C. Fisher, "A Christmas Amnesty," *Nation,* 14 Dec. 1946, 694.

35. CFA, "Of Amnesty," 4. See also CFA, *Still No Amnesty* ([New York: Committee for Amnesty, 1948]), CFA Papers, Box 2.

36. Minutes, CFA, 15 Dec. 1945; 20 Mar. and 20 Apr. 1946, all in CFA Papers, Box 1; CFA, "Of Amnesty," 1, 3; "Leading Negro Actors and Artists Urge Truman to Grant Amnesty," 31 Aug. [1946]; "Top Authors Call upon Truman to Grant Amnesty," 23 Sept. 1946; and "Amnesty for Conscientious Objectors," [1946], all in CFA Papers, Box 2; *Amnesty Bulletin,* 1945–48, especially June-Dec. 1946; and Albon Man, interview by author, 23 Apr. 1995.

37. For CO activism at Danbury, see Bennett, "Pacifism Not Passivism," 346–47. For Axford, see also *Amnesty Bulletin* 18 (Sept. 1946).

38. For a list of Amnesty Committee actions, see V. Roodenko to Allen Early, 24 Sept. 1948, WRL Papers, A/13. For the Freedom Train, see clippings in CFA Papers, Box 2; and *Amnesty Bulletin,* 27 Sept., 13 Nov., and 5 Dec. 1947; and 13 Apr. and 18 June 1948.

39. For the 11 May demonstration, see clippings and photographs in folder marked "Publicity, Washington May 11, 1946, Demonstration," CFA Papers, Box 2; *Amnesty Bulletin,* 20 Mar., 1 May, and 15 May 1946; Minutes, CFA, 30 Mar. 1946; and Minutes, Washington CFA, 27 Mar. 1946, both in CFA Papers, Box 1.

40. I. Roodenko et al., "Statement of Five War Objectors at Sandstone, Minn. Prison Prior to Beginning a Hunger Strike," 11 May 1946, Roodenko Papers. See also CFA press release, 16 May [1946], Roodenko Papers. The original fasters were Roodenko, John Hampton, Malcolm Parker, Charles Worley, and Dick Zumwinkle. Henry Dyer, Walter Gormley, and Glenn Hutchinson joined later.

41. I. Roodenko et al. to Clare Booth Luce, 4 July 1946; I. Roodenko to Senator Homer J. Capehart, 10 July 1946; and I. Roodenko et al. to Senator Claude Pepper, 10 Apr. 1946, all in CFA Papers, Box 1. Vivien Roodenko suggested members of Congress to whom Igal and others should write, and in some cases she wrote follow-up letters.

42. I. Roodenko, "Amnesty the Only Solution," *Pacifica Views,* 15 Nov. 1946.

43. Ibid.; and Roodenko, "Discloses Error in Mrs. Lazarus' Letter." After two weeks, prison authorities force-fed Roodenko. See [Tom C. Clark] to Clare Boothe Luce, 25 June 1946, Roodenko Papers; and I. Roodenko to ————, 12 Mar. 1947, CFA Papers, Box 1.

44. Sibley and Jacob, *Conscription of Conscience,* 396.

45. Ibid., 392–96; and Dunar, "Harry S. Truman and the Issue of Amnesty," *NYT,* 23 Dec. 1946, 8. When the board was commissioned, three hundred COs remained in jail and more than five thousand prison COs faced impaired civil and political rights.

46. E. Thomas to Harry S. Truman, 26 Dec. 1947, WRL Papers, A/19. Both the board's report and the presidential proclamation appeared in *NYT,* 24 Dec. 1947, 1, 8. For pacifist responses, see CFA, *Still No Amnesty*; and "Statement of the [WRL] Executive Committee to the President's Amnesty Board," 20 Feb. 1947, WRL Papers, A/30.

47. Albon Man to Scott Bennett, 14 July 1995 and 5 Mar. 2001; Minutes, CFA, 5 May and 9 June 1948, CFA Papers, Box 1; Roy Kepler to Waldo S. Chase, 2 Sept. 1948, WRL Papers, A/12; and Roy Kepler to Robert H. Albright, 2 Sept. 1948, WRL Papers, A/11. The CCCO was formed as a service organization to complement NSBRO and assist COs, especially those not recognized as COs by the new law. Caleb Foote, a WRL member and former prison CO, was named executive secretary of CCCO; nearly half the members of its executive committee also belonged to the WRL. See Central Committee for Conscientious Objectors Papers (hereafter CCCO Papers), Boxes 1 and 4, DG-73, SCPC.

48. Sibley and Jacob, *Conscription of Conscience,* 392–94; Dunar, "Harry S. Truman and the Issue of Amnesty," 293–94; Albon Man to Dorothy C. Fisher, 2 Jan. 1947, CFA Papers, Box 1; and Albon Man, interview by author, 23 Apr. 1995.

49. Rex Corfman et al., "Call to a Conference[:] Preliminary Announcement," [Autumn 1945], *Direct Action,* Autumn 1945, 15–17. For CO correspondence and the Call, see materials in Committee for Nonviolent Revolution Papers (hereafter, CNVR Papers, GDC-A, SCPC); and folder marked "Study Conf. on Revolutionary Pacifism, Stielacoon, WA, Feb. 1945," FOR Papers, II/A-1. For information on CNVR, see Wittner, *Rebels Against War,* 154–56; Isserman, *If I Had a Hammer,* 136–37; and Tracy, *Direct Action,* 51–52.

50. I. Roodenko to V. Roodenko, 6 Feb. 1946, Roodenko Papers. See also loose pages from Chicago Conference Report (Draft), n.d.,; CNVR, "Where Radicalism in the Next Five Years?" 8–10 Aug. [1947]; and CNVR, "Reports of the Feb. Conference on Non-Violent Revolution," 6–9 Jan. 1946, both in CNVR Papers.

51. CNVR, "Where Radicalism in the Next Five Years?" 8–10 Aug. 1947; CNVR-NY, "New York Has Its Concentration Camp," [1946–47], CNVR Papers; *Absolutist,* Apr. 1946, 5; *Politics,* Nov. 1946, 338; *NYT,* 24 Oct. 1946, 9; and R. Finch, interview by author, 29 Jan. 1994. CNVR-NY members who picketed the Hotel Savoy Plaza included Robert Auerbach, Marian Davis, David Dellinger, Ralph DiGia, Mathias Kauten, George Kingsley, Albon Man, Robin Myers, and Jim Peck.

52. CNVR-NY, "Peace[,] Plenty[,] Freedom[,] Revolution[,]" n.d., CNVR Papers.

53. CNVR-NY, "NOAH HAD AN ARK! WHAT HAVE YOU GOT?" [1946–47], CNVR Papers.

54. CNVR-NY, "George Washington Struck Against the Government[.] Why Can't We?" [June 1946], CNVR Papers.

55. CNVR-NY, "RESIST CONSCRIPTION," [1946–47], CNVR Papers.

56. CNVR-NY, "BECAUSE THE PEOPLE OF THE WORLD ARE TIRED OF THIS: THE RULERS OF THE WORLD HAVE CONCOCTED THE UNO," [1946–47], CNVR Papers.

57. For the new social movements, see Epstein, *Political Protest and Cultural Revolution,* especially 1–57, 227–78; and Boggs, *Social Movements and Political Power.*

58. "Letter from Lewis Hill, received too late to be incorporated in pre-Conf. report," 4 Aug. 1947, CNVR Papers.

59. Albon Man to Scott Bennett, 14 July 1995; and CNVR, "Bulletin No. 6," 1 June 1946, CNVR Papers. For the full Brockway quote, see chapter 1.

60. Albon Man to Scott Bennett, 14 July 1995. For the CNVR and its impact on the WRL, I have benefited from interviews with Albon Man, Roy Finch, Ralph DiGia, Vivien Roodenko Lang, Ernest R. Bromley, and Marion Bromley.

61. Wittner, *Rebels Against War,* 156.

62. Ibid.

63. For Peacemakers, see Wittner, *Rebels Against War,* 156–58, 226–27; Tracy, *Direct Action,* 60–67; and Neil H. Katz, "Radical Pacifism and the Contemporary American Peace Movement: The Committee for Nonviolent Action, 1957–1967" (Ph.D. diss., Univ. of Maryland, 1974), 11–14. For Peacemakers' literature, see Peacemakers Papers, CDG-A, SCPC.

64. "Peacemakers: A Declaration to the American People," [1948–49?], Peacemakers Papers.

65. Peacemakers Tax Refusal Committee, *Why We Refuse to Pay Taxes for War,* Aug. 1956, Peacemakers Papers; Ernest R. Bromley to Kaufman, 1 Aug. 1947; Abe [Kaufman] to Ernest R. [Bromley], 25 Sept. 1947; Kaufman to [Horace] Champney, 29 July 1947, all in WRL Papers, A/19; and Ernest R. Bromley, "Tax Refusal Gets a Push Ahead," 16 Apr. 1948, WRL Papers, A/11. WRL members of the Tax Refusal Committee included Walter Gormley, Valerie Riggs, Ralph Templin, Caroline Urie, and perhaps the Bromleys.

66. For example, see Ernest R. Bromley, "The Case for Tax Refusal," *Fellowship,* Nov. 1947, 171–73.

67. Ernest R. Bromley and Marion Bromley, "Tax Refusal—A Way to Resist War," July 1948, 1, Peacemakers Papers.

68. Ernest R. Bromley, "How Movement on Nonpayment Began," 3 Mar. 1962, Peacemakers Papers.

69. Tax Refusal Committee, "Questions and Answers on Tax Refusal," Oct. 1948, 2, Peacemakers Papers.

70. E. R. Bromley and M. Bromley, "Tax Refusal—A Way To Resist War," July 1948, 2, Peacemakers Papers; Ernest Bromley and Marion Bromley, "Tax Refusal—A Way to Resist War," 1; and Ernest Bromley, "How Movement on Nonpayment Began," 3 Mar. 1962, Peacemaker Papers.

71. Ibid.

72. Ernest R. Bromley, "Is Tax Refusal Effective?" *Fellowship,* Dec. 1947, 190.

73. Caroline Urie to Editor of *Fellowship,* Oct. 1948, 39.

74. Gormley, quoted in E. Bromley and M. Bromley, "Tax Refusal—A Way to Resist War," July 1948, 3, Peacemakers Papers.

75. Riggs, quoted in E. Bromley and M. Bromley, "Tax Refusal—A Way to Resist War," July 1948, 6, Peacemakers Papers.

76. *Fellowship,* June 1948, 20.

77. Tax Refusal Committee, "A Year in Review," 21 June 1950, Peacemakers Papers.

78. Ibid., 7.

79. Ibid., 8.

80. E. Bromley and M. Bromley, "Tax Refusal—A Way to Resist War," July 1948; "41 Refuse to Pay Income Tax," 14 Mar. 1949; "No Taxes for War: The Choice Is Ours," n.d.; and Tax Refusal Committee, "Why We Refuse To Pay Taxes for War," Aug. 1956, all in Peacemakers Papers. For additional citations of statements by WRL members, see Bennett, "Pacifism Not Passivism," 42n. 231.

81. *WRL News,* 16 Jan. 1948, See also ibid, 8 Apr., and 10 May 1948, and 28 Apr. 1949; Minutes, WRL-EC, 7 Apr. 1948, WRL Papers, A/2; Frances R. Ransom to Marion C. Frenyear, 26 Feb. 1948, and attached donation form, WRL Papers, A/13; Robert C. Friend to WRL, 15 Mar. 1948, WRL Papers, A/13; Frances R. Ransom to J. William Hawkins, 24 May 1948, and attached donation form, WRL Papers, A/14; Caroline F. Urie to President Truman, 10 Mar. 1948, WRL Papers, A/11; and V. Roodenko to George Yamada, 30 Nov. 1948, WRL Papers, A/20.

82. Ammon Hennacy, "Statement to the Collector of Revenue of Albuquerque, N.M. upon My Refusal to Pay Taxes for War or Conscription," 13 Jan. [1945?] (attached to Kaufman to Ammon Hennacy, 22 Mar. 1945), WRL Papers, A/14.

83. Ammon Hennacy, *The Book of Ammon: The Autobiography of a Unique American Rebel* (Salt Lake City: [Ammon Hennacy Publications], 1970), passim, quotation at 121.

84. Kaufman to Ammon Hennacy, 22 Mar. 1945, WRL Papers, A/14.

85. Hennacy, *Book of Ammon,* 43, 141, 166, 216, 397.

86. [Kaufman] to Caroline Urie, 19 Dec. 1947, WRL Papers, A/19. See also Minutes, WRL-EC, 18 June, 6 Oct., and 30 Oct. 1949, WRL Papers, A/2; Rustin, Charles Bloomstein, Nat Hoffman, and Roy Kepler, "Report and Recommendation of Sub-Committee on Tax Withholding," [Oct. 1949], in Minutes, WRL-EC, WRL Papers, A/2; and *WRL News,* 1 Dec. 1949.

87. Selective Service Act of 1948, quoted in *WRL News,* 26 June 1948. For information on the 1948 law, see also Chambers, "Conscientious Objectors and the American State," 38–39; Flynn, *The Draft, 1940–1973,* 88–109; and Stephen M. Kohn, *Jailed for Peace: The History of American Draft Law Violators, 1685–1985* (Westport, Conn.: Greenwood Press, 1992), 63–67.

88. Resist Conscription Committee (RCC) statements; George M. Houser to Dear Friend, 30 Apr. 1948; Roy Kepler to Dear Friend, 2 July 1948; and Cecil Hinshaw, Muste, and David Dellinger to Dear Friend, 4 May 1948, all in Resist Conscription Committee Papers, CDG-A, SCPC; Minutes, Resist Peacetime Conscription Meeting, 2 Jan. 1948, Roodenko Papers; Roy Kepler to Herbert and Charlotte Ruben, 13 July 1948, WRL Papers, A/18; *WRL News,* 10 May 1948; *NYT,* 10 June 1948, 2; and *Alternative,* June 1948. The Resist Conscription Committee apparently grew out of the Break-With-Conscription Project, which returned or destroyed draft cards.

89. Minutes, WRL-EC, 19 Mar. 1948, WRL Papers, A/2.

90. Minutes, WRL-EC, 12 July 1948, WRL Papers, A/2.

91. The leaflets, which were withdrawn following passage of the 1948 draft law, are attached to Julien Cornell to War Resisters League, 23 June 1948, WRL Papers, A/12. See also ibid.

92. Julian Cornell to War Resisters League, 23 June 1948, WRL Papers, A/12.

93. Minutes, WRL-EC, 9 Aug. 1948, WRL Papers, A/2.

94. Ibid.

95. For instance, see Kepler to Herbert and Charlotte Ruben, 13 July 1948, WRL Papers, A/18. To placate members who opposed illegal actions, the WRL did not officially advocate non-registration, but it did support those members who took that position.

96. Meier and Rudwick, *CORE,* 35.

97. *WRL News,* 15 May 1947. See also Houser, interview by author, 18 May 1995; and "You Don't Have to Ride Jim Crow" (documentary on Journey of Reconciliation), first broadcast in 1995 by PBS/New Hampshire Public Television, produced by Robin Washington. Black WRL members included Rustin, Wally Nelson, and William Worthy; the white members were Houser, Peck, Roodenko, Joseph Felmet, and Homer Jack.

98. Bayard Rustin and George M. Houser, "We Challenged Jim Crow," in Bayard Rustin, *Down the Line: The Collected Writings of Bayard Rustin* (Chicago: Quadrangle, 1971), 17.

99. Ibid. See also "Journey of Reconciliation[:] Very Confidential"; George M. Houser to Participants in the Journey of Reconciliation, 28 Mar. 1947; George M. Houser, "Publicizing the Coming of the Interracial Deputation of the Journey of Reconciliation," n.d., and attached "Legal Questions about the Southern Bus Trip," "Questions on Strategy," and "Preparation for the Project," all in Roodenko Papers.

100. Rustin and Houser, "We Challenged Jim Crow," quotations on 22–24.

101. [George Houser and Bayard Rustin], "Journey of Reconciliation," [Draft Report, "We Challenged Jim Crow"], [Apr. 1947], Roodenko Papers.

102. Rustin and Houser, "We Challenged Jim Crow," 24–25.

103. Theodore D. Walser to I. Roodenko, 6 Apr. 1949, Roodenko Papers. See also George M. Houser Press Release, June 27, 1947; FOR-CORE Press Release, 20 Mar. 1949; *NYT,* 9 Mar. 1949, 21, clipping, all in Roodenko Papers.

104. Meier and Rudwick, *CORE,* 33–39, quotation on 38.

105. For information on the Journey of Reconciliation, in addition to works cited above, see George M. Houser, "A Personal Retrospective on the 1947 Journey of Reconciliation," [Sept. 1992], CORE Papers/George Houser's Correspondence, CDG-A, SCPC; James Peck, *Freedom Ride* (New York: Simon and Schuster, 1962), 14–27; and Houser, interview by author, 18 May 1995.

106. WRL Press Release, 9 Apr. 1948, WRL Papers, A/4.

107. "17th Annual Conference of the War Resisters' [sic] League" (report), 14–16 June 1946, 5, WRL Papers, A/4.

108. Ibid.; program, 1946 Annual WRL Conference, WRL Papers, A/9. See also folder marked "Seventeenth Annual Conference, 1946," WRL Papers, A/9; and *WRL News,* 22 June 1946. Information on social events at WRL conferences was drawn from Edward Gottlieb, untaped conversations with author.

109. *WRL News,* 24 June 1947; Minutes, WRL-EC, 16 June 1947, WRL Papers, A/12.

110. Ibid.

111. See Minutes, WRL-EC, 16 June 1947, WRL Papers, A/2.

112. "Proposed Resolutions," [June 1947}, WRL Papers, A/9.

113. See folder marked "Eighteenth Annual Conference, 1947," WRL Papers, A/9; Minutes,

WRL-EC, 16 June 1947, WRL Papers, A/2; Sandy Katz to WRL Executive Committee, 7 July 1947, WRL Papers, A/15; Irving Ravin to [Kaufman], 23 July 1947, WRL Papers, A/18; and *WRL News,* 24 June 1947.

114. Dellinger, quoted in M. Finch, Minutes, Sunday Morning Session, [20 June 1998], WRL Papers, A/9.

115. Minutes, WRL-EC, 12 July 1948, WRL Papers, A/2.

116. Ibid.

117. See folder marked "Nineteenth Annual Conference, 1948," WRL Papers, A/9; Minutes, WRL-EC, 20 June and 12 July 1948, WRL Papers, A/2; and *WRL News,* 26 June 1948. For the Danish general strike, see Ackerman and Kruegler, *Strategic Nonviolent Conflict,* 213–49.

118. Dellinger, quoted in Notes, "First Session: Is Pacifism Practical?" [18 June 1949], WRL Papers, A/9.

119. Albon Man, interview by author, 23 Apr. 1995.

120. Program, 1950 Annual WRL Conference, WRL Papers, A/9.

121. "Notes on the Purpose and Approach at the June Conference of the WRL," 4 May 1950, WRL Papers, A/9.

122. "A Question and Suggestion Sheet to Help Prepare You for the WRL Conference," [1950], WRL Papers, A/9.

123. Ibid.

124. Bloomstein, quoted in Minutes, War Resisters League, 21st Annual Summer Conference at the Homestead, Crafts, N.Y. (Saturday session), 3–4 June 1950, WRL Papers, A/9.

125. Dellinger, quoted in *WRL News,* July 1950.

126. Bloomstein, quoted in *WRL News,* July 1950.

127. *WRL News,* July 1950. See also folder marked "Twenty-first Annual Conference, 1950," WRL Papers, A/9.

128. Kaufman to E. Thomas, 21 Apr. 1946, Kaufman Papers.

129. Kaufman to [WRL] Executive Committee, 8 Sept. 1947, in Minutes, WRL-EC, WRL Papers, A/2; Minutes, WRL-EC, 24 Apr. 1946, WRL Papers, A/2; Kaufman to Frieda [Lazarus], 30 Apr. 1946, WRL Papers, A/16; Kaufman to Evan Thomas, 21 Apr. 1946; Kaufman to Dear Friend, 17 Nov. 1947; Kaufman to Michael Young, 26 Dec. 1974, all in Kaufman Papers.

130. [Frieda Lazarus] to Kaufman, 13 Sept. 1947, Lazarus Papers, Box 2.

131. [Kaufman] to F[lorence] L[.] L[atimore], 2 July 1948, Kaufman Papers. See also Kaufman, interview by author, 24 Aug. 1997.

132. Kaufman to WRL Executive Committee, 8 Sept. 1947, in Minutes, WRL-EC, WRL Papers, A/2; and Minutes, WRL-EC, 5 Mar. 1948, WRL Papers, A/2.

133. Kaufman, "Manuscript," Kaufman Papers. Roy Kepler replaced Kaufman as executive secretary in 1948. Frances Rose Ransom was acting executive secretary from 1 Jan. 1948 to July 1948. In Oct. 1950, Sidney Aberman (a World War II CPS CO) succeeded Kepler.

134. F. M. [Frances M. Witherspoon] to [Kaufman], [recd. 6 Aug. 1948], WRL Papers, A/20.

135. Ibid.

136. [Kaufman] to F. M. [Witherspoon], 6 Aug. 1948, Kaufman Papers.

137. For personality differences as an explanation of Kaufman's and Lazarus's behavior, see E. [Thomas] to [Muste], 4 Feb. 1945, FOR Papers, A/11; and V. Roodenko to Roy [Kepler], 17 Jan. 1951, WRL Papers, B/10.

138. Minutes, WRL-EC, 8 May and 8 June 1950, WRL Papers, B/1.

139. James Peck to Kaufman, 17 May 1950; See also Kaufman to James Peck, 20 May 1950, Kaufman Papers.

140. Kaufman to James Peck, 20 May 1950.

141. James Peck to Kaufman (Postcard), [14 June 1950], Kaufman Papers. See also James Peck to Kaufman, [June 1950?], WRL Papers, A/10.

142. This paragraph is based on interviews with Ralph DiGia, Edward Gottlieb, George Houser, Abraham Kaufman, Vivien [Roodenko] Lang, and Albon Man.

143. See Letterhead and other materials in folder marked "Policy, Minutes, Lit., etc., 1940–1945," in Metropolitan Board for Conscientious Objectors Papers, Box 1, CDG-A, SCPC; and M[artin] Goldwasser, "History of Metropolitan Board for C.O.'s," 25 Oct. 1971, Kaufman Papers.

144. Minutes, WRL-EC, 9 Nov. 1950, WRL Papers, B/1.

145. Ibid.

146. Draft Minutes, WRL-EC, 9 Nov. 1950, WRL Papers, B/1.

147. See draft and official Minutes, WRL-EC, 9 Nov.; and Minutes, WRL-EC, 11 Dec. 1950, WRL Papers, B/1.

148. Minutes, WRL-EC, 9 Nov. 1950, WRL Papers, B/1.

149. Ibid.; and Kaufman to Sidney Aberman, 10 Nov. 1950, WRL Papers, A/2.

150. Kaufman to Sidney Aberman, 12 Feb. 1951, Kaufman Papers.

151. Ibid.

152. Lazarus, quoted in Minutes, WRL-EC, 11 Dec. 1950, WRL Papers, B/1.

153. Minutes, WRL-EC, 11 Dec. 1950, WRL Papers, B/1.

154. Frieda Lazarus to Roy [Finch], 18 Apr. 1951, WRL Papers, A/2.

155. E. Thomas to Sidney Aberman, 12 Dec. 1950, WRL Papers, A/2.

156. E. Thomas, "A Pacifist Looks at the Future," 1 Mar. 1950, Kaufman Papers; Frieda Lazarus to Sidney Aberman, 8 Jan. 1951, WRL Papers, A/2; Minutes, WRL-EC, 9 Nov. 1950, 11 Jan. 1951, WRL Papers, B/1; and *WRL News,* Apr. 1951. On the three resignations as a turning point, see Peck, *We Who Would Not Kill,* 188; and M. Young, "Wars Will Cease When Men Refuse to Fight," 174.

157. Minutes, WRL-EC, 11 Jan. 1951, WRL Papers, B/1.

158. "The WRL Working Program for the Immediate Future," 19 Mar. 1951, *WRL News,* Apr. 1951.

159. Ibid.; Minutes, WRL-EC, 11 Jan.–19 Mar. 1951, WRL Papers, B/1; and Frances R. Ransom to Charles Mackintosh, 1 May 1951, WRL Papers, A/10.

160. Mackintosh, quoted in *WRL News,* May-June 1951.

161. Ibid.

162. Frances R. Ransom to Charles Mackintosh, 1 May 1951, WRL Papers, A/10.

163. Ibid.

164. Minutes, WRL-EC, 12 Mar. 1951, WRL Papers, B/1. See also Minutes, WRL-EC, 26 Feb. 1951, WRL Papers, B/1.

165. *WRL News,* July-Aug. 1953, and Jan.-Feb. 1955.

166. Anderson, *Bayard Rustin,* 153.

167. Ibid., 153–65, 171; and Minutes, WRL-EC, 27 Apr. 1953, WRL Papers, B/1.

168. Dave Dellinger to Roy Finch, 6 Sept. 1953, WRL Papers, B/12.

169. Hughan, quoted in R. Finch, "Confidential Memo to Executive Committee and National Advisory Council," [Aug. 1953], in Minutes, WRL-EC, WRL Papers, B/1.

170. *WRL News,* May-June 1954. For the debate over Rustin's appointment, see folder marked "Correspondence re. Bayard Rustin as Ex. Sec. 1953," WRL Papers, B/12.

171. *WRL News,* May-June 1955.

### Chapter 7. Nonaligned International Pacifism

1. For the phrase "one world community," see WRL, "Statement of Purpose and Program," 10 Mar. 1947, in Minutes, WRL-EC, WRL Papers, A/2. Lawrence Wittner explores this theme in *One World or None: A History of the World Nuclear Disarmament Movement Through 1953* (Stanford: Stanford Univ. Press, 1993).

2. *WRL News,* 13 Nov. 1946.

3. Wittner, *One World or None.* For a general treatment of opposition to Cold War "containment" by the peace movement, see E. Timothy Smith, *Opposition Beyond the Water's Edge: Liberal Internationalists, Pacifists and Containment, 1945–1953* (Westport, Conn.: Greenwood, 1999).

4. Revisionist accounts of the 1950s, which argue that the decade contained radical currents that resisted the dominant culture and provided a seed bed for later social change, include Isserman, *If I Had a Hammer*; Dan Wakefield, *New York in the 50s* (New York: Houghton Mifflin/Seymour Lawrence, 1992); Andrew Jamison and Ron Eyerman, *Seeds of the Sixties* (Los Angeles: Univ. of California Press, 1995); and Richard H. Pells, *The Liberal Mind in a Conservative Age: American Intellectuals in the 1940s and the 1950s* (New York: Harper & Row, 1985). For the link between the 1950s peace movement and the New Left, see also Tracy, *Direct Action*; Isserman, "You Don't Need a Weatherman But a Postman Can Be Helpful: Thoughts on the History of SDS and the Antiwar Movement," in *Give Peace a Chance: Exploring the Vietnam Antiwar Movement,* ed. Melvin Small and William D. Hoover, 22–34; Todd Gitlin, *The Sixties: Years of Hope, Days of Rage* (New York: Bantam Books, 1987); Terry H. Anderson, *The Movement and the Sixties* (New York: Oxford Univ. Press, 1995); James Miller, *Democracy in the Streets: From Port Huron to the Siege of Chicago* (New York: Simon and Schuster, 1987); Edward J. Bacciocco, Jr., *The New Left in America: Reform to Revolution, 1956–1970* (Stanford: Hoover Institute Press, 1974); Irwin Unger, *The Movement: A History of the American New Left* (New York: Dodd, Mead & Co., 1974); Charles DeBenedetti and Charles Chatfield (assisting author), *An American Ordeal: The Antiwar Movement of the Vietnam Era* (Syracuse: Syracuse Univ. Press, 1990); James J. Farrell, *The Spirit of the Sixties: The Making of Postwar Radicalism* (New York: Routledge, 1997); and Allen Smith, "Present at the Creation . . . and Other Myths: The Port Huron Statement and the Origins of the New Left," *Peace and Change* 25 (July 2000): 339–62.

5. Wakefield, *New York in the 50s,* 83.

6. Dellinger, *From Yale to Jail,* 152.

7. *WRL News,* 26 Sept. 1949.

8. Ibid., 13 Nov. 1946.

9. Ibid., 10 Oct. 1946.

10. Ibid.

11. Ibid., and "Jottings," *Fellowship,* Nov. 1946, 184.

12. *WRL News,* 20 Aug. 1946.

13. Gregory D. Sumner, *Dwight Macdonald and the Politics Circle: The Challenge of Cos-*

*mopolitan Democracy* (Ithaca: Cornell Univ. Press, 1996), 179–92, quotations on 179, 186–87, 192. See also Minutes, WRL-EC, 8 Oct. 1945, WRL Papers, A/2; and *WRL News,* 20 Aug. 1946, 16 Apr. 1947; and May-June 1951.

14. *WRL News,* 10 Apr. 1946 and inserted Theodor Michaltscheff, "German Democracy in Peril." See also *WRL News,* 11 May 1946, 16 Apr. 1947, and 10 Dec. 1948.

15. *WRL News,* 16 Oct. 1945.

16. Ibid., 24 June 1947.

17. Ibid., 13 Sept. 1945.

18. Ibid., 10 Apr. 1946.

19. Ibid., 13 Sept. 1945.

20. Ibid., 10 Apr. 1946.

21. In addition to the sources cited in notes 15–20, see Hughan to Editor of the *World-Telegram,* 14 Jan. 1945 [sic/1946?], WRL Papers, A/15; and Michael Wreszin, *A Rebel in Defense of Tradition: The Life and Politics of Dwight Macdonald* (New York: Basic Books, 1994), 192.

22. *WRL News,* May-June 1951.

23. Frances R. Ransom, "Six Months Summary: Jan.-June, 1947," 10 July 1947, in Minutes, WRL-EC, WRL Papers, A/2; *WRL News,* 20 Aug. 1946; 14 Jan., 13 Mar., and 8 Dec. 1947; 18 Oct. 1948; Feb. 1950 (Insert: "Report to Members and Contributors on How Your WRL Money Is Spent"); and May-June 1951; Frances R. Ransom to William Rickel, 2 Apr. 1948, WRL Papers, A/18; and folder marked "Foreign Correspondence," WRL Papers, B/10.

24. *Peace News,* 4 July 1947, 1; and *WRL News,* July-Aug. 1952.

25. *WRL News,* July-Aug. 1952.

26. Ibid.; and *WRL News,* Sept.-Oct. 1952; May-June 1953.

27. Minutes, WRL Interim Administrative Committee (hereafter, WRL-IAC), 7 Aug. 1950, WRL Papers, B/1.

28. Minutes, WRL-EC and Minutes, WRL-IAC, 10 Feb. 1947; 23 Apr. and 22 Nov. 1948, and 7 Aug. 1950, WRL Papers, A/2 and B/1; *WRL News,* 12 Feb. 1947 and 8 Mar. 1948; and Robert A. Divine, *American Immigration Policy, 1924–1952* (New York: Da Capo Press, 1972), 110–45.

29. *WRL News,* May-June 1952.

30. Ibid., July-Aug. 1953.

31. Minutes, WRL-EC, 4 June 1953, WRL Papers, B/1. See also *WRL News,* Nov.-Dec. 1952 and Sept.-Oct. 1953.

32. Flynn, *The Draft,* cited, p. 269n. 12; Frank Kofsky, *Harry S. Truman and the War Scare of 1948: A Successful Campaign to Deceive the Nation* (New York: St. Martin's Press, 1995), 195–96; and Wittner, *Rebels Against War,* 162–64.

33. Harry B. Sell to Dear WRL, 19 May 1947 (and attached matchbooks), WRL Papers, A/18. See also "There are things to do AGAINST CONSCRIPTION" [1948?], WRL Papers, A/4; *WRL News,* 10 Sept. 1947, 8 Apr. and 10 Aug. 1948.

34. Kepler, quoted in House Committee on Armed Services, Selective Service Extension: Hearings on H.R. 6826, 81st Cong., 2d sess., 1950, 5278–79; and Roy Kepler, Testimony Before Senate Committee on Armed Services, Selective Service Extension Act of 1950 and Manpower Registration and Classification Act: Hearings on S. 2861 and H.R. 6826, 81st Cong., 2d sess., 1950, 33.

35. *WRL News,* 10 Oct. 1946.

36. Ibid., 12 Feb. 1947. See also *Politics,* Jan. 1947, 31; and "Draft Card Burning" (flyer), WRL Papers, A/12.

37. Dellinger, quoted in the *Absolutist,* Mar. 1947, 2; and Dwight Macdonald, "Why Destroy Draft Cards?" *Politics,* Mar.-Apr. 1947, 54–55. See also *WRL News,* 13 Mar. 1947; *Fellowship,* Apr. 1947, 64; and *NYT,* 13 Feb. 1947, 20.

38. *Washington Post,* 6 June 1948, 4; *WRL News,* 26 June, 18 Oct. 1948; Roy Kepler to Dear Friend, 14 May 1948, WRL Papers, A/4; and *NYT,* 31 Aug. 1948, 1.

39. Peck, *Underdogs vs. Upperdogs,* 98–101.

40. Caleb Foote, "The Gara Case," *Fellowship,* July 1949, 4–9, quotation on 5. See also *News Notes* (CCCO), Nov. 1950; and Larry Gara and Lenna Mae Gara, eds., *A Few Small Candles,* 91–93.

41. For the quotations in this paragraph, see *WRL News,* 10 Aug. 1949 and 19 Jan. 1950. See also *WRL News,* 28 Apr. and 28 June 1949; 19 Jan. 1950; and Roy Kepler and Muste to Dear Friend, 5 July 1949, WRL Papers, A/4. Although the *WRL News* quotation—in response to the court's ruling—refers to the related case of Kansas minister Wirt Warren, the only other person convicted for counseling nonregistrants (his son), it is equally applicable to Gara.

42. *WRL News,* 15 May and 10 Sept. 1947; and Minutes, WRL-EC, 12 May 1947, WRL Papers, A/2.

43. Minutes, WRL-EC, 12 July 1948; 5 Jan. and 30 Oct. 1949, WRL Papers, A/2; *WRL News,* 10 Dec. 1948; 28 Oct. 1949; and Apr. 1950; "U.S. Pacifists Urge Israel to Recognize Rights of Conscientious Objectors," 22 Apr. 1949; and George W. Hartmann to Chaim Weizmann, 22 Apr. 1949, WRL Papers, B/11.

44. *WRL News,* 1 Dec. 1949. See also *WRL News,* 17 Mar. and 28 Oct. 1949.

45. Minutes, WRL-EC, 23 Oct. 1946, WRL Papers, A/2.

46. WRL statement in Senate Committee on Foreign Relations: Hearings on the Charter of the United Nations, 79th Cong., 1st sess., 1945, revised, 686–88.

47. Ibid., 688.

48. "[Report], 17th Annual Conference of the War Resisters League," 14–16 June 1946, 6, WRL Papers, A/9.

49. Wittner, *One World or None,* 161.

50. Ibid., 67–68, 70, 74, 160–62, quotation on 70. See also Frances R. Ransom to James Cassels, 16 Mar. 1948, WRL Papers, A/12; and V. Roodenko to Esther S. Frankel, 6 Nov. 1948, WRL Papers, A/13.

51. Orlie Pell to Kaufman, 9 Oct. 1946; Tracy [Mygatt] to [Kaufman], 10 Oct. 1946; Frances Witherspoon to Executive Committee, 9 Oct. 1946, in Minutes, WRL-EC; Minutes, WRL-EC, 10 Mar. 1947 (emphasis added); and Minutes, WRL-EC, 12 July, 19 Sept. 1948, all in WRL Papers, A/2.

52. Garry Davis, *The World Is My Country* (New York: G. P. Putnam's Sons, 1961), 246; and *NYT* [13 Sept. 1948], clipping in Garry Davis Papers (hereafter, Davis Papers), CDG-B (France), SCPC.

53. Sarrazac, quoted in Davis, *The World Is My Country,* 246.

54. G. Davis, *The World Is My Country,* 86; and Garry Davis, *From War Pilot to World Citizen,* 2d. ed. (Glen Gardner, N.J.: Libertarian Press [1950]), 6, 22–[23], clippings, Davis Papers.

55. G. Davis, *The World Is My Country*, 102. See also Davis, *From War Pilot to World Citizen*, 2d ed. (Glen Gardner, N.J.: Libertarian Press, [1950]); G. Davis, *Over to Pacifism* (London: Peace News, 1949); Wittner, *One World or None*, 113–15, 137, 160, 162–63, 179, 293, 327–28; *Peace News*, 4 Mar. 1949, 1; *NYT*, 2 Oct. 1950, 6; and clippings in Davis Papers.

56. Minutes, WRL-EC, 20 Mar. 1950, WRL Papers, B/1.

57. *Alternative*, Nov. 1949.

58. [Liberation Press Publishers], preface to *From War-Pilot to World Citizen*, by Davis. See also *Peace News*, 4 Mar. 1949, 1; and Minutes, WRL-EC, 31 July 1950, WRL Papers, B/1.

59. *Washington Post*, 5 Oct. 1949, 13; and *Hunterdon Republican* (Flemington, N.J.), 6 July 1950, 1. See also G. Davis, *Over to Pacifism*; *WRL News*, 28 Oct. 1949; Minutes, WRL-EC, 6 Oct. 1949, WRL Papers, A/2; "What Garry Davis Has Done" [Sept. 1949], Peacemakers Papers; *Washington Post*, 6 Oct. 1949, 8B; and *NYT*, 5 Oct. 1949, 18; and 6 Oct. 1949, 14.

60. Dellinger, introduction to *From War Pilot to World Citizen*, by G. Davis.

61. Ibid. See also Dellinger, *From Yale to Jail*, 164; "World Citizens 'Quit' U.S.," clipping in Davis Papers; Glen Gardner, "Stop the Korean Crisis and World War Three," [5 July 1950], Fast for Peace Committee Papers, CDG-A, SCPC (hereafter, Fast for Peace Committee Papers); and Garry Davis, interview by author, 3 Apr. 1996.

62. Minutes, WRL-EC and WRL-IAC, 6 Oct. 1949; 8 May, 31 July, and 7 Sept. 1950, WRL Papers, A/2 and B/1; Caroline Urie to James Peck, 12 Aug. 1950, WRL Papers, B/10; and *WRL News*, Dec. 1950.

63. Mildred Fahrni, "Report on the World Pacifist Movement in India," [Dec. 1949-Jan. 1950?], WRL Papers, B/10; Minutes, WRL-EC, 18 June 1949, WRL Papers, A/2; and *WRL News*, 19 Jan. 1950.

64. R[oy] K[epler] to [?], 15 Sept. 1949, WRL Papers, B/11; and Minutes, WRL-EC, 19 Oct. 1949, WRL Papers, A/2. See also Minutes, WRL-EC, 28 July and 12 Sept. 1949.

65. *WRL News*, 28 Oct. 1949; Roy [Kepler] to I. [Roodenko], 18 Jan. 1950, Roodenko Papers; and [I. Roodenko] to V. [Roodenko], 14 and 18 Nov. 1949, and 4 Feb. 1950, all in WRL Papers, B/11.

66. Letter, quoted in *WRL News*, 13 Mar. 1947. See also Dwight Macdonald, "Notes on the Truman Doctrine," *Politics*, May-June 1947, 85–87; James Peck, "Should Pacifists Vote for Henry Wallace? Yes!" *Fellowship*, Mar. 1948, 13; *Fellowship*, May 1947, 81; and *Peace News*, 28 Mar. 1947, 5.

67. Letter, quoted in *WRL News*, 13 Mar. 1947.

68. [George W. Hartmann and Hughan] to Dear Mr. President, 19 Apr. 1948, WRL Papers, A/4. See also WRL Press Release, 19 Apr. [1948], WRL Papers, A/4.

69. Both quotations from Olmstead, Assistance to Greece and Turkey: Hearings, 300–307.

70. *Politics*, May-June 1947, 85–86.

71. Ibid., 86.

72. *Politics*, Summer 1948, 148; and Peck, quoted in *Fellowship*, Mar. 1948, 13.

73. George Hartmann to President Truman, 4 Apr. 1949, in *WRL News*, 28 Apr. 1949; and Edward C. M. Richards, Testimony Before Senate Committee on Foreign Relations, North Atlantic Treaty: Hearings on Executive L, North Atlantic Treaty, 81st Cong., 1st sess., 1949, 1081–86. The WRL does not seem to have been preoccupied with NATO, though WRL executive committee minutes for the first half of 1949 are missing.

74. George Hartmann to President Truman, 4 Apr. 1949, in *WRL News,* 28 Apr. 1949.

75. Richards, North Atlantic Treaty: Hearings, 1949, 1081–86, quotations on 1083 and 1082 respectively.

76. Muste, Testimony Before Senate Committee on Foreign Relations, Convention on Relations with the Federal Republic of Germany and a Protocol to the North Atlantic Treaty: Hearings on Executive Q and R, 82nd Cong., 2nd sess., 1952, 171–76. Although representing the FOR, Muste's remarks also reflected the WRL's position.

77. "The Atomic Bomb" (WRL executive committee statement), 11 Feb. 1946, in Minutes, WRL-EC, WRL Papers, A/2. Both Frank Olmstead and A. J. Muste (the latter representing the FOR) wrote to atomic scientists. See *WRL News,* 20 Aug. 1946; folders marked "Correspondence, Atomic Bomb," in FOR Papers, A/12; and Wittner, *One World or None,* 60, 64.

78. *WRL News,* 10 Dec. 1948.

79. WRL Press Release, 24 Feb. 1950, WRL Papers, B/10.

80. All quotations from "WRL Statement on the Hydrogen Bomb," [1950], WRL Papers, B/10.

81. *Alternative,* Feb. 1950.

82. Ibid.; and *WRL News,* Feb. 1950.

83. Peacemakers Fast Committee, "A Call to a Seven-Day Fast for Peace" [Spring 1950], Peacemakers Papers; Fast For Peace Committee Papers; and *WRL News,* Apr. 1950.

84. Peacemakers Tax Refusal Committee, "A Year in Review," 21 June 1950, 2–3, Peacemakers Papers.

85. Ibid., 3–4. See also *WRL News,* Apr. 1950.

86. WRL, Peacemakers, and Catholic Worker Movement to Dear Friends of Hiroshima and Nagasaki, 6 Aug. 1954, Peacemaker Papers.

87. Peacemakers Press Release, 20 Sept. 1954, Peacemakers Papers.

88. "War Can Be Stopped: A Statement on Korea by the War Resisters League," Aug. 1950, Kaufman Papers.

89. Ibid.; James Peck, "Report by Jim Peck," 26 June–21 Aug. [1950], in Minutes, WRL-EC, WRL Papers, B/1; Minutes, WRL-IAC, 21 Aug. 1950, WRL Papers, B/1; *WRL News,* 1 Sept. 1950; and Glen Gardner, "Stop the Korean Crisis and World War Three" [5 July 1950], Fast for Peace Committee Papers.

90. Minutes, WRL-IAC, 26 June 1950; Peck, "Report by Jim Peck," 26 June–21 Aug. [1950], in Minutes, WRL-EC, WRL Papers, B/1; and Bayard Rustin, "Report on World Citizenship Deputation to Washington, D.C." [8 Aug. 1950], Fast for Peace Committee Papers; *WRL News,* 1 Sept. 1950.

91. All quotations from the two versions of the strikers' statement: Glen Gardner, "Stop the Korea Crisis and World War Three" [5 July 1950], Fast for Peace Committee Papers; and Glen Gardner, in *Hunterdon Republican* (Flemington, N.J.), 6 July 1950, 1.

92. Dellinger offers his account and reprints the leaflet (which differs in formatting from the original) in *From Yale to Jail,* 158–69; the leaflet is on 472–73. See also *Peace News,* Sept. 21, 1951, 1.

93. David Dellinger, Ralph DiGia, Arthur Emery, and Bill Sutherland, "American Peacemakers Reach Soviet Army," 5 Nov. 1951, Peacemakers Papers.

94. Ibid.

95. WRL, "War Can Be Stopped," Aug. 1950, Kaufman Papers. Several members submitted

drafts, which prompted sharp debate over the relative blame to assign the Soviet Union and the United States for the Korean conflict. For the drafts, see folder marked "Korea Leaflet," WRL Papers, B/10. For more on this debate, including a postwar exchange between Dellinger and Kaufman, see Bennett, " 'Pacifism Not Passivism,' " 523–24n. 188.

96. WRL, "War Can Be Stopped," Aug. 1950, Kaufman Papers; Minutes, WRL-EC, 10 July 1950, WRL Papers, B/1; and *WRL News,* 1 Sept., Oct. 1950.

97. *WRL News,* Oct. 1950.

98. N.a. to Mr. and Mrs. Devere Allen (Postcard), 30 Nov. 1950, Allen Papers. See also WRL Press Release, 1 Dec. 1950, WRL Papers, A/4.

99. *WRL News,* Sept.-Oct. 1953.

100. *WRL News,* 18 Oct. 1948.

101. *WRL News,* 10 Oct. 1946; 10 Sept. 1947; 18 Oct. 1948; 1 Dec. 1949; Feb. 1950; May-June and Nov.-Dec. 1951; Jan.-Feb. and Mar.-Apr. 1952; May-June 1953; Minutes, WRL-EC and WRL-IAC, 14 Apr. 1947; 19 Sept. 1948; and 1 Nov. 1950, WRL Papers, B/1. For annual WRL conferences and dinners, see folders in WRL Papers, A/9–10 and B/8.

102. *NYT,* 7 Apr. 1947, 7; 29 Mar. 1948, 13; and 18 Apr. 1949, 1 and 3; *New York Daily News,* 7 Apr. 1947, 4; *Fellowship,* May 1947, 81 and July 1947, 120; *WRL News,* 16 Apr. 1947; May-June 1951; and May-June 1952.

103. Minutes, WRL-EC, 19 Nov. 1953, WRL Papers, B/1.

104. Minutes, WRL-EC, 16 May 1953, WRL Papers, B/1; Anderson, *Bayard Rustin,* 140–41, 143; George Houser, *No One Can Stop the Rain* (New York: Pilgrim, 1989), 10–14, 20, 26–28, 67; and Sutherland, interview by author, 12 Feb. 1994.

105. Dellinger, *From Yale to Jail,* 169; and Sutherland, interview by author, 12 Feb. 1994.

106. *WRL News,* Sept.-Oct. 1953; and Minutes, WRL-EC, 16 May and 19 Nov. 1953, WRL Papers, B/1.

107. *WRL News,* Sept.-Oct. 1953; Jan.-Feb. and Mar.-Apr. 1954; Minutes, WRL-EC, 16 May and 19 Nov. 1953, WRL Papers, B/1; Sutherland and Meyer, *Guns and Gandhi in Africa*; Dellinger, *From Yale to Jail,* 169; and Sutherland, interview by author, 12 Feb. 1994.

108. Muste, I. Roodenko, and Sidney Aberman to Dear Friend, 8 June 1955, WRL Papers, B/8. See also Wittner, *Rebels Against War,* 231–32.

109. *WRL News,* Nov.-Dec. 1955. See also *WRL News,* Sept.-Oct. 1955.

110. Minutes, WRL-EC, 26 Oct. 1954, WRL Papers, B/1. See also Minutes, WRL-EC, 4 Oct. 1950. For additional examples of WRL anticommunism, see Bennett, "Pacifism Not Passivism," 504–5, 527–28n. 236.

111. For a general treatment of this theme, see Robbie Lieberman, *The Strangest Dream: Communism, Anticommunism, and the U.S. Peace Movement, 1945–1963* (Syracuse: Syracuse Univ. Press, 2000).

112. For the Communist peace movement, see ibid., 57–113; and Wittner, *One World or None,* 171–90, 182–86, 202–9.

113. Minutes, WRL-EC, 10 July 1950, WRL Papers, B/1.

114. Minutes, WRL-IAC, 1 Nov. 1950, WRL Papers, B/1.

115. *WRL News,* Dec. 1950.

116. Minutes, WRL-EC and WRL-IAC, 10 July and 1 Nov. 1950, WRL Papers, B/1; and *WRL News,* Dec. 1950.

117. Dwight Macdonald, *Henry Wallace: The Man and the Myth* (New York: Vanguard Press, 1948), 31.

118. Dwight Macdonald, "Should Pacifists Vote for Henry Wallace? No!" *Fellowship,* Mar. 1948, 7; and Donald Harrington, "Pacifists Should Vote Socialist," *Fellowship,* May 1948, 9.

119. Harrington, "Pacifists Should Vote Socialist," 7, 12.

120. A. J. Muste, "A Vote for Wallace Will Be—A Vote for the Communists," *Fellowship,* July 1948, 7.

121. Macdonald, "Should Pacifists Vote for Henry Wallace? No!" 9. Dwight Macdonald, "The Wallace Campaign: An Autopsy," *Politics,* Summer 1948, 178. See also R. Finch, "What about Wallace?" *Alternative,* Apr. 1948; *Fellowship,* May 1948, 25; and Wreszin, *Rebel in Defense of Tradition,* 192, 198–205, 224, 232–39, 248.

122. Peck, "Should Pacifists Vote for Henry Wallace? Yes!" 13.

123. Ibid., 6, 13–15, quotations on 15.

124. No aggregate voting figures exist for WRL members, but see John M. Mecartney to Editor of *Fellowship,* Oct. 1948, 38; Independent Voters for Norman Thomas to Dear Friend, [1948?], Lang Papers; Harrington, "Pacifists Should Vote Socialist," 9–12; Macdonald, "The Wallace Campaign," 179; Kaufman to Rose Sanders, 21 June 1948, WRL Papers, A/19; and interviews with WRL members.

125. *WRL News,* May 1950; and "Protests Beating of Pacifist" (annotated copy of Bernard D. Davis to Editor of *New York Herald Tribune*), 4 May 1950, WRL Papers, B/10.

126. *WRL News,* 1 Sept. 1950.

127. WRL, "Statement on Civil Rights," 30 Oct. 1949, in Minutes, WRL-EC, WRL Papers, A/2.

128. Ibid.

129. Ibid. See also Minutes, WRL-EC, 19 Oct. 1949. The WRL statement was a near-verbatim version of a draft that Muste prepared for the FOR. However, the FOR statement invoked "religious grounds" for its pacifism; the WRL statement did not. For a robust defense of communists and their importance to the radical movement (along the lines of Peck in 1948) by WRL members, see Roy Finch, Sandy Katz, David Dellinger, and Robert Auerbach in *Alternative,* Apr.-May 1950.

130. Minutes, WRL-EC and WRL-IAC, 5 Jan., 20 Apr., 14 Aug., and 4 Oct. 1950, WRL Papers, B/1. See also folder marked "Putnam County News," WRL Papers, B/12.

131. Minutes, WRL-EC, 8 June 1950, WRL Papers, B/1.

132. *WRL News,* July 1950.

133. WRL, "There are things to do for PEACE," [1954?], WRL Papers, A/4.

### Chapter 8. Present at the Creation

1. I have borrowed the phrase "powerful historical symbol" from Dee Garrison, " 'Our Skirts Gave Them Courage': The Civil Defense Protest Movement in New York City, 1955–1961," in *Not June Cleaver: Women and Gender in Postwar America, 1945–1960,* ed. Joanne Meyerowitz (Philadelphia: Temple Univ. Press, 1994), 201. For the link between the 1950s peace movement and the 1960s social movements, see chapter 7, note 4.

2. Wittner, *Rebels Against War,* 235–37, 240–41, 255–56, quotaton on 235.

3. *WRL News,* May-June 1957.

4. *WRL News,* July 1950. See also [draft of *WRL News* conference report], [4 June 1950?], WRL Papers, A/9.

5. "War Resisters League Membership Report—1956," in Minutes, WRL-EC, 1 Apr. 1957, WRL Papers, B/1. I could not locate membership numbers for 1963.

6. Paul Boyer, *By the Bomb's Early Light: American Thought and Culture at the Dawn of the Atomic Age* (New York: Pantheon Books, 1985), 352.

7. Ibid., 352–67, quotations on 352 and 355.

8. Editors, "Tract for the Times," *Liberation,* Mar. 1956, 4.

9. Ibid., 3, 6.

10. "Report of Sub-Committee on Magazine," [Nov. 1955]; Editors, "Report to W.R.L.-E.C. on First Year of Liberation," [Nov. 1956]; "Ideological Basis of Magazine," [1955], all in Minutes, WRL-EC, WRL Papers, B/1; and Minutes, WRL-EC, 15 Sept. and 7 Dec. 1955, WRL Papers, B/1. For *Liberation,* see also Editors, "Tract for the Times," 4; Roy Finch, "The Liberation Poll," *Liberation,* Nov. 1959, 14–17; and Paul Goodman, ed., *Seeds of Liberation* (New York: George Braziller, 1964), an anthology.

11. Minutes, WRL-EC, 23 Apr. 1956 and 6 May 1957, WRL Papers, B/1; "Policy on War Tax Refusal by WRL and WRL Employees[:] Support for Resisters and Organizational Response to IRS Levies and Other Collection Efforts," Dec. 1988 (provided by Ralph DiGia); Ed Hedemann, ed., *Guide to War Tax Resistance,* 2 ed. (New York: WRL, 1983), 78–79, 117; and DiGia, interviews by author, 9 May 1995 and 23 Mar. 1998. DiGia refused to pay one-third of his income tax (the amount that he calculated was used to fund the military).

12. Quoted in *New York World-Telegram,* 15 June 1955, 1.

13. Ibid. Other press accounts include *WRL News,* July-Aug. 1955; *Peacemaker,* 4 July 1955; and *Catholic Worker,* July-Aug. 1955.

14. Guy Oakes, *The Imaginary War: Civil Defense and American Cold War Culture* (New York: Oxford Univ. Press, 1994).

15. Oakes, *Imaginary War.*

16. Hennacy, *The Book of Ammon,* 286.

17. Dorothy Day, A. J. Muste, Ralph DiGia, and Kent Larrabee to Abraham Stark, 15 June 1955, WRL Papers, B/8f.

18. PDC, *What Happened on June 15?* (New York: Provisional Defense Committee, [1956]), [6].

19. Ibid., [5].

20. Ibid.

21. "Minutes of the strategy meeting held June 19," [1955]; Muste to Kenneth A. Greenawalt [PDC lawyer], 15 Aug. 1955; and PDC, "Memo to Defendants," 22 Sept. 1955, all in WRL Papers, B/8f; and *News Notes* (CCCO), July-Aug. 1955, 3.

22. Minutes, WRL-EC, 13 July 1955, WRL Papers, B/1.

23. Ibid.

24. "Memo to Defendants," 22 Sept. 1955, WRL Papers, B/8f.

25. PDC, *What Happened on June 15?* [10].

26. Ibid., [12]. See also *New York v. Parilli* (New York Mag., Arrest Pt. 1955, [unpublished opinion]), 180–81, copy in Civil Defense Committee Papers, CDG-A, SCPC.

27. PDC, What Happened on June 15? [7–8]; Kenneth W. Greenawalt to Whom It May Concern, 26 Apr. 1961, WRL Papers, B/8f.

28. For 1956–59 protests, see Hennacy, *Book of Ammon,* 289–93; and accounts in *WRL News* and *Catholic Worker.*

29. WRL, "The Only Real Defense: Your Part in the Civil Defense Drill," 20 July 1956, WRL Papers, B/8f.

30. Ibid.

31. Roy Finch to Dear WRL Member and Supporter, June 1959, WRL Papers, B/3.

32. *New York Post,* quoted in Hennacy, *Book of Ammon,* 293.

33. Hennacy, *Book of Ammon,* 290–91; *WRL News,* May-June 1959; and Garrison, "Our Skirts Gave Them Courage," 201–26.

34. For instance, see WRL, "Civil Defense Plans," [1956], WRL Papers, B/8f.

35. Clippings in WRL Papers, B/9; Edward Gottlieb and Muste to Dear Friend, Jan. 1961, and attached "Action for Peace," [1961], WRL Papers, B/3; CDPC, "A Call to Sanity," [1960], WRL Papers, B/8f.

36. Kempten, quoted in [*Village Voice*], [1960], clipping, WRL Papers, B/9. See also [*New York Post*], [4 May 1960], clipping, WRL Papers, B/9; and CDPC, "A Call to Sanity," [1960], WRL Papers, B/8f.

37. Boyle, quoted in [*Tribune*], [4 May 1960], clipping, WRL Papers, B/9.

38. Mailer, quoted in [*New York Post*], [4 May 1960], clipping, WRL Papers, B/9.

39. Morrissett, quoted in [*Village Voice*], [1960], clipping, WRL Papers, B/9.

40. MacDonald, quoted in ibid.

41. Ibid. See also [*The Worker*], [8 May 1960], clippings, WRL Papers, B/9.

42. Susan Pines, "30 Years of Activism: Overcoming Capitalism with Nonviolent Change: An Interview with David McReynolds," *The Nonviolent Activist,* Jan.-Feb. 1991, 3.

43. Ibid., 4.

44. [David McReynolds] to Douglas M. Pomeroy, 10 July 1955, David McReynolds Papers (hereafter, McReynolds Papers, Series roman number/Box Arabic number), Series I, Box 1, DG-134, SCPC.

45. David McReynolds to Vern Davidson, 4 July 1956, McReynolds Papers, I/1.

46. David McReynolds to IRS District Director, 15 Mar. 1957, McReynolds Papers, I/2; David McReynolds to Don Reeves, 15 Aug. 1956, McReynolds Papers, I/1.

47. This portrait of McReynolds is based on Pines, "30 Years of Activism," 3–12; biographical sketches of McReynolds in McReynolds Papers, V/1; and McReynolds, interview in *Protest: Pacifism and Politics: Some Passionate Views on War and Nonviolence,* by James Finn (New York: Random House, 1967), 206–22.

48. David McReynolds, "There Is Still Time, Brother," [*Village Voice*], [1960], clipping in WRL Papers, B/9.

49. Ibid.

50. CDPC, "Civil Defense Protest Day," [1960], WRL Papers, B/8f.

51. *National Guardsman,* 30 May 1960; [*New York Post School and College News*], [27 May 1960], clippings in WRL Papers, B/9.

52. [*Village Voice*], [1960], clipping in WRL Papers, B/9.

53. *WRL News,* May-June 1960; [*Village Voice*], [1960], clipping in WRL Papers, B/9; and Garrison, "Our Skirts Gave Them Courage."

54. *NYT,* [8 May 1960], clipping, WRL Papers, B/9. See also [*Village Voice*], [1960], clipping, WRL Papers, B/9.

55. [*The Nation*], 14 May 1960, clipping in WRL Papers, B/9.

56. CDPC, "BRAVE MEN DO NOT HIDE," [1961], and attached David McReynolds and Mary Sharmat to Dear Friend, 20 Apr. 20, 1961, WRL Papers, B/8f.

57. [? Journal], [29 Apr. 1961], clipping, WRL Papers, B/9.

58. Ibid., and other clippings in WRL Papers, B/9.

59. David McReynolds, "Neither Run Nor Hide: II," *Village Voice,* 27 Apr. 1961.

60. Ibid. See also Minutes, WRL-EC, 21 Mar. 1961, WRL Papers, B/1; and McReynolds, "Neither Run Nor Hide," *Village Voice,* [20 Apr. 1961].

61. McReynolds, "Neither Run Nor Hide: II."

62. "Statement in Court by David McReynolds," [1961]. See also *Daily News,* 17 May 1961, clipping, WRL Papers, B/9.

63. [David] McReynolds to Muste, [Bayard] Rustin, [Ralph] DiGia, and [Robert] Gilmore, [1961?], WRL Papers, B/8f. See also Minutes, CDPC, 13 Oct. 1961, WRL Papers, B/8f; and Minutes, WRL-EC, 18 Oct. 1961 and 21 Feb. 1962, both in WRL Papers, B/1. Like McReynolds, Muste recognized the value of civil defense protests in enlisting popular support and building the peace movement. "Experience has shown," he contended, "that civil defense protest is a cause [in] which popular support can be enlisted and opens up opportunities for peace education among new sectors and for increasing the ranks of anti-war forces." See Muste, "Civil Defense in 1961," [1961], WRL Papers, B/8f.

64. "Excerpts from the speech by Dr. Martin Luther King delivered in New York at the 36th annual dinner of the War Resisters League," 2 Feb. 1959, Lang Papers.

65. Ibid.

66. "FOR Secretaries and Key Persons in the FOR in Race Relations," [1961], FOR Papers, E/16; and Alfred Hassler to Robert J. D. Robertson, 9 May 1968, FOR Papers, E/17.

67. David J. Garrow, *Bearing the Cross: Martin Luther King, Jr., and the Southern Christian Leadership Conference* (New York: Vintage, 1988), 11–82; Taylor Branch, *Parting the Waters: America in the King Years, 1954–63* (New York: Simon & Shuster, 1988), 120–205; and Howell Raines, *My Soul Is Rested: The Story of the Civil Rights Movement in the Deep South* (New York: Penguin, 1983), 37–74.

68. Isserman, *If I Had a Hammer,* 144.

69. Rustin, interview in *My Soul Is Rested,* by Raines, 52; Martin L. King, Jr., *Stride Toward Freedom: The Montgomery Story* (New York: Harper & Brothers, 1958), 101; Anderson, *Bayard Rustin,* 185–86; and Garrow, *Bearing the Cross,* 68, 72–73.

70. King, *Stride Toward Freedom,* 90.

71. Ibid., 91.

72. Ibid., 95.

73. Ibid., 98. For Chalmers (an FOR and WRL member), see also Glenn [Smiley] to John [Swomley] and Al [Hassler], 29 Feb. 1956, FOR Papers, E/16.

74. King, *Stride Toward Freedom,* 101.

75. Ibid.

76. Alfred Hassler to Robert J. D. Robertson, May 9, 1968, FOR Papers, E/17; Glenn [Smiley] to John [Swomley] and Al [Hassler], 29 Feb. 1956, FOR Papers, E/16; and Jack, quoted in Bayard Rustin, "Report on Montgomery, Alabama," 21 Mar. 1956, WRL Papers, B/3. See also Rustin, interview in *My Soul Is Rested,* by Raines, 53; Garrow, *Bearing the Cross,* 72–73; and Tracy, *Direct Action,* 88–98.

77. All quotes from Minutes, WRL-EC, 20 Feb. 1956, WRL Papers, B/1. See also Rustin, "Report on Montgomery," WRL Papers, B/3; and *WRL News,* Mar.-Apr. 1956.

78. John M. Swomley to Wilson Riles, 21 Feb. 1956, FOR Papers, E/16.

79. John W. Swomley, Jr., to Glenn E. Smiley, 29 Feb. 1956 (two letters, same date), FOR Papers, E/16.

80. Rustin, quoted in Anderson, *Bayard Rustin,* 190.

81. Anderson, *Bayard Rustin,* 189–92.

82. Rustin, "Report on Montgomery," 21 Mar. 1956, WRL Papers, B/3.

83. Minutes, WRL-EC, 26 Mar. 1956, WRL Papers, B/1.

84. Ibid., 26 Mar. and 11 June 1956, WRL Papers, B/1; *WRL News,* May-June and July-Aug. [1956]; and Anderson, *Bayard Rustin,* 195.

85. "Report to W.R.L.-E.C. on First Year of Liberation," [Nov. 1956?], in Minutes, WRL-EC, WRL Papers, B/1. See also Minutes, WRL-EC, 11 June, 8 Oct., 12 Nov., and 17 Dec. 1956; and 21 Jan. 1957, all in WRL Papers, B/1; *WRL News,* May-June 1956; Anderson, *Bayard Rustin,* 194–96; and folder marked "Committee for Non-Violent Integration," CDG-A, SCPC.

86. *WRL News,* May-June 1956.

87. Ibid., Sept.-Oct. 1956.

88. Ibid.

89. Anderson, *Bayard Rustin,* 197.

90. *WRL News,* Jan.-Feb. 1957.

91. King, quoted in Anderson, *Bayard Rustin,* 207. See also Minutes, WRL-EC, 1 Apr. 1956 (and attached Bayard Rustin Memorandum to [WRL], n.d.), and 6 May 1957, WRL Papers, B/1; and *WRL News,* May-June 1957.

92. Minutes, WRL-EC, 10 Sept. and 22 Oct. 1957, WRL Papers, B/1.

93. Minutes, WRL-EC, 8 Sept. 1958, WRL Papers, B/1. See also Youth March Letterhead, FOR Papers, E/20; Minutes, WRL-EC, 7 Oct. 1958, WRL Papers, B/1; and *WRL News,* Nov.-Dec. 1958; Mar.-Apr. and May-June 1959; and Mar.-Apr. 1960.

94. *WRL News,* Nov.-Dec. 1958.

95. Anderson, *Bayard Rustin,* 210–11.

96. *WRL News,* Mar.-Apr. 1960.

97. Minutes, WRL-EC, 10 Sept. 1960 (which includes a typescript copy of Nat Hentoff, "Adam Clayton Powell: What Price Principle?" *Village Voice,* 14 July 1960), WRL Papers, B/1. For both the SCLC and the Youth Marches, see Anderson, *Bayard Rustin;* Garrow, *Bearing the Cross;* Adam Fairclough, *To Redeem the Soul of America: The Southern Christian Leadership Conference and Martin Luther King, Jr.* (Athens: Univ. of Georgia Press, 1987); and Branch, *Parting the Waters.*

98. Minutes, WRL-EC, 1 Nov. 1960, WRL Papers, B/1. See also Minutes, WRL-EC, 10 Oct. 1960; "W.R.L. Staff Memo on '60 Elections," n.d., in Minutes, WRL-EC [1960], WRL Papers, B/1; and folder marked "Election Protest (1960)," WRL Papers, B/13.

99. Minutes, WRL-EC, 10 Oct. 1960, WRL Papers, B/1; and *WRL News,* Nov.-Dec. 1960.

100. 1961 WRL Peace Calendar (New York: WRL, 1960), frontispiece, WRL Papers, B/7.

101. Minutes, WRL-EC, 21 Mar. 1961, WRL Papers, B/1.

102. Minutes, WRL-EC, 10 Sept. 1960; 19 Sept. 1961; and 18 Sept. 1962, WRL Papers, B/1; Peck, *Underdogs vs. Upperdogs,* 123–43; and Anderson, *Bayard Rustin,* 235–38.

103. Minutes, WRL-EC, 12 Nov. 1963. See also Minutes, WRL-EC, 10 Dec. 1963, WRL Papers, B/1.

104. Minutes, WRL-EC, 26 June 1963, WRL Papers, B/1.

105. Bloomstein, quoted in Anderson, *Bayard Rustin,* 264; and Rustin, quoted in Minutes, WRL-EC, 10 Sept. 1963, WRL Papers, B/1.

106. *WRL News,* Sept.-Oct. 1963; and *Life,* 6 Sept. 1963. For information on Rustin and the march, see Anderson, *Bayard Rustin,* 239–66; Levine, *Bayard Rustin and the Civil Rights Movement,* 130–48; and Garrow, *Bearing the Cross,* 276–85.

107. Anderson, *Bayard Rustin,* 283–98; Tracy, *Direct Action,* 129–33; and *WRL News,* Mar.-Apr. 1965. For a shrewd assessment of Rustin's political move to the Right, see David McReynolds, review of *Bayard Rustin,* by Anderson, in *The Nonviolent Activist,* Nov.-Dec. 1997, 19–21.

108. Milton S. Katz and Neil H. Katz, "Pragmatists and Visionaries in the Post-World War II American Peace Movement: SANE and CNVA," in *Doves and Diplomats: Foreign Offices and Peace Movements in Europe and America in the Twentieth Century,* ed. Solomon Wank (Westport, Conn.: Greenwood, 1978), 265–88.

109. Wittner, *Rebels Against War,* 240.

110. Scott, quoted in *Liberation,* May 1957, 14–15.

111. For SANE/CNVA, see CNVA, "What Is CNVA?" [1961 or after], Committee for Nonviolent Action Papers (hereafter, CNVA Papers, Series roman number/Box Arabic number), Series II, Box 2, DG-17, SCPC; NVAANW Letterhead, [June 1957], CNVA Papers, I/1; CNVA, "Report of Nominating Committee," [28 Dec. 1959], CNVA Papers, VI/13; Minutes, WRL-EC, 4 Nov. 1958, WRL Papers, B/1; *WRL News,* May-June 1957; *Liberation,* May 1957, 14–15; N. Katz, "Committee for Nonviolent Action"; M. Katz and N. Katz, "Pragmatists and Visionaries," 265–88; Wittner, *Resisting the Bomb,* 51–60; Wittner, *Rebels Against War,* 241–56; and Milton S. Katz, *Ban the Bomb: A History of SANE, the Committee for a Sane Nuclear Policy, 1957–1985* (New York: Greenwood, 1986).

112. N. Katz, "Committee for Nonviolent Action," 36; Minutes, WRL-EC, 6 May and 4 June 1957, WRL Papers, B/1; and *WRL News,* May-June and July-Aug. 1957.

113. Lawrence Scott, "My Reasons for Civil Disobedience in Nevada," [1957], CNVA Papers, VI/11. See also N. Katz, "Committee for Nonviolent Action," 42–45;

114. Muste quoted in Peck, *Underdogs vs. Upperdogs,* 110. See also N. Katz, "Committee for Nonviolent Action," 42.

115. Peck, *Underdogs vs. Upperdogs,* 108–11, quotation at 110. See also *Catholic Worker,* FOR-NY, Non-Violent Action Against Nuclear Testing [NVAANW], Jewish Peace Fellowship, and WRL to Interested Persons, [1957], WRL Papers, B/13.

116. For the WRL's endorsement and promotion of the project, see Minutes, WRL-EC, 30 Dec. 1957; and 28 Jan. and 3 Mar. 1958, WRL Papers, B/1; "Summary of Emergency [NVAANW] Executive Committee Meeting," 22 Feb. 1958, CNVA Papers, VI/11; and *WRL News,* Jan.-Dec. 1958.

117. Albert S. Bigelow, "Why I Am Sailing This Boat into the Bomb-Test Area," reprint, first publ. in *Liberation,* Feb. 1958.

118. Albert S. Bigelow, *The Voyage of the Golden Rule: An Experiment with Truth* (Garden City, NY: Doubleday, 1959), 47.

119. Ibid., 42. See also George Willoughby, Lawrence Scott, Albert Bigelow, and William Huntington to President Dwight D. Eisenhower, 9 Jan. 1958, CNVA Papers, VI/11.

120. Peck, *Underdogs vs. Upperdogs,* 111–18; and Bigelow, *Voyage of the Golden Rule,* 59–207.

121. Robert W. Gilmore to New York Committee for a SANE Nuclear Policy, 9 May 1958, CNVA Papers, VI/11. See also Minutes, WRL-EC, 5 May 1958, WRL Papers, Box 1; and *WRL News,* May-June 1958.

122. Reynolds, quoted in Wittner, *Rebels Against War,* 249. For support of the *Phoenix* by the WRL and its members, see *WRL News,* July-Aug. 1959; James Peck to Lyle [Tatum], 14 July 1958; and NVAANW Letterhead, CNVA Papers, VI/11.

123. NVAANW Press Release, 17 Feb. 1958, and attached "Statement of Intention in Our European Witness"; and "Summary of Events to June 11, 1958," [June 1958], both in CNVA Papers, VI/11.

124. Minutes, WRL-EC, 2 Dec. 1958, WRL Papers, B/1; *WRL News,* Jan.-Feb. 1959.

125. *WRL News,* July-Aug. 1958.

126. Wittner, *Rebels Against War,* 249.

127. Fellowship (Peace Information Edition), 15 July 1959, CNVA Papers, VI/12; Minutes, WRL-EC, 4 May and 9 June 1959, WRL Papers, B/1; and *WRL News,* May-Dec. 1959.

128. "Call to Nonviolent Action Against Nuclear Missile Policy at the Omaha, Nebraska, ICBM Bases and Throughout the United States," [1959], WRL Papers, B/13; "This is Omaha Action[:] Nonviolence Against Nuclear Missile Policy" [1959]; clippings, both in CNVA Papers, VI/12; and N. Katz, "Committee for Nonviolent Action," 78–85.

129. For legal developments, see *Peacemaker,* 1 Aug. 1959; "Five Given Suspended Sentences of Six Months and $500, Probation for One Year, . . ." 9 July 1959, CNVA Papers, VI/12.

130. Jehle, quoted in [*Lincoln Journal*], [21 June 1959], clipping, CNVA Papers, VI/12.

131. Clippings, in CNVA Papers, VI/11 and VI/12.

132. Direct Action Committee Against Nuclear War (DACANW), "Memorandum on Sahara Protest Entry," [1959]. See also Michael Randle et al. to General Charles D. DeGaulle, 9 Sept. 1959; CNVA, "Summary Information on the Sahara Nuclear Bomb Protest Team," 22 Dec. 1959, CNVA Papers, VI/13; Wittner, *Resisting the Bomb,* 265–68, 336; and Sutherland and Meyer, *Guns and Gandhi in Africa.*

133. In addition to sources listed in n. 132, see "Sahara Protest Bulletin I," 10 Nov. [1959]; Bayard Rustin et al., "Progress Report [#2] on Sahara Africa," [1959]; [Bayard Rustin] to [Ralph DiGia], 22 Nov. 1959, all in CNVA Papers, VI/13; and Muste, "Africa Against the Bomb," *Liberation,* Jan. 1960, 4.

134. Minutes, WRL-EC, 5 Oct. 1959; Minutes, Emergency WRL-EC, 8 Oct. 1959, both in WRL Papers, B/1; and Sutherland and Meyer, *Guns and Gandhi in Africa,* 36–40.

135. Rustin et al., "Progress Report [#2] on Sahara Africa," [1959], CNVA Papers, VI/13.

136. Bayard Rustin to George Willoughby, Muste, Stanley Levison, Ralph DiGia and Tom Marcel, 5 Nov. 1959, CNVA Papers, VI/13.

137. James Peck to [Bayard Rustin], 16 Nov. 1959; Rustin, "Report No. 3[:] Sahara Project," 16 Nov. 1959, CNVA Papers, VI/13.

138. DiGia, quoted (with brackets) in Anderson, *Bayard Rustin,* 222.

139. James Peck to [Bayard Rustin], 16 Nov. 1959, CNVA Papers, VI/13.

140. A. J. Muste, "Africa Against the Bomb (II)," *Liberation,* Feb. 1960, 13.

141. DACANW Press Release, 22 Dec. 1959; Michael Randle, Cables, 8 Jan.–29 Feb. 1960, all in CNVA Papers, VI/13; and *Liberation,* Jan. 1960, 4–7.

142. "PEOPLE OF AFRICA! AFRICA IS IN DANGER!" [1959], CNVA Papers, VI/13.

143. WRL, "FRANCE, DON'T TEST THE BOMB!" (flyer), [Dec. 1959], CNVA Papers, VI/13,

attached to WRL, "SUPPORT SAHARA BOMB PROTEST PROJECT" (flyer), [Dec. 1959], WRL Papers, B/1. See also Michael Randle, Cables, 8 Jan.–29 Feb. 1960; and Minutes, WRL-EC, 7 Dec. 1959, WRL Papers, B/1.

144. Michael Randle, Cable, 19 Feb. 1960, CNVA Papers, VI/13.

145. Muste, "Africa Against the Bomb," 5.

146. Ibid., 4.

147. Sutherland and Meyer, *Guns and Gandhi in Africa,* 36–37.

148. David McReynolds, "Memo on Possible WRL-CNVA Merger," [1964], WRL Papers, B/18.

149. Ibid., and N. Katz, "Committee for Nonviolent Action," 219.

150. David McReynolds, "Memo on Possible WRL-CNVA Merger" [1964], WRL Papers, B/18. See also Charles Bloomstein, "Reaction to David McReynold's Memo on Possible WRL-CNVA Merger," 24 Nov. 1964, WRL Papers, B/18; *WRL News,* Mar.-Apr. 1968; and N. Katz, "Committee for Nonviolent Action," 215–24.

151. "Minutes of the War Resisters League Evaluation Conference," 16 Dec. 1961, in Minutes, WRL-EC, WRL Papers, B/1.

152. Ibid.

153. Ibid.

154. *WRL News,* Mar.-Apr. 1959. For the evaluation conferences, see also materials in Minutes, WRL-EC, 8 Jan. 1959 and 16 Dec. 1961, WRL Papers, B/1.

155. For instance, see R. Finch to WRL Member and Supporters, June 1959; Edward Gottlieb and A. J. Muste to Dear Friend [Jan. 1961] (and attached "Action for Peace"), WRL Papers, B/3.

156. Bayard Rustin to Dear Friend, Apr. 1964, WRL Papers, B/3.

157. "Report of Special Committee on WRL-Program," 12 Mar. 1964, in Minutes, WRL-EC, WRL Papers, B/1.

158. Isserman, *If I Had A Hammer,* 128.


## Epilogue and Conclusion

1. Morris, *The Origins of the Civil Rights Movement,* 139–73; for references on the WRL, see pages 57, 140, 159.

2. DeBenedetti and Chatfield, *An American Ordeal,* 68. Besides the WRL, this peace coalition included the FOR, AFSC, WILPF, SANE, CNVA, and SPU.

3. For the WRL and tax resistance, see Ed Hedemann, ed., *Guide to War Tax Resistance,* 2d ed. (New York: WRL, 1983); WRL, *History of the War Resisters League* ([New York: WRL], 1980), 13, copy in WRL Papers, B/1.

4. Marilyn B. Young, *The Vietnam Wars: 1945–1990* (New York: HarperCollins, 1991), 96.

5. DeBenedetti and Chatfield, *An American Ordeal,* 176. For a study of draft resistance in Boston during the Vietnam War, see Michael S. Foley, *Confronting the War Machine: Draft Resistance During the Vietnam War* (Chapel Hill: Univ. of North Carolina Press, 2003).

6. For the Fifth Avenue Parade Committee and Mobe, see *WRL News,* May-June 1967, May-June 1968, and May-June 1971; DeBenedetti and Chatfield, *An American Ordeal,* 163, 174–77, 180–85, 188, 196–98, 215, 224–31; and Tracey, *Direct Action,* 136–51.

7. WRL, *History of the War Resisters League,* 13.

8. This overview is based on the *WRL News* during the Vietnam Era (1963–75); David McReynolds, "Pacifists and the Vietnam Antiwar Movement," in *Give Peace a Chance,* ed. Small and Hoover, 53–70; DeBenedetti and Chatfield, *An American Ordeal;* Marty Jezer, *Fifty Years of Nonviolent Resistance: The Story of Radical Pacifism in the United States from the Conscientious Objectors of World War I to the Present* (1973 WRL Peace Calendar; New York: WRL, 1973), [39–52]; and Lewy, *Peace and Revolution: The Moral Crisis of American Pacifism,* 89–105, passim.

9. For the link between the 1950s peace movement and the 1960s New Left, see chapter 7, note 4.

10. The WRL's embrace of the counterculture was shown by its sponsorship of *WIN* magazine ("Workshop in Nonviolence"). See WRL, *History of the War Resisters League,* 10.

11. Wendy Schwartz, "Bringing the Women Together," *WRL News,* July-Aug. 1971.

12. For the feminist perspective on the WRL, see ibid. Several months earlier, Schwartz noted that "the sexual revolution [h]as—in a small but nevertheless significant way—finally touched the League. For over a year now, the all-male bastion of Lafayette Street has been integrated"; Wendy Schwartz, "A Memo on 'Dear Sir,' " *WRL News,* Mar.-Apr. 1971.

13. Schwartz, "Bringing the Women Together"; Schwartz, "A Memo on 'Dear Sir' "; *WRL News,* Jan.-Feb. 1973; and DiGia, interview by author, 9 May 1995. The first female WRL vice chair was Frieda L. Lazarus, who held one of the three vice chairs in 1944, and at other times during the 1940s.

14. Vicki Leonard and Tom MacLean, eds., *The Continental Walk for Disarmament and Social Justice* (New York: Continental Walk for Disarmament and Social Justice, 1977).

15. Ed Hedemann, "The Seventies," in Ruth Benn et al., eds., *War Resisters League, 1923–98: 75 Years of Nonviolent Resistance* (1998 WRL Peace Calendar; New York: WRL, [1997]). For information on the WRL's position on nuclear power, see WRL, "War Resisters League: Seventy Years of Nonviolent Action" [1993?]; DiGia, interview by author, 9 May 1995.

16. For information on the WRL's activities from the 1970s on, see Hedemann, "The Seventies"; Mandy Carter, "The Eighties"; and Melissa Jameson and Oliver Hydon, "The Nineties," all in WRL, *War Resisters League: 1923–98* (1998 WRL Calendar); and WRL, *History of the War Resisters League,* 14–20.

17. Chambers, "Conscientious Objectors and the American State," 42.

18. Ibid.

19. Ibid., 35–46; Kohn, *Jailed for Peace,* 111–14; and Charles F. Howlett, "Case Law Historiography in American Peace History," *Peace and Change* 22 (Jan. 1997): 60–61.

20. Ackerman and Duvall, *A Force More Powerful,* 4 and passim. For Sharp and other scholars in his tradition, see Introduction, note 10. For a statement on the realism of nonviolence by a leading scholar of international relations, see Richard Falk, *Explorations at the Edge of Time: The Prospects for World Order* (Philadelphia: Temple Univ. Press, 1992).

21. Wittner, *Resisting the Bomb,* ix. For more information on world disarmament, see Wittner, *One World or None,* and *Resisting the Bomb*; and Lawrence S. Wittner, *Toward Nuclear Abolition: A History of the World Nuclear Disarmament Movement, 1971 to the Present* (Stanford: Stanford Univ. Press, 2003).

22. Chatfield, *American Peace Movement,* 180. For the "prophetic" role of radical pacifism, see also ibid., 170.

23. DeBenedetti, *Peace Reform in American History,* 108–37.

# Selected Bibliography

Since this study is based on unpublished manuscript sources, this selected bibliography does not list published sources. In addition to the selected bibliography and endnotes in the present volume, references to the full range of documents, pamphlets, books, journal articles, and periodicals used in this study may be found in Scott H. Bennett, " 'Pacifism Not Passivism': The War Resisters League and Radical Pacifism, Nonviolent Direct Action, and the Americanization of Gandhi" (Ph.D. dissertation, Rutgers University, 1998).

## Manuscript Collections

I conducted most of my research at the Swarthmore College Peace Collection (SCPC). At SCPC, the War Resisters League Papers constituted the most important manuscript collection for this study. Several other SCPC collections proved especially valuable for multiple chapters; these included the Devere Allen Papers, FOR Papers, Jessie Wallace Hughan Papers, Abraham Kaufman Papers, and Igal Roodenko Papers. The Devere Allen Papers and Igal Roodenko Papers were unprocessed when I used them; both have since been processed. The FOR Papers have been reorganized since I used them; minor changes were also made to the organization of the WRL Papers during my research.

Swarthmore College Peace Collection, Swarthmore, Pennsylvania

Jane Addams
Devere Allen
American Friends Service Committee: Civilian Public Service, 1940–1946
American Union Against Militarism
Anti-Enlistment League
Break With Conscription Committee
A. Fenner Brockway
Central Committee for Conscientious Objectors
Horace Champney
Civil Defense Committee

Civilian Public Service
Committee for Amnesty For All Objectors to War and Conscription
Committee for Nonviolent Action
Committee for Non-Violent Revolution
CORE Papers/George Houser's Correspondence
Garry Davis
Albert Einstein
Fast For Peace Committee
Fellowship of Reconciliation/U.S. Section
Roy Finch
Larry Gara
Edward P. Gottlieb
Richard B. Gregg
John Haynes Holmes
Jessie Wallace Hughan
Paul Jones
Abraham Kaufman
Roy Kepler
Mary Stone McDowell
David McReynolds
Metropolitan Board for Conscientious Objectors
Tracy D. Mygatt and Frances Witherspoon
Scott Nearing
New York Bureau of Legal Affairs
No-Conscription Fellowship
No More War Movement
Peacemakers
Peace Now Movement
Mercedes M. Randall
Resist Conscription Committee
Igal Roodenko
SANE
John Nevin Sayre
Student Peace Union
Evan W. Thomas
United States Miscellaneous Peace Material, 1944–1954
Caroline Foulke Urie
War Resisters' International
War Resisters League
Wilfred Wellock
Woman's Peace Party

Women's Peace Society
Women's Peace Union

New York Public Library, New York, New York

Frieda L. Lazarus

Barnard College, New York, New York

Jessie Wallace Hughan

**Personal Collections**

Charles Bloomstein (New York)
August Gold (Croton-on-Hudson, New York)
Edward P. Gottlieb (New York, New York; and SCPC)
Abraham Kaufman (Minneapolis, Minnesota; and SCPC)
Vivien Roodenko Lang (Glenside, Pennsylvania)

**Micromaterials**

Norman Thomas (microfilm)
"The Reminiscences of Norman Thomas," Columbia University Oral History Collection (microfiche)
Socialist Party Papers (microfilm)
War Resisters' International (microfiche)

**Newspapers and Periodicals**

*Absolutist*
*Alternative*
*American Socialist Quarterly*
*Amnesty Bulletin*
*CNVR Bulletin*
*The Conscientious Objector*
*Direct Action*
*Fellowship*
*Liberation*
*The New Leader*
*The New York Times*
*The Nonviolent Activist*

*Pacifica Views*
*Peace News*
*Politics*
*Weekly Prison News Letter*
*Socialist Call*
*The War Resister*
*The Washington Post*
*WRL News*
*The World Tomorrow*

**Interviews and Personal Communications**

I have benefited from taped interviews, untaped conversations, and written correspondence with the following WRL members. The number of taped interviews I conducted with each is in parentheses. I conducted taped personal or telephone interviews with Charles Bloomstein (2), Ernest Bromley (3), Marion Bromley (1), Ralph DiGia (2), Margaret Rockwell Finch (1), Roy Finch (2), August Gold (2), Edward P. Gottlieb (16), George Houser (1), Abraham Kaufman (20), Vivien Roodenko Lang (2), Richard Lazarus (1), Albon Man (1), Jules Manson (1), Annabel Sidman (1), and William Sutherland (1). In addition, I have benefited from untaped conversations with Ralph DiGia, Seymour Eichel, Edward P. Gottlieb, Philip Isely, Abraham Kaufman, Vivien Roodenko Lang, Brad Lyttle, and David McReynolds. I have also benefited from written communications with Margaret Rockwell Finch, Abraham Kaufman, and Albon Man. Finally, I have benefited from interviews with Carlos Cortez (6) and Garry Davis (1), and a conversation with August Tyler, none of whom was a WRL member.

# Index

Abalone Alliance, 242
Abbot, John H., 101
Aberman, Sidney, 172
abolitionism, 7–8
absolute pacifism. *See* radical pacifism
*Absolutist* (publication), 89
Acheson, Dean, 180
Ackerman, Peter, 250n. 13
ACLU. *See* American Civil Liberties Union
*Action* (camp publication), 111
Addams, Jane, 8–9, 14
African Americans: abolitionism, 7–8;
    Brotherhood of Sleeping Car Porters, 95.
    *See also* civil rights movement; racism
African independence movement, 196–97,
    231
African National Congress, 196
Africa Project, 196
AFSC. *See* American Friends Service
    Committee
A. J. Muste Memorial Institute, xi
Alexander, Myrl E., 115
Allen, Clifford, 10
Allen, Devere, 30–33; on armed revolution,
    52, 57, 65; as bridge between WRL and
    Socialist Party, 30, 63–67; on class war,
    59, 61–62; in debate with Socialist Party
    over Spanish Civil War, 61–62, 63; on
    Debs Column, 64; "Declaration of
    Principles" of Socialist Party, 30, 53;
    *The Fight for Peace,* 32–33; and
    Friends of the Debs Column, 65;

on legitimate uses of armed power, 52,
    59–60, 61–62, 63, 65; No-Frontier
    News Service, 31–32, 33, 44; on
    nonviolent resistance, 32–33, 58–59;
    on peace and labor movements, 32,
    36–37; on Spanish Civil War, 30, 31, 52,
    56, 57, 59–60, 64–65; on Sudetenland
    crisis, 58; war resistance literature of
    1930s of, 46; on WRI world council, 30,
    65, 67
Alonso, Harriet, 7
Alpha Omicron Pi, 2
*Alternative* (publication), 154, 161, 183
Altman, Jack, 54
Amalgamated Textile Workers of America
    (ATWA), 35, 39–40
America First Committee, 78
American Civil Liberties Union (ACLU): on
    amnesty for conscientious objectors, 142;
    Danbury strike supported by, 118;
    Holmes as leader in, 27, 244; and Legal
    Service for Conscientious Objectors, 87,
    105; and National Civil Liberties
    Bureau, 34; World War I pacifists in
    establishment of, 145; WRL members in
    founding of, 244
American Federation of Labor, 6, 35, 36
American Friends Service Committee
    (AFSC): liberal pacifism of, 257n. 2; and
    Morris tour of U.S., 177; and
    Nonviolent Action Against Nuclear
    Weapons/Committee for Nonviolent